DATE DUE

Hemispheric American Studies

Hemispheric American Studies

Edited by

CAROLINE F. LEVANDER

and ROBERT S. LEVINE

RUTGERS UNIVERSITY PRESS

NEW BRUNSWICK, NEW JERSEY, AND LONDON

LIBRARY OF CONGRESS CATALOGING-IN-PUBLICATION DATA

Hemispheric American studies / edited by Caroline F. Levander and Robert S. Levine.
    p.   cm.
    Includes bibliographical references and index.
    ISBN 978-0-8135-4222-5 (hardcover : alk. paper) — ISBN 978-0-8135-4223-2 (pbk. :
alk. paper)
    1. America—Civilization.   2. America—Study and teaching (Higher)   3. Western
Hemisphere—Study and teaching (Higher)   4. United States—Study and teaching
(Higher)   5. America—Race relations.   6. Migrations of nations.   7. America—
Intellectual life.   8. American literature—History and criticism.   9. Latin
American literature—History and criticism.   10. Ethnic groups in literature.
I. Levander, Caroline Field   II. Levine, Robert S. (Robert Steven)
    E20.H46   2008
    970—dc22   2007012715

A British Cataloging-in-Publication record for this book is available
from the British Library.

CONTENTS

ACKNOWLEDGMENTS

We are grateful for the assistance we have received from a number of individuals and institutions. Our thanks to the Andrew Mellon Foundation for funding a year-long graduate seminar on Hemispheric American Studies at Rice University. The members of the Mellon seminar—Elizabeth Fenton, Gale Kenny, Cory Ledoux, David Messmer, Molly Robey, and Benjamin Wise—provided a lively critical forum for a number of our contributors. We thank Gordon Hutner for his support of this project in its early stages, and we are grateful to participants of the University of Toronto's Andrew Mellon Sawyer Seminar, "Envisioning a Global Americas," for their responses to a preliminary version of our introduction. For funding research costs related to the book's completion, we thank Gary S. Wihl, Dean of Humanities at Rice University, and the Department of English and the College of Arts and Humanities at the University of Maryland. We are also pleased to thank the National Endowment of the Humanities for helping to sustain the conversation on hemispheric studies by funding a summer NEH seminar on the topic. Our editor at Rutgers University Press, Leslie Mitchner, has inspired us with her professionalism and enthusiasm for the project. We would also like to thank Alison Hack, Alicia Nadkarni, Carey Nershi, and Marianna Vertullo for their invaluable assistance with the preparation of the manuscript. Finally, we are pleased to thank our contributors, whose hard work, collegiality, and commitment to the project have made coediting this volume a pleasure and an education.

Hemispheric American Studies

Introduction

Essays Beyond the Nation

CAROLINE F. LEVANDER AND ROBERT S. LEVINE

In 1973 an editorial team at Yale University published *American Literature: The Makers and the Making*, the most influential American literary anthology of the decade.[1] This two-volume work both exemplified the state of the field and set the direction of Americanist literary criticism for the next ten to fifteen years. As framed by the editors, Cleanth Brooks, R. W. B. Lewis, and Robert Penn Warren, the selections in the first volume charted a tripartite literary development beginning with the Puritans' "Pre-National Literature (1620–1743)," proceeding to the revolutionaries' "Emergent National Literature (1743–1826)," and culminating with the triumphal achievement of "A National Literature and Romantic Individualism (1826–1861)." For those authors and texts that didn't quite fit their nation-based teleological schema, Brooks et al. created an oxymoronic subcategory, "Literature of the Nonliterary World," where supposedly nonliterary and non-national African American and Native American writers were collected. Race therefore emerged as an ancillary but not irrelevant excess within an anthology that sought to present seamless connections among race, nation, and literature. Native American writers, for example, complicated the various ideas of the national espoused by the Puritans and American Revolutionaries, while Frederick Douglass's position within the anthology as a figure of the "nonliterary world" signaled the extent to which the literary itself lay uneasily within the editors' national frame.

But perhaps the editors were simply prescient in relegating Douglass to their non-national grouping, for their selected text, an excerpt from *My Bondage and My Freedom* (1855), was published only a few years before Douglass began to express an interest in emigrating to Haiti. Though he never did emigrate, he retained his fascination, traveled to Hispaniola in 1871 to ask inhabitants what they thought about becoming a black state in a hypothetical American Union, and served as U.S. minister and consul general to Haiti from 1889 to 1891. He was so admired by Haitian leaders that they chose him as their

1

official representative to the World's Columbian Exposition in Chicago in 1893. Outraged and alienated by the upsurge of whites' antiblack racism during the 1880s and early 1890s, Douglass in his capacity as Haiti's representative celebrated the Haitian revolution as "one of the most wonderful events in the history of this eventful century, and . . . in the history of mankind," and extolled Haiti as "the only self-made Black Republic in the world."[2] His critique of U.S. racism from within the space of the Haitian pavilion suggests that Douglass's position in U.S. history cannot be separated from his position in Haitian history—that his relatively recent relocation from the margins to the center of American literature anthologies should necessitate a rethinking of both the national and the literary.

Though it is easy to critique older anthologies that so blatantly uphold traditional notions of nation-based literary history, subsequent revisionary scholarship of the 1980s and 1990s has nonetheless tended to argue that marginalized texts by minority authors like Frederick Douglass should be central to the American canon without addressing the larger question of what constitutes "America." In other words, much current scholarship now features hitherto forgotten or marginalized writers but continues to take the nation as the key organizing unit for literary and cultural studies. Douglass's engagement with Haiti over a nearly forty-year period, however, suggests the larger hemispheric framework in which one of the U.S. nation's most canonical figures worked and the importance of this framework to the various literary and cultural traditions to which he has subsequently become essential. Douglass was hardly alone among key U.S. literary and cultural figures for his keen interest in the interconnections among nations, peoples, institutions, and intellectual and political movements in the larger context of the American hemisphere. His very interest in those interconnections, as disruptive as such thinking may have been to his U.S. nationalism, helped him to see the nation's potential and limitations within a fuller history of race in the Americas. For Douglass, to move beyond the nation was not to abandon it but instead, through an engagement with overlapping histories and geographies, to better understand it. At the Columbian Exposition, Douglass holds up a Haitian black republican mirror to Chicago's White City of 1893 in order to represent the larger inconsistencies underpinning late nineteenth-century U.S. racialized nationalism.

Hemispheric American Studies takes a similarly strategic comparativist approach to consider the overarching shape and texture of American literary and cultural history. The collection as a whole focuses on the complex ruptures that remain within but nonetheless constitute the national frame, while at the same time moving beyond the national frame to consider regions, areas, and diasporan affiliations that exist apart from or in conflicted relation to the nation. Our collection thus seeks to disrupt the temporal sequence of what Eddie Glaude has termed "nation time"[3] by putting different national and extra-national histories and cultural formations into dialogue. By examining the intricately intertwined geographies, movements, and cross-filiations among peoples, regions, diasporas, and nations of the American hemisphere, the collection seeks to contextualize what can sometimes appear to be the artificially hardened borders and boundaries of the U.S. nation, or for that matter, any nation of the American hemisphere. We bring together a range of scholars working in the fields of Latin American, Asian American, African diasporan, Canadian, and U.S. literary and cultural studies to address the urgent question of how scholars might reframe disciplinary boundaries within the broad area of what is generally called American Studies. Collectively, the essays draw on current critical work in inter-American and hemispheric studies and suggest future possibilities and directions for comparativist and dialogical approaches to the Americas. One of the large goals of the anthology is to chart new literary and cultural geographies by decentering the U.S. nation and excavating the intricate and complex politics, histories, and discourses of spatial encounter that occur throughout the hemisphere but tend to be obscured in U.S. nation-based inquiries. In short, the essays in this collection approach distinct regions in the Americas, many of which now lie within U.S. borders, as products of overlapping, mutually inflecting fields—as complex webs of regional, national, and hemispheric forces that can be approached from multiple locations and perspectives and that can help us to reframe American cultural analysis.

Although many of the essays in this collection address the United States in some form or other, we contend that analysis of the United States's engagements with a wide and surprising array of geographic entities helps to contextualize and clarify, rather than reproduce, the exceptionalism that has long been central to the nation's conception of its privileged place in the American hemisphere. These hemispheric engagements, as our contributors demonstrate, are multidirectional and involve overlapping interactions among various peoples, regions, and nations. In subjecting such interactions to close scrutiny, our collection seeks to consolidate and extend important work in hemispheric studies, and thus to serve as a sort of handbook (or guidebook) to a burgeoning field.[4] Some of the best recent critical work in the field has responded to the challenges posed by Janice Radway's 1998 presidential address to the American Studies Association, "What's in a Name?" In that address, Radway called on scholars in American Studies to move beyond nation-based analysis in order to consider the ways in which U.S. nationality is "relationally defined and historically and situationally variable," and particularly to relinquish "the idea that [U.S.] culture can be adequately conceived of as a unitary, uniform thing, as the simple function of a fixed, isolated, and easily mapped territory." She also encouraged scholars to resist taking "America" as a default term for the United States.[5] We share Radway's concerns about equating "America" with the United States and we share her sense of the importance of recognizing the limits of a hermetically defined nation-based analysis. The title of our anthology, *Hemispheric American Studies*, means to put pressure on the word "American" by tightly linking it with the larger hemispheric world that American Studies has often seemed to exclude—a world that, very much like the United States itself, emerged out of a series of colonial conflicts and engagements. The "invention" of a seemingly autonomous and exceptionalist U.S. nationality developed in relation to the more expansive geographies and longer histories of the Americas, and it is the relation of the U.S. nation to that often elided context that is one of the large subjects of this collection.

As the work of a number of historians and critical theorists has made apparent, the ideas of America, Latin America, and the Western hemisphere are invented rather than found—constructed rather than natural. Such a distinction is not merely rhetorical but has deep meaning for current Latin American Studies, transnational inquiry, American Studies, and post-national commentaries. Edmundo O'Gorman's *The Invention of America* first popularized the idea that America was not a continent waiting to be discovered but rather an "invention" or conceptual category necessary to the consolidation of a Western worldview. Scholars from Immanuel Wallerstein to Walter Mignolo concur that the modern world-system generated in the long sixteenth century depended upon the invention/creation of the Americas as a geographical and cultural construct.[6] Collectively, Wallerstein and like-minded theorists approach this history not so much as a linear process of discovery but rather as evolving theses that culminated in the dramatic moment when the need to give meaning to the land mass that we now refer to as America became more urgent than the need to continue to see the world as one Island of the Earth or an Orbis Terrarum. From this perspective, then, America as a conceptual entity literally did not exist until people made it. This making was a process even for Columbus, who believed that he had arrived at the eastern shores of the Orbis Terrarum or Asia, and not "America," because the land mass he saw was imbued with a particular ontological meaning meant to further the one Island of the Earth hypothesis of geographers of the time.

If America was invented rather than discovered, so too were Latin America and the Western hemisphere, ideas that accrued their own particular ontological meanings over time. From Arthur Whitaker's description of how the Western hemisphere emerged as a concept in the late eighteenth century to Mignolo's account of the "creation" of Latin America in the early to mid-nineteenth century, scholars have suggested that we recognize that the past is transmitted forward through a spatial as well as a linear process. The Western hemisphere idea, for example, was a slow genetic process that required not only the acquisition of knowledge but also the development of a new feeling of spatial compatibility, not only the spread of Enlightenment political philosophy to North and South America but also the belief that, as Mexican statesman Lucas Alamán declared in 1826, "the similarity of their political institutions has bound [the countries of America] even more closely together, strengthening in them the dominion of just and liberal principles."[7] Just as this process of developing shared spatial consciousness inevitably involved occluding, repressing, and appropriating other modes of depicting the past and the numerous other constituencies that occupied space within a temporal frame, so too did the process through which Latin America emerged require the erasure or subordination of indigenous populations. A story of creole and mestizo elites embracing a modernity that required the simultaneous embracing of racism, the idea of Latin America did not so much stand in opposition to as further articulate, and even enable, the invention of America. While independence in all the Americas, including the United States, helped to bring an end to external colonialism, it also facilitated internal colonialism through institutionalized slavery of certain portions of the population and through the repression of indigenous histories, knowledge, and cultural forms. The recovery of such occluded and contested histories remains a crucial project of hemispheric studies.

With its emphasis on taking account of overlapping and sedimented histories, hemispheric studies has profound implications for current scholarly reconsiderations of area studies as a disciplinary practice, as well as for thinking about the possibilities of revitalizing conversations between Latin American and American Studies scholars and between Latin Americanists working in the United States and those working in Latin America. From a spatio-temporal vantage point, we see that location is always crossed—that Latin Americanists as well as U.S. Americanists have historically tended to think from a colonial discourse that emerges from and all too often depends upon histories of conquest and colonization. The historic complaints by Latin Americanists that the United States has appropriated the name "America" to refer to itself as a country and in so doing has marginalized Latin America, for example, insufficiently capture the sometimes shared and sometimes conflict-ridden colonial histories that shaped the Americas. Precisely because colonialism has not been the sole province of the United States, efforts to "invert . . . the naturalized view of the Americas," with the South occupying a more privileged position, ultimately only "changes the content, but not the terms of the conversation," as Mignolo has pointed out. In short, such an approach finally proves an inadequate response to the historical processes that have yielded the ideas of nation and hemisphere in the first place. Because area studies typically emphasizes space (or geographical locale) over time, it has tended to uphold a constant, crystallized idea of national identity.[8] Once we recognize that the nation is not the realization of an original essence but a historical configuration designed to include certain groups and exclude others, we are able to see the nation as a relational identity that emerges through constant collaboration, dialogue, and dissension. Such a relational approach to national identity attends to the uneven power relations that form and are too often erased within concepts of national unity.

Humanities departments have historically tended to reinforce the idea of the separate and free-standing nation-state, with attention to geopolitical interchange generally following formal structures of colonialism. French departments, for example, focus on French literature and culture, Hispanic Studies departments on primarily Spanish, Central American, and South American national traditions, and English departments on American and English literature, as separate if sometimes parallel genealogical entities. Within such an intellectual milieu, area studies as practiced by Latin Americanists in particular has offered the promise of crossing such national and disciplinary boundaries and creating research fields that were organized around rubrics other than the nation. Border studies, for example, has focused on the particular locales that spring up at the crossroads of national cultures. Yet, as Alberto Moreiras reminds us, the abandonment of the national referent has not necessarily introduced new modes of thinking, but rather has offered a series of alternative identities and localities that all too often inadvertently replace and reinforce rather than unseat the "more traditional tools for U.S. cultural domination."[9] This collection seeks to avoid some of the pitfalls of those area studies models in which, as Susan Gillman elaborates in her closing commentary, language studies stand in for method, geographical area stands in for disciplinary theory, and indigeneity offers the utopian promise of authenticity. Rather, we approach the hemisphere and the shifting, evolving nations and regions within it from a spatio-temporal vantage point where comparative approaches bring out the contingency of both the nation and region. From such a perspective, retaining a national referent—a national literature in the context of a hemispheric paradigm, for example—of necessity entails an ongoing recognition of the processes through which nations are embedded in and develop gradually out of local and transnational circumstances. In short, by attending to multiple and sometimes competing conceptions of geography and chronology, we are able to see that the idea of a national literature and culture emerges out of a series of subordinations, alliances, and cross-fertilizations that make the nation a richly suggestive but hardly an autonomous entity.

The essays collected in *Hemispheric American Studies* in various ways chart the interdependencies between nations and communities throughout the Americas. A central goal of the collection is to enlarge the critical frame of Americanist debate by moving beyond traditional area studies paradigms through analyses of the multiple geopolitical terrains encompassed by the hemisphere. Accordingly, the volume is less concerned with documenting the tangible, net effects of U.S. power—the inclusion, exclusion, appropriation, marginalization, domination, exploitation, and invasion of other "neighbor" nations—and instead asks such questions as: What happens to U.S. and American literary and cultural studies if we recognize the asymmetry and interdependency of nation-state developments throughout the Americas? What happens if we let this recognition of the nation as historically evolving and contingent—rather than already formed—revise our conceptions of literary and cultural genealogies? Finally, what happens if the "fixed" borders of a nation are recognized not only as historically produced political constructs that can be ignored, imaginatively reconfigured, and variously contested but also as component parts of a deeper, more multilayered series of national and indigenous histories? We believe that addressing such questions opens up the possibility of developing not only a broader definition of what the United States includes but also a more historically complex view of the creative tensions and interdependencies that are embedded within and threaten to undo any fixed notion of "America." Such an approach shifts the critical focus from the terms under which various constituencies are included or excluded within an already established U.S. governing body to how those seemingly other constituencies actually operate as dynamic parts of multiple nations, some of which deny their presence. Such an approach, not surprisingly, also acts as a corrective to critical endeavors to understand geographic encounters in the hemisphere in terms of a developing U.S.-centered world system, because it suggests the importance of doing literary and cultural history from the perspective of a polycentric American hemisphere with no dominant center.

In this conceptualization, then, to attempt to move beyond the U.S. nation in American studies is not to abandon the concept of the nation but rather to adopt new perspectives that allow us to view the nation beyond the terms of its own exceptionalist self-imaginings. It is to take full account of the contingency of nation formation, the unpredictability of national histories, and the protean character of the nation itself. Prasenjit Duara remarks that "[w]hen we consider national identity in its changeability, fungibility, and interplay with other identifications, we see that it can be as subversive of the nation-state as it has been supportive." Interpretive views of the nation from without can be as fungible as from within, and in this regard recent tendencies to conceive of the United States in the American hemisphere solely in terms of empire and imperialism tend to overlook the complex series of encounters that collectively comprise national communities in the Americas. The Monroe Doctrine, for example, has typically been taken as a key starting point of U.S. hemispheric expansionism, but it is important to recognize that the doctrine emerged in response to the very real threat posed by European colonialism. As Rodrigo Lazo points out, "the separation of America as a hemisphere promoted by the Monroe Doctrine worked hand in hand with opposition to Spain in some sectors of Latin America."[10] From such a perspective, the U.S. nation can be understood in relation to nationalistic Latin American liberation movements of the early to mid-nineteenth century. A recognition of this intertwined history of nations in formation presses us to abandon a simple binary that pits the United States as a fully formed, homogeneous entity against the myriad peoples and nations of the rest of the hemisphere.

Recognizing the overlapping national formations occurring within a hemispheric context likewise highlights the importance of race to the idea of the nation and the cultural formations that represent, contest, and consolidate national identities. Political theorists, historians, and social commentators have long acknowledged the tensions between race and nation. From the observation of the late nineteenth-century political philosopher Ernest Renan that "race marks and orders the modern nation-state," to the work of twentieth-century scholars like Ernest Gellner and Anthony Marx on the ethnic and racial origins of nation-states, critics have consistently observed the powerful ways in which racial identity promotes and at times threatens the idea of the nation. Yet coincident with such commentary on the racial origins of the nation is an overlapping commentary on the hemispheric dimensions of such racialized national origins. Jose Martí, for example, challenges readers of "Our America" to think of the nations that comprise America from a comparative, hemispheric perspective—to think of the hypothetical villager's relation to the larger "American" cosmos. Developing a multilayered positionality in relation to local, national, and hemispheric cultures is, in Martí's opinion, the only way to realize full civic representation in a hybrid American world. Almost twenty years later, Randolph Bourne recognized that America was "coming to be, not a nationality but a trans-nationality, a weaving back and forth, with other lands, of many threads of all . . . colors," and it was in this larger political world—and more particularly in Cuban independence efforts—that W. E. B. Du Bois found powerful models for rethinking the place of blacks in the United States.[11] Important social thinkers from Martí to Bourne and from Martin Delany to Du Bois consistently located the racial nation-state within the larger flows of hemispheric culture and recognized the importance of hemispheric parameters in thinking about and helping to develop alternative nationalisms.

Literary texts can offer uniquely rich evidence of the hemispheric resonances that these alliances (and tensions) between race and nation create. For literary nationalists of the eighteenth and nineteenth centuries, nationality was almost always tied to race. As Appiah remarks, there thus developed in the thinking of the time a "dual connection . . . between, on the one hand, race and nationality, and, on the other, nationality and literature. In short, the nation is the key middle term in understanding the relations between the concept of race and the concept of literature." This set of interconnections among race, nation, and literature is clearly evident by the late eighteenth century and has important origins in the writings of Johann Gottfried Herder, particularly his 1767 *On the New German Literature*, which presents the literary, as Appiah puts it, as "the sacred essence of nationality."[12] Yet analyses of a rich array of literary and cultural documents reveal that nationality, as we have seen with Frederick Douglass, is embedded within hemispheric cultural flows—that nations are intra- as well as interdependent entities. Taking account of such dynamic series of ever-shifting and mutually embedding logics and subordinations through a hemispheric approach of necessity opens up literary, cultural, and national frames and requires the development of new ways of conceptualizing archives, texts, and contexts. Such an approach, as the essays in this collection demonstrate, invariably asks us to reorient ourselves in relation to that which has hitherto seemed familiar and known.[13]

As we hope is clear, moving beyond the nation does not mean abandoning the idea of nation but rather recognizing its dynamic elements and fluid, ever-changing, essentially contingent nature. Still, one might ask: What is "Hemispheric American Studies" and how does one assay to move "beyond" the nation? How can one de-center the United States in American Studies, and how can American Studies become transnational without bringing about what George Handley has called "a neoimperialist expansion into the field of Latin American studies?"[14] We pose these questions to suggest the nature of this anthology. We are not grandly declaring a new field ("Hemispheric American Studies"), nor are we presenting a utopian solution to the problems and constraints of nation-based literary and cultural inquiry ("Beyond the Nation"). Instead, the title of the collection is intended to point to the broad interpretive and disciplinary challenges that the essays as a group seek to address. Hemispheric American Studies, as represented in the critical practices of the contributors to this volume, complicates questions of the national, and thus raises rather than resolves interpretive problems. In this sense hemispheric studies can be regarded as a heuristic rather than a content- or theory-driven method; it allows for discovery of new configurations rather than confirmation of what we think we already know. Although the essays present strongly articulated and theorized visions of this protean field or heuristic, they do not issue dictums or argue for one "correct" way of undertaking hemispheric inquiry. Rather, the essays, in the manner of case studies, insist on paying close attention to archives and texts, the local and the global, with an emphasis on developing interpretive perspectives on mutually inflecting literary and cultural histories. Collectively, the essays explore the rich archival evidence of the obscured, often palimpsestic cultural geographies out of which similitude and disparity develop and out of which the nation takes shape as an alternately assumed, imagined, and enduringly important category—but ultimately just one category in a broader interpretive field. Still, if nations and hemispheres are ideas or inventions, they are also social realities with very real consequences for individuals and communities. Our collection thus takes up questions such as: What happens to citizens of one nation when they enter another? How do bodies migrate across nations? Most importantly for our purposes, how are these migrations represented in a diverse range of textual and cultural forms? With essays that interrogate stamps, cartoons, novels, film, art, music, travel documents, and governmental and non-governmental organization publications, *Hemispheric American Studies* seeks to excavate the complex cultural history of texts, discourses, and bodies in motion and at rest across the ever-shifting and multilayered geopolitical and cultural fields that collectively comprise the American hemisphere.

Such an approach yields new insights into what has traditionally been called "Early American Studies." The collection begins with essays by Anna Brickhouse and Ralph Bauer on colonial encounters and exchanges in the Americas, and their analyses point to the limits of what Brooks, Lewis, and Warren (and many other anthologists and literary historians before and since) have conceived of as the pre-national and emergent national periods. As Brickhouse and Bauer make clear, the very concept of the "pre-national" requires an ahistorical importing of 1776 onto colonial encounters and creole cultures in an extended Caribbean in which national and cultural histories were intermingled, complex, and confused, collectively offering anything but a unitary starting point for a teleological history that would culminate in the U.S. nation. Brickhouse and Bauer challenge those hermetic narratives that present the United States as emerging inevitably from the British settlements of the early seventeenth century, and instead focus on transcultural conflicts involving colonial powers and indigenous peoples in the larger field of the Americas. These are precisely the histories (of imperialism, polyculturalism, multilingualism, and race) that exceptionalist national histories obscure but that nonetheless need to be understood as constitutive of the nation.

In her essay on "Hemispheric Jamestown," for instance, Brickhouse complicates conventional understandings of Jamestown as the "mother" of slavery and the U.S. nation by considering the crucial role of a Spanish Jesuit settlement that had preceded the English settlement at Jamestown. Through her close consideration of the interactions between the Spanish settlers and the indigenous peoples they encountered, she restores to our understanding of Jamestown a complicated history of Spanish priority and native-creole biculturalism, and thus encourages us to read the English history of Jamestown in relation to larger imperial histories of the Americas, particularly with respect to cross-cultural and bilingual interactions that the English writers themselves failed to discern. That hidden history implicates the Pocahontas story and Anglophone chroniclers of Jamestown in a wider hemispheric milieu, helping to disclose indigenous agency and imperial conflict at a site that for too long has been regarded in U.S. nation-based histories as the promulgator of the nation. While Brickhouse shows how indigenous cultures were in active dialogue with and appropriated the very terms of colonial discourse, Ralph Bauer argues that we can only see the full complexity of modern ideas of race by recognizing a "triangular," circum-Atlantic discourse of colonial difference that emanated from Spanish America both north across the hemisphere as well as east across the Atlantic. Bauer thus challenges U.S. nation-based understandings of race by illustrating how birthplace or point of origin continued to play an important role in distinguishing American-born creoles from European peoples in the Americas, and therefore how, by extension, peoples in the

Americas became "white," "red," or "black" only after having come in extended contact with colonial cultures. Through readings of Jorge Juan and Antonio de Ulloa's *Noticias secretas* and Thomas Jefferson's *Notes on the State of Virginia*, Bauer charts an understanding of race in the early Americas that emerged not only from the (proto-)scientific models of European imperialism in the New World but also from a geopolitical counterdiscourse of creole patriotism that would remain of central importance to nineteenth-century nationalisms throughout the Western world.

Brickhouse and Bauer ask us to rethink "origins" geospatially by revealing how discourses that seem to reinforce a center/margin paradigm of dominance work against what we actually know about the origins and workings of nations. Rodrigo Lazo and Jesse Alemán explore what such a doubled, overlaid approach to American origins reveals about early nineteenth-century print culture and the gothic narrative form, respectively. Lazo suggests how Hispanophone conceptions of Philadelphia and its printing industry might dislodge the United States from its position as the too-often assumed nodal point for the consideration of power relations in the Americas. While it might seem initially counterintuitive to conduct such a rethinking from the seat of U.S. nation-making (Philadelphia), Lazo shows how Americanism during the 1820s becomes a hemispheric process rather than a U.S. ideology for such writers and political figures as Vicente Rocafuerte, future president of Ecuador, and the Cuban poet José María Heredia. Describing "la famosa Filadelfia" as a symbol of hemispheric aspirations for breaking away from European monarchical rule, Heredia and other Latin American exiles in Philadelphia used the printing industry to generate and disseminate political material that to some extent subsumed the United States to their larger political vision of a vibrantly democratic and free Hispanophone "America." Alemán considers another key moment in the advent of the American hemisphere—the moment when Mexico's antiquity becomes the United States's hemispheric history following the revolutionary break from England—and analyzes how this blending is represented in and through the particular narrative form of the gothic. Approaching the gothic from a hemispheric perspective reveals a repressed historical presence within the U.S. nation and challenges us to rethink the hemisphere not as cleft in two but as our America and the other America at the same time. Through readings of early nineteenth-century narratives such as Robert Montgomery Bird's *Calavar*, William Prescott's *History of the Conquest of Mexico*, and the anonymously published *Xicoténcatl*, Alemán illustrates that inter-American gothic anxiety is uncannily *intra*-American because it emerges not only from without but also from within the United States.

The inevitable blending and overlaying of national histories is in some ways most acute in the geographic area of the U.S. South, described by some in the nineteenth century as the "American Mediterranean." Matthew Guterl, Jennifer Greeson, and Kirsten Gruesz explore the literary and social history of this multi-layered, gateway area between North and Central America, paying particular attention to how debates in the United States about slavery, emancipation, citizenship, and corporate capitalism were structured not just by internal political disputes but also by hemispherically shared experiences. As Guterl demonstrates, during the antebellum period a sense of "Southern exceptionalism" co-existed quite easily and naturally with a conviction that the planter class shared a common fate less with the U.S. nation than with slaveholders elsewhere in the hemisphere, a Southern version of manifest destiny that even included Cuba and the empire of Brazil. But what the planter class also shared with the slaveholders of the southern hemisphere was a vision, exacerbated by the "nightmare" of the Haitian Revolution, of imminent collapse. (For African American leaders such as David Walker and Martin Delany, however, who likewise looked south in their efforts to create transnational diasporas, Haiti and the prospect of a free Cuba remained sources of inspiration.) The U.S. South emerges as a liminal and unbordered space not only during the antebellum era, but also during the Reconstruction and post-Reconstruction period, when the South entered U.S. literature as an imaginative geographic site for conceptualizing U.S. empire. Through analysis of George Washington Cable's local color fiction, Greeson suggests that local color writing's emergence in the post-bellum United States was integral to the development of a popular hemispheric expansionist imaginary. In this model, Southern locales like Louisiana and local color fiction as a genre are embedded within and fuel the national machinery of empire. But as is clear from Gruesz's long history (from the late nineteenth through the twentieth century) of New Orleans as a hemispheric "center," empire is never a simple matter of one nation imposing its desires on others. From the moment when bananas and coffee came to replace cotton as an engine of U.S. and Latin American trade, New Orleans became the focus of the geographic imaginings and desires of political and business leaders from Honduras, El Salvador, Guatemala, Nicaragua, Costa Rica, Panama, and the United States. In her discussion of texts by O'Henry, Máximo Soto Hall, Annie Proux, and many others, Gruesz asks what it might mean to conceive of New Orleans, and the Gulf of Mexico itself, as a broadly conceived "Central" America where multiple interests and worldviews are constantly clashing. She also underscores the centrality of race and ethnicity to the many immigration narratives that take the Gulf as a central point of hemispheric transit.

Race, whether conceived nationally or diasporically (or both), is central to the essays by Michelle Stephens and Ifeoma Nwankwo. Though drawing meaning from a national history of slavery that pitted U.S. South against U.S. North, African American writers, performers, and political activists have regularly engaged larger hemispheric frameworks. Taking the career of Paul Robeson as her subject, Stephens explores how his various performances—whether in song, in the press, onstage, or onscreen—resonated both nationally for white and black American audiences and hemispherically in black communities throughout the diaspora. His representations of the New World slave, during the 1920s and 1930s, highlight the hemispheric dimensions of black masculine identity and reveal how discourses of race, gender, and nation operate throughout the Atlantic world *as* discourses of political freedom. Like Stephens, Nwankwo suggests that recent scholarship has focused primarily on unequal relations between the United States and Latin American nations, thereby ignoring relations between U.S. African Americans and the rest of the Americas. Nwankwo begins to address such a gap by tracing a hemispheric genealogy of slavery that covers over 150 years and that aligns African American writers from Martin Delany to Gayl Jones. Showing how both writers' engagements with Latin America served as a basis of their advocacy for collective action against racial oppression, Nwankwo argues that Latin America functioned as a powerful political as well as geographic midpoint between Africa and the United States and therefore became a privileged site for U.S. African American writers who wished to claim both an American citizenship and an international network. Her readings of Martin Delany's *Blake* and Gayl Jones's *Mosquito* in particular reveal that U.S. African American authors were cognizant of and integrally engaged in theorizing a diasporic consciousness that shows nation and hemisphere to be simultaneously enforcing and complicating concepts.

The complicated relations between and across nations' interests and identities in the Americas are the central concerns of the essays by Deborah Cohn, Claire Fox, and Robert Irwin, which address the tightly interwoven and often symbiotic interactions between U.S. and Latin American artists, politicians, administrators, and cultural impresarios from the Cold War to the present. Focusing on a writing congress, the art world, film, stamps, and dance, these essays as a group demonstrate what Cohn terms "the limitations of scholarly approaches that are confined within the national or regional boundaries set by area studies, themselves products of the Cold War." The essays also underscore the need to take account of Latin American agency rather than simply surrendering to notions of U.S. domination. In her case-study of the 1966 International PEN writing congress in New York City, for example, Cohn shows how the artists of the Latin American "Boom" (Carlos Fuentes, Mario Vargas Llosa, and others) sought to use a congress, which to some extent was intended by the host nation to serve the ends of U.S. Cold War nationalism, as a platform to advance their own literary agenda and to air the ongoing debate among Latin American intellectuals about the Cuban Revolution of 1959. Claire Fox examines similar interplay in her study of the Cuban critic and curator José Gómez Sicre's efforts to create a hemispheric arts circuit in the Americas. As Fox shows, the "hemispheric success" of Sicre's prodigy, the young Mexican artist José Luis Cuevas, was revealingly asymmetric. Whereas Cuevas was regarded in the United States as an angst-ridden modernist whose vision corresponded with the Cold War universalism of the Pan American Union, in Mexico he was seen along more particularist lines as a parodist and critic of national culture. Fox's archival research illuminates just how canny Cuevas was in working with and through Sicre in exploiting the burgeoning postwar international art market in both venues. Competing and complexly intercultural interpretive frames are also crucial to Irwin's essay on the controversy surrounding the Mexican government's 2005 issuing of four postage stamps commemorating the Afro-Mexican comic book antihero Memín Pinguín. Just as Cuevas was regarded differently in Mexico and the United States, so were the images on these stamps. For U.S. Americans, Memín Pinguín was simply another in a long line of stereotypical minstrel images intended to denigrate people of African descent, whereas for many Mexicans, the comic antihero spoke to ideals of racial tolerance. Irwin's essay provides a deep history of the image in the context of Mexico's vexed relationship to Afro-Cuban culture, showing how classic Mexican film and dance of the mid-twentieth century attempted to create a Mexican national imaginary that excluded blackness by constructing a threatening (albeit seductive) Afro-Cuban other. In this respect, Yolanda Vulgas Dulché and Alberto Cabrera's Memín Pinguín, which drew on these images, assumed importance as one of the few unambiguously positive representations of blackness and racial tolerance in Mexican culture. For Irwin, then, who regards U.S. attacks on the image as misguided because blind to this larger cultural history, the controversy on the Memín Pinguín commemorative stamps underscores the limits of viewing cultural discourses in the American hemisphere through the lens of supposedly autonomous national histories.

For the most part, the essays in this collection collectively adopt a North-South rather than East-West perspective to analyze the contingency and diversity of nation-formation in the American hemisphere. But the opening essays by Brickhouse and Bauer in particular remind us to pay heed to what Paul Giles has termed "hemispheric partiality," the risk of "replacing nationalist essentialism predicated upon state autonomy with a geographical essentialism predicated on physical contiguity."[15] The essays by Timothy Marr, Kandice Chuh, and Rachel Adams make a special point of enlarging the frame beyond borders and boundaries, underscoring the crucial importance of the global to the hemispheric as well as of considering the hemisphere's extended and sometimes neglected northern reaches. In his study of Islam in what he terms a "transhemispheric" context, Marr links European exploration of the New World to fantasies of displacing or overcoming the contentious challenge of Islam, showing how the Islamic foundations of the Spanish past have remained a submerged presence within Latin American and U.S. American literary and cultural genealogies. According to Marr, the "irruption" of this haunted and haunting past in writings by Melville, Twain, Paul Bowles, and other writers of the literary Americas suggests the integral relation of Islam to "New World" cultural imaginings. Kandice Chuh takes a similarly broad North-South/East-West perspective in her discussion of the writings of Karen Tei Yamashita, an

Asian American writer living in and writing about Brazil. As Chuh elaborates, Asian American studies require a radical rethinking in relation to hemispheric studies, and vice versa, precisely because Asianness remains immutably "foreign" despite nativity, citizenship, or acculturation within the United States. Rachel Adams's account of the Argentinian Canadian author Guillermo Verdecchia, whose plays and short stories conceive of an "America" that extends from Toronto to Tierra del Fuego, similarly complicates questions of national identity. As Adams argues through her close readings of Verdecchia, geography is never literal, borderlands can be exported from expected locations along the U.S.-Mexico border to a range of locales in the United States, Canada, the Southern Americas, and beyond, and the hemisphere itself can be regarded as a "contact zone where Anglo and Latin America meet up, clash, and interpenetrate."

It is precisely the literary, cultural, and historical consequence of those meetings, clashes, and interpenetrations in the American hemisphere that is the subject of this volume.

NOTES

1. *American Literature: The Makers and the Making*, ed. Cleanth Brooks, R. W. B. Lewis, and Robert Penn Warren (New York: St. Martin's Press, 1973).

2. Frederick Douglass, "Haiti among the Foremost Civilized Nations of the Earth: An Address Delivered in Chicago, Illinois, on 2 January 1893," *The Frederick Douglass Papers: Series One: Speeches, Debates, and Interviews. Volume 5: 1881–95*, ed. John W. Blassingame and John R. McKivigan (New Haven: Yale University Press, 1992), 506.

3. See Eddie S. Glaude, Jr., *Is It Nation Time?: Contemporary Essays on Black Power and Black Nationalism* (Chicago: University of Chicago Press, 2002).

4. This note can only touch on some of the more influential recent contributions to hemispheric studies. An important book, which provided a foundation for much of the work done in the 1990s, is Bell Gale Chevigny and Gari Laguardia, eds., *Reinventing the Americas: Comparative Studies of Literature of the United States and Spanish America* (Cambridge: Cambridge University Press, 1986). Key recent books include Amy Kaplan and Donald E. Pease, eds., *Cultures of United States Imperialism* (Durham: Duke University Press, 1993); Joseph R. Roach, *Cities of the Dead: Circum-Atlantic Performance* (New York: Columbia University Press, 1996); Jeffrey Belnap and Raúl Fernández, eds., *"José Martí's "Our America": From National to Hemispheric Cultural Studies* (Durham: Duke University Press, 1998); Eric Wertheimer, *Imagined Empires: Incas, Aztecs, and the New World of American Literature, 1771–1870* (Cambridge: Cambridge University Press, 1999); Doris Sommer, *Proceed with Caution, When Engaged by Minority Writings in the Americas* (Cambridge, Mass.: Harvard University Press, 1999); John Carlos Rowe, ed., *Post-Nationalist American Studies* (Berkeley: University of California Press, 2000); Walter Mignolo, *Local Histories/Global Designs: Coloniality, Subaltern Knowledges, and Border Thinking* (Princeton: Princeton University Press, 2000); Shelley Streeby, *American Sensations: Class, Empire, and the Production of Popular Culture* (Berkeley: University of California Press, 2002); Amy Kaplan, *The Anarchy of Empire in the Making of U.S. Culture* (Cambridge, Mass.: Harvard University Press, 2002); Kirsten Silva Gruesz, *Ambassadors of Culture: The Transamerican Origins of*

Latino Writing (Princeton: Princeton University Press, 2002); Ralph Bauer, *The Cultural Geography of Colonial American Literatures* (Cambridge: Cambridge University Press, 2003); Jon Smith and Deborah Cohn, eds, *Look Away: The U.S. South in New World Studies* (Durham: Duke University Press, 2004); Anna Brickhouse, *Transamerican Literary Relations and the Nineteenth-Century Public Sphere* (Cambridge: Cambridge University Press, 2004); Rodrigo Lazo, *Writing to Cuba: Filibustering and Cuban Exiles in the United States* (Chapel Hill: University of North Carolina Press, 2005); Maria DeGuzman, *Spain's Long Shadow: The Black Legend, Off-Whiteness, and Anglo-American Empire* (Minneapolis: University of Minnesota Press, 2005); Debra Castillo, *Redreaming America: Toward a Bilingual American Culture* (Albany: State University of New York Press, 2005); and Don H. Doyle and Marco Antonio Pamplona, eds., *Nationalism in the New World* (Athens: University of Georgia Press, 2006). See also the 2003 special issue of *PMLA* edited by Djelal Kadir, on "America, the Idea, the Literature"; the 2003 special issue of *Modern Fiction Studies* edited by Paula Moya and Ramón Saldivar, on "Fictions of the Trans-American Imaginary"; the 2004 special issue of *Radical History Review* edited by Sandhya Shukla and Heidi Tinsman, on "Our Americas: Political and Cultural Imaginings"; the 2005 special issue of *Comparative American Studies* edited by Claire F. Fox, on "Critical Perspectives and Emerging Models of Inter-American Studies"; and the 2006 special issue of *American Literary History* edited by Caroline F. Levander and Robert S. Levine, on "Hemispheric American Literary History."

5. Janice Radway, "What's in a Name?: Presidential Address to the American Studies Association, November 20, 1998," *American Quarterly* 51 (1999): 10, 15.

6. See Edmundo O'Gormon, *The Invention of America: An Inquiry into the Historical Nature of the New World and the Meaning of Its History* (Bloomington: Indiana University Press, 1961); Anibal Quijano and Immanuel Wallerstein, "Americanity as a Concept: Or the Americas in the Modern World-System," *ISSA* 1:134 (1992), 549–556; and Walter Mignolo, *The Idea of Latin America* (Oxford: Blackwell, 2005).

7. Qtd. in Alberto Moreiras, *The Exhaustion of Difference: The Politics of Latin American Cultural Studies* (Durham: Duke University Press, 2001), 2. See also Arthur Whitaker, *The Western Hemisphere Idea: Its Rise and Decline* (Ithaca: Cornell University Press, 1954).

8. Area studies in its many incarnations, as Harry Harootunian suggests, "failed to provide . . . a persuasive attempt to account for its privilege of space (and place) and its apparent exemption from an encounter with time" ("Some Thoughts on Comparability and the Space-Time Problem," *boundary 2*, 32:2 [2005]: 29).

9. Moreiras, *The Exhaustion of Difference*, 10.

10. Prasenjit Duara, *Rescuing History from the Nation: Questioning Narratives of Modern China* (Chicago: University of Chicago Press, 1995), 9; Lazo, *Writing Cuba*, 5. For the expansionist perspective, see Gretchen Murphy, *Hemispheric Imaginings: The Monroe Doctrine and Narratives of U.S. Empire* (Durham: Duke University Press, 2005).

11. Ernest Renan, "What Is a Nation?," (1882), in *Nations and Identities: Classic Readings*, ed. Vincent Pecora (Malden, Mass.: Blackwell, 2001), 162–177; Randolph Bourne, "Trans-National America," *Atlantic Monthly* (1916), rpt. in *The American Intellectual Tradition: A Sourcebook*, ed. David Hollinger and Charles Capper (New York: Oxford University Press, 2006), 171–181; Ernest Gellner, *Nations and Nationalism* (Ithaca: Cornell University Press, 1983); Anthony Marx, *Making Race and Nation: A Comparison of South Africa, the United States, and Brazil* (New York: Cambridge University Press, 1998); José Martí, "My Race," in *Jose Martí: Selected Writings*, ed. Esther Allen (New York: Penguin, 2002), 319–322.

12. Kwame Anthony Appiah, "Race," in *Critical Terms for Literary Study*, ed. Frank Lentricchia and Thomas McLaughlin (Chicago: University of Chicago Press, 1990), 283, 284.

13. See Carolyn Porter's seminal "What We Know That We Don't Know: Remapping American Literary Studies," *American Literary History* 6 (1994): 467–526.

14. George Handley, *Postslavery Literatures in the Americas: Family Portraits in Black and White* (Charlottesville: University Press of Virginia, 2000), 28. See also Peter Schimdt, Deborah Cohn, George Handley, and others, "Concluding Roundtable: Postcolonial Theory, the U. S. South, and New World Studies," *Mississippi Quarterly: The Journal of Southern Cultures* 57, no. 1 (Winter 2003–2004): 171–194.

15. Paul Giles, "Commentary: Hemispheric Partiality," *American Literary History* 18 (2006): 649.

1

Hemispheric Jamestown

ANNA BRICKHOUSE

Near the middle of the earliest known novel of the African American literary tradition, William Wells Brown's 1853 *Clotel*, the narrator looks back across the centuries and juxtaposes two ships, the *Mayflower* and an unnamed vessel, both in mid-transatlantic route and approaching the eastern shores of the future United States. The *Mayflower*, bound for Plymouth Rock, projects "the voice of prayer . . . and the glorious music of praise"; the other vessel, "a low rakish ship hastening from the tropics," resounds by contrast with the "cry of despair and . . . the crack of the flesh-cutting whip": the historical echoes of slavery's first arrival in the English colonies on the banks of Jamestown, Virginia, in 1619. For Brown, formerly enslaved and writing from exile in Britain, the ships bear all the weight of two opposed historical trajectories emerging out of Plymouth Rock and its ostensible antithesis in Jamestown: "Each a parent, one of the prosperous, labour-honoring, law-sustaining institutions of the North; the other the mother of idleness, lynch-law . . . and the peculiar institution of the South."[1] Yet Brown recasts this North-South divide—a New England–Jamestown opposition that has underwritten many of our most enduring literary-historical narratives—by highlighting not the moment of actual arrival in the new land, but the transit of the two ships from their respective points of departure in England and the Caribbean.[2] As maritime "parent[s]," the ships embody alternative sites of American origin that remain nevertheless inextricable within the genealogy of international conflicts and transcultural relations their union engenders. At the same time, while merely implying the nation's (always unknowable) paternity in Plymouth Rock, the scene registers in a jarring maternal metaphor the unsettling certainty of Jamestown's role as the dark "mother" of both slavery and nation.

Clotel thus locates Jamestown both upon the historical map of the nation—site of the first permanent English settlement in the New World, the putative birthplace of America—and within the distinctly transnational geography implied by its unspecified and "rakish" affiliation with the "tropics," from which America's first slave ship hastens. This latter geography inscribes Jamestown as a crossing-point of the hemispheric axes that define what Immanuel Wallerstein has called the extended Caribbean, a formation designated not by current or past European claims, nor by postcolonial political boundaries, but by environmental, economic, and historical affiliations that connect the region stretching from Bahia, Brazil, to the tidewater coasts of Virginia through the shared production of tropical crops and a plantation economy generating lines of commerce and trade as well as cultural transmission.[3] The extended Caribbean, then, both gives shape to and lies encrypted within the scene sketched out by *Clotel*'s narrator. More broadly, the scene itself suggests that while Jamestown's status as a marker of American beginning has imbued the English settlement with varying degrees of political and cultural capital within a changing national narrative, this narrative remains always in tension with a less visible but nonetheless informing hemispheric story.

This chapter tracks a single strand of Jamestown's hemispheric history, drawn from a series of Spanish colonial writings about a sixteenth-century Jesuit settlement on the Chesapeake Bay that was established in preparation for a Spanish attempt at colonization of the area. The archival record of this Jesuit mission exposes the fictionality of Virginia as the site of what the English themselves, first in Roanoke and then in Jamestown, often imagined as an originary moment of European-indigenous encounter. And while scholars of early American history have long recognized that the English were indeed preceded by rival European powers in that part of the Americas, the story of the Spanish Jesuit settlement marks a compelling symbolic and genealogical aporia within prevailing narratives of American *literary* history. Indeed, the colonial writings devoted to the Spanish in (what would become) Virginia invite us to reposition the literary trajectory emerging from the settlement at Jamestown and its anglophone chroniclers within a wider hemispheric milieu of textual relations. At the same time, the textual record of the Spanish settlement, defined by the exchange, circulation, and withholding of knowledge—and the transmission of profound doubt—offers a kind of allegorization of narrative interpretation in the colonial moment as well as, perhaps, our own. The various accounts of the episode reveal a process of dense mediations and a set of twinned, internal narrators that undermine and reshape the larger meaning of their collective, external narrative. This narrative is ultimately riven not only by conflicting stories about the event in question but by a polyvocality that demands a certain degree of self-consciousness in relation to the geopolitics of our own contemporary narratives of literary history. As I will suggest in conclusion, the archive of the Spanish in Virginia embeds a powerful counternarrative—told in this case, quite literally, from the margins of colonial historiography—that may have an ongoing critical significance for the varied projects subsumed under the rubric of Hemispheric American Studies.

* * *

In 1570—decades before the anglophone literary history generated out of the
Roanoke and Jamestown ventures in the writings of Thomas Harriot, John
Smith and William Strachey—a group of Spanish Jesuits sailed from Santa
Elena, a small island off what is now South Carolina, up the Atlantic coast
and into a body of water they knew as the Bahía de Santa María (later the
Chesapeake Bay), to establish a settlement among the coastal Indians in a
place they had for some time called Ajacán—the Virginia tidewater region of
the Algonquian-speaking Powhatan Indians.[4] Nearly forty years prior to the
arrival of the English, then, the Spanish had established a settlement in the
land where Jamestown would be founded. The manuscripts of the letters and
relaciones connected to this settlement, written between 1570 and 1622, were
transcribed and translated into English, and then collected in a dual Spanish-
English edition in 1953 by Clifford M. Lewis and Albert J. Loomie, two Jesuit
Fathers writing explicitly from the perspective of the "Christian historian."
Their history follows "the dictum of St. Paul," they avow, in forming its argument through "all that rings true, all that commands reverence, and all that
makes for right . . . wherever virtue and merit are found": they present the 1570
mission, accordingly, as "one of the noblest events in all of early American
history."[5]

The Ajacán mission was undertaken before the adoption in Paraguay and
other parts of Latin America of the Jesuit *reducción* system, which compelled
Indians to work on permanent settlements under missionary supervision; and
its relations were also produced decades before the much better known *Relations de ce qui s'est passé en la Nouvelle-France*, the annual printed records of the
French Jesuit missionaries in Canada that would become a massively popular
collective account of New World encounter in seventeenth-century France.
Occupying a mid-Atlantic space between the Latin American and the Nouvelle
France models, the Virginia Jesuit mission produced a fascinatingly hybrid
genre in a narrative repository that merges the classical traditions of ethnographic description and exoticizing travel account with the Christian conceits
of witness, prophesy, miracle, self-sacrifice, affliction, and martyrdom. All of
these become vehicles of rhetorical transformation in the Jesuit relations of
the Ajacán mission—and enable in this set of texts the elision of profound
native resistance as the triumph of missionary devotion.

The central Native figure represented in these relations is a young Virginia Powhatan who traveled to Spain; who lived for nearly a decade in Cuba
and Mexico; who learned to speak and, according to some of the accounts, to
read and write in Spanish; who was ostensibly converted and christened Don
Luis; and who eventually returned to live permanently among the Algonquian-
speaking Indians of Ajacán. According to one strand of historical scholarship
on Virginia before the arrival of the English, Don Luis may have been none

other than Opechancanaugh: the brother of the future Chief Powhatan, as the English would come to know him, and thus the uncle of Pocahontas herself.[6] Whatever his specific filial relation to the Powhatan ruling elite, however, Don Luis appears in the Jesuit writings as an uncanny and violent figuration of the complex hemispheric history that underwrites even the romance narrative most central to the insular and nationalist accounts of Jamestown's legacy.

As the Jesuit documents tell his story, the man later called Don Luis came to live with the Spaniards—either willingly, in a trade, or by force—as a young boy or teenager in 1561, when a Spanish ship sailed into the Chesapeake Bay, hunting for rival imperial settlements. The Algonquian-speaking boy apparently told the Spaniards that the name of his homeland was Ajacán and that he was the son of a chief. The boy then traveled with the Spaniards to Mexico, where he became the godson of the Mexican viceroy as well as an ostensibly faithful devotee of the Spanish missionaries, to whom he apparently suggested the project of returning to the Chesapeake Bay to convert the natives of Ajacán through his own navigational and interpretive labor.

In 1566, under the authority of the colonial governor of Cuba and *adelantado* of Florida, Don Luis accompanied a group of Dominican missionaries—along with considerable military backup—on a voyage to return to Ajacán. The Dominicans reported that Don Luis was unable to recognize the coastline sufficiently to find an entrance to the bay. The group afterward sailed on to Spain, where Don Luis continued his education in the royal court before returning to Cuba later that same year. Four years later, in 1570, two Jesuit priests, Father Juan Baptista de Segura, vice-provincial of the order in Florida, and his assistant, Luis de Quirós, requested permission from the colonial governor to make their own attempt at a settlement in Ajacán. Unlike the Dominicans, they chose—against all advice to the contrary from Jesuit and colonial authorities alike—to undertake their mission without the accompanying presence of Spanish soldiers. This time around, Don Luis successfully found his way into the bay and located his apparent homeland.

Immediately after their arrival in Ajacán, Fathers Quirós and Segura wrote the first text related to the Jesuit expedition, a letter reporting on their progress to the royal treasurer of Cuba; dated September 12, 1570, their missive is also the only surviving document written by any of the Ajacán settlers. In a fascinating and multivalent account of Don Luis's return to his home and his people, this letter introduces a minor, unnamed figure into the story of the Spanish in Ajacán that nevertheless holds a heavy significance for the future colonization of Virginia by the English:

> We find the land of Don Luis in quite another state than expected, not because he was at fault in his account of it, but because our Lord has chastised it with six years of famine and death, which has made it less populated than usual. . . . So the Indians have nothing else to offer us

but good will, and certainly these Indians have shown that in a kind manner. (89)

The letter recounts in detail the Indians' "opinion that Don Luis has risen from the dead, and come down from heaven, and since all who are left are his relatives, they are very greatly consoled in him . . . and hope that God may seek to favor them" (89–90). But it introduces a new figure into the story when it notes that "the chief has kept a brother of Don Luis, a boy of three years, who lies very ill 6 or 8 leagues from here and now seems certain to die. He has requested that someone go and baptize him, for which reason it seemed good to Father Vice-Provincial to send last night one of Ours to baptize the boy so close to death" (90).

The information transmitted here is of course contingent upon the mediation of Don Luis himself, the only bilingual Spanish-Algonquian translator available for communication with the Chesapeake Powhatans. Enlisting the Christian trope of deathbed conversion, Don Luis directs the Jesuits' attention to a child—hidden from view of the settlers and named only as the younger "brother of Don Luis"—and the occasion of a potential last-minute salvation before an imminent demise. Yet the child, who disappears from future Jesuit accounts of the mission, either recovers and survives or was never ill to begin with, if we choose to believe those historians who postulate that Don Luis was the future Opechancanaugh: for the "boy of three years" would thus prove to be Opechancanaugh's much younger brother and grow up to become the leader of the Powhatan Indians, known to the English as "Powhatan" and as Pocahontas's father. Through this record of Don Luis's first act of mediation, then, the major Native interlocutor for the English in Jamestown nearly forty years later may have entered the written record in the Spanish Jesuit documents of a pre-English Virginian past.

At the same time, the letter of Quirós and Segura introduces from its outset a deep-seated problem of polyvocality in the tension between internal and external narrators, a tension that deforms the intended story told in the letter and that will persist throughout all future Jesuit accounts documenting the story of the Spanish in Virginia. This tension registers most obviously in Don Luis's insistent presentation of himself to the Jesuits through the putative perspectives and emotions of the Natives: phrases like "it is their opinion" signal his own characterizations of indigenous frames of mind that he in turn narrates for the Jesuit writers in familiarly European frames of reference. Don Luis avowedly appears to the Natives as "risen from the dead, and come down from heaven"—an apotheosis that at once recalls the resurrection of Christ and the alleged Aztec identification of Cortés as the god Quetzalcoatl, returning from afar—a conflation that became a recurring staple of both Spanish and English colonial discourse.[7] Quirós clearly presents this Native perception of Don Luis as evidence of a general ripeness for conversion; yet it is equally plausible to read Don Luis's configuration as a motivated adaptation of colonial tropes to a new situation, one in which Don Luis, rather than the Fathers, has now assumed narrative control of the very discursive apparatus of the Jesuit missionaries. The possibility of such misguidance becomes explicit in the next lines of the relation, where Quirós warns that any new supply ship must follow a different route into the mainland of Ajacán: "It is not convenient to enter by the river as we did," he warns darkly, "for we did not have as good information from the Indians as was necessary about the place we should have entered" (90).

Indeed, the Jesuit narrators themselves seem to sense Don Luis's translative usurpation of the story they are trying to tell. The letter notes, on the one hand, that their interpreter "performs as well as was hoped, and is most obedient regarding that which Father orders him to do, and with much respect for Father, as also for the rest of us here." On the other hand, relations with the Natives seem to have deteriorated since their arrival:

> before the Indians whom we met on the way would give to us from their poverty, now they are reluctant when they see there are no trinkets for their ears of corn. They brought the ears of corn and other foods and asked that they be given something when they handed them over. . . . Since Father had forbidden this, so that they would not become accustomed to it and then afterwards want to bargain with us, the Indians took [the food] away with them. (92)

Despite their "most obedient" interpreter, then, the Jesuits are losing confidence in their understanding of the Native point of view and the meaning of their interactions. The letter conjectures that this problem with the Indians must be "Due to an error . . . made by whom on the ship I don't know[:] . . . some poor trade in food was made, which therefore brought the disadvantage that followed" (92). But the Jesuits' external narrative of some seaman's "error" in trading with the Indians for food is underwritten by the trace of a more motivated form of communication—a trace that resides in the striking absence of any explanation from their interpreter of the Natives' new economic position. There runs throughout this initial letter a deforming tension, in other words, between Don Luis's supporting interpretive role in the narrative of conversion and redemption that the Jesuits seek to inscribe and his central and in fact quite autonomous role as an internal narrator of the indigenous point of view. If that point of view is left pointedly untold here, the Natives' choice to barter rather than "give . . . from their poverty" is clear enough, for it leaves the Jesuits entirely without sustenance, and in a situation grown increasingly dire. In a mysterious postscript to the colonial commander based in Havana, the Jesuit narrators write a firm refusal to what was apparently a request to find and bring back another young Powhatan to send to the base for a colonial education (and a future career as a translator): "In no way does it seem best to me to send you any Indian boy, as the pilot will explain, and for other reasons, too" (91–92).

What the pilot will explain, and what might be the unspecified reasons for not sending another cross-cultural apprentice and Native ambassador, is never made clear. But the later fate of the Ajacán settlers sheds light both on the Jesuit narrators' reservations about training a new Native interpreter and on the subverting polyvocality shaping their letter. For when the supply ship returned in 1571 under the direction of the original pilot, he found no trace of the Jesuits within sight of the ship. According to a Jesuit priest who came to the Chesapeake the following year to seek the missing settlers, "The Indians, noticing that [the Spanish] were wary and watching for the appearance of the Fathers, used this stratagem. Taking the robes of the dead fathers, they put them on and walked upon the shore and the rest of the Indians called out that there were the Fathers and to come ashore" (120).[8] Quickly deciding to return to Cuba for reinforcements, the Spanish crew captured and took with them two Powhatan hostages, one of whom committed suicide by jumping into the sea. The other eventually conveyed the news that the Cuban colonial authorities and Jesuits most feared: the settlers in Ajacán had apparently been killed by their own translator, the Christian convert and godson of the Mexican viceroy, Don Luis himself.

Yet the Powhatan captive also informed his interrogators that one member of the Jesuit expedition had been spared: a young boy named Alonso de Olmos, who was the Creole son of a Santa Elena settler and who had served in the mission as an expert woodsman. When colonial Cuban authorities returned to Virginia the next year, in 1572, to find Alonso and the remains of the apparently slaughtered Ajacán settlers, they directed their soldiers to seek retribution while recovering the boy. Safely returned to the Spanish during this punitive mission, Alonso became the sole surviving Spanish-speaking eyewitness to the events in Ajacán over the previous year.

The first and most immediate version of what happened between Don Luis and the Spanish Fathers was recorded by a Jesuit priest accompanying the 1572 punitive mission, Juan Rogel, who wrote a report of the trip directly from the Chesapeake Bay, just after the recovery of Alonso. As figured by Rogel, Alonso supplements and provides a kind of double for Don Luis's role as an internal narrator—and like its counterpart, Alonso's internal narration registers a similarly deforming tension between the Jesuit and indigenous points of view.

> I will now relate . . . how came the death of Ours . . . as this boy tells it. He says that . . . Don Luis abandoned them . . . he did not sleep in their hut more than two nights nor stay in the village . . . for more than five days [before] he went off to live with [the Indians] . . . a day and a half away. Father [Segura] sent a message . . . two times to the renegade.

Don Luis never came, and Ours were in great distress, for they had no one by whom they could make themselves understood to the Indians. They were without . . . support, and no one could buy grain from [the Indians]. (109)

In this initial account, Rogel foregrounds the dependence of his own status as a narrator upon that of Alonso: the ensuing story can only be told "as this boy tells it." Drawing upon familiar religious and colonial tropes, this internal narration figures Don Luis's gradual physical movement away from the Jesuits in correspondence with his return to Native culture and his final emergence as a "renegade": from the two nights of intimacy in the same sleeping hut, to his five days in the Christian space of the Jesuit village, and finally to the journey away, where he is "liv[ing] with [the Indians]," Don Luis's apostasy signifies both spatially and temporally—just as his spiritual transformation, from agent of Christian conversion to murderous savage, is both corporeal and discursive. Alonso's internal narrative thus privileges the Jesuits' loss of their translator as a source of "great distress" even over the problem of starvation: "*no tenían con quien poderse entender con los indios*"—a phrase that evokes, in this particular context, the Jesuits' central problem as that of making themselves understood rather than that of understanding.

This tension between narration and comprehension also marks the ensuing versions of the story that the Jesuits would tell, which—unlike Rogel's first relation, written in the moment, on the waters of the Bahía de Santa María— were written often decades after the fact, some by eyewitnesses to the punitive expedition that recovered Alonso, and some by those who only learned the story afterward in Santa Elena or elsewhere. As the relations move in time from the event of Alonso's recovery, the larger narrative repository begins to flatten out and elide the mediations and polyvocality marking its earliest texts by introducing increasingly self-conscious literary qualities and more subtle modes of characterization alongside more heavily allegorical meanings. Don Luis becomes "a ravening wolf, tossing aside the sheep's clothing," a "Judas" whose actions are elaborated through exegesis of specific biblical passages; and the names of the Jesuit fathers are, through the texts' self-reflexive metaphors of inscription, "written into the heavens" when not remembered specifically.[9] The fathers are tortured in elaborate ways before they are killed, the killings themselves embellished with competing forms of symbolism. In one version, it is on the Sunday after the feast of the Purification, when Don Luis—"himself . . . the first to draw blood with one of those hatchets which were brought along for trading with the Indians"—destroys the masters with their own tools of colonial enterprise, choosing a particular holy day to taint with his apostasy. In another, Don Luis degenerates into a primitive savage, merely "arriv[ing] with his tribe armed with clubs and lances[:] . . . Raising his club and giving his greeting were really one gesture, and so in wishing [Father

Segura] well, he killed him." In still another version, Don Luis approaches the Jesuits the day before "the solemn feast of Candlemas" and requests hatchets to distribute among the Natives as "he wished to go with all the Indians to cut wood in order to construct a church for the Virgin" during the morning mass; with Segura kneeling at the altar, Don Luis—in a premeditated and symbolic desecration of the chapel—"came and gave him a heavy blow."[10]

As the Jesuit writings struggle to contain the subversive meanings of Don Luis's actions, their collective narrative elaborates a carefully balanced structural reversal that provides closure to the tale: three of Don Luis's followers miraculously fall down dead after attempting to open a chest belonging to the slain Jesuits, which contains a large crucifix. As the relations proceed, this miracle story becomes more detailed and rhythmic, each of the three Indians approaching the chest individually and meeting their fates sequentially rather than at once. Through this corrupted trinity and the powers attributed to the sacramental chest, the relations thus grapple with an unsettling problem of genre that threatens to undermine the stability of the Christian colonial discourse upon which their New World narrative depends: How does one tell a conversion story in which the central figure of redemption apparently converts back?

By the time the first printed account of Don Luis's story appeared, in Pedro de Ribadeneyra's *Life of Father Francis Borgia*, first published in Madrid in 1592, the question of how to explain Don Luis's conversion and his subsequent actions in Ajacán appears as two opposing conjectures: "Don Luis and his relatives and friends fell upon the said Fathers and slew them," Ribadeneyra explains, "either because Don Luis had already apostatized and returned to idolatry and so was embarrassed, or because he had already been conspiring and weaving this evil plan."[11] Don Luis's alleged killing of the Jesuits resulted, in other words, either from the shame of his failing conversion, his apostasy to Native idolatry—or there was never a conversion to begin with, and it was only staged as the means to a wicked end.

The early seventeenth-century Peruvian mixed-race poet and historiographer, the Inca Garcilaso de la Vega, apparently arrived at the latter interpretation in his own gloss of the story. When he wrote his influential account of the De Soto expedition, *La Florida del Inca* (1509–1605), he was so taken with Ribadeneyra's story of Don Luis that he added a final section to his already complete manuscript.[12] In a dark revisionist twist, Garcilaso depicts his own anonymous informant for the entire history of *La Florida*—a purported survivor of the De Soto expedition—coming across Don Luis long before his return to Ajacán, while the young Powhatan travels with a group of seven Indians throughout Spain.[13] This group of Natives is displayed to the wonderstruck public as "perfectly friendly," and "wearing the same clothes that . . . they wear in their native land," "carrying bows and arrows . . . for their greater adornment."[14] When Garcilaso's informant hears of the Indians, he hastens to meet them, and what follows is an ambiguous scene of unambiguous foreshadow-ing—made all the more astonishing by the utter absence of anything like it in Garcilaso's source text (Ribadeneyra's *Life of Borgia*):

> The Indians . . . recognized that he . . . had accompanied . . . de Soto, and . . . with evil eyes, replied: "Having left those provinces as desolate as you did, . . . you want us to give you news of them?" [The Indians] would not answer . . . another word, but among themselves, they [said] (according to the interpreter . . . accompanying them): "We would more willingly give him arrow blows than the information he requests . . ." Then (in order to make this man realize their desire to shoot arrows at him and the skill with which they might so do) [they] discharged great arrows . . . with so much force that they were lost from sight. (641)

In this shattering scene of recognition, the Indians understand Garcilaso's informant, just as the soldier hopes, as someone "who had been in Florida." What they recognize, however, is not their mutual knowledge of a coastal world across the Atlantic (they are ostensibly from the Chesapeake Bay area, after all, not Florida) but instead their interlocutor's status as a returning explorer and thus a would-be conqueror. As Garcilaso stages this scene, then, Don Luis (with his fellow Indians) knows long before returning to Ajacán that he would choose battle with Spanish colonizers over any disclosure of information to them: in other words, that a mere parry for news from Florida is, in the hemispheric point of view from which the Peruvian Garcilaso writes, a practical equivalent to military aggression in Ajacán or any other part of the indigenous Americas. The strategy of the Indians is paradoxically both to refuse "another word" and to clarify, through an interpreter and then with gestures, their message of refusal and retribution. Rewriting his source text, Garcilaso thus introduces an entirely new episode, one that retroactively casts the murder of the Ajacán Jesuits as an act not of volatile barbarity but of premeditated and, perhaps more crucially, *prearticulated* revenge for the "desolate" state of La Florida after De Soto's expedition. In Garcilaso's version, therefore, when Don Luis kills the Ajacán Jesuits, he falls "upon them with great impetus and fury, as if he were attacking *a squadron of armed soldiers*."[15]

Perhaps Garcilaso was also drawn to the cross-cultural and translational mediations presented in Don Luis's story, as much as to the fatal outcome of the Jesuit Fathers. Garcilaso knew well and firsthand the ways in which the monolingual shortsightedness of the Spanish had visited tragic historical consequences upon the Peruvian Incas.[16] Don Luis, too, possessed a cross-cultural and bilingual understanding that might be considered analogous to Garcilaso's—as did the only other survivor from the Jesuit mission, Alonso de Olmos. At the time of his recovery, Alonso had lived among the Natives of Ajacán for two years, and he spoke their language fluently. Only Alonso, moreover, could tell the full story of the Jesuits' demise to the Spanish;

and all accounts of their deaths, from the moment of his recovery on, rest
on Alonso's narration alone. Yet in a seemingly inscrutable revision of his
source text, Garcilaso chooses to omit Alonso from the story entirely—and at
the expense of the story's credibility: for without Alonso, there is no witness
to tell the story of what happened in Ajacán. Thwarting the early modern
historiographical impulse to establish eyewitness sources of information as
forms of corroboration and verification and means of evaluation, Garcilaso's
story floats unmoored from these modes of knowledge and becomes instead
epigraphical (though its brief summation of Don Luis's story concludes rather
than begins the larger work): it reprises its more general theme—violent
indigenous resistance to religious conversion and imperial acquisition—by
dangerous but indirect association rather than explicit statement or logical
analogy. That Garcilaso's text was later banned during the Tupac Amaru indigenous rebellion in the eighteenth century for allegedly advocating violence
suggests, then, perhaps not *just* that Spanish and Creole readers interpreted it
so, but that it may have *also* signified within another, indigenous genealogy of
thought, even if we now have access only to the Spanish and Creole reading of
what that signification was.[17]

As does Garcilaso's text in eliding Alonso, the Jesuit relations of Ajacán, too, refuse to acknowledge the strangely twinned roles of Don Luis and
Alonso as bilingual interpreters and cross-cultural internal narrators. But the
structural similarity of the two figures pulses anxiously through the story of
Alonso's recovery:

> When Alonso de Olmos . . . heard the report of ships . . . he fled at
> night. . . . At daybreak he came to the beach . . . swam out to the flag-
> ship . . . and climbed aboard. Since he arrived naked and browned by
> the sun, no one recognized him. . . . [The Spanish] understood him to
> be an Indian. Gazing about the ship, [Alonso] . . . recognized his father
> . . . threw himself at his feet . . . kissed him and cried: "Here is my
> father!" Because he had not used our language for five [*sic*] years, and
> was so happy on being in the protection of Christians, he could hardly
> speak.[18]

If Alonso is unrecognizable to the Spanish after living among the Indians for
two years—stretched by this account into five, as if to better account for the
consequences—the slippage between European and Indian, Christian and
heathen, is neatly contained by the narrative frame of the passage, which
establishes Alonso's fervent desire to return to the Spanish through his flight
in the dark of night and his daybreak swim to the ships, a rebaptism into his
former identity, "in the protection of the Christians," as he emerges, naked
and reborn, from the sea, and utters the words that establish his paternity
as a Christian and a Spanish subject: "Here is my father!" Yet the concluding
sentence of this natal scene undermines the representation of Alonso's filial

pronouncement with its recognition that the boy can no longer speak—"*de repente no acercava hablar*"—or rather, that his language is no longer "*nuestra lengua*," no longer primarily Spanish, but Algonquian.

Alonso never made such a breathtaking escape from the Indians, however: other Jesuit relations make it clear that the colonial Cuban authorities had to drive a hard bargain with the Powhatans over Alonso, and not until the Spanish took hostages was the boy apparently *brought* to the ship. Most accounts also suggest that because of his youth, and possibly also his lay status, the natives of Ajacán protected Alonso, and he was adopted into the family of a Powhatan leader, where he lived until the arrival of the punitive expedition. Rogel's first account, written immediately after Alonso's return, accordingly emphasizes the boy's linguistic utility for the Jesuits' future colonial ambitions:

> We are keeping this boy with us. He is very fluent in the [Native] language and [has] almost forgotten his Spanish. After he was freed from his captivity, we asked . . . if he wished to be with us [the Jesuits], or go with his father [back to Santa Elena]. He said he wanted to be with us only. In order to make sure that he retains the language and does not forget it, I am debating whether to bring along . . . an Indian boy, who has come along with Alonso, leaving his parents and home to be with him, and so he might practice the language. (111)

Here again, the repetitive exchange of young boys groomed to translate for the Spanish bears obvious structural similarities to the initial story of Don Luis. As Don Luis did, Alonso is now separating both from his Powhatan father, the leader who, in Rogel's own words earlier in the letter, "would treat him well and hold him as a son" (110), and from his birth father, who has accompanied the punitive expedition. And as Don Luis did, Alonso chooses here to follow the Jesuits. Most remarkably, a young "Indian boy" in the company of Alonso—perhaps an adoptive brother—may be "leaving his parents and home" in order to facilitate Alonso's growth as an interpreter for future settlements in Ajacán—where Rogel is "confident" that the Spaniards should settle, "provided they would frighten the natives that threaten harm" (111).

But by the time Rogel writes his second account, between 1607 and 1611, his cross-cultural internal narrator and future interpreter has nearly dropped out of the story, retained only in a few lines as a minor source of information: "This was learned from a boy. . . . His name was Alonso, and because of his youth or by God's design, the Indians did not kill him" (119). Why has the figure of Alonso been diminished rather than embellished in the second and more elaborate of Rogel's accounts—especially given that he was, after all, the sole Spanish-speaking eyewitness source of information about the Jesuits' fate, and thus the *single* source for all of the ensuing accounts of the Jesuit mission in Virginia—including *all* our contemporary historical accounts of this episode of Spanish colonial history?

The only clue as to Alonso's near disappearance from the story is a cryptic note scrawled in the margin of Rogel's first text from August of 1572 alongside his description of Alonso's satisfaction in being returned to the Spanish Jesuits. "*En esto me e engañado, porque se a estragado mucho despues que a vivedo solo entre indios, ni quiere estar con nosotros, no conviene,*" writes Rogel: 'In this I was mistaken, for he was much corrupted after living alone among Indians, he does not want to be with us, it doesn't suit him"—or, more ominously, if we don't assume a tacit "le" before "conviene": "he is not suitable."[19] Rogel apparently found this later commentary upon Alonso significant enough, in other words, that he returned to his original text in order to inscribe a marginal gloss critiquing his own internal narrator as both deceptive and utterly destroyed—for *engañado* can also mean "deceived," and *estragado* implies both corruption and destruction, as from a military conquest. Alonso's remarkable transculturalism thus ultimately subverts Rogel's narrative confidence in documenting the outcome and the larger meaning of the mission—a seemingly insurmountable problem given that Alonso's internal narration bears sole responsibility for remembering and transmitting the very story of Christian martyrdom that ended the Jesuit mission in Virginia.

*　*　*

This single inscription throws the entirety of the collective, colonial Jesuit narrative into doubt—as well as the historical narrative we now have available in contemporary scholarship—opening the possibility for a new story altogether, one apprehended in reading, quite literally, from the margins, and suggestive of an emphatically different point of view on the part of Alonso, the young Creole son of a Santa Elena settler. The untold story suggested in this marginal note forms a compelling counternarrative to the official colonial story the Jesuits themselves wanted to tell: a counternarrative of adoption, kinship, and identification with the Natives, and a story of feigned allegiance to the Spanish—"I was deceived," says Rogel—that parallels the more consuming story of Don Luis's false conversion and his violent resistance to the colonizers. At the same time, the stories of both Don Luis and Alonso provide an illuminating Spanish harbinger of the English story of Pocahontas at Jamestown—also a captive, a translator, an informant, and an ostensible convert to Christianity. As a collection, the relations present the sedimented layers of their shared connective story as a single strand of hemispheric colonial discourse over time, written from Virginia, Santa Elena, and Cuba, in addition to Spain, and crystallized in one narrative whose shifting contours offer an alternative vision of colonial Virginia than the one now enshrined in most literary-historical narratives.

First, and perhaps most obviously, the relations dramatically alter both the traditional reading of European-Native cultural encounter generated by the Jamestown legend of Pocahontas and the numerous ethno-historical but nevertheless nationally demarcated readings that seek to unmask that legend's ethnocentrism. The relations beg the question of what it would mean to understand Powhatan and the Chesapeake Indians as on some level familiar not simply with European culture but with the comparative history of colonialism in other parts of the Americas *prior to the arrival of the English*, via their exposure to the cultural and political experiences that Don Luis accumulated over his many years abroad: in Spain, the seat of European empire in the New World; in Mexico, indelibly marked by the violent legacy of indigenous slavery and the *encomienda* system; and in Cuba, where the near extinction of the indigenous population was almost complete by the mid-sixteenth century.[20] An increasingly interdisciplinary collaboration among anthropologists, historians, and literary critics in recent years has proposed modes of rereading colonial literature to discern the places where Native voices, influences, epistemologies, and structures of meaning impose upon and powerfully shape the text of the colonizer. But what the particular case of the Jesuit writings suggests, I think, is the possibility of reading the subsequent Jamestown literature not just for the modes of indigenous agency shaping its texts, but for signs of an informing Native-European and colonial polyculturalism that the English writers themselves could never discern. To put this another way, the Jesuit writings cast a different light on the very origins of anglophone American literature—an English tradition rooted in a story of Native-European contact that not only had a historical precedent in the precise geographical location as the Jamestown settlement but was already embodied in a series of hispanophone narratives about the same native population and locality. The Jesuit relations thus challenge our literary-historical tradition to consider what it would mean to restore to (U.S.)-American letters this ambivalent history of Spanish colonial priority and Native-Creole biculturalism at the site of the future nation's ostensible English founding in Jamestown.

It is no coincidence, after all, that the story of English Jamestown, and of Pocahontas in particular, became prominent in the nineteenth-century Anglo-American public sphere at the very height of its promotion of the Black Legend and its polemical insistence upon the legacies of Spanish incompetence and cruelty in the years leading up to the U.S.-Mexican War. Nor is it a coincidence, I would argue, that the story of the sixteenth-century Spanish exploration of the Chesapeake, long hidden successfully from the English by the Spanish, first entered—precisely to be dismissed from—the anglophone scholarly record when discovered by an influential linguist and historian working for the U.S. State Department during the U.S.-Mexican War: Robert Greenhow, who used his multilingual and historical proficiencies for translating colonial history into contemporary geographic surveys—for researching land claims and jurisdiction in order to facilitate the expansionist interests of the U.S. government.[21] By the time the tercentennial of Jamestown's English founding arrived, the president of the 1907 Jamestown Exposition explicitly acknowledged that the "object" of the national festivities, held at what would become the Norfolk Naval Base, was "primarily to celebrate and commemorate the 300th anniversary of the founding of the first permanent English settlement in America, and secondarily to demonstrate to the world our right to claim supremacy." The 1907 Jamestown Exposition ostentatiously overlapped its displays of Jamestown history with exhibits of U.S. naval and marine prowess in the wake of the Spanish-American war and the nation's acquisition of Puerto Rico and the Philippines, directing its remembrance of Jamestown quite self-consciously toward U.S. imperial ends in the hemisphere and beyond.[22] "Hemispheric Jamestown," then, is in a sense what Jamestown has always been: freighted with mutually informing roles as site of exceptionalist national memory and axis of hemispheric relations—and thus pointing to some of the political and intellectual stakes of undertaking a hemispheric American studies in our own moment, as we make sense of Jamestown, 2007, and "America's 400th Anniversary."

Among these stakes is the problem of perpetuating the United States as the default center of the scholarly narratives we create—however much we may acknowledge that center to be multilingual, internally riven, and hemispherically traversed, on the one hand, and imperialistic, on the other. The story of Ajacán that underwrites Jamestown offers a particularly acute case in point. It would be all too easy to note (with some degree of pleasurable irony) that the Spanish were in Virginia before Virginia existed—and to offer this up as a supplement and corrective to the anglophone (and subsequently anglophilic) literary narrative of Jamestown, restating in this way what we already (think we) know: that the nation's self-described site of origin has always been a site of mixture and crossing. But as this chapter has tried to show, the Ajacán documents also offer us a series of alternative narratives, attendant to the figures of Don Luis and Alonso, that inherently displace the prolepsis of nation as the absent center of analysis. Foregrounding instead the geopolitics of knowledge, these alternative narratives engendered by Don Luis and Alonso both represent and enact the production of what Walter Mignolo has termed "border gnosis," or the subaltern critical thought that emerges in response to the discursive violence of imperialism—a "fractured locus of enunciation," as Mignolo envisions it, "embedded in indigenous . . . experiences and genealogies of thought" and existing in tense dialogue with the very colonial idiom seeking either to control or suppress it.[23]

To recognize the internal narration of Don Luis and Alonso is thus to find in the Ajacán archive more than another, predictably unreliable colonial narrative; it is to understand both figures in a complex, multivalent, and powerfully active engagement with the very terms of colonial discourse. And as Rogel's bewildered marginal commentary on Alonso's corruption and unsuitability reveals, the bicultural, hybridized frameworks of knowledge within which Don Luis and Alonso acted and narrated in the sixteenth century cannot be fully excavated or transparently understood from inside the perspective of

Western modernity, or through its forms of knowledge alone. Approaching the Ajacán documents with this in mind, I would propose the story of Don Luis and Alonso as a gloss on the field of Hemispheric American Studies—largely written from inside the United States, and usually in English—and its responsibility to consider and make self-conscious the geopolitics of knowledge delimiting the work that we do. This is not, of course, a sufficient critical endpoint for the field—but neither is it a rote posturing of monolingual culpability and the institutional privileging of English. It is instead a first step toward recognizing and trying to give audience to perspectives and forms of knowledge formed beyond the scholarships of Western epistemology, produced at the margins of the modern Western world, and lying, in this particular case, in the literal margins of the written account of what happened in sixteenth-century Ajacán. To open up the category of knowledge in our own work means recognizing our failure to see beyond the perspectives of our various disciplines and the modes of knowing the past they have invented. Otherwise, we are, like Rogel, "engañado" (mistaken and, perhaps, deceived), simply assimilating the margins of our collective epistemological text, dismissing the faint but indelible inscriptions that trouble the historical and critical narratives we think we already know.

NOTES

1. William Wells Brown, *Clotel; Or, The President's Daughter: A Narrative of Slave Life in the United States*, ed. Robert S. Levine (Boston and New York: Bedford/St. Martin's, 2000), 180, 181.

2. Until recently, historians agreed that the first Africans in Virginia arrived on a Dutch warship transporting them from the West Indies. New evidence, however, suggests they were brought directly from Angola on a Portuguese slave ship that was seized at sea by British pirates.

3. Immanuel Wallerstein, *The Modern World System* (New York: Academic Press, 1974), II:47.

4. Throughout, I will be following Charlotte Gradie, among other historians, in assuming that the Ajacán natives are the Virginia Powhatans. Gradie, "The Powhatans in the Context of the Spanish Empire," in *Powhatan Foreign Relations, 1500–1722*, ed. Helen Rountree (Charlottesville: University of Virginia Press, 1993), 154–172.

5. Clifford M. Lewis and Albert J. Loomie, *The Spanish Jesuit Mission in Virginia, 1570–1572* (Chapel Hill: University of North Carolina Press, 1953), xi. All future citations will be internal to Lewis and Loomie's English translations—though I have changed some of their wording in consultation with the original Spanish. One of the earliest historians to draw upon Lewis and Loomie's collection of the Jesuit accounts was Carl Bridenbaugh, who fails to mention contradictory versions of events, instead choosing to cite from the accounts with the most sensational details. See *Jamestown 1544–1699* (New York: Oxford University Press, 1980), 10–33. For a more helpful historical analysis of the Spanish in Virginia, see Gradie as well as Camilla Townsend, *Pocahontas and the Powhatan Dilemma* (New York: Hill and Wang, 2004), 7–11; and Frederick W. Gleach, *Powhatan's World and Colonial Virginia: A Conflict of Cultures* (Lincoln: University of Nebraska Press, 1997), 18–22.

6. Following the lead of Lewis and Loomie, Bridenbaugh asserts that Don Luis took the name Opechancanaugh, allegedly meaning "He whose soul is white" in Algonquian, to signal a newfound "hatred of all Spaniards and Christians" (17); Bridenbaugh thus reads the 1622 Powhatan attack on Jamestown led by Opechancanaugh as a follow-up to his alleged murder (as Don Luis) of the Jesuits in 1571, "Opechancanaugh's first 'massacre.'" In the story as I recount it here, I have drawn from what more recent historians have considered the most reliable of the primary documents involved— primarily, the letter of Quirós and Segura and the two relations of Juan Rogel.

7. The idea that the Aztecs perceived Cortés as a God has persisted in the popular imagination as well as in academic scholarship, despite many studies showing otherwise. Camilla Townsend, "Burying the White Gods: New Perspectives on the Conquest of Mexico," *American Historical Review* 108 (2003): 1106–1144. The trope of the divine European dazzling a bewildered indigenous audience was canonical in accounts of the conquest by the 1550s (in other words, a decade before Don Luis began his sojourn among the Spanish), and it was clearly inflected by the Christian narrative of apotheosis. On the prevalence of this conflation in English colonial writings, see William M. Hamlin, "Imagined Apotheoses: Drake, Harriot, and Ralegh in the Americas," *Journal of the History of Ideas* 57 (1996): 405–428.

8. The priest is Juan Rogel, discussed later.

9. See the 1610 relation of Bartolomé Martínez (159) and the relation of Luis Gerónimo de Oré, composed between 1617 and 1620 (181–182), in Lewis and Loomie, *Spanish Jesuit Mission in Virginia*.

10. See, respectively, the August letter of Juan Rogel, 1572, 110; the relation of Juan Rogel, from between 1607 and 1611, 119; and the relation of Luis Gerónimo de Oré, composed between 1617 and 1620, which can be found in Lewis and Loomie, *Spanish Jesuit Mission in Virginia* (181–182).

11. Ribadeneyra, *Life of Father Francis Borgia*, Book III, ch. 6 (145–146), in Lewis and Loomie, *Spanish Jesuit Mission in Virginia*.

12. Lewis and Loomie note that El Inca Garcilaso de la Vega had already completed *La Florida del Inca* when he decided to add the story of the Jesuits in Ajacán (*Spanish Jesuit Mission in Virginia*, 147).

13. Garcilaso's informant is thought to be Gonzalo Silvestre, who participated in the De Soto expedition. See Lisa Voigt, "Captivity, Exile, and Interpretation in *La Florida del Inca*," *Colonial Latin American Review* 11 (2002): 251.

14. This translation is from *The Florida of the Inca*, trans. John and Jeanette Varner (Austin, University of Texas Press, 1951), 641. Future citations are internal.

15. Garcilaso, p. 642, my emphasis. On the ending of *La Florida*, though not its relation to the story of Don Luis as told by the Jesuits, see also Voigt, 251–273.

16. On Garcilaso and the "rhetoric of particularism," see Doris Sommer, *Proceed with Caution, When Engaged by Minority Writing in the Americas* (Cambridge, MA: Harvard University Press, 1999), 61–91.

17. See John Varner, *El Inca: The Life and Times of Garcilaso de la Vega* (Austin: University of Texas Press, 1968), 379–383.

18. Relation of Bartolomé Martínez, in Lewis and Loomie, *Spanish Jesuit Mission in Virginia*, 1610, 160.

19. See Lewis and Loomie, *Spanish Jesuit Mission in Virginia*, 114 n. 17. As far as I can tell, no later historians have noted the existence of this commentary from the margins (or, at any rate, elaborated on its implications).

20. On what kinds of observations Don Luis would likely have made upon his arrival in Mexico, see Gradie's excellent analysis in "The Powhowtans in the Context of the Spanish Empire," 166–168.

21. Robert Greenhow, "Memoir on the First Discovery of the Chesapeake Bay, Communicated to the Virginia Historical Society, May, 1848," *An Account of Discoveries in the West until 1519, and of Voyages to and along the Atlantic Coast of North America, from 1520 to 1573*, ed. Conway Robinson (Richmond: Shepherd and Colin, 1848), 481–491. On Greenhow's work as a translator for the State Department, see David Rankin Barbee, "Robert Greenhow," *William and Mary Quarterly*, 2nd ser., 13, no. 3 (July 1933): 182–183; as well as Mark J. Stegmaier, "Treachery or Hoax? The Rumored Southern Conspiracy to Confederate with Mexico," *Civil War History* 35 (1989): 28–38.

22. On the 1907 Jamestown Exposition, see in particular Amy Waters Yarsinske, *Jamestown Exposition: American Imperialism on Parade* (Charleston, SC: Arcadia, 1999).

23. Walter Mignolo, *Local Histories/Global Designs: Coloniality, Subaltern Knowledges, and Border Thinking* (Princeton: Princeton University Press, 2000), x, and Walter Mignolo, *The Idea of Latin America* (Oxford: Blackwell Publishing, 2005), 34.

2

The Hemispheric
Genealogies of "Race"

Creolization and the Cultural Geography of Colonial
Difference across the Eighteenth-Century Americas

RALPH BAUER

In the wake of the postcolonial studies movement, early American literary scholarship across disciplinary boundaries has focused on the role that "race" played in European imperial expansionism and colonialism in the New World. Literary scholars and historians alike have generally proceeded from a historical notion of race as it emerged in the nineteenth century—as a transnational discourse of identity and difference based on biological factors, such as skin color (i.e., the "white," "black," "red," "brown," or "yellow" race)—and then traced the "origins" of this modern concept back to English colonialism in the seventeenth century,[1] the Spanish conquests of the sixteenth century, and even to the Christian reconquest of Spain from the Moors and the expulsion of the Jews from Spain during the late fifteenth century.[2] While these accounts have generally acknowledged "race" as an arbitrary and socially constructed category that is historically contingent and "ever-changing and adaptive," they have also regarded the discourse of race as "remarkably resilient" and "persistent,"[3] thus positing a continuous intellectual genealogy that connected pre-modern discourses of difference, such as the Spanish *estatutos de limpieza de sangre* (statues of the purity of blood) with the modern scientific racism of the nineteenth and twentieth centuries. Recently, however, some scholars have disputed the notion that the "modern concept of race is . . . simply a continuation of age-old prejudices,"[4] insisting that it is anachronistic to speak of "race"—in the modern sense of the word—before the nineteenth century. Indeed, as they have pointed out, the word "race" itself had a very different meaning before the nineteenth century, pertaining not to transnational groups of people distinguished by biological factors such as skin color but rather to various ethnic groups distinguished primarily by cultural practice. Thus, scholars have begun to place common metaphors conceptualizing human differences such as "blood"—all too quickly associated with the modern idea of race—within their proper historical context, showing that in early modern social hierarchies their meaning approximates more closely what we today might call "ancestry" or "lineage," whose quality ("good" or "bad" blood) was seen to manifest not biological but rather cultural and social difference.[5]

While this brief essay can obviously not offer a definitive resolution to this historical controversy, I do want to revisit the question of the modern concept of race from the hemispheric perspective of the eighteenth-century Americas. For this purpose, I will bring into the conversation two key discursive sites that have often been discussed in connection with the emergence of a modern concept of race in their respective realms: the writings of Antonio de Ulloa and Jorge Juan about their voyage to South America (1748/1772) and Thomas Jefferson's *Notes on the State of Virginia* (1785). When read in the context of their hemispheric genealogies, Jefferson's emergent ideas about race present themselves less as "The White Man's Burden" that modern Americans allegedly inherited from the early modern (European) colonial encounter with an American "other." Instead, such a hemispheric perspective will bring into focus the dialectical relationship between the modern idea of race and an older ("early modern") circumatlantic discourse about (Spanish) American "creolization," in which the geography and sociology of birth continued to play an important role in distinguishing American-born creoles from Europeans and that emanated from Spanish America both north across the hemisphere as well as east across the Atlantic.[6] In other words, Jefferson's emergent ideas about race will appear not as the (proto-)scientific product of the European imperial legacy in the New World but rather as a geopolitical counterdiscourse—that of creole patriotism—that would ultimately become the dominant ideology of nineteenth-century nationalism throughout the Western world in the process of hemispheric and transatlantic cultural diffusions.[7] The idea of "whiteness," in particular, became hereby central to a discourse of creole patriotism across the hemisphere, as European American colonials sought to assert new Enlightenment ideas of "equality" within colonial geographies. In the first section of this essay, I turn to the writings of Juan and Ulloa about South America and focus on what they reveal about the sociology of the creole discourse of whiteness; in the second, I discuss the historical translation of the debate about creolization into the British American context; and in the third, I take up the rhetorical construction of Jefferson's discourse of race in its dialectical engagement with the discourse of (Spanish American) creolization.

Creole Subjects and the Idea of "Whiteness" in Spanish America: Jorge Juan and Antonio de Ulloa's *Noticias Secretas*

In 1735, two Spanish naval officers, Antonio de Ulloa and Jorge Juan, accompanied a French scientific expedition to South America under the leadership of the French naturalist Charles de Condamine, whose charge it was to take measurements of the terrestrial meridian on the equatorial line that were supposed to lead to a determination of the exact shape of the globe. The two Spanish naval officers, however, were charged with an additional mission by the newly ascended Spanish Bourbon monarchy under Philip V: they were to write up a report on the state of Spanish possessions in South America, with observations on the state of colonial society, economy, and political administration that would be instrumental in the Bourbons' attempt to salvage Spain's decaying empire in the Americas through conservatively Enlightened reforms. Their observations resulted in various accounts, most notably the (co-authored) *Relación histórica del viaje á la América Meridional* (Madrid, 1748) and Ulloa's *Noticias Americanas* (1772). While these works contained a vast amount of information about South American geography, natural history, and economy, some of Juan and Ulloa's observations on viceregal society and politics were too sensitive for public consumption and therefore omitted from their public accounts. After their eventual return to Spain, however, they were commissioned by the Marques de Ensenada, the Spanish Bourbons' secretary of state, to write a secret report about the problems of the empire. The resulting work, *Discurso y reflexiones políticas sobre el estado presente de los reinos del Perú* (1748), provided a graphic indictment of corruption and misrule, particularly the abuses visited upon the indigenous peoples, which the authors claimed to have witnessed during their eleven-year sojourn in the Viceroyalty of Peru. The exposé was prohibited from publication by the Bourbon government, but—like so many other Spanish reports about the Americas in previous centuries—it became literary "contraband" when the manuscript fell into the hands of the Englishman David Barry, who subsequently published it in an English translation as *A Secret Expedition to Peru* in London in 1826. It has since come to be known as the *Noticias secretas* in Spanish American literary scholarship.

One of the most troubling chapters of the *Noticias secretas* about the society that had emerged in the New World concerned the "Partisan animosity in Peru between Europeans and creoles." "No dejará de parecer cosa impropia," they wrote, "que entre gentes de una misma nación y de una misma religión, *y aun de una misma sangre*, haya tanta contrariedad y encono como la que se deja percibir en el Perú, donde las ciudades y poblaciones grandes son un teatro de discordia y de continua oposición entre españoles y criollos" (Nothing can seem more inappropriate than that among a people of the same nation and of the same religion, *and even of the same blood*, there should be such an enmity and rancor as the one that can be perceived in Peru, where the cities and large populations are a spectacle of discord and continual opposition between the Spaniards and creoles).[8] According to Juan and Ulloa, there were two main causes for this animosity between creoles and peninsular Spaniards: on the one hand, the ease with which the European immigrants, who arrived in Peru in a "mísero y desdichado estado" (a mean and wretched condition), are quickly able to rise above their lowly social condition (429); on the other hand, "la demasiada vanidad, presunción y soberanía que reina en los criollos" (the excessive vanity and overbearing manners of the creoles), which "se encumbra a tanto que cabilan continuamente en la disposición y orden de sus gene-alogías, *de modo que no tengan que envidiar en nobleza y antigüedad a la de las prim-eras casas de España*" (rise to such a height that they are perpetually discussing the order and line of their descent, so that it would appear, *as it respects nobility and antiquity, they have nothing to envy in the most illustrious families in Spain*) (429; my emphasis). In truth, however, the creoles' lofty pretensions to a noble ancestry rest on rather thin ice, as it was a commonly known fact among them, Juan and Ulloa wryly observe, that "es rara la familia donde falte mezcla de sangre" (a family can rarely be found that has no mixed blood) (429).

Thus, what in effect rationalizes the creoles' social ascendancy vis-à-vis the other sectors of viceregal society, such as Indians, blacks, and the varie-ties of mixed peoples, is not so much their "lineage," which they knew to be intertwined, but rather their claim to "whiteness": "No tienen los criollos más fundamento para tal conducta que *el decir que son blancos*, y por esta sola prerrogativa son acreedores legítimos a tanto distintivo, sin pararse a considerar cuál es su estado" (In pursuing such a course the creoles have no better ground to rest upon than *merely to say that they are white*, and this sole prerogative entitles them to some distinction) (432; my emphasis). Ironically, then, Juan and Ulloa observe, "son ellos mismos [los criollos] los que dan a los europeos toda la estimación, autoridad y convenencias que disfrutan" (it is they—the creoles—themselves who give to Europeans all the esteem, authority, and advantages which they enjoy) (431). In this respect, while the discourse of racial identity ("whiteness") upholds the creoles' social ascen-dancy vis-à-vis the "non-white" sectors of viceregal society, its logic inevitably places the Europeans, even low-born ones, into a position of social privilege that erases all considerations of social birth. For, "siendo europeo, sin otra más circunstancia, se juzgan merecedores del mismo aplauso y cortejo que se hace a los que van allá con empleos, cuyo honor los debería distinguir del común de los demás" (being European, without any other consideration, they are judged as being worthy of the same courtesy and esteem that is due to the more distinguished individuals who go there with an appointment from the government, the honor of which ought to distinguish them from the bulk of commoners) (433).

Thus, Jorge Juan and Antonio de Ulloa's troubled observations about vice-regal society in Spanish South America suggest that in the Peruvian creoles' social imaginary, the metaphor of "blood" has assumed a meaning very dif-ferent from what it meant to the two peninsular Spanish authors themselves. Whereas in the social imaginary of the Old World "blood" still stood for family lineage ("noble" blood), religion ("Christian" blood), or nationality ("Span-ish" blood), in the creoles' New World it has come to denote a new difference that we might recognize as an emergent, though not yet fully articulated and theorized, modern essentialist discourse of race—"whiteness." Its ideological function in viceregal Peru is to realign old geographic and social distinctions (i.e., "Americans" vs. "Europeans;" "nobility" vs. "commoners") through a fiction of a transnational kinship between Europeans and creoles across social and ancestral distinctions based on their common "whiteness," even though this discourse still privileges, as Juan and Ulloa observe, Europeans, whose "whiteness" is (unlike that of the creoles') beyond suspicion.

Before we further explore this connection between a creole subjectivity and the discourse of race in eighteenth-century Spanish America, a brief clarification may be in order about Juan and Ulloa's use of the word "creole." While Juan and Ulloa's Spanish eighteenth-century use of the word—denoting here a "white" but not "European" person—will be familiar enough to early (Latin) Americanists, it may at first seem surprising to scholars specializing in American literature and culture during the nineteenth and twentieth centuries, as nowadays the word is typically used to denote a "black" person or a person of mixed racial heritage. This modern meaning, however, is the result of a semantic shift that took place only in the context of the nineteenth-century post-colonial United States and Caribbean, primarily Haiti.[9]

In the imperial world before the nineteenth century, by contrast, the word as it was used in all Western languages ("criollo," "créole," "creole") had primarily a broadly *geographic* connotation—referring to a person who is "native" (though not "Native in the sense of "aboriginal") to a European territorial possession outside Europe, either of European or African descent. Most likely derived from a Latin root (*creare*, to make, to create, i.e., something new), the word "creole" made its first appearance in modern Western languages as a Portuguese neologism (*crioulo*) in a colonial New World context—to distinguish Black slaves born in the Americas from those brought from Africa. While, as property, creole slaves were sometimes favorably compared to the "unseasoned" African slaves because of their lower mortality rate, they also had a reputation of being more cunning, rebellious, and untrustworthy. In the course of its sixteenth-century translation into the Spanish context, "*criollo*" came to designate not only slaves of African descent but also, and primarily, settlers of European ancestry born in the Americas. Its earliest documentations in this sense appear in letters written during the 1560s by Spanish officials from New Spain, who observed that the Spanish sector of the colonial population was now "different from that before" because the "creoles, who are those that are born there, . . . have never known the king nor ever hope to know him, [and] are quick to hear and believe those who are mal-intentioned." Its earliest documentation in print has been traced to the *Geografía y descripción universal de las Indias* (1570), written by the royal chronicler Juan López de Velasco, who claimed that the Spaniards born in the Indies, "who are called Creoles, turn out like the natives even though they are not mixed with them [by] declining to the disposition of the land."[10] By the end of the sixteenth century, the American-born creoles had come to be regarded as a distinct group in most regions of the Ibero-American empire—a group believed to have assumed, as one historian puts it, a "single, if varied, character" that had acquired "all those supposed shortcomings of the Indians that were thought to derive from psychological weakness or deformation, above all their moral and social instability."[11] As the famous Franciscan missionary Bernadino de Sahagún wrote,

> I do not marvel at the great defects and imbecility of those who are born in these lands ... because the Spaniards who inhabit them, and even more those who are born there, assume these bad inclinations; those who are born there become like the Indians, and although they look like Spaniards, in their constitution they are not; those who are born in Spain, if they do not take care, change within a few years after they arrive in these parts; and this I think is due to the climate or the constellations in these parts.[12]

Thus, while modern scholars have often celebrated creolization in the New World as "creative adaptations," evidencing human innovativeness and cultural diversification,[13] in early modern times the fact that transplanted Europeans underwent cultural change in the Americas was seen as profoundly disturbing—as evidence of a cultural "degeneration."

This early modern "dispute of the New World" is familiar enough and does not need a detailed rehearsal here.[14] It will suffice to note that the idea of cultural degeneration was based on two suppositions in early modern natural history, both of which ultimately had roots in classical antiquity. The first one, humorial theory, was derived from the scientific thought of Aristotle, Hippocrates, Polybius, Galen, and others, and held that a person's physiological and psychological constitution was determined by the qualities of the natural environment or astrological constellation; and the second one, rooted in Greco-Roman notions of civility and barbarism in classical natural history (mainly Herodotus and Pliny the Elder) and corroborated by contemporary reports alleging the "barbarity" of the New World's indigenous population, held that the natural environment and the skies of the New World were inauspicious to the development of human culture. Cultural changes observed in transplanted Europeans were in this early modern ethnological scheme inevitably interpreted as a cultural "decline." The polemic about creolization culminated during the eighteenth century, when it became a prominent topos in Enlightenment philosophy in the works of Montesquieu, Raynal, Voltaire, Buffon, and Robertson, who concluded that due to New World climates and soils, Americans of whatever ancestry were "destined to remain uncivilized."[15] While, during the sixteenth and seventeenth centuries, remarks about the negative influences of the New World environment were usually qualified by reflections on the efficacy of human moral choice to overcome them, in the

eighteenth century the thesis found further development in the environmental determinism of the Enlightenment philosophes. Thus, the abbé Raynal
famously argued that the "degeneration" of biological and cultural forms in
some parts of the New World, due to the adverse effects of its air and soil, had
even diminished male ardor for the female and led to a biological degeneration of all species.

> The men there are less strong [he wrote], less courageous, without beard
> or hair; degenerate in all the signs of manhood, feebly endowed with
> this lively and powerful sentiment, with this delicious love which is the
> source of all loves, the beginning of all attachments, the prime instinct,
> society's first bond, without which all other liaisons have neither depth
> no durability. . . . The indifference of the male toward that other sex
> to which Nature has entrusted the place of reproduction suggests an
> organic imperfection, a sort of infancy of the people of America similar
> to that of the individuals of our continent who have not reached the age
> of puberty.[16]

Within this epistemic paradigm of neoclassical natural history, and especially with regard to its environmentalist understanding of human difference
(creolization), the emerging fiction of "whiteness," observed by Juan and Ulloa
in the creole social imaginary of eighteenth-century Spanish America, points
then to a new and different—a modern and proto-anthropological— discourse
of identity and difference that would become elevated as "science" in the context of nineteenth-century nationalism: "race." Its early manifestations in the
eighteenth century, however, must be understood as ideologically contingent
on a developing creole patriotism as it emerged out of its engagement with an
early modern economy of identity and difference, particularly the theory of
creolization. Whereas in neoclassical natural history, physiological differences
such as that of skin color were seen as environmental in origin, the essentialist discourse of "whiteness" in the creole social imaginary carved out a "third
space" in the early modern economy of identity and difference,[17] in which creoles, though presumably subject to the *same* environmental influences, could
nevertheless see themselves as essentially *different* from Indians, Africans, and
racially mixed peoples who shared a geographic space with them. We might say
that it realigned the distributive boundary in this discursive economy of natural history between New World peoples (Native Americans, as well as European
American and African American creoles) and Old World peoples (mainly Europeans) by identifying European American creoles with Europeans through the
fiction of "whiteness" (*el decir que son blancos*).

Of course, racial categories such as the creole idea of "whiteness" must in
the colonial American (or any other) context be thought of primarily in social
and legal terms that were highly variable according to local cultural perceptions. In colonial Spanish America, where the particular colonial exchanges

between Spanish, Native American, and African cultures had produced a regionally highly variable mosaic of cultural and racial *mestizaje*, the category *criollo* was used to distinguish American-born peoples "of European descent" not only from peninsular Spaniards, Africans, and Indians, but also (and often primarily) from those of "mixed" ancestry (mainly mestizos) in an elaborate system of *castas* (castes) within the taxonomy of which the criollos inhabited a highly ambiguous position as "Spaniards." On the one hand, the creoles were frequently regarded by the peninsulars as subordinate, despite the fact that Spanish law made no distinction between peninsulars and creoles, as the *república de españoles* included all those born of (purely) "Spanish" ancestry. On the other hand, the social category of *criollo* always existed in counterdistinction to racially other and mixed people—to signify "pure" European ancestry and, as such, social privilege vis-à-vis peoples of mixed origin (and, of course, Indians and Africans). However, allegations of the creoles' inferiority with respect to the peninsulars was furthered precisely in part by an "unofficial" miscegenation and in part by the increasingly common practice on the part of imperial officials in the eighteenth century to sell "certificates of Whiteness" (*cédulas de gracias al sacar*) to those who could not otherwise assume to be identified as such. Thus, it was not unusual to hear about the "dark origin" of some creoles, as somewhere between 20 and 40 percent of all defined as "criollo" were in fact biologically *mestizos* whose assimilation as "creoles" was linked to their Spanish fathers' efforts to retain certain privileges in colonial society. This "unofficial" miscegenation had the effect that the category of "creole" (i.e., "white") was gradually expanded in strictly biological terms and had, by the eighteenth century, become semi-official.[18]

This process is illustrated in many of the eighteenth-century "casta paintings," which were intended to explain to curious Europeans the complex social structure of colonial Spanish America. In an anonymous eighteenth-century series about New Spain, for example (which represents a total of sixteen different castas), a "Spaniard" mixing with an "Indian" woman is said to produce a "mestiza"; if that "mestiza" were to mix with a Spaniard, their offspring would be a "castiza"; and if that "castiza" were to mix with a Spaniard, their offspring would be considered to be a "Spaniard" (see Figures 1, 2, and 3). What is significant about these casta paintings, which are a distinctly *European* genre, is that they never use the term "white" (which would have had a de-familiarizing ring to a Spanish audience) but rather use "Spanish." As recent historians have persuasively argued, the casta system was, in the social hierarchy of viceregal Spanish America, a taxonomy based *not* on biological (and thus "racial") but rather on cultural difference.[19] However, the inclusion of the "Spanish" in America (i.e., creoles) in this taxonomy, and their fluid status within it, sheds light on the ideological role fulfilled by the creole discourse of "whiteness." In particular, the conferral of the official status of "Spanish" upon children with a three-quarter "Spanish" descent had the (perhaps unintended) effect

FIGURE 1. "Of a Spanish man and an Indian woman is born a Mestiza." Museo Nacional de Antropología, Madrid.

of biologically expanding the category of "Spanish" (i.e., "white," in the creole social imaginary). It thus tended to lend a distinctly biological component to environmentalist theories about creole degeneracy and to further render the category of "criollo" as social status highly ambiguous and unstable in a social hierarchy based on a principle of inequality in which a person's status or "quality" (*calidad*) determined many aspects of his or her social life (profession, guilds, dress, jurisdiction, etc.).

In one telling incident in New Spain in 1728, for example, a creole by the name of José Sevilla applied for a license to the local authorities to practice as an apothecary, a guild reserved exclusively to "Spaniards" (peninsular and creole). When approaching the parish of Sagrario Metropolitano in order to obtain the necessary copy of his certificate of baptism, however, he was surprised to discover that his certificate had been placed in the book reserved for mestizos and mulattos, rather than that of Spaniards. Knowing that his professional future depended on his status as a "Spaniard," José immediately appealed to the local authorities to have his name erased from the book of mestizos and mulattos and logged into the one for Spaniards. He was asked to

FIGURE 2. "A Spanish man and a Mestiza produce a Castiza." Museo Nacional de Antropología, Madrid.

produce witnesses who could attest to the purity of his lineage. However, as he was a foundling who had been given to a prominent Spaniard, Don Miguel Sevilla, all the witnesses could do was to attest to the fact that he was "white and blond" and that he had been able to marry a very "noble" woman. When authorities nevertheless remained unconvinced, José finally produced a witness who testified that he happened to be present at the house of Miguel Sevilla during the night that José had been left at the doorstep and that, remarkably, he had a note attached to him that stated that he was a "Spaniard" born to "noble" parents. José's nightmare finally came to an end when the judge decided to have his name removed from the book of mestizos, given his "putative" lineage as a Spaniard.[20] While the story had a happy ending for José, it illustrates the creoles' ambiguous position in the hierarchical casta system of viceregal New Spanish society and, as documented by Juan and Ulloa, also of viceregal Peru. In the absence of a clearly documented "lineage," the creoles' only recourse when asserting their claim to social privilege was "*decir que son blancos*," although in New Spain in 1728, this alone was apparently not yet sufficiently persuasive.

FIGURE 3. "Of a Spanish man and a Castiza is born a Spaniard." Museo Nacional de Antropología, Madrid.

Hemispheric Diffusions: Creolization and "Race" in British America

Juan and Ulloa's tracts were read widely across the Atlantic world, appearing in various translations, including John Adams's English translation as *A Voyage to South America* (1758). Thomas Jefferson owned a copy of virtually all of Juan's and Ulloa's writings about their journey and cited from the *Noticias* in his own "noticias"—the *Notes on the State of Virginia*. And, as we shall see, the debate about Spanish American creolization also had a role to play in the history of the concept of "race" in eighteenth-century British America.

During the sixteenth and seventeenth centuries, the differences between peninsular Spaniards and Spanish American creoles had not been lost on the English translators and promoters of Protestant imperialism, who hoped to take advantage of the alleged decline of Spanish virtues and loyalty in the New World. The earliest documentation of the word "creole" in English occurs in E. Grimstone's 1604 translation of José de Acosta's *Historia natural y moral* (1590), which makes reference to "Crollos" as designating "Spaniards borne at the Indies."[21] By the end of the seventeenth century, English writers were also using the word to express their own "deep skepticism" about the survival of "British" character among the English progeny born in the Caribbean, Virginia, and New England, referring to them as "natives," "Creoles," and "country-born." Like their Spanish counterparts a hundred years earlier, English writers remarked that the English in America had "imbibed the Barbarity and Heathenism of the countries they live in" and in the process "brought forth many monstrous births."[22] But, despite the gradual domestication of the word into the English language and its occasional use in reference to British American colonials, until the end of the eighteenth century the word retained a distinctly Hispanic connotation (rather than the Gallicized one that it assumed in the nineteenth century), being associated with Spanish American creoles in New World historiography. This is evident in the spelling of Cotton Mather's famous early eighteenth-century designation of certain behaviors among the colonials by which he found himself surrounded by "*Criolian* degeneracies" (from Spanish "criollo"), which deliberately invoked the notorious Spanish American example of cultural and racial mixture for maximum rhetorical effect in a cautionary tale that was supposed to reinforce his call to regenerate New England's allegedly original Protestant purity.[23]

Despite the substantial cultural diversity that characterized its various colonial regions, in British America the conception of the "creole" as a social category was overall less intricately articulated than in Spanish America. While in British America, too, even elite creoles were frequently regarded as inferior to the "English-born,"[24] the creoles' identity as being of (pure) "European descent" was in British America threatened less by biological mixture than it was by cultural creolization. Observations about the European American creoles' changes in complexion, dress, custom, or morality in comparison with the English born were typically explained not in terms of racial mixture but rather in terms of the influence of climate, environment, and cultural contact with Africans and Native Americans. This difference was due in part to the relatively greater exclusiveness that characterized British American colonial societies from the very beginning. Although, as in Spanish America, in early British America, too, European women were a rare and prized "commodity"—in Virginia, female indentured servants were frequently "bought" out of servitude before the end of their term by free suitors—English colonists arrived in the New World more frequently as family units than did their Spanish counterparts, especially in areas such as New England. Moreover, the institution of indentured servitude provided single English women with a social and economic "opportunity" (for a lack of a better word) of coming to the New World that was not available to their Spanish counterparts. The result of these combined factors has been characterized by comparative historians of early American borderlands (perhaps too schematically) as a "frontier of exclusion" characterizing the British American contact zones, as compared with a "frontier of inclusion" characterizing those of Spanish America.[25] While biological mixture between Europeans, Africans, and Native Americans was also a frequent occurrence in British America, colonial laws such as the Virginia Codes—stipulating that the offspring of a union between a (presumably Black female) slave and a (presumably white male) free person would follow the "condition of the mother"—had the effect that racial mixture in British American creole societies expanded biologically the cultural category of "Black" rather than that of "White," as was the case in Spanish America.

But despite these important differences, in British America, too, creoles inhabited an ambiguous space in the imperial order. They were by and large viewed with suspicion by European imperial administrators and therefore frequently barred from imperial office due to the location of their American birth. As in Spanish America, this imperial order was scientifically underwritten by neoclassical natural history, which theorized alleged differences between creoles and Europeans as the result of environmental influences in the New World. And, as in Spanish America, it was the fiction of "race" in the creole social imaginary that dialectically engaged—and ultimately shattered—the epistemic paradigm of natural history that rationalized human difference in connection to the natural environment.

The Rhetoric of "Race" in Jefferson's *Notes on the State of Virginia*

The dialectical relationship between neoclassical natural history and this emergent proto-modern discourse of race is nowhere more evident than in Thomas Jefferson's *Notes on the State of Virginia*. For his scientific "racism," Jefferson has long been seen as a "man of contradictions," a man whose views on race and culture were, first of all, "complex"—an opponent of slavery and proponent of abolition, admirer of African American moral integrity and defender of Native American cultural achievements on the one hand; on the other hand, one of the earliest theorists of African racial "inferiority." In his important essay, "Thomas Jefferson: Race, Culture, and the Failure of Anthropological Method," Frank Shuffelton, for example, has suggested that "something more complex is at work here [in Jefferson's apparently contradictory statements on Native Americans and Africans] than a mere prejudice against people of color." In order to understand Jefferson's "contradictory attitudes," Shuffelton proposes to "shift the terms of discussion from race, the usual frame of reference, to ethnicity . . . [which] focuses more directly on differences in cultural behavior." As he observes, Jefferson's *Notes* participated in a lively debate among eighteenth-century philosophers about human difference. While most philosophers, such as Montesquieu, explained human difference in terms of climate, religion, laws, and government—in short, in terms of environmental factors—some, such as Johann Friedrich Blumenbach or Lord Kames, embraced newer theories that focused on anatomical differences and categorized humans into a hierarchy of "races" such as the Caucasian, Mongol, American, and Mayalan. Shuffelton, however, sees the latter discourse of race as essentially continuous with, and an extension of, the Enlightenment debate about environmental influence, which "positioned eighteenth-century thinkers on a slippery slope beginning with science and ending in racism, and the difficulties remain alive for us in this century." Ultimately remaining unable to account for Jefferson's "contradictory attitudes" toward race, Shuffelton presents him as a victim of what he sees as an (essentially European) discourse of Enlightenment anthropology, concluding that "Jefferson's blindness [to African American cultural achievements is] complex, but at the outset, no matter how much we admire him as an opponent of slavery, we must recognize his racism. . . . The discourse of anthropological observation fails Jefferson . . . [and] he is betrayed into the language of anatomy and the differentiation between species."[26] I would argue, by contrast, that the logic of Jefferson's arguments about race—Native American "race" on the one hand and African "race" on the other—becomes apparent if we read them not so much as his confessions—what Jefferson "really" believed about human difference—but rather as a rhetorical exercise in theorizing a scientific platform for a hemispheric creole patriotism *against* the circumatlantic discourse of creolization in neoclassical natural history as it underpinned the imperial geography of power in the European settler empires in the Americas.

The title and organization of content of Jefferson's *Notes* suggests that it was conceived very much in the same hemispheric and scientific spirit as Ulloa's "notes." It was written in response to the request of the secretary of the French legation, François de Marbois, for information about Virginia—presumably to aid the latter in his design to write a natural history. Accordingly, Jefferson structured his response into the familiar set of prescribed natural historical headers—rivers, climate, animals, aborigines, (colonial) towns, manners, and so on. However, while working within the generic formal mold of natural history, Jefferson also worked to undermine its underlying epistemology, exploring the contingent relations between the natural environment, the development of biological forms, and human culture.

With regard to Native Americans, for example, Jefferson refuted Enlightenment philosophes such as Buffon, who had represented the "barbarous" state of native cultures as one of his primary exhibits in proof of his thesis that the natural environment of the New World inhibited cultural development. Jefferson, by contrast, stressed that he could not observe any natural differences between Indians and the Europeans, refuting Buffon's claim, for instance, of alleged differences in the size of male genitals. Jefferson refers to the extensive research he had done not only on North American Indians but also on South American Indians in this regard, and one of his primary sources on the latter was the writings of the two Spaniards Juan and Ulloa. At first, Jefferson seems disappointed that Ulloa had portrayed the Indians as "los mas cobardes y pusilánimes" (cowardly and weak), though in the end he still finds an opportunity to enlist his support: "Don Ulloa here admits, that the authors who have described the Indians of South America, before they were enslaved, had represented them as a brave people and therefore seems to have suspected that the cowardice which he had observed in those of the present race might be the effect of subjugation."[27]

Jefferson's noted scientific interest in Native American cultures across the hemisphere and his eagerness to refute European natural historians' disparagements of the Native Americans' physiological constitution and cultural achievements must be understood primarily in the context of his creole patriotism, in particular the implications that the logic of environmental determinism held true for the constitution of European American creoles as well. Indeed, the implications of Buffon's environmental determinism for European American creoles had already been spelled out by the abbé Raynal. As Jefferson observes, "So far the Count de Buffon has carried this new theory of the tendency of nature to belittle her productions on this side the Atlantic. Its application to the race of whites transplanted from Europe, remained for the Abbe Raynal. 'On doit etre etonne (he says) que l'Amerique n'ait pas encore produit un bon poete, un habile mathematicien, un homme de genie dans un seul art, ou seule science.'" Jefferson refutes Raynal's claim by pointing out the relative "youth" of Anglo-American creole culture, while also proudly putting on display some of the "geniuses" that this young culture has already produced in the arts and sciences:

> When we shall have existed as a people as long as the Greeks did before they produced a Homer, the Romans a Virgil, the French a Racine and Voltaire, the English a Shakespeare and Milton, should this reproach be still true, we will inquire from what unfriendly causes it has proceeded. . . . In war we have produced a Washington, whose memory will be adored while liberty shall have votaries, whose name shall triumph over time. . . . In physics we have produced a Franklin, than whom no one of the present age has made more important discoveries, nor has enriched philosophy with more, or more ingenious solutions of the phenomena of nature. We have supposed Mr. Rittenhouse second to no astronomer living; that in genius he must be the first, because he is self taught. As an artist he has exhibited as great a proof of mechanical genius as the world has ever produced. . . . As in philosophy and war, so in government, in oratory, in painting, in the plastic art, we might show that America, though but a child of yesterday, has already given hopeful proofs of genius. . . . We therefore suppose that this reproach is as unjust as it is unkind and that, of the geniuses which adorn the present age, America contributes its full share.

Having defended native and (white) creole American culture from the European charge of degeneration by in effect denying the philosophes' logic of a detrimental influence of the New World environment, Jefferson turns next to a consideration of African creoles in the New World. While expressing admiration for the moral integrity, religious piety, and loyalty of many of the

Africans he personally knew, he belittles Africans' inherent capacity for genius in a series of disparagements, such as his famous attack on the Boston poet Phillis Wheatley: "Religion indeed has produced a Phyllis Whately; but it could not produce a poet. The compositions published under her name are below the dignity of criticism. The heroes of the Dunciad are to her, as Hercules to the author of that poem" (267). Considering the fact that under Roman slavery, some slaves, such as Epictetus, Terence, and Phaedrus, were able to become accomplished writers, Jefferson dismisses the possibility that it might be the institution of slavery itself that inhibits the Africans' cultural development. The difference between Roman and African slaves, Jefferson argues, is that the former "were of the race of whites": "It is not their [the Africans'] condition then, but nature, which has produced the distinction. Whether further observation will or will not verify the conjecture, that nature has been less bountiful to them in the endowments of the head, I believe that in those of the heart she will be found to have done them justice" (200).

Jefferson's patriotic defense of creole (European American) character and culture is thus predicated on a particular rhetorical shift in which the eighteenth-century discourse about cultural creolization and degeneration is displaced by a modern discourse of "race." If the American environment did not have a degenerative influence on human culture (as his discussions of Native American and white creoles intend to demonstrate), but African American creoles were obviously (to Jefferson) inferior, it must be that Africans had arrived in the New World already as a distinct "race," whose inferiority must be seen as essential and independent of environmental and geographical factors or social "condition." Jefferson's *Notes* manifests thus not so much "the failure of anthropological method" as the emergent challenge posed by a modern anthropological method that would ultimately shatter the Enlightenment discourse of natural history by rending its environmental contingencies asunder and by breaking up the study of "nature" into its discreet modern disciplines—geography, botany, zoology, anthropology, and so on.[28]

The fact that this modern discourse of race was far from dominant in the eighteenth-century world—however acceptable to American creoles—is illustrated by the general hesitancy, even "diffidence," with which Jefferson ventured upon (and published) his "opinion, that they [Blacks] are inferior in the faculties of reason and imagination, even where the subject may be submitted to the Anatomical knife, to Optical glasses, to analysis by fire, or by solvents" (200). Jefferson's "diffidence" and hesitancy stand in stark contrast to the confidence with which one of his most prominent adversaries in the debate about human identity and difference could argue that Africans were not, essentially, a different and inferior race. In refuting racialized explanations of human difference such as Jefferson's, Olaudah Equiano, in *The Interesting Narrative of Olaudah Equiano, or Gustavus Vassa, the African* (London, 1789), was able to draw on the most authoritative texts in Enlightenment natural history, as well as (and perhaps most importantly), the Judeo-Christian theological canon. Thus, Equiano, who in his narrative claims to have been kidnapped as a child from Africa and brought to America on the Middle Passage (though his African birth has lately been questioned),[29] employs Enlightenment comparative ethnology by comparing the Ebo to the Jews in order to engage the notion that difference in color may be genetic and a mark of racial inferiority that has been used to justify chattel slavery. He refers within his text to John Mitchel's *Causes of the Different Colours of Persons in Different Climates* (London, 1756), which considers the example of Spanish "creolization" in the New World in order to prove that difference of color is not inherent but rather environmental and that notions of essential racial difference such as those proposed by Jefferson were therefore erroneous:

> "The Spaniards, who have inhabited America, under the torrid zone, for any time, are become as dark coloured as our native Indians of Virginia; of which *I myself have been a witness*." . . . THESE instances, and a great many more which might be adduced, while they shew how the complexions of the same persons vary in different climates, it is hoped may tend also to remove the prejudice that some conceive against the natives of Africa on account of their colour. Surely the minds of the Spaniards did not change with their complexions! Are there not causes enough to which the apparent inferiority of an African may be ascribed, without limiting the goodness of God, and supposing he forbore to stamp understanding on certainly his own image, because "carved in ebony." Might it not naturally be ascribed to their situation? When they come among Europeans, they are ignorant of their language, religion, manners, and customs.[30]

Equiano was not alone in responding to Jefferson. Indeed, after the publication of *Notes on the State of Virginia*, Jefferson received several letters from people who challenged his ideas by resorting to arguments similar to those in Equiano's narrative. One of these letters was written by the Marylander Benjamin Banneker, who, diplomatically, appealed to Jefferson's generally benevolent disposition towards Africans which, Banneker hoped, would incline him to join him in his efforts "to eradicate that train of absurd and false ideas and opinions, which so generally prevails with respect to us," and instead lend support to the evident truth that "one universal Father hath given being to us all; and that he hath not only made us all of one flesh, but that he hath also, without partiality, afforded us all the same sensations and endowed us all with the same faculties; and that however variable we may be in society or religion, however diversified in situation or color, we are all of the same family, and stand in the same relation to him."[31] Quoting back to Jefferson his famous words of the Declaration of Independence, though here with specific reference to the Africans' enslavement—"'We hold these truths to be self-evident, that all men are created equal; that they are endowed by their Creator with certain unalienable rights, and that among these are, life, liberty, and the pursuit of happiness'"—Banneker shrewdly calls attention to Jefferson's apparent inconsistency between his celebrated notions of (white) equality and (Black) inferiority.

In hindsight, it is clear that the scientific logic of Equiano and Banneker, though still persuasive in the eighteenth century, would ultimately lose ground to Jefferson's racialist logic, which became one of the dominant scientific ideologies of the nineteenth century. As the Marxist theorists of race Etienne Balibar and Immanuel Wallerstein have argued, nineteenth-century nationalism was intimately linked to the rise of modern scientific racism. Balibar and Wallerstein see the ideology of race as an emergent mystification of the inherent contradictions between the modern bourgeois social value of "equality" and meritocracy, on the one hand, and the increasing need for labor and a "non-meritocratic basis to justify inequality" in an expanding capitalist economy, on the other.[32] More specifically, the historian Edmund Morgan has argued that it was no coincidence that a proto-Jeffersonian ideology of equality among whites should first emerge not only in a New World society based on a slave economy but also during the early eighteenth century—precisely at a time when African slaves had begun to outnumber white indentured servants in the British American colonies. The emergence of a modern ideology of "equality" among whites was thus based, Morgan argues, on a socioeconomic infrastructure of Black chattel slavery.[33] However, the modern scientific ideas of "whiteness" and "race" on which this modern political ideology of equality were based was not simply already available for early Americans to draw upon as an ideological superstructure that would rationalize the New World economic base. As poststructuralist theorists of race such as Anthony Appiah have suggested, the "science of biology did not exist when Jefferson was writing the *Notes*. What did exist was natural history. . . . To think of race as a biological concept is to pull out of the natural history of humans a focus on the body . . . and to separate it . . . [from] the broader world of behavior and of social and moral life." While I would thus agree with Appiah's argument that Jefferson's discussion is representative of a transition in the way the word "race" is used in reflecting on the characters of different kinds of peoples, I would argue that the modern concept of race is not so much "a natural historical notion" (as Appiah suggests),[34] but rather the product of the creoles' dialectical engagement with the early modern scientific paradigm of natural history that had rationalized the "tri-angular" constellation of geo-political power in the old European settler empires in the Americas. In their engagement with early modern neoclassical natural history, creole patriots throughout the Americas realigned the discursive economy of human identity and difference by shifting the rationalization from the eighteenth-century scientific debate about "creolization" to a nineteenth-century scientific debate about race. This engagement with early modern natural history was not primarily a local or national, but rather a circumatlantic, debate with a distinctly hemispheric genealogy, as the idea of the "creole" traveled from sixteenth-century Brazil, to viceregal Spanish America, to the French circumcaribbean, as well as to the North American British colonies. In the course of these travels throughout the hemisphere, however, the idea of the *Spanish American* creole, with its connotations of cultural and biological mestizaje, remained the constant alter ego of the idea of "whiteness" in the creoles' social imaginary from the eighteenth century onward.

NOTES

1. See Gary Nash, *Red, White, and Black: The Peoples of Early America* (1972; Englewood Cliffs: Prentice Hall, 1982); Winthrop Jordan, *The White Man's Burden: Historical Origins of Racism in the United States* (New York: Oxford University Press, 1974); Winthrop Jordan, *White over Black: American Attitudes toward the Negro, 1550–1812* (Chapel Hill: University of North Carolina Press, 1968); Dana Nelson, *The Word in Black and White: Reading "Race" in* American *Literature, 1638–1867* (New York: Oxford University Press, 1992); and Dana Nelson, *National Manhood: Capitalist Citizenship and the Imagined Fraternity of White Men* (Durham: Duke University Press, 1998). See also Joyce Chaplin, *Subject Matter: Technology, the Body, and Science on the Anglo-American Frontier, 1500– 1676* (Cambridge, Mass.: Harvard University Press, 2001), which is perhaps the most carefully argued and historically comprehensive study of the topic in recent years, though its exclusive focus on "British America" occludes some of the hemispheric genealogies that I am concerned with here.

2. See Richard Hoffman, "Outsiders by Birth and Blood: Racist Ideologies and Realities around the Periphery of Medieval European Culture," *Studies in Medieval and Renaissance History* 6 (1983): 6–34; also Magnus Mörner, *Race Mixture in the History of Latin America* (Boston: Little Brown, 1967).

3. Nelson, *Word,* viii. Acknowledging that "early European representations of Native Americans had much more to do with cultural, rather than so-called racial differences," Nelson argues that "During the mid-seventeenth century, representations of both African and Native Americans began to shift from theories of cultural and climate-imposed physiological difference . . . to speculations about profound and ineradicable racial difference," hereby providing the rationalization for appropriation of Native American lands and enslavement of Africans. She sees in this shift a manifestation of a Foucauldian "rupture" in the history of Western knowledge from the epistemic principle of "similitude and resemblance to identity and difference" in the seventeenth century (6–7).

4. Kenan Malik, *The Meaning of Race: Race, History and Culture in Western Society* (New York: New York University Press, 1996), 55; see also Patrick Wolfe, "Race and Racialization: Some Thoughts," *Postcolonial Studies* 5 (2000): 51–62.

5. Ruth Hill, *Hierarchy, Commerce, and Fraud in Bourbon Spanish America: A Postal Inspector's Exposé* (Nashville: Vanderbilt University Press, 2005).

6. See Ralph Bauer, *The Cultural Geography of Colonial American Literatures: Empire, Travel, Modernity* (Cambridge and New York: Cambridge University Press, 2003).

7. Jorge Cañizares Esguerra has recently made a similar argument with regard to Spanish American creoles in the seventeenth century from a transatlantic perspective, though he also prematurely equates the metaphor of "blood" for "racial" difference when, in fact, his creole sources consistently speak of "Spanish" blood versus

"Indian" or "mixed" bloods ("castas"). He is not interested in the hemispheric diffusions of this new rhetoric of identity and difference. See Cañizares Esguerra, "New Worlds, New Stars: Patriotic Astrology and the Investion of Indian and Creole Bodies in Colonial Spanish America, 1600–1650," *The American Historical Review* 104 (1999): 33–68.

8. Jorge Juan, *Noticias secretas* (Madrid: Historia 16, 1991), 427; my emphasis. Further citations appear parenthetically in the text. Translations are my own.

9. Robert Chaudenson, *Creolization of Language and Culture* (New York: Routledge, 2001), 6–7.

10. Juan López de Velasco, *Geografía y descripción universal de las Indias recopiladas por el cosmógrafo-cronista Juan López de Velasco desde el año de 1571 al de 1574* (Madrid, 1894), 37–38; see also Bernard Lavallé, *Las promesas ambiguas: Ensayos sobre el criollismo colonial en los Andes* (Lima, 1993), 25, 16; and José Juan Arrom, *Certidumbre de América: Estudios de Letras, Folklore y Cultura*, 2nd ed. (Madrid, 1971), 5–54.

11. Anthony Pagden, "Identity Formation in Spanish America," in *Colonial Identity in the Atlantic World, 1500–1800*, ed. Nicholas Canny and Anthony Pagden (Princeton: Princeton University Press, 1987), 57, 81.

12. Bernadino de Sahagún, *Historia General de las Cosas de Nueva España* [compl. 1590], 3 vols. (Mexico City, 1938), 3:82.

13. Timothy H. Breen , "Creative Adaptations: Peoples and Cultures," in *Colonial British America: Essays in the New History of the Early Modern Period*, ed. Jack Greene and J. R. Pole (Baltimore: Johns Hopkins University Press, 1984), 195–234, 221; see also Kamau Brathwaite, *The Development of Creole Society in Jamaica, 1770–1820* (Oxford: Clarendon Press, 1971), especially 295–305. For a discussion of theories of cultural creolization in modern times, see David Buisseret and Stephen Reinhardt, eds., *Creolization in the Americas* (College Station, TX: Texas A&M University Press, 2000), 3–18. On "Atlantic creoles," see Ira Berlin, *Many Thousands Gone: The First Two Centuries of Slavery in North America* (Cambridge, Mass.: Harvard University Press, 1998).

14. See Antonello Gerbi, *The Dispute of the New World: The History of a Polemic, 1750–1900* [1955], trans. Jeremy Moyle (Pittsburgh: University of Pittsburgh Press, 1973); and Gerbi, *Nature in the New World: From Christopher Columbus to Gonzalo Fernandez de Oviedo*, trans. Jeremy Moyle (Pittsburgh: University of Pittsburgh Press, 1985); see also Cañizares Esguerra, "New Worlds, New Stars"; Cañizares Esguerra, *How to Write the History of the New World: Histories, Epistemologies, and Identities in the Eighteenth-Century Atlantic World* (Stanford: Stanford University Press, 2001); and Sean X. Goudie, *Creole America: The West Indies and the Formation of Literature and Culture in the New Republic* (Philadelphia: University of Pennsylvania Press, 2006).

15. William Robertson, *The History of the Discovery and Settlement of America* (1777; New York: Harpe, 1829), 123.

16. Guillaume-Thomas Raynal, *Histoire philosophique et politique des établissemens du commerce des européens dans les deux Indes*, vol. 3, bk. 9, 339.

17. See Michel Foucault, *The Order of Things: An Archaeology of the Human Sciences* (New York: Vintage Books, 1994), 129, 144.

18. See Ralph Bauer and José Antonio Mazzotti, eds., *Creole Subjects in the Colonial Americas: The Ambivalent Coloniality of Early American Literatures* (Chapel Hill: University of North Carolina Press, forthcoming). For discussions of the social significance of racial categories in colonial Latin America, see Mörner, *Race Mixture in the History of Latin America* (Boston: Little Brown, 1967).

19. See Hill, *Hierarchy*, 333 n. 4; also Magali M. Carrera, *Imagining Identity in New Spain:*

Race, Lineage, and the Colonial Body in Portraiture and Casta Paintings (Austin: University of Texas Press, 2003).

20. For a more extensive discussion of this, see Ilona Katezew, *Casta Painting: Images of Race in Eighteenth-Century Mexico* (New Haven: Yale University Press, 2004), 45–46.

21. José de Acosta, *The Natural History of the East and West Indies*, trans. E. Grimstone (London, 1604), 278.

22. Morgan Godwin, *The Negro's and Indians Advocate, Suing for Their Admission into the Church* (London, 1680), "Preface," n.p.; Samuel Groom, *A Glass for the People of New England in Which They May See Themselves* (London, 1676), 16.

23. Cotton Mather, *Magnalia Christi Americana; or, The Ecclesiastical History of New England* (Hartford, 1855), 1:13, 25.

24. Carole Shammas, "English-Born and Creole Elites in Turn-of-the-Century Virginia," in *The Chesapeake in the Seventeenth Century: Essays on Anglo-American Society*, ed. Thad Tate and David Ammerman (Chapel Hill: University of North Carolina Press, 1979), 274–296, 284; see also Michael Zuckermann, "Identity in British America: Unease in Eden," in *Colonial Identity in the Atlantic World, 1500–1800*, ed. Nicholas Canny and Anthony Pagden (Princeton: Princeton University Press, 1987), 115–157, 156. One of the negative connotations that the word "creole" assumed in the Protestant context of British America is still reminiscent today in one of the *Oxford English Dictionary*'s definition of the verb "to creolize" as "to spend the day in a delectable state of apathy."

25. See Alistair Hennessy, *The Frontier in Latin American History* (Albuquerque: University of New Mexico Press, 1978), 19; see also David Weber, *The Spanish Frontier in North America* (New Haven: Yale University Press 1992), 12; Paula H. Covington, ed., *Latin American Frontiers, Borders and Hinterlands* (Albuquerque: University of New Mexico Press, 1990); and Jane M. Rausch and David Weber, eds., *Where Cultures Meet: Frontiers in Latin American History* (Wilmington: University of Delaware Press, 1994).

26. Frank Shuffelton, "Thomas Jefferson: Race, Culture, and the Failure of Anthropological Method," in *A Mixed Race: Ethnicity in Early America*, ed. Frank Shuffelton (New York: Oxford University Press, 1993), 257–278; 258–259, 260, 273.

27. Thomas Jefferson, "Notes on the State of Virginia," in *The Writings of Thomas Jefferson*, 20 vols. (Washington, D.C.: Thomas Jefferson Memorial Association, 1905), 2:83–84. Further citations from this text appear parenthetically in the text.

28. For a discussion of this modern breakup of natural history in the nineteenth century, see Foucault, *Order*, 129–144.

29. Vincent Carretta, "Olaudah Equiano or Gustavus Vassa? New Light on an Eighteenth-Century Question of Identity," *Slavery and Abolition* 20 (1999): 96–105.

30. Olaudah Equiano, *The Interesting Narrative of the Life of Olaudah Equiano, or Gustavus Vassa, the African, written by himself* (London, 1789), 42–43.

31. Benjamin Banneker, *Copy of a Letter from Benjamin Banneker to the Secretary of State, with His Answer* (Philadelphia: Printed and sold by Daniel Lawrence, no. 33. North Fourth-Street, near Race, 1792), 4–5.

32. Etienne Balibar and Immanuel Wallerstein, *Race, Nation, Class: Ambiguous Identities* trans. of Etienne Balibar by Chris Turner (New York: Verso, 1991), 34.

33. Edmund Morgan, *American Slavery, American Freedom: The Ordeal of Colonial Virginia* (New York: Norton, 1975).

34. Anthony Appiah, *Color Conscious: The Political Morality of Race* (Princeton: Princeton University Press, 1996), 48–50.

3

"La Famosa Filadelfia"

The Hemispheric American City and Constitutional Debates

RODRIGO LAZO

Ten days after he arrived in "la famosa Filadelfia" in April 1824, José María Heredia penned a letter to an uncle in which he offered a descriptive map and architectural account of the city. "A thousand times you must have heard that it is one of the most uniform cities in the world, and it is true," wrote Heredia, in exile after authorities in Cuba discovered his participation in a revolutionary plot.[1] As if recounting an afternoon stroll, Heredia methodically noted the most important features of Philadelphia: its banks, churches, and public works. "Without doubt," he exclaimed about the Bank of the United States, "it's the most beautiful [building] I have seen on earth; and I enjoy strolling under its portico, where a delicious breeze reigns at all times. I believe that in its make-up it took the model of the Parthenon in Athens; but I doubt that the latter, even during its pinnacle, can rival the American building in simple elegance and beauty."[2] Heredia was right that the bank had been modeled on the Parthenon, albeit with marble from the quarries of Montgomery County, Pennsylvania.[3] Praising the "simple elegance" of the adaptation as well as its "magnificent columns," Heredia elevated the "*American*" building over its Greek predecessor, and thus echoed the competitive response to Europe that appealed to many anticolonial revolutionaries of the period. In Heredia's estimation, the building had come to represent "the triumphant achievement of human ingenuity." Celebrating the conjunction of economic power and architectural accomplishment of the bank, Heredia's letter exemplifies the affection shared by writers from the southern Americas who made their way to "la famosa Filadelfia" in the early nineteenth century and viewed it as representative of hemispheric aspirations for breaking away from European monarchical rule.

Philadelphia was "famosa" because it had come to be well known as a hotbed of opposition to the Spanish monarchy, a gathering place for supporters of independence throughout the Americas. After 1794, when a notorious book against the Spanish crown called *El Desengaño del Hombre* (*Man Undeceived*) was published, Philadelphia also became one of the most important Spanish-language print culture centers in the hemisphere. Travelers to the city associated it with the founding documents of the United States and the composition of the U.S. Constitution. When Vicente Rocafuerte, future president of Ecuador, called Philadelphia the "bastion of liberty," he was attempting to present the political foundations and commercial conditions of this "first city" as a hemispheric model that could inspire other cities and nations.[4] Writers regarded Philadelphia as an opportune place to publish materials that could be deployed in debates over the political and social future of emerging nations.[5] Philadelphia's printers and booksellers offered everything from Spanish-language writing primers to translations of Rousseau, as well as political tracts by eminent thinkers from the southern Americas, including Peru's Manuel Lorenzo de Vidaurre and Cuba's Felix Varela. The membership roll of the American Philosophical Society shows that from 1794 to 1804 more than a dozen liberals from Spain joined the society, an indication of a growing connection between Spanish-speaking intellectuals and Philadelphia.[6] By the 1820s the publication of books and other materials in Spanish was a part of what William Charvat has called the "publishing axis" of New York-Philadelphia.[7]

Hispanophone Philadelphia reminds us of the multinational and multilingual dimensions of independence movements and debates over republicanism in the hemisphere. But more to the point of this essay, Philadelphia radiated outward. It was a hemispheric American city because intellectuals seeking to establish a north-south constitutional continuum and develop new political institutions in the southern Americas embraced its representative power—its symbols, foundational national documents, and printing presses. These thinkers engaged in the exchange of ideas about philosophy and government by publishing texts in the United States while concurrently attempting to address local conditions in their home countries.[8] Accordingly, Philadelphia's print culture can help to illuminate the productive tension between cosmopolitan Enlightenment thought and the exigencies of emergent communities after the wars of liberation in the Americas. Benedict Anderson has associated the establishment of national communities with the rise of local print culture, particularly daily newspapers.[9] A standard print language that differed from Latin and the vernacular contributed to the emergence of national consciousness, Anderson argues. But in the multilingual exchanges of Philadelphia, another role of languages also noted by Anderson becomes apparent. Colonial languages (English, Spanish) were a vehicle for articulating the importance of the U.S. and French revolutions and transmitting republicanism.[10] Consistent with this historical development, the writers who populated Hispanophone Philadelphia worked bilingually, publishing translations of what they viewed as the most important works of political theory. As a result of the double engagement with the U.S. Constitution and the home countries, the Hispanophone writings of Philadelphia often present a temporal frame that differs from the notion of simultaneous time that Anderson associates with the nation. Rather than create the "meanwhile" of the novel or daily newspaper (the sense of constituents of a nation moving forward together), "Filadelfia" connected the revolutionary discourses of the 1770s and 1780s with the Latin American revolutions and political developments of the second and third decades of the nineteenth century.

These texts in a sense constitute an anticolonial mentality, or hemispheric commonality, spanning roughly fifty years and in certain respects collapsing the 1770s with the 1820s. The linkage of 1776 to 1821 is precisely the point of Rocafuerte's *Ideas Necesarias a Todo Pueblo Americano Independiente, Que Quiera Ser Libre* (1821), a collection that includes translations of Tom Paine's *Common Sense* and the U.S. Constitution, among other documents. While Hispanophone writers proclaimed that the authors of the Declaration of Independence and the U.S. Constitution had bestowed on the Americas (and the world) documents that would bring "light" to places still under colonial rule, they emphasized the hemispheric dimensions of the word "American" and situated themselves in a Creole community with the likes of Paine. The United States was not the only source of influence; as Jaime Rodriguez and other historians have noted, the southern Americas drew political inspiration from a variety of sources, including Hispanic legal and political theorists.[11] Certainly the constitutional debates in Spain in the second decade of the century influenced much of the discussion. Nevertheless, many of the intellectuals who made their way to Philadelphia valued the contributions of the United States, a position at odds with contemporary analyses that emphasize the ways U.S. imperialism creates an economic divide between the North and South.[12] As Gretchen Murphy has noted in her analysis of the Monroe Doctrine, the notion of hemispheric commonality in the early nineteenth century has been interpreted retroactively in tension with North-South divisions that emphasize the imbalances created by U.S. imperial domination.[13] While the economic imperatives of U.S. expansionism are an important dimension of conditions in the nineteenth century, in this essay I show how "la famosa Filadelfia"—and the Hispanophone print culture it has motivated—became a symbol for leaders in countries moving out of colonial rule. Instead of emphasizing a border demarcating differences between the U.S. empire and its southern neighbors, the elite Latin American intellectuals who made their way to Philadelphia engaged the city's print culture to propose a hemispheric commonality that could translate to other contexts.

"Segars" for Books: Philadelphia's Spanish-Language Print Culture

Philadelphia presented a tripartite connection of print culture, political ideology, and urban development. It was attractive as a symbol because some writers from the southern Americas did not see the exceptionalism of the U.S. Revolution in nationalist terms. They proclaimed that the authors of the Declaration of Independence and the U.S. Constitution had bestowed on the Americas (and the world) documents that would bring "light" to places still under colonial rule. By these terms, the U.S. national constitution could be conceived of as having a multinational potential and hemispheric influence. In contradistinction to Europe, Philadelphia was a presumed material manifestation of republican government, a type of progressive laboratory and urban space where liberal thinkers from the southern Americas and Spain could gaze at the architecture of a newly emergent country.

Philadelphia was a major printing center in the U.S. colonial period, and when the nation's capital moved there from New York in 1790, printers benefited from the governmental business. "Until 1800, when the capital moved to Washington, D.C., Philadelphia was alive with political publishing and publishing schemes directly connected to political patronage," writes Rosalind Remer.[14] This created a momentum that trickled down to nonpolitical works and continued until the 1820s and 1830s, when the city was eclipsed by the publishing houses of New York and Boston. In her study of print culture in Philadelphia, Remer shows that the early U.S. national period saw the ascension of publishing houses, which acquired and marketed works; however, printing could also be undertaken by individual authors and civil or religious groups that sought to circulate a particular kind of book.[15] While publishers sought works that could be sold in other parts of the United States and abroad, writers from the southern Americas sometimes commissioned the printing of materials for circulation in other countries. Hispanophone writers who had enough money to pay for a run of several hundred books seemed to have developed relationships with printers such as Thomas and George Palmer and "Juan" Hurtel, whose names appear regularly in the title pages of Spanish-language books. This type of publication-by-commission served a function that was comparable to that attributed by Nicolás Kanellos to the U.S. exile press. "The raison d'etre of the exile press has always been to influence life and politics in the homeland," Kanellos writes, "by providing information and opinion about the homeland, changing or solidifying opinion about politics and policy in the *patria*, assisting in raising funds to overthrow the current regime."[16] As a result, Spanish-language texts published in the early U.S. republic often engaged multiple audiences in the United States and other countries.

Philadelphia's publishers, printers, and booksellers (sometimes these were one and the same) participated in the Spanish-language market. Perhaps the most prominent publisher in Philadelphia in the early nineteenth century was the house run by the Carey family, which went through several names and incarnations: Mathew Carey, M. Carey and Sons, and Carey & Lea, among others. The Carey house published not only spelling and grammar books such as *El Pequeño Director de los Niños, Para Aprender á Deletrear y Leer* (1811), a pocket-sized edition of the lengthier *El Director de los Niños* (1811), but also novels and political books such as Rousseau's *El Contrato Social* (1821). In 1824 one of the Careys made a trip to Europe and arranged for the Philadelphia store to receive a large shipment of books in French, Italian, and Spanish.[17] Among the titles included the following year in the Carey catalog were Antonio de Solís's *Historia de la Conquista de Mexico* and *Don Quixote*.[18] Solis's book was a historical source for the celebrated anonymous novel *Jicoténcal* (1826), published in Philadelphia, which includes passages quoted verbatim from *Historia de la Conquista*. One can envision the anonymous author of *Jicoténcal* walking to the Carey house and purchasing a copy of the book, then using it as a source for the novelistic account of the fall of Tlascala.

In addition to selling Spanish-language titles in Philadelphia, Carey attempted to open new markets across the United States and Canada as well as other parts of the globe.[19] The account books for the firm in 1821 and 1822 show that the Carey house was trying to set up a regular export business with Chile, Brazil, Puerto Rico, Haiti, and "Buenos Ayres," among other destinations in South America and Asia. In 1822, the outgoing letters from the Carey publishing house to a bookseller in Havana named Louis Castagnino grew increasingly enthusiastic. Carey had sent Castagnino merchandise on consignment and was seeking the most expedient way to receive payment. "If you can procure segars of the manufacturer of Cabanas, they will always sell without difficulty at a fair price," one letter said.[20] Castagnino was among the most successful of the contacts outside of the United States, and Carey figured cigars would be a convenient commodity to exchange. "It is necessary that they be genuine," the letter said about the Cabana brand, "as we are informed that many imitations of them we make but they will not sell here."[21] Carey's letters not only provide insight into the refined taste of early republican cigar smokers in Philadelphia, they also display the primacy of commercial interests in the printer's dealings with sellers in other countries. Carey encouraged Castagnino to sell pens and other supplies, in part because books could always be proscribed. The sale of books with subversive content was bound to run into problems with authorities in colonial Cuba, and thus the Carey house also sought to move products that they could sell with the least interference.

Politically charged Spanish-language materials coming out of Philadelphia had faced censorship and reprisals as early as 1794. That was the year the Spanish Inquisition banned Santiago Felipe Puglia's *El Desengaño del Hombre*, an energetic argument against divine sanction for monarchs. Puglia, an immigrant from Italy naturalized in the United States, became the first prominent figure in the publishing world of Hispanophone Philadelphia. In 1793, Puglia distributed a call for subscribers to *El Desengaño*, publishing a pamphlet with the following appeal:

The Author conceives that the greater part of the Friends of Liberty in this country having no knowledge of the Spanish will become Subscribers merely to encourage the publication, without wishing to have all the copies they may subscribe for . . . The generous light of Democracy which eminently shines forth in the American Stars, will in the publication of this work find a favourable opportunity of shewing how inclined it is to the propagation and support of the Rights of Man.[22]

This call was handed out on Philadelphia street corners, but it took several months before Puglia could collect the money for publication.[23] When 500 copies of the book were published, the list of subscribers included "Alexandro Hamilton," "Tomas Jefferson," "P. Freneau," and one "true friend of liberty and independence for all nations" who paid for 130 copies.[24]

Puglia's *El Desengaño del Hombre* mounted a scriptural argument against the monarchical right to govern by linking it to despotism. He dedicated the book to an "all powerful God," thanking the "Supreme Being" for giving him the energy to defend rights granted to humans. The opening chapter quotes freely from the Old Testament in order to establish a difference between "divine law" and "human law," the latter being the result of the faculty of reason that God has given to humans. Puglia argued that the "law of monarchy" claimed divine sanction but was actually a tool to benefit royal families. Instead of divine sanction, he argued, the authority of the law came from "some anonymous scribe."[25] Drawing freely from Enlightenment principles, *El Desengaño* did not quote directly from any French philosopher, nor did it directly attack Spain; the indirectness was no doubt a rhetorical strategy for appealing to Catholic readers. As Merle E. Simmons has noted, "Puglia, in an effort to pretend that his ideological attack is coldly objective and directed at despotism and the monarchical system wherever found, seeks as part of a studied prose to avoid, whenever possible, any direct reference to Spain or Spanish America by name."[26] Nevertheless, a Spanish-language book attacking tyranny, courtly privilege, and the intrigue of priests was bound to catch the attention of censorious readers in the southern Americas.

On October 24, 1794, about eight months after *El Desengaño del Hombre* was published, the Spanish Inquisition issued an order of excommunication for anyone holding a copy of Puglia's book. A broadside with the order was posted on church doors in Mexico City, signed and sealed by five church authorities; it critiqued Puglia's use of the Spanish language, calling him a "merchant turned pedantic writer," and then accused him of inciting rebellion among Spain's colonies:

SABED: QUE CON ASOMBRO, Y GRAVE dolor de nuestro corazon, hemos leído y exâminado, y hecho exâminar â nuestros zelosos, y sabios Calificadores un Libro en octavo, intitulado: Desengaño del Hombre, impreso en Filadelfia en este presente año, su Autor D. Santiago Felipe

Puglia. Este infame autor se manifiesta por su Obra, orgulloso, altivo, inobediete, flasfemo, traidor, y con todos los demás caractéres con que describe San Pablo en la segunda Carta á Timoteo, capítulo tercero, aquella casta de hombres que aparecerán en los último dias, que segun parece se acercan, é instan yá, â vista de tantos monstruos, como ha producido este siglo, quienes despues de blasfemar de toda Religion natural, y revelada: despues de destronar á la Suprema Magestad de Dios del Solio de su divino Poder: y a la Católica Religion, de su divina Autoridad, ê institucion, calificandola de fanatismo, han emprehendido ultrajar, hacer odiosa, y aun arrancar desde los cimientos la Autoridad, y Magestad Real.[27]

(Let it be known that with great pain in our hearts and amazement we have read and examined and asked our wise and zealous theological censors to examine an octavo volume titled Man Undeceived, printed in Philadelphia this year, its author Don Santiago Felipe Puglia. In this work the infamous author shows himself to be proud, haughty, disobedient, blasphemous, treacherous, and to have all of the other traits that St. Paul, in his second letter to Timothy, third chapter, attributes to that class of men that appeared in the days before judgment, which it appears is imminent when one considers that this century has produced so many monsters who after desecrating all Religion, after disenthralling the Supreme Majesty of God from the throne of his Divine power and the Catholic church from its divine authority, calling the latter fanaticism, have undertaken to disdain, to inspire hatred against, and to tear out from its roots the ruling authority and his royal majesty.)

The Inquisitors took the opportunity to renew an earlier edict of 1790 banning any book focusing on France and, more generally, any book that could inspire sedition. They then positioned El Desengaño del Hombre as the most seditious of all. Anyone with a copy of the book who did not turn it in within six days would be sentenced to excommunication, and in case that was not enough of a deterrent, would also be fined five hundred ducats to be paid to the Church.[28] In addition, the Spanish government sent a letter of protest to President Washington demanding that Puglia and the printer of the book be punished. Washington replied that he could not interfere with freedom of the press in the United States.[29]

The ideological dimensions of Puglia's project and the commercial interests of the Carey house came together in the 1820s. Puglia, then in his sixties, published three books, all with Carey: Sistema Político-Moral de Santiago Felipe Puglia (1821), a book that included a translation of Constantin François de Volney's catechism on the "law of nature"; El Derecho del Hombre (1821), a translation of Paine's Rights of Man; and a new edition of El Desengaño del Hombre (1822). For Puglia, this was an opportunity to contribute to the ongoing struggles for independence in the Americas. In his introductory note to *Sistema Político-Moral*, Puglia notes that Mathew Carey had asked him to translate the book. Carey was in the business of commissioning translations when they appeared profitable; his publishing house, for example, had paid for the 1811 translation from the French of the writing primers *El Director de los Niños* and *El Pequeño Director*. Where Puglia saw an opportunity to continue his political work, Carey saw a profit margin, and the two worked together. That convenient marriage of commodity production and political goals was materialized in many of the Spanish-language books produced in Philadelphia. In turn, the books themselves helped circulate a purported ideological union between liberal economics and republican government.

Vincente Rocafuerte's *Federalist*

In 1821, Vicente Rocafuerte took the rhetoric of Philadelphia's promise to a new height. "I cannot contain the joy in my heart that I experience upon knowing that the glorious standard of independence waves over the promising shores of aqueous Guayaquil," he writes in the opening line of his *Ideas Necesarias a Todo Pueblo Independiente Que Quiera Ser Libre*. The mention of his home city of Guayaquil sets up the second sentence, in which he asks his "beloved compatriots" to "permit me to send my most heartfelt good wishes from this capital of Pennsylvania." Rocafuerte then delivers a sentence overblown not only in its praise but in the connection it proposes: "And where would I find memories more sublime, lessons more heroic and more worthy of imitation, and situations more analogous to our actual political situation, than in the celebrated Philadelphia?"[30] Rocafuerte quickly mentions 1776 and then quotes from the Declaration of Independence. For him, Philadelphia radiates the "spirit of independence." That sequence prompts an important question about what exactly is the relationship between Philadelphia and Guayaquil, but before addressing that I want to consider the publication of *Ideas Necesarias*.

The book, which went through two editions in three years, had a history that spanned the hemisphere in that its composition, publication, and circulation involved numerous countries. Rocafuerte wrote in his memoir that after Mexico declared independence in 1821, "I went to the United States to publish a tract that I composed and is titled, *Ideas Necesarias a Todo Pueblo Independiente Que Quiera Ser Libre*."[31] The place he left was Havana, which might explain why some scholars have surmised that *Ideas Necesarias* was published in Havana with an apocryphal imprint on the title page.[32] The editor of Rocafuerte's memoir even assumes that Rocafuerte's memory failed him when the latter wrote that he published the book in the United States.[33] The evidence points to publication in the United States, but the more interesting point is that the debate about the place of publication shows the fluidity in the hemispheric book trade. The title page of the 1821 edition bears Philadelphia as city of publication, with "D. Huntington" as publisher and "T. & W. Mercein" as print-ers.[34] Since both David Huntington and Mercein printers were based in New York and not Philadelphia, a more likely alternate place of publication was New York City, which had its own Spanish-language book trade. Was it possible that Rocafuerte composed his prologue in Philadelphia and then asked New York printers to put "Philadelphia" on the title page? If so, Rocafuerte sought to intertwine the importance of Philadelphia as a print culture center with the city's symbolic power. In other words, the city's printing presses did not just produce the symbols of hemispheric republicanism but were themselves part of the symbolism.

Because of its connection to the U.S. Revolution, Philadelphia allowed Rocafuerte to emphasize an anti-monarchical position, which spoke directly to the context in Mexico. Mexico's declaration of independence had been accom-panied by a political compromise that would retain Catholicism as the coun-try's official religion and keep open the possibility of a monarchy in the future. The Mexican theater became divided between republicans who opposed all monarchies and those who supported either the institution of a new Bourbon king or the ascendancy of Agustín de Iturbide as Mexico's new monarch. "The defenders of monarchical power," Rocafuerte writes, "have lost their argu-ment before the court of reason; fifty years have passed since the genius of independence led to the Constitution of the United States as the only hope of oppressed people."[35] The use of "only" speaks not so much to U.S. excep-tionalism as to other political models circulating at the time. In Rocafuerte's hemispheric context, the U.S. Revolution and Constitution became an attack on supporters of a monarchy in Mexico. The monarchical question also begins to explain why the first text printed in *Ideas Necesarias* is *Common Sense*, which offers a lively attack on the English monarchy. The choice of writings included in *Ideas Necesarias*—translations of both the Articles of Confederation and the U.S. Constitution—betrays a bent toward constitutional theory.

Rocafuerte published two other books that engaged significantly with how republican traditions contained in the U.S. Constitution could be adapted in southern American contexts: *Ensayo Político* (New York, 1823) and *Cartas de un Americano Sobre las Ventajas de los Gobiernos Republicanos Federativos* (London, 1826) (*Letters of an American on the Advantages of Federal Republican Governments*).[36] These books take up political theory in detail and discuss constitutions in Mexico, Colombia, and Peru, among other places. Perhaps most interesting is that over the years Rocafuerte drifted toward a federalist position, although in the southern Americas that did not convey the same position as in the United States in 1787. While in U.S. debates over ratification of the Constitution the federalists were the more fervent supporters of a strong national government, in Mexico, Colombia, and other parts of the Americas the strong nationalist position was often described as "central" or "unitary." In other words, to be a federalist in the southern Americas in the 1820s was to support a division of power between the national government and state governments as modeled on the U.S. Constitution. In trying to promote a federal system, Rocafuerte inserts translations of passages from *The Federalist* into *Cartas de un Americano*. Proposing that the U.S. model of government marks a development from ancient republicanism, Rocafuerte translates the following passage from "The Federalist No. 9":

> The regular distribution of power into distinct departments—the introduction of legislative balances and checks the institution of courts composed of judges, holding their offices during good behavior—the representation of the people in the legislature by deputies of their own election—these are either wholly new discoveries or have made their principal progress towards perfection in modern times. They are means, and powerful means, by which the excellencies of republican government may be retained and its imperfections lessened or avoided.[37]

Particularly striking is the fact that Rocafuerte repeats the assertion that these are "new discoveries" almost forty years after the U.S. Constitution has been ratified. The implication is that the ideas remain new in the Americas. In this framework, the late eighteenth-century United States and early nineteenth-century southern Americas share a new republican era, opposed in tandem to centuries of monarchical rule but also distinct from classical republicanism. Rocafuerte suggests that the U.S. example can "lessen" the imperfections of republicanism, but he is clear that he does not see the U.S. Constitution as flawless. Rather, he sees it as offering the best model for structuring a government in the present revolutionary moment. For Rocafuerte, that moment stretches from 21 November 1787, the date of "Federalist No. 9," to 20 November 1825, the date of the letter written in Philadelphia in which he discusses the relationship of new constitutions to classical forms of government. Drawing from *The Federalist*, Rocafuerte nudges U.S. foundational documents away from their nationalist associations and circulates them in other parts of the hemisphere.

But the question that remains is what exactly is the relationship between Philadelphia and Guayaquil? Although both are port cities, the specific comparison is not clarified until the end of the anti-monarchical prologue:

> La provincia de Guayaquil por su situacion geográfica, por la feracidad de su suelo, por la riqueza de sus producciones, por la actividad de su industria, por la variedad de sus maderas, y por la abundancia de sus aguas, y facilidad de transportes y conducciones, está destinada por la naturaleza a ser el centro mercantil de la costa occidental de la América.[38]

> [The province of Guayaquil, due to its geographic location, the fecundity of its soil, the richness of its products, the eagerness of its industry, the

variety of its woods, and the ease of transport and conveyance in its deep waters, is destined by nature to be the mercantile center of the west coast of America.]

The implication is that Guayaquil can become to the western coast of the hemisphere what Philadelphia purportedly will become to the eastern coast, with both cities accomplishing this through commercial enterprise. Rocafuerte describes commercialism as the enemy of privilege—in other words, the enemy of monopolies, royal companies, and royalty itself. In this picture, free commerce stands in opposition to the types of advantages granted to those who receive favors from the Spanish crown.

The purported connection between "Filadelfia" and liberal economics was common in the discourse of "la famosa Filadelfia," but it is important to note that Rocafuerte remains within the realms of political theory. He does not approach a type of proto-Weberism that emerges in the writings of travelers who emphasized the cultural dimensions of the city. A decade after Rocafuerte published *Ideas Necesarias*, Lorenzo de Zavala celebrated Philadelphia in a book that echoed some of the most insulting and racist accounts of Mexico in the nineteenth century. Zavala's account of his passage through the city retraces the footsteps of "Filadelfia" discourse: "The city of Philadelphia is cut perfectly in parallel lines that form streets in the figures of parallelograms. . . . The Bank of the United States is of beautiful white marble, an imitation, although imperfect, of the Parthenon of Athens," he writes in *Viaje a los Estados Unidos del Norte de América* (1834) (*Journey to the United States of North America*).[39] Like Heredia before him, Zavala goes on to note a visit to the museum: "Exhibited there is ancient clothing of the Indians of the country, very similar to that of the Egyptians, and also the complete skeleton of the biggest mammoth that I have seen up to this time" (97–98). In several pages he describes Philadelphia as "the city of capital" whose banks were formed through a system of shareholder subscriptions and the subsequent issuance of notes without gold or silver to back them.

Zavala's description of banking is in keeping with his stated principal purpose: "presenting to Mexicans the customs, manners, institutions, and establishments of the United States as a nominal model, to put it thus, for Mexican legislators" (101). With respect to "customs," Zavala offers the following tirade:

> The Mexican is easy going, lazy, intolerant, generous almost to prodigality, vain, belligerent, superstitious, ignorant and an enemy of all restraint. The North American works, the Mexican has a good time; the first spends less than he has, the second even that which he does not have; the former carries out the most arduous enterprises to their conclusion, the latter abandons them in the early stages; the one lives in his house, decorates it, furnishes it, preserves it against the inclement

weather; the other spends his time in the street, flees from his home, and in a land where there are no seasons he worries little about a place to rest. (2–3)

John-Michael Rivera has proposed that the account above of national differences be read rhetorically in light of Zavala's focus on the effects of colonialism in Mexico.[40] That point would seem to be in keeping with the *Journey*'s complicated and contradictory responses to both the United States and Mexico. (Zavala, for example, is very critical of slavery in the United States.) But perhaps Rivera is too generous. Zavala unapologetically compels his readers to take the passage as transparent. If Mexicans want him to change his opinion, he says, they should "Get rid of those eighty-seven holidays during the year that you dedicate to play, drunkenness and pleasure. Save up capital for the decent support of yourselves and your families in order to try to give guarantees of your concern for the preservation of the social order" (3). As the emphasis on capital suggests, Zavala praises in Philadelphia the type of economic order and competition that he seeks in Mexico. Emphasizing the role of Quakers in the political foundations of Pennsylvania, Zavala concludes, "The important thing is that in general they are charitable, hardworking, and honorable" (100). As in many sections of the *Journey*, Protestants are presented not only with tolerance and respect but also as integral to the political system and customs of the country. Ultimately, Zavala invokes Philadelphia to suggest a desired continuum between economic conditions and cultural norms.

Like Rocafuerte, Zavala can also be read as writing "Filadelfia" (and the United States more generally) in response to conditions in Mexico. He had left for the United States as a political refugee after conservatives rose to power.[41] But while Zavala saw in the urban order of Philadelphia a contrast to the practice of everyday life in Mexico, Rocafuerte opted for a symbolic association leading to constitutional engagement. Ultimately, constitutional debates offer the most important context for reading the texts of "la famosa Filadelfia." "Justice demands that we should acknowledge the intrinsic advantages and practical utility of the Constitution of the United States," wrote José María Salazar in *Observations on the Political Reforms of Colombia* (Philadelphia, 1828), published in both English and Spanish versions, "but it is an absurdity to suppose it [can be] adapted to those countries differing in circumstances, and where elements of social state are contradictory."[42] The occasion for the Philadelphia publication of Salazar's observations was a forthcoming constitutional convention in Colombia.

"Brilliant Irregularity": Another City

Several visitors to Philadelphia in the early nineteenth century noted the city's order, particularly its grid-like streets and regularity of construction. Order had always been an important dimension of the city in colonial Spanish America, going back to the sixteenth century. As Angel Rama argues, cities founded by the Spanish and Portuguese were constructed to bring order to colonial settings "as a hierarchical society transposed by analogy into a hierarchical design of urban space."[43] Men of letters attempted "to dominate and impose certain norms on their savage surroundings" to promote colonial expansion and a "civilizing mission."[44] Philadelphia presented a different scenario for the cosmopolitan intellectuals and liberal thinkers of the early nineteenth century: its regularity signified a move toward the anticolonial dawn of new constitutions. Order had come to represent national sovereignty. Despite its regularity, the city gave birth to a type of difference that I have tried to evoke through the use of the word "Filadelfia" and that points to the multilingual history of hemispheric relations.

Philadelphia contained within it the seeds of a Hispanophone culture because its urban print culture allowed visitors and exiles to recreate "Filadelfia" from a hemispheric perspective. This process is illustrated in a curious moment described by Heredia in the already quoted letter to his uncle. After walking through the city, Heredia takes a significant detour; he enters a museum and sees the skeleton of a mammoth. "All my previous visions disappeared upon seeing it," Heredia writes. The mammoth sends Heredia into a flight of the imagination as he tries to estimate the date of the animal's existence on earth. In turn, he reflects on an indigenous legend about the mammoth as a "race of invincible and monstrous creatures" that roamed the earth bent on destruction, threatening to annihilate humans. According to this legend, the Great Spirit shot lightning at the "oppressors of the earth" and felled them all. Heredia calls attention to a lapse in his memory; he doesn't remember where he has read about this "legend of the north American Indians." But his retelling is similar to Thomas Jefferson' account of the mammoth legend in *Notes on the State of Virginia*: "That in ancient times a herd of these tremendous animals came to the Big-bone licks, and began an universal destruction of the bear, deer, elks, buffaloes, and other animals . . . the Great Man above, looking down and seeing this, was so enraged that he seized his lightning."[45] Jefferson discusses the mammoth to refute the Comte de Buffon's claim that animals in the Americas are smaller than those in Europe. That type of old world/new world dispute should have fed into Heredia's desire to elevate the Bank of the United States over the Parthenon, so it is curious that the mammoth moves Heredia in a different direction, into what he calls "regions of conjecture in which understanding is lost and even imagination is extinguished." He imagines a future time when "we" will be extinct and other beings will seek information about us in vain. A romantic poet, Heredia seeks this temporal sublime, a speculation about a future scene that will parallel his own moment only in that both he and the imagined future interlocutor reach an epistemological uncertainty. The result is a letter that both establishes a common ground with the United States, based on geographic and political contradistinctions to Europe, but at the same time displays discomfort with "la famosa Filadelfia" and imaginatively moves to some other "American" place not necessarily tied to the United States.

The notion of Philadelphia as a place in the early nineteenth century was in tension with the potential disruptions brought on by the temporal and spatial movements of its Spanish-speaking visitors and residents. Heredia's ruminations on the mammoth are followed by a second detour. Toward the end of the letter, as he offers population figures and describes the streets, he notes again that the city is *bellísima* and envisions even more stunning scenery emerging when the trees that line its streets are in full bloom. Then he abruptly remarks: "Nevertheless, the same regularity of its streets and almost total uniformity of its buildings brings on some type of fatigue to those who contemplate it." Initially oppressed by the specter of extinction conjured by the mammoth, Heredia is now oppressed by thinking about the cumulative repetitive effort exerted by the men who built rows of uniform houses. He suddenly confesses a preference for the "brilliant irregularity of New York."[46] What are the implications of this turn toward irregularity? We could say it is Heredia's romantic spirit taking flight, but it might be more accurate to say that the detours in his letter point to a contradiction built into the discourse of "la famosa Filadelfia." The hemispheric American city was conceived as a site that both conveyed its temporal limits and pushed against those limits: Heredia's restless moments are in tandem with efforts to transport and transpose "Filadelfia" to other contexts.

The movement of texts in and out of the city and the presence of the Spanish language in a site generally associated with the so-called U.S. founding fathers alter Philadelphia, both as a space that we can read historically and as a set of conditions that existed in the early nineteenth century. Hispanophone Philadelphia disrupts the city by shifting it away from its nationalist associations. In "Walking in the City," Michel de Certeau analyzes the tension between the organization of a city and elements that disrupt that order. On the one hand, the city produces a space of "rational organization" that must "repress all the physical, mental, and political pollutions" that would compromise it.[47] Philadelphia, as it was conceived in the early national period, is exemplary of Certeau's point that the "discourse of the city serves as a totalizing and almost mythical landmark for socioeconomic and political strategies." But the construction of a city is not a final take. Walking itself enacts a kind of reproduction of a city, but one that necessarily veers from a totalizing model. Like walkers, Hispanophone writers appropriated the space of Philadelphia, using it for their own purposes while tapping into the city's conception of itself as the birthplace of independence. As a result, writers like Heredia and Rocafuerte left documents that point to a little-known part of U.S. history: Spanish-language print culture. "La famosa Filadelfia" offers an alternate—perhaps "irregular," to quote Heredia—account of a point in history before nations became a primary influence on constitutions of the self.

NOTES

I thank the Balch Institute for Ethnic Studies at the Historical Society of Pennsylvania for a fellowship that helped me conduct part of the research for this article. I am indebted to James N. Green of the Library Company of Philadelphia for his help with archival materials.

1. My translation. "Mil veces habrás oído decir que es una de las ciudades más regulares del mundo, y es verdad." Heredia to Ignacio Heredia y Campuzano, Philadelphia, 15 April 1824, *Antología Herediana*, ed. Emilio Valdés y de la Torre (Havana: Imprenta El Siglo XX, 1939), 102.

2. Ibid., 103. "Sin duda es el más bello que he visto sobre la tierra; y me gozo en pasearme debajo de su pórtico, donde siempre reina una deliciosa frescura. Creo que en esta fábrica se tomó por modelo el Partenón de Atenas; pero dudo que este, aun en tiempo de su mayor lustre, igualase en sencilla elegancia y belleza al edificio americano."

3. *Views of Philadelphia and its Environs from the Original Drawings Taken in 1827–1830* (Philadelphia: C.G. Childs, 1827), 82.

4. Vicente Rocafuerte, prologue to *Ideas Necesarias a Todo Pueblo Americano Independiente, Que Quiera Ser Libre* (Philadelphia: D. Huntington, 1821), 1.

5. For two articles that focus on the work of José Alvarez de Toldeo Y Dubois (1779–1858) in relation to Hispanophone intellectual circles in Philadelphia, see Nicolás Kanellos, "José Alvarez de Toledo y Dubois and the Origins of Hispanic Publishing in the Early American Republic" (ms., forthcoming) and Kristin A Dykstra, "On the Betrayal of Nations: José Alvarez de Toledo's Philadelphia *Manifesto* (1811) and *Justification* (1816)," *CR: The New Centennial Review* 4 (2004): 267–305.

6. Harry Bernstein, *Making an Inter-American Mind* (Gainesville: University of Florida, 1961), 178–186.

7. Charvat writes,

> I identify as publishing centers during the first half of the nineteenth century those cities in which publishers, seeking the trade not only of the coast but of the interior, discovered (in a sense, established) the common denominators in the literary taste of the whole country. These cities were Philadelphia and New York, which, close together and connected by abundant ocean, river, and road transportation, formed what I shall call the publishing axis. (*Literary Publishing in America, 1790–1850* [Philadelphia: University of Pennsylvania Press, 1959], 23)

This paradigm may begin to explain the movement of Spanish-language writers from Philadelphia to New York and back. Two periodicals, *El Habanero* (1824–26) and *El Mensajero Semanal* (1828–29), began publishing in Philadelphia and then moved to New York. While both cities were important to Hispanophone writers, Philadelphia offered more symbolic potential for writers attempting to conceive new political forms of organization. A third important site where intellectuals congregated and published their works was London.

8. Writers such as Heredia, Rocafuerte, and Varela were part of a lettered elite that traveled widely in Europe and the United States. Familiar with one another, they committed themselves to the rigors of philosophical, political, and literary study in multiple languages. In the case of Rocafuerte, an impressive fortune allowed him to

mention trips to Paris as if they had been weekend excursions. The passion of these cosmopolitan intellectuals for books (both their own and those written by others) could be indulged in Philadelphia, where writers and publishers operated without governmental restrictions.

9. In the case of South American republics, he also notes the influence of colonial administrative units on the importance of local economic zones. Benedict Anderson, *Imagined Communities* (New York: Verso, 1991), 24–25, 52.

10. Ibid., 44–51.

11. See, for example, Jaime E. Rodríguez O., ed., *The Divine Charter: Constitutionalism and Liberalism in Nineteenth-Century Mexico* (Oxford: Rowman & Littlefield, 2005).

12. I refer here to the tradition of Latin American criticism of U.S. imperialism that stretches from the nineteenth to the twentieth centuries and is perhaps embodied most forcefully in the writings of José Martí and Che Guevara. But I am also talking about recent studies of the Americas that emphasize that critique. José David Saldívar's *The Dialectics of Our America* (Durham: Duke University Press, 1991), one of the most influential interventions, offers a masterful comparative model that brings together writers such as Gabriel García Márquez and Ntozake Shange by drawing a conceptual connection between U.S. social movements and Latin American struggles against imperialism. We see echoes of anti-imperialism in the opening page of Anna Brickhouse's *Transamerican Literary Relations and the Nineteenth-Century Public Sphere* (Cambridge and New York: Cambridge University Press, 2004). Brickhouse opens with a speech by Ronald Reagan in which he praises Simón Bolívar; she quickly unmasks Reagan's ideology by pointing to the U.S. attacks on Nicaragua and El Salvador during his administration—in turn, reminding us of Bolívar's own vexed response to the United States. The economic and military realities of twentieth-century U.S. imperialist expansion are marshaled against what Brickhouse regards as the hemispheric idealism of Pan-American unity that circulated in the early nineteenth century.

13. Gretchen Murphy, *Hemispheric Imaginings: The Monroe Doctrine and Narratives of U.S. Empire* (Durham: Duke University Press, 2005), 3–9.

14. Rosalind Remer, *Printers and Men of Capital: Philadelphia Book Publishers in the New Republic* (Philadelphia: University of Pennsylvania Press, 1996), 7.

15. Ibid., 2–4.

16. Nicolás Kanellos, Introduction to *Herencia: The Anthology of Hispanic Literature of the United States* (New York: Oxford University Press, 2002), 22.

17. Donald Kaser, *Messrs. Carey & Lea of Philadelphia: A Study in the History of the Book Trade* (Philadelphia: University of Pennsylvania Press, 1957), 37.

18. *Catalogue of an Extensive Collection of Books, in the English, French, Spanish, and Italian Languages, Sporting Prints, Books of Caricatures, & c., Recently Imported and for Sale by H.C. Carey and I. Lea* (Philadelphia: Carey and Lea, 1825).

19. "Attempts were made to establish agencies abroad," Kazer writes. "Representatives were soon selling Carey's books in Canton and Gibraltar, Buenos Aires and Calcutta" (*Messrs. Carey & Lea*, 19).

20. Carey publishing house to Louis Castagnino, 18 April 1822. Carey Letterbook for Jan. 1–June 24, 1822, Lea and Febiger Collection. Historical Society of Pennsylvania.

21. Ibid.

22. Quoted in Merle E. Simmons, *Santiago F. Puglia: An Early Philadelphia Propagandist for Spanish American Independence* (Chapel Hill: North Carolina Studies in the Romance Languages and Literatures, 1977), 19.

23. Ibid., 20–21.

24. Santiago Felipe Puglia, *El Desengaño del Hombre* (Filadelfia: Imprenta de Francisco Bailey, 1794), v.

25. Puglia, *El Desengaño*, 22–23.

26. Simmons, *Puglia*, 26.

27. "Nos Los Inquisidores." The broadside is in the Library Company of Philadelphia.

28. Ibid.

29. Simmons, *Puglia*, 47.

30. My translation.

> Amados paisanos mios: no cabe en mi pecho el vivo gozo que esperimento al saber que tremola ya el glorioso estandarte de la independencia sobre las risueñas márgenes del caudaloso Guayaquil. Permitidme que desde esta capital de Pensilvania os envie mi mas espresivo parabien, acompañado de los ardientes votos que dirijo al cielo por la felicidad de mi patria. ¿Y en dónde puedo encontrar recuerdos mas sublimes, lecciones mas heróicas, mas dignas de imitacion, y ejemplos mas análogos a nuestra actual situacion política, que en esta famosa Filadelfia? (Vicente Rocafuerte, Prologue to *Ideas Necesarias A Todo Pubelo Americano Independiente Que Quiera Ser Libre* [Philadelphia: D. Huntington, 1821], 1)

31. "Yo fui a los Estados Unidos a publicar un opúsculo que compuse y lleva por título: *Ideas Necesarias*" Vicente Rocafuerte, *Vicente Rocafuerte, Un Americano Libre*, ed. José Antonio Fernandez de Castro (Mexico: Secretaría de Educación Pública, 1947), 32.

32. The nineteenth-century Cuban scholar Antonio Bachiller y Morales says that *Ideas Necesarias* was published in Havana and not in Philadelphia, as stated on the title page. He references a 194-page edition, which presumably differs from the 180-page edition that bears an 1821 Philadelphia imprint. Bachiller y Morales might be referring to another edition of the book. Antonio Bachiller y Morales, *Apuntes Para la Historia de las Letras y de la Instrucción Pública en la Isla de Cuba*, 3 vols (Havana: Cultural, 1937), 3:342.

33. "Aquí, a tantos años de distancia, Rocafuerte comete un error de memoria." José Antonio Fernandez de Castro, ed., *Vicente Rocafuerte, Un Americano Libre*, 73 n. 15.

34. David Huntington was a New York-based publisher and T. W. Mercein was a printer with an office on Gold Street, also in New York.

35. Rocafuerte, *Ideas*, 9.

36. Vicente Rocafuerte, *Ensayo Político* (New York: A. Paul, 1823); [Vicente Rocafuerte and José Canga Argüelles], *Cartas de un Americano Sobre las Ventajas de los Gobiernos Repúblicanos Federativos* (London: Imprenta de Calero, 1826).

37. Alexander Hamilton, "The Federalist No. 9," *The Federalist with Letters of "Brutus,"* ed. Terence Ball (Cambridge and New York: Cambridge University Press, 2003), 36. Rocafuerte and Argüelles, *Cartas de un Americano*, ed. Neptalí Zúñiga (Quito: Gobierno del Ecuador, 1947), 12.

38. Rocafuerte, *Ideas*, 15.

39. Lorenzo de Zavala, *Journey to the United States/ Viaje a los Estados Unidos del Norte de América*, trans. Wallace Woolsey (Houston: Arte Público Press, 2005), 97; hereafter cited parenthetically by page number.

40. Rivera proposes that Zavala is deploying the Greek concept of *theoria*, the production of cultural and political knowledge through a travel account that presents a utopia.

See his introduction to Zavala, *Journey to the United States of North America*, xix, xxiv–xxv.

41. Rivera, introduction to Zavala, *Journey*, xv–xvii.

42. José María Salazar, *Observations on the Political Reforms of Colombia*, trans. Edward Barry (Philadelphia: William Stavely, 1828), 19. The Spanish-language version appeared as *Observaciones Sobre las Reformas Politicas de Colombia* (Filadelfia: Imprenta de Guillelmo Stavely, 1828).

43. Angel Rama, *The Lettered City*, ed. and trans. John Charles Chasteen (Durham: Duke University Press, 1996), 3.

44. Rama, *Lettered City*, 12–13.

45. Thomas Jefferson, *Writings*, ed. Merrill D. Peterson (New York: Library of America 1984), 165.

46. Heredia, "Letter," 104. "Sin embargo, aquella misma regularidad de sus calles y casi completa igualdad de sus edificios, causan no sé qué fatiga al que los contempla."

47. Michel de Certeau, *The Practice of Everyday Life* (Berkeley: University of California Press, 1984), 94.

4

The Other Country

Mexico, the United States, and the Gothic History of Conquest

JESSE ALEMÁN

The idea of the "Western Hemisphere" . . . establishes an ambiguous position. America simultaneously constitutes difference and sameness. It is the other hemisphere, but it is Western. It is distinct from Europe (of course, it is not the Orient), but it is bound to Europe. It is different, however, from Asia and Africa, continents and cultures that do not form part of the Western hemisphere. But who defines such a hemisphere?[1]

In the introduction to Robert Montgomery Bird's 1834 *Calavar, or, The Knight of the Conquest*, an American wandering through Mexico sits on Chapultepec hill and muses on Mexico's pre-conquest history. The Toltecs first populated Mexico, the American imagines, and were "the most civilized of which Mexican hieroglyphics . . . have preserved in memory." Other tribes followed, but none brought civilization until the Aztecs. "[F]rom this herd of barbarians," the American thinks, "grew . . . the magnificent empire of the Montezumas, . . . heaving again with the impulses of nascent civilization." Finally, the "voice of the Old World" rolls over the eastern mountains, but instead of fully civilizing the Aztecs, the "shout of conquest and glory was answered by the groan of a dying nation." So goes Mexico's romantic history of conquest for the dreamy American. Spanish colonialism killed the "incipient greatness," the potential for new world civilization, in the Aztec empire and left Mexico in the hands of "civilized savages and Christian pagans." Mexico must "rekindle the torches of knowledge," the American thinks out loud, and he is not alone in his idea. A Mexican curate has overhead the American's musings and agrees that Mexico must regenerate itself from its post-revolutionary "Pandemonium" of ambitious rulers and servile citizens to reassert its past, indigenous potential as a civilized new world nation. Until then, Mexico is a "gust of anarchy," the curate explains, that will "disease thy imagination, until thou comest to be disgusted with the yet untainted excellence of thine own institutions, because thou perceivest the evils of their perversion."[2]

The curate presses the American to leave Mexico and to take with him, to translate and publish, several volumes of Mexican history, "which will teach thee to appreciate and preserve . . . the pure and admirable frame of government, which a beneficent power has suffered you to enjoy." A historian and descendent of Montezuma, the curate has penned a history that finds no favor in Mexico because Mexicans are too benighted to appreciate the nascent civilization of their indigenous past. "Your own people," the priest explains, "are, perhaps, not so backward." Written as an Aztec palimpsest, the volumes span pre-conquest to the 1821 revolution and assert that "reason reprobates, human happiness denounces, and God abhors, the splendour of contention." The American accepts the volumes—with rights to the profits accrued from their republication, of course—and returns to the United States where he unsuccessfully attempts to crack the palimpsests until he reads of the curate's death in a Mexican newspaper. The padre, it turns out, is a genius historian whose manuscript pages were "arranged like those in the form of a printer," and once the American has unfolded the volumes, "he beheld the chaos of history reduced to order." He transcribes the hieroglyphic text and discovers among the volumes a story about the cavaliers of the conquest, which he translates, edits, and republishes, after deleting much of the curate's philosophy and changing the title to fit the "intellectual dyspepsia" of American readers. The result is *Calavar, or, The Knight of the Conquest*, which the American calls a *Historia Verdadera* (à la Bernal Diaz del Castillo), a fitting subtitle, the Introduction insists, because "the history of Mexico, under all aspects but that of fiction, is itself—a romance."[3]

Calavar's opening scene invokes a common frame for historical romances in which the ghostly voices of bygone times inhabit a locale and impress themselves on the mind of a romantic wayfarer; and Chapultepec in particular is a significant site for hemispheric musings. Linked by a causeway to Tenochtitlán, Chapultepec hill served as a fortified retreat and burial ground for Aztec emperors, but during the nineteenth century, it became a contested symbolic space that embodied the living history of Mexico's indigenous past.[4] Cuban poet José María Heredia's 1820s poem "Las sombras," for instance, features a nineteenth-century democrat on a pilgrimage to Chapultepec, where he encounters the shades of past "indigenous rulers of the Americas," who debate and denounce tyranny and empire in a series of monologues.[5] Frances Calderón de la Barca's 1839 visit to Chapultepec likewise conjured the sublime continuity between Mexico's indigenous past and its post-independence present: "Could these hoary cypresses speak," Calderón de la Barca muses on the hill's trees, "what tales might they not disclose, standing there with their long gray beards, and outstretched venerable arms, century after century: already old when Montezuma was a boy, and still vigorous in the days of Bustamante!" The link between Montezuma and President Anastasio Bustamante is an apt juxtaposition, for while Calderón de la Barca fancies that "the last of the Aztec Emperors wandered with his dark-eyed harem" at Chapultepec, Bustamante's presidential reign is rapidly collapsing: he will be pushed out of office in 1840, exiled by 1841, and succeeded by Antonio López de Santa Anna the same year. And Montezuma and Bustamante are not the only troubled spirits of Chapultepec: "the shade of the conqueror's Indian love, the far-famed Doña Marina," roams the area, too.[6] For Calderón de la Barca, Mexico's pre-conquest tranquility and post-independence instability converge on the ghost of La Malinche, who haunts the caves and woods of Chapultepec and functions as a reminder of the damning, subversive space women occupy when they literally and symbolically traverse two cultures and languages.[7]

Calavar's introduction thus marks the cultural moment when Mexico's antiquity becomes the hemispheric history of the United States following its revolutionary break from England. As Eric Sundquist explains, the "romantic primitivism that permeated much American literature in the antebellum period . . . provoked echoes of revolutionary rhetoric about breaking the constraints of British and European custom."[8] Yet, even as the United States turned away from Europe and the mother country, it turned to another country, Mexico, to stage its romantic primitivism and in the process generated an alternative literary and national narrative that placed the legacy of the Spanish conquest of Mexico strangely at the heart of the historical emergence of the United States. As *Calavar*'s introduction makes clear, the United States and Mexico share the same revolutionary spirit and hemispheric, republican ideals. Yet, the *translatio studii* assimilates Mexico's past and rearticulates it as Anglo-America's hemispheric story in a literary act that sets the stage for continental colonization of the Americas by the United States. In this sense, Mexico functions as the nation's "*imago*," to recall María DeGuzmán's argument about the United States' relationship to the image of Spain. But where DeGuzmán sees Spain as a "virtual or mirror image in front of which, in a libidinal dynamic of identification and disavowal, Anglo American culture, despite its fragmentation and initial fragility, ascends toward a seemingly unified and coherent imperial identity," Mexico more appropriately stands in as an uncanny figure for the United States because the continental proximity of the two countries and their shared revolutionary histories make them estranged national neighbors.[9]

Freud's definition of the uncanny as "*unheimlich*"—the "unhomely"—is especially apt here because the fluidity of national borders collapses the otherwise clear distinctions between native and foreigner, domestic and international, America and América, making Mexico in particular a strangely familiar place that troubles the trans-American imaginary of the United States.

"The 'uncanny' is that class of the terrifying which leads back to something long known to us, once very familiar," writes Freud, and then he continues to explain that the German word for "home" embodies two contradictory meanings: "that which is familiar and congenial" and "that which is concealed and kept out of sight." The uncanny occurs when that which was concealed emerges as a familiar object that has been repressed.[10] *Heimlich* also means "native," however, so that the notion of "home" can be extended to the idea of nation, as when Juan Seguín characterized his position in Texas after the 1848 signing of the Treaty of Guadalupe Hidalgo as being a "foreigner in my own land."[11] Seguín was emphasizing the haunting unhomeliness of colonial displacement that continues to trouble Mexican Americans. It is a dispossession, to be sure, but not strictly in the sense of being without a home; rather, it is an estrangement from the home, a momentary recognition that the foreign rests at the center of the familiar, leading to "the discovery that 'home' is not what or where we think it is," Priscilla Wald explains, "and that we, by extension, are not who or what we think we are."[12]

Postcolonial theory, especially following Homi Bhabha, often uses keywords such as *ambivalence, hybridity*, or *mimicry* to express the troubling doubleness between colonizer and colonized, while the uncanny also characterizes American studies as a field "conceived on the banks of the Congo."[13] Yet the hemispheric *unheimlich* I am describing in nineteenth-century U.S. cultural production is not so much the disturbing presence of a double or an other that reflects the imperial self as much as it is the haunting realization that the self is the other—not a projection, reflection, or abstraction but a repressed historical presence within. "The categories of subaltern and imperialist, particularly in the American hemisphere, are not mutually exclusive, but often overlaid," explains Jeff Karem in his critique of the applicability of postcolonial theory to Pan-American studies.[14] But his point also serves as a reminder that sameness rather than difference haunts the Americas and challenges us to rethink the hemisphere not as cleft in two but as our America and the other America at the same time. The "uncanny hybridity" of the U.S. South that Jon Smith and Deborah Cohn discuss, for instance, is an equally apt description of the western hemisphere as "a space simultaneously (or alternately) center and margin, victor and defeated, empire and colony, essentialist and hybrid, northern and southern (both in the global sense)."[15] As only a palimpsest map might show, our America is also the other America, but instead of a happy hemispherism, the presence of the other felt and discovered within rather than outside of the borders of self, home, and nation generates an inter-American gothic anxiety from "inside the monster," as Martí once described the United States.[16]

My understanding of early nineteenth-century narratives such as Robert Montgomery Bird's *Calavar*, William Prescott's *History of the Conquest of Mexico*, and the anonymously published *Xicoténcatl* runs the risk of reproducing a hemispheric paradigm that centers the United States in relation to national

"Others." Claudia Sadowski-Smith and Claire F. Fox put the problem this way: "we fear that an Americanist-led hemispherism will only promote a vision of the Americas in which all academic disciplinary configurations are subordinate to those of the United States and in which every region outside the United States is collapsed into a monolithic other."[17] But I want to encourage an approach to "inter-American" studies that considers "inter" not as the prefix "across" but as the word for "burial" in order to emphasize the idea that the presence of the other in the nation is "that which is concealed and kept out of sight" but always felt as a haunting history that must be excavated. "Inter" Americanism understands that the nations of the western hemisphere already contain *within* ("intra") their borders national others whose formative presence is subsequently buried (interred) but nonetheless felt and often expressed through gothic discourse. While liberal Mexican leaders fashioned Mexico's 1821 independent system of governance loosely on the United States, for instance, *Calavar*'s opening reminds us that the United States likewise imagined its place in the hemisphere by way of Mexico's antiquity. The United States and Mexico thus share a familial relation that vexes citizenship as much as it troubles their national literary histories, for their confluences indicate how one country is already embedded within the history of the other perhaps because the borders across the Americas are so porous.

As the hills of Chapultepec remind us, specters of empire characterize the hemispheric *unheimlich*, and narratives about the Spanish conquest of the Aztecs are particularly uncanny because the sixteenth-century conquest seemed strangely familiar to the United States, especially after the Monroe Doctrine imagined hemispheric solidarity against Europe in the form of U.S. imperialism throughout the Americas. Often described as historical romances, *Calavar*, *The History of the Conquest of Mexico*, and *Xicoténcatl* become gothic in the context of "inter-Americanism" because each work exhumes the legacy of conquest and racial rebellion that haunts the hemispheric presence of the United States. Rebellious Moors, republican Indians, and heroic Aztecs become horrifying in U.S. conquest narratives written in the context of the Indian removal, the annexation of Texas, and black slavery—the home becomes unhomely as *Calavar* and *Conquest* link the Spanish empire in the Americas to U.S. imperialism. Yet both U.S. narratives are related to another "inter-American" text, the anonymously published *Xicoténcatl*, which was only recently disinterred from literary history to express what *Calavar* and *Conquest* would rather keep buried: that the inter-American gothic emerged in the first place because republicanism became empire in the Americas.

Specters of Empire

A physician interested in abnormal psychology, Robert Montgomery Bird is often celebrated as the first successful U.S. playwright, though mostly by default considering the dearth of early Anglo-American dramatists, and is best known for his 1837 *Nick of the Woods*, a gothic narrative about a seemingly inoffensive Quaker, Nathan Slaughter, who doubles as a demonic Indian killer. But between the years of his plays and his frontier novels, Bird imagined a native U.S. literary history rooted in Spanish America. His last two popular plays, *Oralloosa, Son of the Incas* (1832) and *The Broker of Bogota* (1833), signaled Bird's growing interest in the Americas, and though the Philadelphian only got as far as New Orleans during his 1833 planned trip to Mexico, he was already imagining its landscape, political history, and potential for romance in his first historical novel, *Calavar, or, The Knight of the Conquest*. Written mostly in 1833, *Calavar* was published in Philadelphia by Carey, Lea, and Company in 1834, and was meant to be the first of at least eight historical romances about Mexico, spanning its conquest to its 1821 revolution for independence.[18] As with his trek south, however, Bird's literary plans fell short: he followed *Calavar* with its two-volume sequel, *The Infidel, or The Fall of Mexico* (1835), but never returned again to Mexico's antiquity.

While *The Infidel* is more recognizable as a gothic thriller, with its doublings, incest, and homicidal monks, *Calavar* particularly interests me here, for it expresses the repressed histories of conquest the United States inherits from the Old World and reproduces across the New World. A novice knight, Don Amador enters the New World in 1520 to find Calavar, his father-knight who, following his participation in the conquest of Granada, has fled to Mexico to help defeat the Aztecs. Calavar, however, is a skeleton of his former self, a ghostly relic who embodies the demise of the Spain's Old World codes of chivalry in the New World:

> He was in full armour, but the iron plates were rusted on his body, and in many places shattered. The plumes were broken and disordered on his helmet; the spear lay at the feet of his steed; his buckler was in the hands of his attendant; and instead of the red tabard which was worn in a season of war by the brothers of his order, the black mantle of peace, with its great white cross, hung or drooped heavily from his shoulders. . . . [H]e presented the appearance of a ruin majestic in decay.[19]

Alienated from himself and his fellow Spaniards, the knight suffers from the guilt of bloodlust, for he believes he killed Alharef-ben-Ismail, a Moorish noble, and his lover Zayda in a jealous rage during the conquest of Granada. His apprentice knight, Don Amador, fares no better. He too battled at Granada, where he fell in love with Leila, a Christianized Moor the knight believes to have been captured by infidels at the end of Granada's fall. Already unsettled by the conquest of Granada, Calavar and Amador find further estrangement in the New World when Amador arrives in Mexico, and the first battle the novice knight joins in Mexico is not between Spanish Christians and Aztec barbarians but between Cortés and Navarez, two Spaniards warring against each other for the right to conquer Mexico.

Specters of empire thus haunt the narrative as the Spanish colonization of Granada and the Moors mirrors the conquest of Mexico and the Aztecs. Roughly thirty years after Spain's 1492 Reconquista of Granada led to the large-scale persecution of Moriscos under the Inquisition, Abdalla the Moor and his son Jacinto are reminders, especially to Calavar and his novice knight, that the Spanish crusade in the New World is a legacy of a crusade waged for centuries in the Old World.[20] This legacy of empire, however, troubles Calavar and Amador to the point that they see ghosts of their Moorish princesses in Aztec temples leading pagan rituals of human sacrifice. As Amador explains to Jacinto of these ghostly sightings: "I am almost quite convinced, that she is a spectre, and an inhabitant of hell, sent forth upon earth to punish me with much affliction, and, perhaps, with madness. For I think she is the spirit of Leila; and her appearance in the guise of a pagan goddess, or pagan priest-ess,—the one or the other,—shows me, that she whom I loved, dwells not with angels, but with devils."[21]

The conquest of Mexico literally conjures the Moorish dead, bringing them back to life in the form of strangely familiar Aztecs, but in this case, Amador's pale specter is nothing more than the return of the repressed. As it turns out, the pagan priestess is none other than Jacinto, who, it turns out, is none other than Leila. Amador finds his lost Morisco lover in Mexico in drag as Calavar's page boy, who cross-dresses as a pagan Aztec priestess as part of a plot devised by Abdalla to "inflame the [Mexican] people with fresh devotion and fury against the Spaniards." The transvestite terror Leila/Jacinto inspires in Amador is both sexual and transnational. That is, Leila's drag performance fosters queer desire that shores up the adage that conquest works under the logic of fear and desire. "But, father," Amador confesses to a priest,

> here is another circumstance that greatly troubled me; and, in good sooth, it troubles me yet. It is known to thee that my kinsman had, until yesterday night, a little page—a Moorish boy, greatly beloved by us both. As for myself, I loved him because he was of the race of Leila; and . . . unnatural as it may seem, I bore not for my young brother a greater affection than for this most unlucky urchin. A foolish fellow charged him to be an enchanter; and sometimes I bethink me of the accusation, and suppose he has given me magical love-potions.[22]

Eventually, the narrative forecloses the subversive element of Leila's trans-vestism, for in the end, she embraces her Christian identity at the expense of her Moorish background and marries Don Amador, and the lovers, as his name suggests, relocate to Spain. Nevertheless, the event shores up the "inter-American" *unheimlich* as the buried history of Spain's conquest of Granada emerges from beneath the conquest of the Aztecs as a specter of empire that haunts the literary appropriation by the United States of Mexico's history and literal acquisition of Mexican territory, first by way of Texas and later through the U.S.-Mexico War. Indeed, Leila's transvestism signals two interrelated terrors: that Mexico will be to the United States what Granada was to Spain, a conquered nation of racialized subjects who were subsequently incorporated into the Spanish empire; and that Mexico's indigenous people are Moors in disguise—that is, more black than white in a U.S. racial system dominated by the logic of slavery. On the one hand, the conquest of Mexico threatens the self-proclaimed republicanism of the United States, and on the other, the fear of slavocracy lingers as the ambiguous racialization of Mexicans places them in between U.S. citizenry and chattel slavery.

And Leila is not the only cross-dressed Moor. Her father, Abdalla, is none other than Alharef-ben-Ismail, the Morisco prince Calavar believed he had killed in Granada. In love with Zayda, Calavar "slew! slew! slew!" her when he learned she had slept with Alharef-ben-Ismail, though Calavar did not know that Alharf-ben-Ismail and Zayda were betrothed at the time. The guilt of bloodlust that Calavar attempts to escape in Mexico returns in the form of Abdalla cum Alharef-ben-Ismail, who betrays the Spaniards by siding with the Aztecs to seek revenge for the fall of Granada. The "black legend" takes on a whole new meaning in the text as Abdalla and several other Moors escape from their Spanish masters and teach the Aztecs modes of European warfare that help them expel the Spaniards from Tenochtitlán during *la noche triste*. Theirs is a racial rebellion that traverses histories of conquest as the Moors revenge the fall of Granada and help the Aztecs in the process take back their capitol city in an anti-imperial war for freedom that echoes the revolutionary rhetoric of the United States even as it expresses the threat of slave rebellion: "This is not a war of heaven against hell," says Abdalla, "but of tyranny against freedom." It is thus fitting that Abdalla and Calavar meet at the battle of Otumba, where the conquest of Mexico becomes a strangely familiar reenactment of the conquest of Granada that leaves Abdalla dead on the field and Calavar mortally wounded as the Spaniards rout the Aztecs in the background:

> [F]uriously descending the slope of the hill . . . [there] seemed [to be] a Christian cavalier in black armour, mounted on a noble horse, and couching a lance like a trained soldier, only that, behind him, there followed, with savage yells, a band of several thousand Indians, bearing the well-known colours of Tenochtitlan itself. . . . [At] the opposite mountain . . . a mounted cavalier descend[ed] with lance in rest, and with the speed of thunder, as if rushing to a tournay with him of the black armour, but without being followed by any one, excepting a single youth, who staggered far behind.[23]

Adballa is all the more terrifying because his radical republican rhetoric echoes the revolutionary spirit that fueled the break of the United States from

England, but this time, a black subject of Spanish colonialism uses the rhetoric of republicanism to lead the Aztecs in collective racial resistance against the Spaniards in an act that speaks to early nineteenth-century fears that blacks and Indians would unite in a war against Anglo-America. The terror of slavery and slave revolt that the narrative imagines raises the threat the United States stands to inherit if it follows Spain's hemispheric legacy. In the wake of Nat Turner's rebellion, the Cherokee Trail of Tears, and the Seminole Wars, Bird's narrative situates blacks and Indians between anti-colonial insurgents and semi-barbaric infidels. Their anti-imperial resistance echoes Anglo-American revolutionary rhetoric, but their racialized proto-republicanism generates a race war that, as in Melville's "Benito Cereno," sees the gothic threat of racial rebellion as the legacy of colonialism in the Americas. The cross-dressed Moors, in other words, link the Aztecs to the Moors and Mexico to Granada and disclose a history of empire that, by Bird's preface to the 1847 edition of *Calavar*, the United States stands to reproduce. "There is, indeed, a remarkable parallel between the invasions of the two great captains," Bird says of Cortés and General Winfield Scott:

> There is the same route up the same difficult and lofty mountains; the same city . . . as the object of attack; the same petty forces, and the same daring intrepidity leading them against millions of enemies, fighting in the heart of their own country; and, finally, the same desperate fury of unequal armies contending in mortal combat on the causeways and in the streets of Mexico. We might say, perhaps, that there is the same purpose of conquest: but we do not believe that the American people aim at, or desire, the subjugation of Mexico.[24]

At the height of the U.S.-Mexico War, Bird returns to his narrative about the Spanish conquest of Mexico in an ambivalent recognition that the United States is both following and not following in Spain's footsteps, while on the congressional floor in 1847, Lewis Cass articulated a similar ambivalence to the stipulations of the Treaty of Guadalupe Hidalgo: "It would be a deplorable amalgamation [uniting the United States and Mexico]. No such evil will happen to us in our day. We do not want the people of Mexico, either as citizens or subjects. All we want is a portion of territory, which they nominally hold, generally uninhabited, or, where inhabited at all, sparsely so, and with a population which would soon recede, or identify itself with ours."[25] Cass's contradictory stance balances the desire of the United States for Mexican territory and its fear of racial miscegenation through a gothic discourse that has its roots in *Calavar*'s *mestizo* nation, where blacks and Indians unite and scare the hell out of white people until they end up dead, like Calavar, or exiled back to the home, like Amador, whose domestic bliss with Leila and their mixed-blood child back in Spain concludes with the news that "Mexico has become a Spanish city."[26] The home is not home after all.

Gothic History

It is literary commonplace to assert that romance characterizes William H. Prescott's *History of the Conquest of Mexico*. It is less commonplace to argue that Prescott's three volumes move from romanticism to the gothic as his narrative progresses through the history of Mexico's conquest, and the shift is probably indicative of Prescott's post- and neo-colonial "discovery" of empire in the Americas. Of course, as John Eipper notes, Prescott scholars usually view his history as pro-imperialist and often conflate his life with his works to come to the following conclusion: "namely, Prescott demonstrates how Christian (West) triumphed over Pagan (non-West) because History destined it to be that way, in both the sixteenth century and the now romantic, now 'scientific' nineteenth."[27] Every U.S. navy ship library carried Prescott's volumes during the U.S.-Mexico War, and undoubtedly, his historical narrative fanned the romantic flames of U.S. army volunteers in Mexico; his narrative also acted as travel guide and ethnography during the invasion, though Prescott never set foot in Mexico. Yet as a Bostonian Whig, Prescott opposed the annexation of Texas—for fear that it would extend slavery—and found the pro-war expansionist spirit fueling the U.S.-Mexico War distasteful. He even refused to write a history of the war, despite General Winfield Scott's request and offer to open his war papers to Prescott.[28] Prescott's *Conquest* suffers from the same ambivalence: it sees much to admire in the Spanish conquest of Mexico and much to abhor about it in the same way that the narrative wavers between recognizing the Aztecs as a civilized, indigenous empire and characterizing them as savage barbarians.

This racial "equivocation," to recall Vera M. Kutzinski's phrase, haunts *Conquest* in the form of competing racialized body politics whose battle over Mexico becomes a gothic, if not grotesque, event that seems strangely familiar to Prescott's 1840s historical moment.[29] "The gothic's connection to American history," Teresa Goddu explains, "is difficult to identify precisely because of the national and critical myths that America and its literature *have* no history."[30] Ironically, *Conquest* may prove this to be the case as Mexico's history stands in for the history of the United States and in the process invokes the quintessentially gothic terror, race, but places it within an "inter-Americas" context that, as with *Calavar*, is unsettling because one national identity is buried within another. In much the same way that the "Africanist presence" accounts for the U.S. gothic, the inter-American gothic emerges when the hemispheric horrors of the Spanish conquest of Mexico return in narratives, such as Prescott's, that sense how the United States stands to inherit the monstrous race war hidden beneath the romantic veneer of Mexico's history.[31] This process is all the more disturbing, I maintain, because it transforms Prescott's native country into another country that anxiously exposes the historical presence of racial rebellion that should otherwise remain hidden.

The three-volume history does not begin gothic, but it becomes it as the Aztecs under Guatemozin fight to keep the Spaniards out of Tenochtitlán after expelling them during *la noche triste.* To be sure, before then, the specter of Aztec religion spooks the Spaniards, as when Cortés and the Spaniards first visit the Aztec temples and find the walls "stained with human gore," while "the frantic forms of priests, with their dark robes clotted with blood . . . seemed to the Spaniards to be those of the very ministers of Satan." As if to match gore with gore, the Aztecs gather in an annual festival that celebrates Huitzilopochtli, the war god, but while Cortés is away from the capitol, the Spaniard in charge, Alvarado, orchestrates an Indian massacre that leaves the "pavement" covered with "streams of blood, like water in a heavy shower." The "massacre by Alvarado," as Prescott calls it, leads directly to the revolt of the Aztecs as they unite to expel the Spaniards from the city in what is known as "*la noche triste,*" the sad night when Cortés, his fellow Spaniards, and their Indian allies suffered their greatest loss during the conquest of Mexico. But even this night, which has all the potential of the grotesque, keeps the gothic at bay as "many an unfortunate victim" during the night-long Spanish retreat "was dragged half-stunned on board [Aztec] canoes, to be reserved for a protracted but more dreadful death" in the form of human sacrifice.[32]

The narrative thus buries much of the potentially gothic elements that might portray the Spaniards as emphatically within the black legend or the Aztecs as too barbaric to be an example of an indigenous American civilization.[33] Cannibalism, sacrifice, and Spanish bloodlust are all mentioned, of course, but in measured language that frames the historical narrative within the purview of genteel romance—until the Spanish return to retake Tenochtitlán. Fortified with Spanish troops and Indian allies, the soldiers set out on a *reconquista* of the Aztec empire, and the narrative slides into the gothic. During the second siege of the city, for instance, Alvarado and Sandoval find themselves separated from Cortés and the main field of battle but within earshot of its tide against the Spaniards:

> The two captains now understood that the day must have gone hard with their countrymen. They soon had proof of it, when the victorious Aztecs, returning from the pursuit of Cortés, joined their forces to those engaged with Sandoval and Alvarado, and fell on them with redoubled fury. At the same time they rolled on the ground two or three of the bloody heads of the Spaniards, shouting the name "Malinche." The captains, struck with horror at the spectacle . . . instantly ordered a retreat.

Heads abound during the fight, for while the Aztecs toss three Spanish heads down in front of Alvarado and Sandoval, claiming that one of the heads belongs to Cortés ("Malinche," as they call him), two more heads tumble before Cortés as the Aztecs lob at him "the heads of several Spaniards, shouting at the same time, 'Sandoval,' 'Tonatiuh,' the well-known epithet of Alvarado. At the sight of the deadly trophies, [Cortés] grew deadly pale."[34]

Undoubtedly the Aztecs understand that decapitation functions as a symbolic act that severs from the body the part most associated with power, ideas, and leadership, but while Indian dismemberment occurs occasionally in the previous parts of the history, Spanish heads are not thrown about so amply and easily as they are in *Conquest*'s last volume. Even horses lose their heads in what is a blatant display of Aztec power: "Guatemozin sent several heads of the Spaniards, as well as of the horses, round the country, calling on his old vassals to forsake the banners of the white men, unless they would share the doom of the enemies of Mexico." With the Aztecs united in a fierce indigenous resistance against the Spanish conquest, the narrative gapes at the terror of human sacrifice:

> On its convex surface, [the captive's] breasts were heaved up conveniently for the diabolical purpose of the priestly executioner, who cut asunder the ribs . . . and tore away the heart, which, hot and reeking, was deposited on the golden censer before the idol. The body of the slaughtered victim was then hurled down the steep stairs of the pyramid . . . and the mutilated remains were gathered up by the savages beneath, who soon prepared with them the cannibal repast which completed the work of abomination![35]

What was previously concealed about human sacrifice is now revealed in gory detail, as the greatest horror of the conquest—collective racial resistance by the Aztecs—is visited on the Spaniards in full force.

This explains why *Conquest* becomes gothic. Before the second siege of Tenochtitlán, the story of the Spanish conquest of Mexico is romantic because Mexico's Indians, save for the Tlascalans, an ostensibly independent republican nation, cannot muster an effective resistance to Spanish wile and warfare. Prescott's debt to the black legend at first favors the Aztecs, for as Anna Brickhouse explains, the legend "cast the Spanish conquistadores as bloodthirsty, Catholic villains who preyed mercilessly upon the hemisphere's indigenous races, who were simultaneously characterized as gentle and culturally advanced to an extent that ostensibly set them apart from the indigenous races of the United States."[36] But when the Aztecs unite under Guatemozin, whose bellicosity is a far cry from Montezuma's "pusillanimity," the romance of indigenous adversaries darkens as their terrifying resistance inspires the gothic in the romantic historian whose greatest fear in the 1840s may very well be collective racial rebellion against Anglo imperialism.[37] Perhaps, then, the three volumes of *Conquest* can be considered as a narrative of disinterment whereby the genteel historian is shocked to find mutilated white corpses beneath the romantic history of Mexico's fall; equally disturbing is that the

United States stands to inherit such a gothic genealogy on the eve of its own conquest of Mexico.

Similia Similibus Curantur

In a scene recounted in Bernal Diaz del Castillo's 1632 narrative, an Aztec governor serving as ambassador under Montezuma arrives at the Spanish camp near the port of San Juan de Ulúa to greet the Spaniards, exchange gifts, and reconnoiter the invaders. Tendile brings with him "some clever painters" who "make pictures true to nature of the face and body of Cortés and all his captains." Aware of the power of symbol, Cortés orders the cannons fired and the horses galloped across the sand to intimidate the Aztec ambassadors, but a week later, Montezuma responds with his own trick:

> Then one morning, Tendile arrived with more than one hundred laden Indians, accompanied by a great Mexican Cacique, who . . . bore a strong likeness to our Captain Cortés and the great Montezuma had sent him purposely, for it is said that when Tendile brought the portrait of Cortés all the chiefs who were in Montezuma's company said that a great chief named Quintalbor looked exactly like Cortés and that was the name of the Cacique, who now arrived with Tendile; and as he was so like Cortés, we called them in camp "our Cortés" and "the other Cortés."[38]

This encounter is a small reminder that the conquest of Mexico involved two empires—the Spanish and the Aztec—that mirrored each other in their determination to dominate Mexico's indigenous people. They are strangely familiar enemies more alike than different, haunting reflections of conquest that, as the Cortés twins imply, collapse the difference between Old and New World imperialisms, for if the Spanish find an "other" Cortés in Mexico, the Aztecs recognize their Quintalbor among the foreigners.

The scene is also an apt way of returning to the *unheimlich*, especially in relation to Mignolo's opening question: "Who defines such a hemisphere," which is situated ambiguously between "difference and sameness?" For Mignolo, Saxon and Iberian colonial Creoles defined the hemisphere in the early nineteenth century through a "double consciousness" that was "geopolitical" insofar as the Creoles imagined the hemisphere in opposition to Europe (England and Spain, respectively) and racial insofar as the Creoles consolidated their whiteness against indigenous groups, African Americans, and black Creoles.[39] This double logic works through a process that in effect renders the hemisphere unhomely, for, on the one hand, it characterizes the hemisphere by what it is geo-politically not (Europe) and, on the other, represses the presence of what the hemisphere geo-racially is (indigenous and *mestizo*). Estranged from itself, the western hemisphere is doubled—European but not Europe; native but not indigenous. The doubling itself is uncanny, but what I have been emphasizing with *Calavar* and *Conquest* is how this doubling becomes especially haunting when it manifests itself in sameness rather than difference, to reverse Mignolo's phrase. That is, difference maintains the borders across the Americas that distinguish one nation from the other, but sameness produces an inter-American gothic hemisphere that emerges when native nationalist writings uncover as their origin the history of an other country.

Paula Moya and Ramón Saldívar explain this dichotomy in their discussion of the "trans-American imaginary": "it is first necessary . . . to recognize the influence on literature of competing nationalisms . . . *within* the borders of the nation. But it is also the case that much American literature responds to ideological pressures from *outside* the geopolitical borders of the sovereign United States." But if the presence of the other is already buried within the nation, the distinction between "within" and "outside" collapses into a hemispheric *unheimlich* that vexes the definition of a national literature based on geopolitical borders. Instead, as Moya and Saldívar remind us, the trans-American imaginary recognizes the "shared fates" of the Americas, which I understand as a history of conquest and resistance that troubles the difference between one nation and the other within the Americas.[40] Take, for example, *Xicoténcatl*. The narrative was published in Philadelphia in 1826, nearly a decade before Bird's *Calavar*. It was written in Spanish and certainly penned by a Creole, though the exact authorship remains a toss-up between an unknown Mexican author, the Cuban priest Félix Varela, the Cuban poet José María Heredia, or even Vincente Rocafuerte, a political exile of dubious hemispheric origins who, if he didn't write the text, may have helped to complete it.[41] Its political stance about the fall of the Tlaxcalan republic is applicable equally to the past and early nineteenth-century present of Cuba, Mexico, and the United States insofar as they all share a history of radical republicanism threatened by empire. The narrative is thus an "inter-American" text in more ways than one. The anonymity of its authorship is a standing reminder that the presence of the other is not always fully exhumed from history. The narrative itself has only recently been recovered and republished in Spanish and English editions. And perhaps most importantly, *Xicoténcatl* collapses the distinctions of national histories to imagine a trans-American republican hemisphere made unhomely by conquest.

Of course, *Xicoténcatl* generates a critique against the Spanish conquest by viewing it as a force outside of the Americas that has ostensibly corrupted the indigenous republicans within the Americas. Thus, the narrative reproduces much of the black legend in its description of Cortés and his conquistadors. They are, quite literally and liberally throughout the text, "monsters," "inhuman," "evil," "treacherous," "tyrants," and, in a string of invectives reserved for Cortés in particular, "the most abominable of monsters ever aborted by the abyss!" Their monstrosity encompasses their sexual desire, as when Teutila rebuffs Cortés's advances with "'Monster! . . . You are more inhuman than a tiger and more vile and treacherous than a snake. How can you not be horrified by your impudence?"; their duplicity, as when Teutila again rebukes Cortés: "In what kind of hell have you learned such hypocrisy and such evil?"; and their actions, as when Cortés cuts off the ears, noses, fingers, and toes of captured Tlaxcalan soldiers and then sends them back to terrify the indigenous republic. The gothic monstrosity of Cortés and his fellow Spaniards even extends to their system of governance:

> But a king is a man, [Xicoténcatl explains;] he has passions and can get to be a monster. Look at what is happening to that great Mexican empire. Moctezuma was virtuous, with an honest heart and with great generosity, and this same man . . . now has become a haughty tyrant; he has forgotten that he is a man. . . . Those who are bad join him; the good become corrupted and evil is irreparable, and if it is not, it exacts incredible convulsions, blood, and horrors.[42]

Oddly enough, Moctezuma and the Mexican empire appear at the center of Xicoténcatl's republican critique of the Spanish crown, suggesting that the conquest of Mexico occurred because empire was already within the hemisphere. In fact, *Xicoténcatl* is only nominally about the Spanish conquest of the Aztecs; it is more clearly about Tlaxcala's fall, which, the narrative reveals, has very little to do with forces outside of the republic. "When internal divisions destroy the unity of a people," the narrator explains, "they inevitably become the victims of their enemies, and more so if the practitioners of political shrewdness and craftiness are able to take advantage of that discord." Recall that, even before the Spaniards arrive, Tlaxcala and the Aztec empire are at warring odds, and personal revenge divides the Tlaxcalan senate between Xicoténcatl the elder's ideal republicanism, the military republicanism of his son, and the political machinations of Magiscatzin, whose corruption culminates with his conversion to Christianity and subsequent tormented death. "Passions presided in the nation's council, and the Tlaxcalans at the end became the victims of their discord."[43]

Tlaxcala's internal fissures explain the narrative's double consciousness, its haunting sense of sameness instead of difference between republicanism and empire. Teutila's loyalty to republicanism and love for Xicoténcatl, for instance, lead her to betray both inadvertently when, during her first interview with Cortés, she reveals Tlaxcala's instability to him: "As a good politician, he especially turned his attention to a great project that the division and discord in the Tlaxcalan senate suggested to him and, all the while, with his eyes he devoured the young American's attributes." With the information he hears from Teutila, Cortés flatters Magiscatzin into treason, and he keeps Xicoténcatl in check by holding Teutila hostage. The narrative stages an even more telling event that externalizes the republic's internal, colonial doubleness. Fray Bartolomé de Olmedo and Diego de Ordaz first meet Teutila at the entrance of a "grotto," where she often waits for Xicoténcatl; the site alone literally invokes the grotesque, if we can trust the English translation of the Spanish original to trace accurately "grotto" as the Latin root of "grotesque." Yet, when Teutila returns to the cave near the end of the narrative, she finds it covered with brush and stones and hears "a sad lament that seemed to be coming from the grotto." She uncovers the cave's entrance, clambers in, and "What she saw before her shocked her modesty and filled her with compassion at the same time. It was a man, entirely naked and so tightly bound that it was impossible for him to move. The wretch was a Spaniard."[44]

He is not just any Spaniard either: he stood guard over Teutila when she was imprisoned in the Spanish camp, but he now finds himself a captive because he has raped a Tlaxcalan woman. Teutila orders him unbound and released, but his presence there in the first place is what is important, for he serves as a symbolic reminder that empire was already buried beneath the indigenous Americas before Spain's arrival. The fact that he is there because of rape is equally important. Throughout the narrative, the Spaniards rape or attempt to rape indigenous women, but instead of framing the fall of Tlaxcala as a sexual violation, which would be consistent with the Spaniards' behavior, the narrator explains the republic's demise as a result of sexual solicitation:

> From that moment on, the Republic of Tlaxcala ceased to exist as a nation. The sovereignty of states is like a woman's honor: when people maintain it intact, they are respected and esteemed . . . but when self interest, corruption, weakness, or any other cause make them yield their appreciable jewel, neither one nor the other is more than the object of contempt. . . . Nevertheless, the wretched Republic of Tlaxcala was condemned, for the time, to suffer for a long while the worthy punishment of its vile act of prostitution.[45]

The narrator's misogyny articulates the hemispheric *unheimlich* that troubles *Xicoténcatl*, for the indigenous Americans are not what they seem. The Tlaxcalans, those "enem[ies] of effeminacy," turn out to be feminized; Teutile, the "beautiful Indian maiden," finds a double in the form of a Spanish conquistador; and Xicoténcatl, the narrative's republican hero, turns malinche by letting his passion divide him between Teutile and Doña Marina: "In one word: without ceasing to love his Teutila, he fell in love with the graces with which Doña Marina had beautified herself in her dealings with the Europeans, and speaking with one about the other, he spread his passion toward the two of them."[46] Ironically, La Malinche proper, Doña Marina, who is at first figured as an indigenous traitor, has a change of heart after motherhood, rejects Cortés, and, with her two *mestizo* children, stands as a symbol of a hybrid American hemisphere that, as Debra Castillo puts it, gives "a new twist" to the "old historical narrative" of the Spanish conquest.[47]

It is true, then, when Xicoténcatl the elder tells his son, "Your homeland is no longer Tlaxcala" (84), but perhaps it never was, and it took the conquest to unearth the fact that indigenous republicanism and European empire are more similar than different in the Americas. This is a tragic realization for the novel's indigenous republicans, but for the Spaniards, it invokes a chiaroscuro gothic terror embodied best in Cortés's response to Teutila's death scene: "As pale as a corpse, his hair standing on end, his mouth agape, his eyes wide open, his arms half raised, not daring to either move backward or forward, his whole body trembling, Cortés was left stupefied, his external self well depicting the mortal anguish inside his black soul." During Cortés's brief bout of guilt, inside turns out, white becomes black, and his evil concealed is now revealed in an inter-American gothic moment that strikes an uncanny resemblance to Magiscatzin's tortured demise: "the Evil Spirit burns his black torches, filling this room with its foul-smelling smoke," Cortés's Indian ally moans on his deathbed, "and hovering above all of these frightening specters, one can see, sparkling like a bolt of lightening, the terrible sword directed against me by the powerful arm of a vengeful God. . . . Oh, what a miserable wretch am I."[48] As Cortés's external whiteness becomes moral blackness, moral lightness briefly illuminates Magiscatzin's guilty conscience, despite the smoke-filled darkness of his death chamber. Two characters who mirror each others' duplicity and colonial complicity throughout the narrative are not doubles after all, however—Cortés and Magiscatzin become self and other on the eve of Mexico's conquest.

Cortés' horror in *Xicoténcatl* is the same terror that haunts Robert Montgomery Bird's *Calavar* and Prescott's *Conquest*—a fear that the republic is an unhomely empire. In this sense, the inter-American gothic that the anonymous novel exhumes has its origins in another familial narrative, the Monroe Doctrine, which distinguished the United States from Europe by situating the new republic within the western hemisphere but also made the hemisphere subject to the New World imperialism. That is, while Monroe's message ostensibly articulated the United States as an anti-imperial republic, it also established the nation's hemispheric neo-colonialism through a double logic that situated the United States *within* the Americas by figuring the United States *as* America. As Gretchen Murphy explains, "the Monroe Doctrine's geographic construction of a Western Hemisphere and its relative locations of Europe and North and South America were crucial to the formation of an ideology of American exceptionalism that both claimed a radical separation from European colonialism and enabled cultural, military, and economic dominance."[49] With the Monroe Doctrine, the United States is and is not empire; western but neither European nor indigenous; apart from and a part of the Americas. In other words, the United States becomes "Cortés acá" and "Cortés acullá" (our Cortés, the other Cortés, as Bernal Diaz del Castillo put it) as the duplicitous doctrine turns the logic of homeopathy, *Similia Similibus Curantur*, into the cause of rather than cure for colonial dis-ease, because one Cortés is the same as the other in the hemisphere's haunting history of conquest.

NOTES

1. Walter D. Mignolo, "Coloniality at Large: The Western Hemisphere in the Colonial Horizon of Modernity," *New Centennial Review* 1:2 (2001): 31.

2. Robert Montgomery Bird, *Calavar; or, The Knight of the Conquest: A Romance of Mexico*, (Philadelphia: Carey, Lea, and Blanchard, 1834), I:v–vi, vii, viii, vii, viii, xiii.

3. Bird, *Calavar*, I:xiv, xix, xxv, xxvii.

4. Here and throughout the use of misnomers, such as "Aztec" for the more historically accurate "Mexica" or "Montezuma" rather than "Moctezuma," slights historical accuracy for the convenience of following the usage consistent with each text under consideration.

5. Kirstin Silva Gruesz, *Ambassadors of Culture: The Transamerican Origins of Latino Writing* (Princeton: Princeton University Press, 2002), 57–58.

6. Frances Calderón de la Barca, *Life in Mexico* (Berkeley: University of California Press, 1982), 80, 81.

7. Nigel Leask notes that Calderón de la Barca haunts William Prescott's *Conquest* in much the same way that Doña Marina haunts Chapultepec, for the historian's three-volume history filched Calderón de la Barca's ghostly description of Chapultepec (Leask, "'The Ghost in Chapoltepec': Fanny Calderón de la Barca, William Prescott and Nineteenth-Century Mexican Travel Accounts," in *Voyages and Visions: Towards a Cultural History of Travel*, ed. Jaś Elsner and Joan-Pau Rubiés [London: Reaktion Books, 1999], 206). Compare Calderón de la Barca's passage above, for instance, with Prescott's:

   > and the grounds are still shaded by gigantic cypresses, more than fifty feet in circumference, which were centuries old at the time of the Conquest. . . . Surely, there is no spot better suited to awaken meditation on the past; none, where the traveller, as he sits under those stately cypresses grey with the moss of ages, can so fitly ponder on the sad destinies of the Indian races and the monarch who once held his courtly revels under the shadow of their branches. (William H. Prescott, *History of the Conquest of Mexico*, vol. 2 [Philadelphia: David McKay, 1892], 114).

8. Eric J. Sundquist, "Exploration and Empire," in *The Cambridge History of American Literature*, ed. Sacvan Bercovitch, Vol. 2 (Cambridge: Cambridge University Press, 1994), 132.

9. María DeGuzmán, *Spain's Long Shadow: The Black Legend, Off-Whiteness, and Anglo-American Empire* (Minneapolis: University of Minnesota Press, 2005), xvii. DeGuzmán's otherwise compelling argument about the United States' anxious imperial relationship with Spain almost entirely elides the significance of Mexico's proximity to the United States and how the continental presence of Mexico formed the U.S. image of Spain and Spaniards. DeGuzmán is not alone in this elision of Mexico. Richard Kagan's "Prescott's paradigm" views Spain as the United States' "antithesis": "America was the future—republican, enterprising, rational; while Spain—monarchical, indolent, fanatic—represented the past," Kagan explains (Kagan, "Prescott's Paradigm: American Historical Scholarship and the Decline of Spain," *American Historical Review* 101 [1996], 430). Yet the argument that Spain is the United States'

"antithesis" overlooks how Mexico functions as the synthesis of both countries. Eric Wertheimer's study remains the most convincing articulation of the imaginary relation between the United States and the Americas in this regard. As Wertheimer explains, early nationalist American literature that viewed Columbus, Aztecs, and Incas as indigenous ancestors of American national identity created "an identitarian crisis of Anglo nativism—of claiming a native proto-republican Other as the anchor of national destiny" (Wertheimer, *Imagined Empires: Incas, Aztecs, and the New World of American Literature, 1771–1876* [Cambridge and New York: Cambridge University Press, 1999], 5). This identity crisis, I maintain, manifests itself in the gothic.

10. Sigmund Freud, "The Uncanny," in *Collected Papers*, ed. Ernest Jones, Vol. 10 (London: Hogarth Press, 1948), 369–370, 375, 394.

11. F. Jesús de la Teja, *A Revolution Remembered: The Memoirs and Selected Correspondences of Juan N. Seguín* (Austin: State House Press, 1991), 73.

12. Pricilla Wald, *Constituting Americans: Cultural Anxiety and Narrative Form* (Durham: Duke University Press, 1995), 7.

13. Amy Kaplan, "'Left Alone with America': The Absence of Empire in the Study of American Culture," in *Cultures of United States Imperialism*, ed. Amy Kaplan and Donald E. Pease (Durham: Duke University Press, 1993), 3.

14. Jeff Karem, "On the Advantages and Disadvantages of Postcolonial Theory for Pan-American Study," *New Centennial Review* 1:3 (2001): 96.

15. Jon Smith and Deborah Cohn, "Introduction: Uncanny Hybridities," in *Look Away! The U.S. South in New World Studies*, ed. Jon Smith and Deborah Cohn (Durham: Duke University Press, 2004), 9.

16. José Martí, *Inside the Monster: Writings on the United States and American Imperialism*, ed. Philip S. Foner, trans. Elinor Randall (New York: Monthly Review Press, 1975). Martí's gothic language here further demonstrates my point: he characterizes Anglo-America as "monstrous" in a reversal of the grotesque racialization the United States often projected south, but at the same time, Martí is not writing from Cuba or Mexico—his critique comes from within the United States' national borders. In the belly of the monstrous empire is the anti-colonial self.

17. Claudia Sandowski-Smith and Claire F. Fox, "Theorizing the Hemisphere: Inter-Americas Work at the Intersection of American, Canadian, and Latin American Studies," *Comparative American Studies* 21:1 (2005): 23.

18. Curtis Dahl, *Robert Montgomery Bird* (New York: Twayne, 1963), 73.

19. Bird, *Calavar*, 1:173.

20. Benjamin Keen explains that the relation between Moors and Aztecs was not uncommon in Spanish conquistador writings:

   The conquistadors were acquainted with one infidel civilization that offered a clue to the posture they should assume towards the Aztecs. This was the advanced Moslem culture, known to the Spaniards through centuries of contact in war and peace. . . . Occasionally [conquistadors] compare Moslem and Aztec cultural achievements, to the advantage of the latter, in order to demonstrate the high level of civilization attained by the Aztecs. (Keen, *The Aztec Image in Western Thought* [New Jersey: Rutgers University Press, 1971], 55–56).

21. Bird, *Calavar*, 2:141.

22. Bird, *Calavar*, 2:142, 85.

23. Bird, *Calavar*, 1:271; 2:169, 265.

24. Bird, "Preface to the New Edition," in *Calavar; or, The Knight of the Conquest: A Romance of Mexico* (Philadelphia: Lea and Blanchard, 1847), iv.

25. Lewis Cass, *The Mexican War. Speech of Hon. Lewis Cass, of Michigan, in the Senate of the United States, February 10, 1847*, 5–6.

26. Bird, *Calavar*, 2:295.

27. John Eipper, "The Cannonizer De-Canonized: The Case of William H. Prescott," *Hispania* 83 (2000): 419.

28. Robert W. Johannsen, *To the Halls of the Montezumas: The Mexican War in the American Imagination* (New York: Oxford University Press, 1985), 248.

29. Vera M. Kutzinski, "Borders and Bodies: The United States, America, and the Caribbean," *New Centennial Review* 1:2 (2001): 58.

30. Teresa A. Goddu, *Gothic America: Narrative, History, and Nation* (New York: Columbia University Press, 1997), 9.

31. Toni Morrison, *Playing the Dark: Whiteness and the Literary Imagination* (New York: Vintage, 1993), 5.

32. Prescott, *History of the Conquest of* Mexico, 2:137, 243, 308.

33. It is worth noting that gothic discourses certainly shaped the black legend the United States inherited from England, especially since England's Hispanophobia corresponds chronologically with the rise of its gothic novel. Consider, for instance, how David J. Weber explains the black legend: "From their English forebears and other non-Spanish Europeans, Anglo Americans had inherited the view that Spaniards were unusually cruel, avaricious, treacherous, fanatical, superstitious, cowardly, corrupt, decadent, indolent, and authoritarian" (Weber, *The Spanish Frontier in North America* [New Haven: Yale University Press, 1992], 336).

34. Prescott, *History of the Conquest of Mexico*, 3:134, 136.

35. Prescott, *History of the Conquest of Mexico*, 3:141, 138–139.

36. Anna Brickhouse, *Transamerican Literary Relations and the Nineteenth-Century Public Sphere* (Cambridge and New York: Cambridge University Press, 2004), 75.

37. Prescott, *History of the Conquest of Mexico*, 2:296.

38. Bernal Diaz del Castillo, *The Discovery and Conquest of Mexico, 1517–1521*, ed. Genaro Garcia, Trans. A.P. Maudslay (London: George Routledge, 1928), 121, 124. In the Spanish original, Diaz del Castillo invokes a spatial difference between the doppelgängers: "Cortés acá, Cortés acullá," which I translate literally as "Cortés from here, Cortés from there" (Diaz del Castillo, *Historia verdadera de la conquista de la Nueva España*, ed. Ramon Iglesia [Mexico City: Nuevo Mundo, 1943], 105). Prescott renders it nationally as the "'Mexican Cortés'" (*History of the Conquest of Mexico*, 1:294). Both translations shore up the uncanny event and suggest the idea that Aztec culture understood and even deployed the duplicity of signs in much the same way that Cortés handled signification, as in his firing of the cannons.

39. Mignolo, "Coloniality at Large," 31, 34–35.

40. Paula M.L. Moya and Ramón Saldívar, "Fictions of Trans-American Imaginary," *Modern Fiction Studies* 49:1 (2003): 4, 17.

41. Brickhouse, *Transamerican Literary Relations*, 53–54.

42. Anon., *Xicoténcatl: An Anonymous Historical Novel about the Events Leading up to the Conquest of the Aztec Empire*, trans. Guillermo I. Castillo-Feliú (Austin: University of Texas, 1999), 13, 34, 50, 83, 140, 142, 34, 50, 44, 57.

43. Anon., *Xicoténcatl*, 79, 9.

44. Anon., *Xicoténcatl*, 29, 18, 132, 133.

45. Anon., *Xicoténcatl*, 118.

46. Anon., *Xicoténcatl*, 8, 18, 59.

47. Debra A. Castillo, *Redreaming America: Toward a Bilingual American Culture* (Albany: State University of New York Press, 2005), 48. The "new twist" is that Doña Marina escapes her otherwise pejorative historical name. Known as "La Malinche," Doña Marina served as translator between the Aztecs and the Spaniards; she was also Cortés's mistress and thus earned the reputation as a cultural and sexual "traitor." In *Xicoténcatl*, however, Doña Marina rejects her cursed history by denouncing Cortés and the Spanish while Xicoténcatl becomes "malinche" by betraying his wife and his republican ideals. In effect, the reversal mirrors the narrative's feminization of the Tlaxcalan republic.

48. Anon., *Xicoténcatl*, 84, 154, 120.

49. Gretchen Murphy, *Hemispheric Imaginings: The Monroe Doctrine and Narratives of U.S. Empire* (Durham: Duke University Press, 2005), 6.

5

An American Mediterranean

Haiti, Cuba, and the American South

MATTHEW PRATT GUTERL

A line from the Delta of the Orinoco to the east end of Cuba is but a thousand miles long; and yet, to the west of it, lies this magnificent basin of water, locked in by a continent that has on its shores the most fertile valleys of the earth. All and more, too, that the Mediterranean is to Europe, Africa, and Asia, this sea is to America and the world.

—Matthew F. Maury, "Gulf of Mexico" (1854)

Octavia Walton was a classic Southern "*belle.*" She was also widely regarded as "one of nature's cosmopolites, a woman to whom the whole world was home."[1] The granddaughter of Virginian George Walton, a signer of the Declaration of Independence, Octavia had been raised in the polyglot surrounds of Pensacola, a frontier naval port in the Florida territory, and schooled in a half dozen languages and literatures by an "old Scottish tutor." She grew up with the children of Anglophone colonists, Spanish settlers, Haitian exiles, mulattoes, slaves, and Seminoles, and earned great fame in the South for her internationalist orientation, her "linguistic versatility" in Spanish, Italian and French, and her "sympathetic and assimilating faculty," which allowed her great rapport with others, and enabled her to find comfort in any location or cultural setting.[2] Henry Clay, Lafayette, Washington Irving, and Fredrika Bremer—a varied group, to be sure—found her utterly enchanting, and marveled at her social dexterity and her global wit. As a young woman, Walton was an object of excitement, it seems, largely because these "talents" accompanied her maturation at that place along the Gulf Coast where the residues of French, Spanish, and English empires were blended. She was, people assumed, a reflection of the near future of the American South, as former colonies and tribal lands were subsumed into the expanding slaveholding region of the United States, and as various cultures and languages and races came together in new and unpredictable ways. In 1836, after moving to Mobile, Alabama, another port city drawing ships, people, and commerce from around the world, she married Henry S. Le Vert, a young French émigré and surgeon, and thereafter styled herself as "Madame Le Vert." As the quintessence of Southern cosmopolitanism, she possessed an extraordinary measure of "social sovereignty," and became, as her contemporaries remembered it, the appointed arbiter of high culture along the outer rim of the Gulf of Mexico.[3] Her carefully orchestrated sitting room "Mondays" were sophisticated affairs, drawing weekly visits from the most polished sorts of people in Mobile, as well as guests from Europe, from the West Indies, and from across the South. In between social appointments, Le Vert labored to translate Cuban poetry into English, corresponded with poets and politicians, and traveled the world.[4] She was, in sum, a peerless exemplar of the hemispherics of the mid-century South—at home in the world of ideas, fluent in myriad languages and literatures, and a literal product of the slave-holding world of the American Mediterranean.

In 1857, after two decades of aristocratic prominence, Le Vert collected her intimate letters—most of them written to friends and family while she was abroad—and had them published with the unassuming title of *Souvenirs of Travel*. Published in Mobile, *Souvenirs* was a rare Southern travelogue, and offers a precious glimpse into the antebellum travels of elite white women. The book was well received, or at least Le Vert's considerable vanity allowed her to claim such a reception. Her missives, when arranged in sequence, provide a rich portrait of her two trips to popular historic sites in Europe, and demonstrate her familiarity with European literature and culture, and her personal friendships with Continental glitterati. Madame Le Vert, it seemed, knew all the right people. In its efforts to document this intimate knowledge of important things and royal personages, then, *Souvenirs* reveals itself to be a part of the pronounced nineteenth-century Southern effort to redefine the region as intellectually serious and cultured, with stronger links to Europe than to the literary nationalism of Emerson, and to overturn its reputation as a crude and uncivilized backwater through the establishment and promotion of ornamental soirées and literary circles. Southerners imagined themselves, Michael O'Brien writes, as "the custodians of empire," and drew deeply from European history and culture to provide "order" for their world, and to establish their place in it.[5] Le Vert's manicured "Monday" salons thus offered a regular chance for the stylized performance of Europe's old imperial "project" in the hybrid New World, and for the deliberate translation of European styles to match the authoritarian and expansionist aims of the master class in the Americas.

On her way to Europe for a second trip, Le Vert paused for a few weeks at "the brilliant city" of Havana, a familiar location for many Southerners of her particular social class. A visit to Europe "back then," Eliza McHatton recalled, writing of Le Vert, was "like taking a trip to Mars."[6] If Le Vert's visit to the Old

World had been "the dream of [her] life," this stopover in Havana was something else—a brief and necessary sojourn to a familiar way station.[7] Le Vert had a deep appreciation for the efforts of the *filibusteros* (filibusters) to liberate the island from the cruelties of Spanish domination.[8] She knew this place well, and could imagine it as a more integral part of the South. She was greeted at the dock by a childhood friend, and speedily conveyed to Sarah Brewer's Hotel Cubano. After a brief respite, Brewer escorted Madame Le Vert to promenade at the *Paseo Tacon*, which they circled in a *volante* driven by "an intensely black negro, with immense boots . . . ornamented with silver." In her commentary on the "big-booted postillions" and the jubilant frolics of the local slave population, and in her repetitious appreciations of the "gallant-looking" lighter skinned Cubans, Le Vert countered the prevailing abolitionist portrait of the gruesome sugar industry and of Cuban Creoles as untrustworthy, less civilized "off-white" people.[9] She provides, in other words, a very Southern and very feminine imagining of the island, sympathetic to slaveholders, replete with risqué and comic "darky" portraits and whispered gossip about the neighboring island, volcanic Haiti, and lacking any in-depth consideration of *el ingenio*, the grim sugar factories of the Cuban countryside. Like many of her slaveholding contemporaries, she may well have assumed that Cuba would inevitably become a part of the South, for when she left the island for Europe, in early February of 1855, she described it, tellingly, as "our last day in America," as if the distinction between Cuba and the South was far less significant than the difference between the Old World and the New.[10]

The extraordinary and exemplary Madame Le Vert was, in many ways, a product of her time, her place, and her social position. With her cosmopolitanism as my starting point, this essay explores the South's relationship to the Caribbean in the tumultuous 1850s, with special attention paid to Cuba and Haiti. As an exercise in "postnational" history, it is shaped by the rich and emerging literature on the South as a borderland between the North American republic, the Caribbean, and Latin America, a literature that has contributed to the more widespread reassessment of the power of the nation-state to fully frame, or to completely enclose, the history and literature of the United States.[11] I offer, here, an assessment of the South *in process*, as it reached out to the Americas, wrangled with the North for control of the republic, and began to establish itself—intellectually, culturally, and socially—as an independent nation-state. Like many of her contemporaries, Madame Le Vert imagined the Gulf states as the northernmost border of an American Mediterranean, a profit-rich and danger-filled region of the hemisphere, "curtained," as another writer put it, "on the east, by a chain of fruitful islands, stretching from Trinidad to Cuba . . . on the north and the south and the west, . . . land-locked by the continent, which has bent and twisted around the sea, so as to fold it within its bosom."[12] With secession and Civil War looming, debates in the United States about the future of slavery, emancipation, freedom, and citizenship

were structured not just by internal political disputes, but also by hemispherically shared experiences and experiences of sharing, by the "failure" of Haiti,
and by the chance that Cuba might become a slaveholding state or, conversely,
home to the largest "free" population of former slaves in the New World. Like
Madame Le Vert, Southern planters, themselves routine travelers in the Caribbean, may have understood the United States to be "exceptional" in the Americas, but they also understood the South itself to be even more unique, with
even greater blessings and an even brighter future. The Caribbean and the
Mississippi appear in their imaginings as a singular American Mediterranean,
"*mare nostrum*" as both the Romans and Thomas Hart Benton would call it, with
the scattered New World colonies and fledgling republics standing in for the
ancient cities and empires of the classical world. The antebellum South, here,
was Rome, with all its vices and appetites, and all its fortune and magnificence.
The sense of "Southern exceptionalism" coexisted, quite easily and naturally,
with a sense that the planter class shared a common fate with slaveholders
elsewhere in the hemisphere, a Southern version of manifest destiny that even
included the empire of Brazil, as Henry Nash Smith once wrote, as "the world's
most promising theater for expansion of the plantation system."[13] This interest
in expansion into the Caribbean rendered the South a liminal place, halfway
between the waving palms of the tropics and the clanging millworks of Lowell.
The region and its dominant planter class were imagined by contemporaries to
be just as William Faulkner would later describe them: a New World amalgam
blended from cold climate and tropical heat, sugar cane and iron, "Latin" passion and "Anglo" reason, brutal bondage and "universal" freedom.

* * *

The port city of Havana, a sister city of sorts to Madame Le Vert's Mobile, sat
at the center of the strengthening network of port cities, trade, and travel. As
the capital of an enormously important Spanish colony, it was often described
as the "finest [port] in the West Indies, or, perhaps, the world," and was the
second most important commercial hub in the New World behind New York.
A deep, narrow channel on the north side of the island was overseen by the
formidable Castle Moro before opening into "a magnificent bay, capable of
accommodating 1000 ships."[14] Sugar and slaves, coffee and coolies, all passed
through that narrow channel, coming and going, turning the harbor into
a switching point for the global trade between the New World, Africa, and
Europe and the hemispheric trade among settler societies and colonies. The
island's safe berth, its location relative to beneficial trade winds and currents,
and its role in the slave trade, had long given it a reputation as "the *boulevard*
of the New World," a phrase coined by the Abbé Raynal and repeated in the
enthusiastic literature of the *filibusteros*.[15] Visitors often came from the United
States, the island's northern neighbor, through New Orleans, a sister city of
sorts located about six hundred nautical miles north and west. Trade with

the United States, one popular reference claimed, had "increased threefold" in the decade prior to 1855, making the United States the largest economic partner with the island colony.[16] A warm climate and reputed health benefits lured many travelers from all over the world, while its brutal slavery and tragic indentured servitude made continued sugar cane and coffee production possible and drew, as if by hypnotism, the rapt attention of all visitors. Images of the Havana harbor, lush with tall ships, are a common staple of mid-century newspapers and travel literatures, and the Castle Moro may well have been one of the most written about New World locations in the nineteenth century.

For many Southerners in the 1850s, travel to the island was as much a matter of prospecting for the near future as anything else. But there was nothing new in this. Cuba and the South had long enjoyed a special relationship as two of the largest and closest remaining slaveholding societies in the New World. Southerners—alongside some New England families—owned plantations in colonial Cuba, ran hotels, and operated businesses in Havana. Southerners were slaveowners in Cuba (Nicholas Trist, the American counsel in the 1830s, owned the Flor de Cuba plantation), and businesspeople (James Robb, president of the New Orleans Gas Light & Banking Company, established a sister company in Havana). Less dramatically, Sarah Brewer's Hotel Cubano was a famous oasis of Southern hospitality. The overlap and cross-pollination are so broad as to defy quick summary, and the resulting "binding familiarities" were hardly limited to the South. The railroad cars, sugar boilers, and locomotives brought in to modernize Cuban sugar production came from American companies along the Atlantic seaboard, and New England mechanics proliferated on the Cuban *cafetals* and *ingenios* that were so often visited by Southerners. The United States–born population in Cuba doubled in the two decades before the Civil War, and the Cuban-born population in New York was the largest, and most significant, in the country. But if Cuba, as one historian summarizes, "entered the North American imagination as the 'tropics' . . . as the opposite of what the United States was," the island could also serve to distinguish "the North" from "the South."[17] As significantly, it entered the Southern imagination as something else: as a future state in the republic, destined to be absorbed by the supposedly predestined advance of Southern slavery into the global South.

For several generations, privateers along the frontier's edge had chafed at the power of the nation-state, and had, through gradual settlement or force of arms, stolen away territory that by treaty belonged to Mexico, or Canada, or some other foreign government. New land meant new opportunity, and less chance that an enslaved population would reach dangerous concentrations. Texas, then, was "politically and economically sublime," and its acquisition was pursued and accomplished by Anglo *filibusteros* who were tired of waiting for manifest destiny to catch up with their desire for a land rich in slaveholding promise.[18] Indeed, despite the mythic images of gamblers, drunks, and washouts popularized in movies and novels about the Alamo, the *filibusteros* and those who followed them in the 1850s were not mere bandits or pirates, or simple homesteaders, but men with dreams and ambition of power. John Quitman, for one, was the governor of Mississippi when he turned to assist Narciso López and Ambrosio Gonzales in their plans to conquer Cuba, and was later a Democratic congressman and advocate for the avoidance of any European entanglements when it came to Pan-American affairs. "We claim the right of expansion," Quitman argued, "as essential to our future security and prosperity . . . [we] require more elbow room, to guard against the possibility that a system of labor now so beneficent and productive might, from a redundant slave population confined to a narrow limits, become an ultimate evil."[19] Filibustering was high politics.

The apogee of this movement came with a spectacularly successful effort by the well-traveled and -respected lawyer, doctor, and editor of the *New Orleans Crescent*, William Walker, to carve a new Anglo-American empire out of Mexico and Central America. Encouraged to join a civil war in Nicaragua in 1854, Walker managed to topple the local government, to establish himself—at least briefly—as the president of the country, to gain the official recognition of the United States, and then to revoke a standing prohibition against slavery, a whirlwind turn of events that made him the cause célèbre for all those who wished to expand slavery into Central and South America. If Walker's death by Honduran firing squad in 1860 was the final chapter in the drive to conquer the American Mediterranean by private army, then Abraham Lincoln's rejection of the Crittenden compromise of 1861, which would have established a northernmost latitude for slavery without any southern limit whatsoever, is most certainly a fitting formal coda. "[I]f we surrender, it is the end of us and of the government," Lincoln predicted presciently; "[a] year will not pass before we shall have to take Cuba as a condition upon which [the South] will stay in the Union."[20] The high-water mark for international ambitions also marked, then, the end of any chance of peace between North and South.[21]

Lincoln understood, perhaps, that slaveholding and restlessness were concomitant phenomena in the antebellum South. Local populations of wealthy slaveholders moved around and, in the case of the filibusters, beyond the South—slaves and capital in tow—at a rate equal to or greater than the migration patterns of poor immigrant workers in New England. Transience, one historian writes, was "a normal part of existence in the Old South."[22] Plantations changed hands regularly, as the rootless planter class moved west to Texas and the Southwest, where land was cheap and slavery could expand rapidly, mirroring the expansion of immigrants across the upper Midwest. Along the way, they gathered in the great port cities of the Atlantic seaboard—in Charleston, Mobile, Savannah, and New Orleans. Most continued on to greener pastures in the West. Others, though, took advantage of the short, two-day journey from New Orleans to Havana, and of the tightening ties between those same port cities and their counterparts in the Caribbean. Some went on to test the waters, hoping that Cuba would be annexed, by force or by treaty. Some simply went on to manage an estate, to visit with friends, or to investigate the methods of sugar production. Either way, there were a great many slaveholders—or those whose shared some interest with slavery itself—who ventured, as it were, further southward. "We have had a charming trip to Cuba," Callie Elliot, the daughter of South Carolina planter William Elliot, wrote to her sister, "it was only too *short*, the country is magnificent, the climate delightful, the people [the Cubans] the nicest in the whole world."[23] For Southerners like Callie, a trip to Cuba was, in some ways, a journey into a possible, better future, offering larger profits, better health, and greater numbers of enslaved Africans. All that, and one could recover one's health, too. "Should you meet any Cubans," Callie Elliot wrote to her brother, William, "do try & get all the information you can respecting the price of lands in Cuba. *I have a cough!*"[24]

Cuba was, then, the next Texas, but with greater short-term promise. Literature produced in the South almost invariably surveyed Cuba as both a contemporary competitor and a future acquisition, and married a hard-edged economic appreciation with the usual proslavery romanticism. John S. Thrasher, a longtime advocate of annexation, suggested that Louisiana's sugar production was a great disadvantage when it competed with Cuba, with its "superior cheapness of labor," and that the appropriation or purchase of the island would return the advantage to the South. Hoping to increase the sense of peril and speed up the debate, Thrasher also noted that Cuba was just then seeking "at all hazards" to bring larger numbers of Chinese coolies and install a "system of African apprenticeship."[25] Cuba, another such report began, was a "valuable island," only "a few days['] sail from the Atlantic Ports of the U.S. and only two and a half days['] steaming from New Orleans." With the completion of the telegraph across the continental United States, the island "will become," Thomas Wilson enthused, "a grand manufactory and depot of sugar, to which orders for sugar may be sent from the most distant parts of the U.S. and which by steam may be filled, in less time, than a little affair could have been accomplished between N. York and Philadelphia, in old times." Southern travelers could, at times, claim to have special, "insider" knowledge of the island, a product of their lengthy history of economic and social relations with all levels of Cuban society. And they could be dismissive of those with abolitionist credentials, hailing from New England, who dallied in Havana for a day or two before painting grimmer portraits of the island's future. "Now any person with the least experience," Wilson continued, "knows that it is impossible to gain much knowledge during a few months spent . . . flying through a vast territory. I have seen many of these gentlemen in their travels, and it appears to me that their time is spent principally in pleading at the bar, and in discussing politics with some funny old quiz, who engaged them in conversation, or in discussing the merits of the os flesh of two countries."[26] Aside from the suggestion that short-term "Yankee" travelers were more interested in drink and sex than anything else—the word "os" is an anatomical reference to an aspect of the vagina—Wilson's account of the island assumes that Southern interest in Cuba was financial or economic before it was anything else, even if the island's supposed desire for annexation by the South was very often styled a matter of seduction and conquest by a comely suitor.

"You cannot reason," Richard Henry Dana had once sniffed dismissively, "from Massachusetts to Cuba."[27] But could the same be said of New Orleans or Mobile? Was it possible to "reason," as Dana put it, from Canal Street to Castle Moro? As a bustling sugar town near the mouth of the Mississippi, the multinational, "imperial" history of New Orleans was captured in Charles Pike's 1847 "Coast Directory," listing the plantations along the river between that city and Baton Rouge, some of them owned by the descendants of French settlers, some by St. Domingo exiles, some by Spanish families, and, furthest upriver, some by planters from the continental United States.[28] By the 1850s, in fact, New Orleans was the keystone city in the "great nation of futurity," a "grand emporium of all the vast tracts traversed by the Mississippi and the Missouri" as well as a rich trading port, with notable national and international connections to New York, Boston, Havana, Vera Cruz, and Liverpool.[29] Despite its role in the westward settlement and internal commerce of the United States, travel accounts often explicitly set New Orleans in a hemispheric—and not a nationalistic—milieu, especially when the subject was related to trade or slavery, or when the focus was on polyglot populations and multicultural lifestyles. Hispanophone sojourners, for instance, often found New Orleans to be far more familiar than New York.[30] Anglophone travelers noted a similar, somewhat sultry tone. "Havana," Anthony Trollope wrote cleverly, "will soon become as much American as New Orleans," a statement that says much about both places.[31] Even as the Civil War loomed and the future of slavery in the United States seemed uncertain, social, economic, and cultural connections between Cuba and the South were strengthening and becoming more richly elaborate.

This was no minor concern. At stake here in the debate over Cuba was the moral position of the South and, by extension, the United States. Where the South seemed an eager conqueror, it expressed a sort of hemispheric superiority. But where the South seemed "tropical," it called into question the future of the region. Portraits of the South that emphasized its Caribbean flavor, or its "eroticism," were, implicitly or explicitly, drawing conclusions about its location in relationship to the "tropics," conclusions that could often emphasize the relationship between hot temperatures, immorality, violence, and sex. To call the South hot-tempered or racially hybrid, in other words, was to draw attention to its history of race mixing, to make it seem "Latin American," and to suggest, as generations of ethnologists and climatologists would later do, that civilization could hardly survive let alone prosper beneath a certain latitude. To find any sort of slaveholding solidarity with Cuba—no matter how fleeting—Southerners would have to elide these representations, and escape the deep-rooted Anglo-American concerns about "black" Spanish character, which manifested themselves in the routine association of Cuban culture with "the medieval."[32] They would, in other words, have to forsake (or set aside) some of their heartfelt commitment to the nation-state and to Europe as the standard of "civilization" in order to be a part of the American Mediterranean.

* * *

Haiti was different. By the 1850s, Haiti had become a Rosetta stone for anyone interested in divining the future of a South with fixed borders, a vast and growing slave population, and surrounded by free "Negro" republics. Indeed, the regular reflection on the meaning of Caribbean history hinted at a deep, thoughtful concern by planters and proslavery apologists for the long-term economic consequences of emancipation elsewhere, and an awareness of the parallel circumstances that were affecting other slaveholding societies. Portraits of lawlessness and bloodthirstiness outside of the South were also a justification in themselves for a tightening, or quickening, of the siege mentality of the South. Indeed, many of the most hard-edged elements of mid-century Southern slaveholding—the increasing use of fear instead of "kindness" to control slaves, the use of brinksmanship and saber rattling in diplomacy with the North, the concern about locating a "safety valve" in the West or the Caribbean to reduce the largest concentrations of slaves, the high-wire opposition to all forms of abolitionism—were drawn from the experiences of slaveholders throughout the Americas. One sometimes gets the perverse impression from this dystopian "proslavery" material that much of the New World was a sort of topsy-turvey slaughterhouse, where slaves butchered slaveholders, and where only the South, Cuba, and Brazil were still breathing. Any reference to Haiti, in short, made the South seem utterly refined and civilized by comparison.

Jamaica and Haiti were the Scylla and Charybdis of this darker American Mediterranean, one of them freed by soft-hearted liberals for whom it was more important to be right than to be careful, and one of them freed by force and racial bloodshed. In both cases, internationally oriented cash-crop agriculture—the life's blood of the planter class—failed completely after slavery. This simple "fact," as it was understood then, was very important to those who were concerned about the future of other slaveholding societies. When we frame the literature on Cuba and the South from this perspective, centering the hemispheric qualities linking both, we call attention to the roiling, uncertain backdrop of the period, which featured the past precedents of Haiti and Jamaica. Cuba, Richard Henry Dana suggested, might be the key to the Gulf of Mexico, but it was just as likely to be the key to Pandora's box: "Close upon her," he wrote, "is the great island of Jamaica, where the experiment of free negro labour in the same products is on trial; near to her is Haiti, where the experiment of negro self-government is on trial; and further off . . . yet near enough to furnish some cause for uneasiness, are the slave states of the Great Republic."[33] "The two islands of St. Domingo and Jamaica," wrote Benjamin Hunt, an "expert" on the West Indies, offered "to the choice of the present slaveholder a sample of the different fruits, one or the other of which will probably compose the final harvest of all slavery which is not timely uprooted. . . . In St. Domingo," he concluded, "the French have been destroyed by the blacks; in Jamaica, the English are being peacefully absorbed by them."[34] Haiti and Jamaica were, by and large, object lessons in failure, the stuff of nightmares, not dreams; they were not so much travel destinations as they were bleak stopping points, future-tense reminders of what might come next for slavery, the planter class, and the much-ballyhooed "civilization" of the Old South. Cuba, in turn, was a dream world of sorts for the South, powerful enough to expel the hellish, otherwise absorbing memories of Jamaica and Haiti. "Hayti and Jamaica," William Henry Hurlbert remarked upon his arrival in Havana, "loomed large upon the horizon of my purpose when I wandered here, but they have gone like a vision of sails."[35]

Of these two reference points, Jamaica, where emancipation and labor flight had reportedly brought Britain's largest sugar-producing colony to its knees, was slightly less sensational. Most of the well-educated traveling class would have known something of the so-called Great Experiment of 1834: legislated emancipation, which was followed by the temporary cruelties of apprenticeship, among them the whip, the treadmill, and the penal system. A generation later, the fate of the island was still unclear, its productive potential offset by the frustrating refusal of former slaves to work for the former masters or on gruesomely familiar plantations. Abolitionists proclaimed the success of individual former slaves on the island, showing far less concern for the exploitive sugar industry. But, all and all, the island was still very much an experiment. "Will the growth of sugar pay in Jamaica or will it not?" wondered the traveloguer Anthony Trollope. Not if the white man made it, he concluded, nor even if the brown man did, so long as slavery existed somewhere else. But "[t]he 'peculiar institution,'" he noted, "will not live for ever. The time must come when abolition will be popular even in Louisiana. And when it is law there, it will be the law in Cuba also. If that day shall have arrived before the last sugar-mill in the island shall have stopped, Jamaica may then compete with other free countries. The world will not do without sugar, let it be produced by slaves or free men."[36] For any visitor to the American Mediterranean, the lure and loathing of this prophetic place, this once-rich and now-poor laboratory for African free labor, was impossible to ignore. "The downward tendencies of the island," wrote John Bigelow, after returning for the first time in sixteen years, "cannot be more rapid than they are at present." If, however, "Jamaica was an American State, she would speedily be more productive and valuable than any agricultural portion of the United States of the same dimension."[37]

Haiti, in contrast, inspired otherwise deeply buried fear, loathing, and rage. Two generations earlier, Haitian slaves had taken the expressed universalism of the French revolution at face value and then engaged in what was remembered—rightly or wrongly—as wholesale racial slaughter. For much of the 1850s, the tiny, diplomatically unrecognized republic on the eastern end of Hispaniola was governed by Faustin Soulouque, a former slave freed as a young man by the decree of Léger-Félicité Sonthonax in 1793, and a soldier in the revolutionary army, who was proclaimed emperor in 1849. "King Soloulouque is a black man," Trollope wrote pointedly, conflating skin tone and civilization, "[o]ne blacker never endured the meridian heat of a tropical sun."[38] In the decade that followed his ascension as emperor, or "king," Soulouque gained an international reputation for barbarism, for the murder of presumably more civilized "mulattoes," and for deep-rooted corruption. Haiti had long been a reminder for all Southerners that the "labor question" could not be resolved so easily where slaves were in the majority, but near universal disdain for Soulouque meant that even liberal-minded, presumably sympathetic persons lamented the state of the republic.[39]

The New World's only free black republic served, in short, as a fascinating visual backdrop for contemporary debates about the future of slavery in the Americas. "We ran down the North coast," Nicholas Trist's wife wrote on her way to Cuba, "within 15 miles of the island all the way. As my ill luck would have it, the weather was very hazy: so as to see the mountains plainly, but only just enough to make me wish for clear weather, when the sight of them would have been a great treat. The mountains rising *up out of the sea*, higher than our blue ridge. What a combination of climate and scenery, land & water! And to think that such a Paradise should be in the hands of such animals!"[40] Tropical health specialist Nathaniel Willis noted the "mountain tops of Hayti visible off the starboard bow—their bases and the main stretch of the isle of Negro-cratic dominion hidden by the cloud-mist of morning." Arriving at Jacmel, Willis suggestively noted that they were greeted by "a negro clad in a suit of black—the suit he was born in—standing erect, shiny and unconscious, on the end of the pier."[41] At its best, Haiti could serve as a possible repository for emancipated Africans from the United States, expatriated, or "colonized," on the island; at its worst, Haiti was a racial nightmare, embodying fears of rape and rebellion, signaling the seriousness of all debate about slavery.[42] Such was the portrait of dark "Hayti," at least until 1859, when the coup d'état led by General Fabre Nicolas Geffrard—styled, in at least one newspaper, as a white man—returned some measure of "stability" and "progress" to the island, leading abolitionists and liberal New Englanders (and even some Southerners) to propose Geffrard's republic as a new home for freed Southern slaves.[43]

The cluster of revolutions at the end of the eighteenth century—the French, the American, and the Haitian, all professing enthusiasm for universal concepts like "liberty" and the "equality of all men"—had left a lingering, equalitarian stamp on New World political culture. But the revolt in St. Domingue was a peculiarly significant one, especially for slaveholders. In the late summer of 1791, inspired by the egalitarian rhetoric of the French Revolution and the brutality of slave labor in sugar cultivation, slaves on the French, western side of the island of Hispaniola had taken up arms against the master class. Some hoped for the seizure of their rights as full citizens, while others simply wished for a chance to be free of the lash. Sonthonax, sent to manage the revolt, first cultivated an alliance with the free mulatto population and then, somewhat to the surprise of his new allies, emancipated the colony's African slaves by decree. Toussaint L'Ouverture, an aging slave, emerged as the Cincinnatus, or George Washington, of the revolution, turning away from his retirement to become the leader of the ragtag revolutionary army and a skilled statesman, parlaying the competing desires of England, France, and Spain into some measure of independence for the island's majority population, before he was captured by trickery and brought to Paris, where he died in prison. The final stages of the revolution—right up to its end in 1804—produced little beyond death and sadism, as French soldiers, dying rapidly from yellow fever, struggled to kill the largest possible number of Africans as quickly as possible. Contemporary and historical accounts of the revolution—including some written in the twentieth century—regularly emphasized the barbaric violence of the former slaves against their former masters, and framed the uncivil revolution as a preface to the island's desultory postemancipation financial state. In proslavery thought, then, the idealism of the abolitionist movement was understood to be historically parallel to that brief moment in the early days of the French revolution, when Brissot, Condorcet, the Abbé Grégoire, and "all that brilliant band" lobbied for the end of slavery in the West Indies and the subsequent incorporation of freed Africans as citizens in the republic.[44] Every subsequent mistake, Southern slaveholders assumed, flowed from that first error in judgment. New England abolitionism, much like the antislavery fulminations of *Le Society Des Amis Des Noir*, was, at best, based on a serious misjudgment of the capacity of Africans for civilization and self-government and, at worst, at cross-purposes with the will of God.

Such parallels between American abolitions and French radicalism were hard to ignore, especially when the most determined forces of the antislavery movement were, at least as some saw it, quite literally and openly searching for an American Toussaint and hoping to encourage the same sort of bloodshed on Southern soil. In late 1859, the broadsword-wielding Kansan John Brown hoped that his occupation of the federal armory at Harper's Ferry would be the beginning of a massive revolt against slavery, something rather like the rebellion at St. Domingue. In the wake of Brown's execution, some measure of financial support came to his widow from Haiti, a reflection of the larger, Pan-American meaning of his "meteor-like" life, "flashing through the darkness."[45] In a public letter, Brown's surviving son expressed his gratitude to "all the good

Haytians," who grieved at the loss of "Capt. John Brown, and his companions in arms." He went on, moreover, to invoke the patronage of the saint of the St. Domingue revolt and to hope, as well, for his strength of spirit to awaken the South.

> [I]t is only the body of Toussaint L'Ouverture which sleeps in the tomb, [he concluded;] his soul visits the cabins of the slaves of the South when night is spread over the face of nature. The ears of our American slaves hear his voice in the wind-gusts which sweep over the prairies of Texas, of Arkansas and Missouri; his voice finds an echo in the immense valleys of Florida, among the pines of the Carolinas, in the Dismal Swamp, and on the mountain-tops, proclaiming that the despots of America shall yet know the strength of the toiler's arm, and that he who would be free must strike the first blow.[46]

For the planter class, there could be no stronger proof of the dangerous mix of abolitionist idealism and the treachery of slaves than the idea, offered repeatedly by Wendell Phillips and others after Harper's Ferry, that John Brown's raid marked a veritable second coming of Toussaint L'Ouverture, with the worst, as the South saw it, yet to come.[47]

If the symbolic reverberations of Brown's raid and his subsequent execution were far in excess of the real chance of widespread revolt, it was, in large part, because enslaved and free Africans in the United States and slaves in the South were already dangerously attuned to the meaning of Toussaint. Indeed, a wide array of pamphleteers, rebels, novelists, and former slaves—among them David Walker, Denmark Vesey, William Wells Brown, Henry Highland Garnet, and Gabriel Prosser—had already found strength and authority in the violent success of the Haitian revolution. In noting the "divisions and consequent sufferings of *Carthage* and of *Hayti*" in his famously provocative *Appeal to the Coloured Citizens of the World*, first published in 1829, and the "butchering" of blacks by whites, David Walker, for instance, invoked Toussaint as a vengeful Old Testament messiah for enslaved African peoples: "The person whom God shall give you," Walker advised, "give him your support and let him go his length, and behold in him the salvation of your God."[48] A "war against the tyrants," William Wells Brown concluded, joining the revolution of slaves to the ideals of the American Revolution, would be sparked by the "indignation of the slaves of the south," and would "kindle a fire so hot that it would melt their chains, drop by drop, until not a single link remained; and the revolution that commenced in 1776 would then be finished."[49] "To black Americans," historian Alfred Hunt notes, "long starved for real heroes, Toussaint . . . showed them that freedom could be won and how it could be done," an object lesson of extraordinary value in the antebellum age, when it often seemed as if the slave power would last forever. Across the color line and throughout the American

Mediterranean, Hunt continues, "Toussaint was the most powerful black symbol of his time."[50] Some proslavery apologists and Southern planters might well have been eager to laud Toussaint for his imposition of martial law after the revolution, and for his farsighted—as they saw it—concern for sugar and coffee production on the western side of the Hispaniola, but none would have wished for a Southern version of the man to appear in the Carolina low country or along the Mississippi River.[51] It was all too easy, in the end, for antislavery activists to describe these same actions, as Frederick Douglass did, in terms of racial uplift and postemancipation "development," or to affirm that the labor and land reforms enacted by the great Toussaint in the wake of the bloodshed had been nobly aimed at "the improvement of the negro race."[52]

Indeed, as common touchstones in antislavery protest, Haiti and Cuba could sometimes become dangerously confused. In 1859, the *Anglo-African Magazine* published the opening chapters of a new novel, titled *Blake; or, The Huts of America*, by Martin Delany, a renowned antislavery activist of radical temper. *Blake* was a response, in some sense, to Harriet Beecher Stowe's exquisitely sentimental *Uncle Tom's Cabin*, which featured light-skinned protagonists, much melodrama, and great tragedy. In contrast to Stowe, Delany featured a global cast of characters, including a dark-skinned revolutionary named Blake, and diverse and representative figures for all aspects of the slavery question. Tellingly, *Blake* begins in a Southern port city, Baltimore, where the Natchez planter Colonel Stephen Franks has come to negotiate with his partners, including Capitan Juan Garcia, who is from Cuba. They are, as Delany describes it, "little concerned about the affairs of the general government," and "entirely absorbed in an adventure of self-interest."[53] They have gathered together to discuss their plans to transform a merchant ship into a slaver, and to debate the relative merits of Baltimore and Havana as the site of this transformation. By the time the sprawling novel is complete, the travels of Blake across the South, throughout the Caribbean, and everywhere in the Atlantic World have enabled him to formulate an internationalist, or "Pan-African" response to the slave power. Among slaves, he has what Robert Levine describes as a unique, or "uncommonly broad view of the problem of slavery in the Americas," which enables him to sow the seeds of rebellion and exile, and to claim a civilized black manhood. He shares the planter's sense of slavery, recognizing it as cosmopolitan and global, primarily self-interested, and prospering, at times, outside of the authority of the nation-state. Beginning the novel with that meeting of slaveholders and their partners, Delany suggested, in contrast to Stowe, that slavery was not contained, that it was borderless and cosmopolitan.[54]

Blake played on the dreams and nightmares of the Old South.

Few people in the world, [Delany editorialized at one point,] lead such a life as the white inhabitants of Cuba, and those of the South . . . [Theirs

is a] dreamy existence of the most fearful apprehensions, . . . dread,
horror and dismay; suspicion and distrust, jealously and envy continually pervade the community; and Havana, New Orleans, Charleston or
Richmond may be thrown into consternation by an idle expression of
the most trifling or ordinary ignorant black.[55]

"A sleeping wake or waking sleep," as Martin Delany put it, "a living death or
tormented life is that of the Cuban and American slaveholder. For them there
is no safety." Slaveholders, he continued, were like "[a] criminal in the midst
of a powder bin with a red hot pigot of iron in his hand, which he is compelled to hold and char the living flesh to save his life, or let it fall to relieve
him from torture." In either scenario, the impending freedom of the slave was
impossible to forestall. "Of these two unhappy communities, the master and
the slave, the blacks have everything to hope for and nothing to fear, since
let what may take place their redemption from bondage is inevitable. They
must and will be free; whilst the whites have everything to fear and nothing
to hope for, 'God is just, and his justice will not sleep forever.'"[56] The master
class of the Americas—slaveowners united by their interest in human bondage
even as they were distinguished by their location in the American Mediterranean—confronted a supposedly common enemy, and feared the possibility
that any African slave, under the right set of circumstances, might become the
next Toussaint L'Ouverture.

In the half-century before the Civil War, the planter class thus labored
to prevent this exact hemispheric convergence, to stave off the prospect of
"another St. Domingue." Fear of mulatto refugees from the former slaveholding colony led Charleston officials in 1803 to arrest one man for distributing a
Haitian "Declaration of Independence," the first step in the South's erection of
"an intellectual blockade against dangerous doctrines." Concern that Denmark
Vesey's planned slave insurrection had sought support from Haiti prompted
the South Carolina legislature to impose new restrictions on the movement
of free black sailors, who were presumed to be agents of the revolutionary
contagion, and to have them jailed while in port. Haiti was a vital cornerstone
of colonization efforts—the relocation of freed slaves to Africa or the Caribbean—that aimed, at the very least, to reduce the largest and most densely
concentrated populations of black bodies and, even more ideally, at the de-
tropicalizing of the South and the establishment of white settlement. Southern
politicians, planters, and proslavery intellectuals, some of them schooled by
white planters now exiled from St. Domingue, labored to produce a consensus
on all matters relating to emancipation, and to thus minimize what was seen
as an omnipresent threat either through the removal of freed slaves and free
blacks or through the complete foreclosure of the very idea of emancipation.
Nearly every single proslavery effort aimed at proving that African peoples in
the New World were incapable of self-government, or of slow tutelage toward

some measure of civilization, or even of the most basic kinds of trust, used Haiti as "proof" or scientific evidence.[57] Long before the Civil Rights Movement, with its disgust for the role of "outside agitators" and "federal men," the slaveholders of the deep South styled themselves as modern-day versions of the French West Indian planter class, as "*southern colonies*" threatened by the sharp-elbowed empire of the North and the resentful, untrustworthy slave population.[58]

* * *

In William Faulkner's *Absalom, Absalom!* the Mississippi planter Thomas Sutpen reminisced about the American Mediterranean as if it were both mythic and concrete, fantastic and utilitarian. "I learned," he recalled of his youth, "that there was a place called the West Indies to which poor men went in ships and became rich, and it didn't matter how, so long as that man was clever and courageous." "So when the time came," he continued, describing a planter's coming-of-age, "when I realised that to accomplish my design I should need first of all and above all things money in considerable quantities and in the quite immediate future, I remembered . . . and I went to the West Indies."[59] The consequences of Sutpen's later return to the South—he carried with him bodies of knowledge, the bodies of slaves, and the ghosts of a past life—are at the core of Faulkner's fictional portrait of the slaveholder-as-synecdoche, with Sutpen's downfall, rooted in a West Indian past, standing in for the fate of the South. It is also, scholar John Matthews reminds us, a reflection of the "open secret" of Faulkner's broader word-painting of the South, a region marked, Matthews assures us, not by "indeterminacy but hybridity."[60] This essay has focused on the meaning and makeup of that hybridity, locating the South in the hemisphere in the angry decade before the Civil War, and identifying its shifting contours and its transnational, composite nature—it was, at once, a "colony" of the North, a state in the union, an imperial aspect of the slaveholding Caribbean, a "custodian" of European tradition, and an emergent nation-state. Antebellum Southern fears and fantasies about the Caribbean can be best understood, then, when they are set in a global context, and when the formal political relationship of the slaveholding states to the North American republic is not always assumed to be the only significant backdrop for the coming of the Civil War.

The Old South's dazzling antebellum hybridity—embodied by the linguist and socialite Madame Le Vert and her Mobile salon—would, in the end, be transformed by the wartime creation of an independent slaveholding republic. "The new Empire is at last fairly launched," announced the *New York Times* in early 1861, after the congressional delegations of a handful of Southern states had, with extraordinarily formality, resigned their service to the United States and removed themselves to Montgomery, Alabama, to draft a new constitution for their "Slaveholding Confederacy." "The seceding States," the *Times* continued, had "assumed the attitude of nationality." The laws, trade regulations, and provisions governing slavery—those in the U.S. constitution of 1860—were immediately "continued" in the new federation, and the North was now subject to the tariffs and penalties that were a consequence of foreign trade and not domestic commerce. Jefferson Davis, first president of this new nation-state, strove during the war that followed to fix the borders of the South as a nation-state, to build up a sense of common culture and unity, and to achieve diplomatic recognition from Britain or France. In the midst of this creation, some of the South's peculiar borderland culture and Caribbean complexion was erased, forgotten, and elided. Thus was the hybridity of the antebellum South—its relationship to a distinctly different slaveholding hemispherics—obscured by the rough embrace of war. At war's end, Le Vert, who famously hoped for an end to the conflict and celebrated the surrender of Lee at Appomattox, found herself labeled a "traitor" and was chased out of Mobile, accused of having not subscribed to the new national ideal of the Confederacy and having failed to cling to the South's postwar nostalgia, the melancholic dream of the "Lost Cause."

The "paradoxes" of the moment were, the *Times* admitted in 1861, "the most extraordinary ever exhibited in history." "Of the thirty-four States," it summed, "twenty-eight are still represented in the National Congress . . . [b]ut within this empire is *another*, assuming equal dignity and power."[61] When, I wonder, does the "assumption" of an "attitude of nationality" become nationality itself? What the South described as a crisis in the "foreign" relations between two sovereign republics, the North imagined as a troublesome passage in "our domestic relations."[62] Where Jefferson Davis referred to "the two countries," Abraham Lincoln responded with a reference to "our common country," as if the South had no right to leave.[63] When we describe the antebellum South as a part of the American Mediterranean, when we probe its commitment to a solidarity of slaveholding nations, or to its own sense of "civilized" privilege in the New World, we are, in a sense, revisiting this debate and asking, once again, "what is a nation?" and "what was 'the South'?" If we establish that the deep South reached out to the Americas, engaged in trade, institution building, and intellectual exchange, and verged on social, economic, and cultural distinction from the rest of the United States, are we, then, illuminating a historic South that was, at one point, politically independent? Or are we simply establishing that the history of the United States—including its various and diverse regions and regional histories—cannot be contained by the national archive? Far weaker claims to national status have weighed heavily upon world history in the years since the Civil War. But there are, too, things other than the nation-state—transgressive, troubling, border-crossing things, worthy of equal discussion in our many histories of the South.

NOTES

1. Virginia Tatnall Peacock, *Famous American Belles of the Nineteenth Century* (Philadelphia: J.B. Lippincott, 1901), 102.

2. Eliza McHatton-Ripley, *Social Life in Old New Orleans, Being Recollections of My Girlhood* (New York: D. Appleton, 1912), 86; Ida Raymond, *Southland Writers: Biographical and Critical Sketches of Living Female Writers of the South* (Philadelphia: Claxton, Revson, and Haffelfinger, 1870), 680.

3. Peacock, *Famous American Belles*, 111.

4. Frances Gibson Satterfield, *Madame Le Vert: A Biography of Octavia Walton Le Vert* (Edisto, S.C.: Edisto Press, 1987), 74, 100.

5. Michael O'Brien, *Conjectures of Order: Intellectual Life and the American South, 1810–1860* (Chapel Hill: University of North Carolina Press, 2004), 1:24.

6. McHatton-Ripley, *Social Life in Old New Orleans*, 86.

7. Madame Octavia Walton Le Vert, *Souvenirs of Travel* (Mobile: S.H. Goetzel & Co., 1857), 1:1.

8. Robert E. May, "Reconsidering Antebellum Women's History: Gender, Filibustering, and America's Quest for Empire," *American Quarterly* 57 (May 2005): 1162.

9. Le Vert, *Souvenirs*, 1:289. "Off-white" is taken from the title of Maria DeGuzmán, *Spain's Long Shadow: The Black Legend, Off-Whiteness, and Anglo-American Empire* (Minneapolis: University of Minnesota Press, 2005).

10. Le Vert, *Souvenirs*, 1:318.

11. See, for example, Jon Smith and Deborah Cohn, ed., *Look Away! The U.S. South in New World Studies* (Durham: Duke University Press, 2004).

12. Edward Bryan, *The Rightful Remedy: Addressed to the Slaveholders of the South* (Charleston, S.C.: Walker and James, 1850), 78.

13. Henry Nash Smith, *Virgin Land: The American West as Myth and Symbol* (Cambridge, Mass.: Harvard University Press, 1950), 154.

14. "Havana, or, Havannah," in J. Smith Homans and J. Smith Homans, Jr., eds., *A Cyclopedia of Commerce and Commercial Navigation* (New York: Harper and Brothers, 1858), 949.

15. John S. Thrasher, *Preliminary Essay on the Purchase of Cuba* (New York: Derby & Jackson, 1859), 14.

16. "Havana, or, Havannah," 951.

17. Louis A. Pérez, *On Becoming Cuban: Identity, Nationality, and Culture* (New York: Harper Collins, 1999), 22.

18. Freehling, *Road to Disunion* (New York: Oxford University Press, 1990), 424.

19. "Speech of John A. Quitman, of Mississippi, on the Powers of the Federal Government with Regard to the Territories: Delivered during the Debate on the President's Annual Message, in the House of Representatives, December 18, 1856," reprinted in J. F. H. Clairborne, ed., *Life and Correspondence of John A. Quitman* (New York: Harper & Brothers, 1860), 2:333.

20. Lincoln to James T. Hale, January 11, 1861, in *Abraham Lincoln: Speeches and Writings, 1859–1865* (New York: Library of America, 1989), 196.

21. Robert May, *The Southern Dream of a Caribbean Empire, 1854–1861* (Baton Rouge: Louisiana State University, 1973).

22. James Oakes, *The Ruling Race: A History of American Slaveholders* (New York: Vintage, 1982), 79.

23. Callie to Emmie, March 28, 1857, Elliott and Gonzales Family Papers, Southern Historical Collection, Wilson Library, University of North Carolina at Chapel Hill.

24. Callie to William, September 8, 1858, Elliot and Gonazeles Family Papers.

25. John S. Thrasher, *Cuba & Louisiana: Letter to Samuel J. Peters, Esq.* (New Orleans: Picayune Print, 1854), 7–8.

26. Thomas W. Wilson, *The Island of Cuba in 1850* (New Orleans, La.: Printing Office of "La Patria," June 1850), 5–6, 9.

27. Richard Henry Dana, *To Cuba and Back: A Vacation Voyage* (London: Smith, Elder, and Co., 1859), 237.

28. Pike Map, Historical New Orleans Collection, New Orleans.

29. "New Orleans," in Homans and Homans, ed., *Cyclopedia of Commerce*, 1417.

30. Kirsten Silva Gruesz, *Ambassadors of Culture: the Transamerican Origins of Latino Writing* (Princeton, N.J.: Princeton University Press, 2001).

31. Trollope, *West Indies and the Spanish Main*, 114–115.

32. De Guzmán, *Spain's Long Shadow*; Ronald G. Walters, "The Erotic South: Civilization and Sexuality in American Abolitionism" *American Quarterly* 25:2 (May, 1973): 177–201.

33. Dana, *To Cuba and Back*, 238.

34. Benjamin Hunt, *Remarks on Hayti as a Place for Settlement of Afric-Americans, and on the Mulatto in the Race for the Tropics* (Philadelphia: T.B. Pugh, 1860), 36.

35. William Henry Hurlbert, *Gan-Eden, or, Pictures of Cuba* (Boston: J.P. Jewett, 1854), 101.

36. Trollope, *West Indies and the Spanish Main*, 90–91.

37. John Bigelow, *Jamaica in 1850; or, the Effects of Sixteen Year's Freedom on a Slave Colony* (New York: G.P. Putnam, 1851), 74.

38. Trollope, *West Indies and the Spanish Main*, 90.

39. David Nicholls, *From Dessalines to Duvalier: Race, Colour and National Independence in Haiti* (New Brunswick, N.J.: Rutgers University Press, 1979), 83.

40. Nicholas Trist to Virginia Trist, December 4, 1834, Trist Papers, Southern Historical Collection, University of North Carolina, Chapel Hill.

41. Willis, *Health Trip to the Tropics*, 260, 267.

42. Hunt, *Remarks on Hayti*.

43. "Hayti," *New York Times*, September 21, 1859; "Free Negroes Leaving for Hayti," *New Orleans Picayune*, January 15, 1860; Nicholls, *From Dessalines to Duvalier*, 82–85.

44. C. L. R. James, *The Black Jacobins: Toussaint L'Ouverture and the San Domingo Revolution* (New York: Random House, 1963), 68.

45. "Letter from Hayti," *New York Times*, March 6, 1860. The quote is from Henry David Thoreau, "The Last Days of John Brown," reprinted in Carl Bode, ed., *The Portable Thoreau* (New York: Viking Press, 1977), 676.

46. "The Haytians and John Brown: Letter from John Brown, Jr., to President Geffrard," *New York Times*, August 8, 1860.

47. David Reynolds, *John Brown, Abolitionist: The Man Who Killed Slavery, Sparked the Civil War, and Seeded Civil Rights* (New York: Alfred A. Knopf, 2005), 109–110.

48. Walkner, *An Appeal in Four Articles; Together with a Preamble to the Coloured Citizens of*

the World, But in Particular, and Very Expressly, to Those of the New World, reprinted in Wilson Jeremiah Moses, ed., *Classical Black Nationalism: From the American Revolution to Marcus Garvey* (New York: New York University Press, 1996), 77.

49. Brown, "History of the Haitian Revolution," reprinted in Richard Newman, Patrick Rael, and Phillip Lapansky, eds., *Pamphlets of Protest: An Anthology of Early African American Protest Literature, 1790–1860* (New York and London: Routledge, 2001), 253.

50. Alfred N. Hunt, *Haiti's Influence on Antebellum America: Slumbering Volcano in the Caribbean* (Baton Rouge: Louisiana State University Press, 1988), 101, 98–101.

51. Hunt, *Haiti's Influence*, 88–92.

52. Douglass, "Toussaint L'Overture," *Fredrick Douglass's Paper*, September 4, 1851.

53. Martin R. Delany, *Blake, or, the Huts of America* (1970; reprint, Boston: Beacon Press, 1859), 3.

54. Robert S. Levine, *Martin Delany, Frederick Douglass, and the Politics of Representative Identity* (Chapel Hill: University of North Carolina Press, 1997), 191, 191–199.

55. Delany, *Blake*, 305.

56. Ibid.

57. Hunt, *Haiti's Influence*, 111, 114, 120, 130, 141–142.

58. D J. McCord, "The Practical Effects of Emancipation, Part II," *De Bow's Review*, May 1855, 595.

59. William Faulkner, *Absalom, Absalom!* (1936; reprint, New York: Vintage, 1990), 196.

60. John T. Matthews, "This Race Which Is Not One: The More 'Inextricable Compositeness' of William Faulkner's South," in Smith and Cohn, ed., *Look Away!* 218.

61. "The New Confederacy," *New York Times*, February 11, 1861.

62. This unoriginal phrase is taken from Charles Sumner, *Our Domestic Relations, or, How to Treat the Rebel States* (Boston: n.p., 1863).

63. Notes dated January 12, 1865, and January 18, 1865, included in "Message of President Lincoln on the Hampton Roads Conference, Including Correspondence," in James D. Richardson, ed., *The Messages and Papers of Jefferson Davis and the Confederacy* (1905, reprint; New York: Chelsea House, 1966), 1:521.

6

Expropriating *The Great South* and Exporting "Local Color"

Global and Hemispheric Imaginaries of the First Reconstruction

JENNIFER RAE GREESON

An exceptionalist narrative of U.S. cultural history poses both the process of Reconstruction following the Civil War, and the so-called local color writing in which it was registered, against the golden age of European empire in the late Victorian era. The denomination "local color" itself indicates—as clearly as does the name "Civil War"—that this most popular form of postbellum writing explores a geopolitical specificity purely of the intra- or subnational variety. In opposition to the global consciousness and designs of Europeans scrambling for Africa in the 1870s, U.S. citizens appear turned inward, recovering from their collective trauma by reading nostalgic accounts of antebellum times in the former Confederate states. Yet scholars working in the published archive of local color writing have for decades noted a paradox that undermines this neat opposition of global/imperial/Europe with local/self-contained/United States. In the pages of popular U.S. magazines of the postbellum period, local color stories are interspersed indiscriminately with accounts of far-flung foreign locales. Reading U.S. local color writing in this context of its original publication thus highlights the formal kinship of the ostensibly subnational genre with imperial discourse, in terms of both proto-ethnographic narrative structure and exoticist aesthetics.

The casually observable link between these two discourses of supposedly opposite geopolitical tendencies is neither coincidental nor counterintuitive. Rather, as this essay proposes, U.S. local color writing—and particularly that writing focused on the Southern states during Reconstruction—served as a primary discursive ground upon which U.S. readers conceptualized the ascendance of U.S. neocolonial intervention in the American hemisphere. By excavating both the global imperial analogues and the hemispheric imperial ambitions underwriting representations of the Reconstruction South, this essay argues that local color writing was never bounded imaginatively by the borders of the United States—and it does so by pursuing a revisionist retelling of one of the main origin stories for local color writing in U.S. literary history: a story that begins with the commissioning of the major Reconstruction travel series *The Great South* for *Scribner's Monthly* in 1872, and ends with the publication of the first group of explosively popular "Creole stories" by Louisianan writer George W. Cable in the pages of the same magazine in 1873–1875. This particular story of origins highlights how intimately connected, in the minds of late nineteenth-century readers and writers of English, were the non-fiction narrative accounts of underdeveloped locales—complete with their catalogs of raw materials and advice on civilizing natives—and the fictions of "local," ostensibly subnational, place.

At the same time, these ostensibly subnational U.S. texts reveal—when read through the double and contradictory popular understanding of the relationship of the United States to its south in the 1870s—that the site of the Reconstruction South allowed for a particularly potent projection of future U.S. empire. The Reconstruction South evoked both a transatlantic transposition of the stature and practices of European empire, and a hemispheric American exception from those practices. To the extent that the Southern states under Reconstruction appeared as "conquered provinces," they constituted a sort of domestic Africa for the United States, a site upon which the nation proved its civilizing might to be the equal of Europe's. But to the extent that the Southern states appeared as an intrinsic part of the nation—soon to reassume full standing as constitutive members of the union—their Reconstruction attested to the role of the United States as anti-imperial liberator of the formerly colonial American hemisphere, and their location at the southern limit of the borders of the nation only directed the desirous gaze of U.S. readers still farther south. In sum, this essay seeks to suggest how it was that the formal methods of definitionally domestic U.S. "local color" writing became so easily exportable by the turn of the century to the imperial and neocolonial adventures of the nation in Latin America, the Caribbean, and the Pacific—and to meditate as well upon why "Reconstruction" has remained, into our present century, a powerful rubric under which to conceptualize the workings of U.S. power beyond the borders of the nation.

Domestic Africa

In 1872, the magazine editor Josiah Gilbert Holland found himself in something of a predicament. Just over a year earlier, he had persuaded the powerful publisher Charles Scribner to discontinue two of the magazines published by his firm and to consolidate their subscription rolls behind Holland's bold new venture: the filially named *Scribner's Monthly*, a magazine that aspired to the moral and literary authority of the *Atlantic*; the illustration quantity and

quality of not just *Harper's*, but the popular London magazines; and the subscription rates to surpass all of its "high-toned" competitors.[1] But now Charles
Scribner had died unexpectedly at age fifty. Control of his firm had passed to
his young sons, whose dispensation toward the upstart magazine was unclear,
and Holland had failed so far to generate much notice for *Scribner's Monthly* at
home or abroad or indeed to produce an increase in circulation substantially
beyond that of the 40,000 subscriptions the elder Scribner had handed him
in November 1870. Holland needed a major editorial innovation that would
catapult his little-noticed new magazine to the position of prominence suited
to the flagship periodical of a major publishing house; he needed a revolution
in content that quickly would push his circulation closer to the goal of 100,000
he optimistically had proposed to Scribner père.[2]

Holland seems to have taken inspiration at this critical juncture from the
great U.S. periodical coup of the moment. British expatriate and Civil War vet-
eran Henry Morton Stanley, traveling on assignment for the *New York Herald*,
had in November 1871 "discovered" the incommunicado British missionary
David Livingstone in interior Africa (present-day Tanzania).[3] Stanley's "expedition" into "darkest Africa" transfixed audiences around the English-speaking
world, despite its origin as a bald publicity stunt designed by *Herald* publisher
James Gordon Bennett to garner a European readership for his newspaper.[4]
Stanley's climactic meeting with Livingstone was dubbed the scoop of the century by Bennett's paper, and it indeed represented an American usurpation
of the most popular form of British imperial travel writing in the 1860s and
'70s: the interior Africa exploration narrative. The *Herald* stunt arrogated the
authority of the great empire on matters of African "discovery," figuratively
transferring that authority to the United States—itself a former British colony
just emerging from a political and military convulsion that almost had disas-
sembled it. While the United States had no immediate material claim in the
scramble for Africa among the European powers, Stanley and Bennett momen-
tarily had bested Britain on the cultural field of empire, and both European
and U.S. readers took notice. Indeed, the Scribner firm rushed to secure the
U.S. rights to publish the book version of Stanley's dispatches, *How I Found
Livingstone*, as an over 700-page, copiously illustrated volume produced by
subscription in late 1872.

As he watched his own publisher angle for a piece of the Stanley sensation,
Holland began plotting a parallel "expedition" for *Scribner's Monthly*.[5] Channeling Bennett's already oft-quoted charge to Stanley to "[d]raw a thousand
pounds now . . . and when you have finished that, draw another thousand, and
so on; but, FIND LIVINGSTONE" (Stanley xviii), Holland laid out "an enterprise
involving an amount of labor and expense unprecedented in popular magazine
literature . . . [with n]either pains nor money . . . spared to make it all that we
promise it should be."[6] And as with the Stanley expedition, Holland projected
that a year-long series of dispatches to the magazine would culminate in "a

beautiful volume, in which the material will be newly arranged . . . and offered to the subscriptions of the public, not only in America, but in Great Britain and nearly all the British colonies" (248). On Bennett's model, in other words, Holland laid out an expedition that both would boost magazine subscriptions as it unfolded and would consolidate the sensation it generated in more enduring, higher profit-generating book form at its end. He followed Bennett as well in stepping into the imperial travel-writing genre and thereby engaging automatically an international, rather than purely domestic, English-speaking readership. At the same time, though, Holland sought to improve on the *Herald* stunt by using his magazine format to best advantage. In particular, he stressed the production of high-quality illustrations from direct artist observation; whereas the 1872 volume *How I Found Livingstone* was illustrated after the fact with artists' renderings ostensibly based upon Stanley's untrained sketches, Holland's *Scribner's Monthly* "expedition" was publicized from the first as a joint venture between correspondent and chief illustrator. A "band" of up to seventeen sketchers and engravers would accompany every leg of the journey, and fresh illustrations from the field would be included with each installment of the series.[7] By the end of 1874, Holland's "enterprise" had "occupied, in all, about four hundred and fifty pages of the magazine, and involved the production of more than four hundred and thirty engravings" (248).

Holland's biggest innovation on Bennett's precedent, though, was his choice of "expedition" locale. Rather than follow the *Herald's* figurative competition with Britain on the final frontier of European empire—in the African interior where the United States had no present prospect of an actual material stake—Holland trained his sights on a territory the nation already possessed: an "immense tract of country" (248) recently subdued in war, currently occupied by the U.S. military, and in the midst of a civilizing process called Reconstruction. *The Great South*, as Holland's expedition series was titled, followed the basic ideological contours of British Victorian travel writing about Africa, positing discovery as the necessary predecessor to development as it boasted that the *Scribner's* team "penetrated regions rarely seen by Northern men" (King, *The Great South*, n.p.). It evoked the transatlantic solidarity of British and U.S. imperial civilizations, by "exhibit[ing], by pen and pencil, a vast region almost as little known to the Northern States of the Union as it is to England."[8] But the cultural authority of *The Great South* dovetailed, as it could not in Stanley's African writings, with real U.S. political and economic authority over the realm being "penetrated," "investigated," and "simultaneously offered to the English-speaking public on both sides of the Atlantic" (King, *The Great South*, n.p.).

The Great South has never before been linked with Stanley's *Herald* stunt, perhaps in part because it exists also within a relatively long and well-established domestic tradition of Southern travel writing within U.S. literature. A quarter-century before his editorship of *Scribner's Monthly*, Holland himself had broken into publishing by converting the only trip he ever took south of the Mason-Dixon line into "Sketches of Plantation Life" for the *Springfield* (Mass.) *Republican*.[9] More recently, the war had spawned a renewed emphasis on Southern travel accounts, most of them focused either on ruin and loss—as in J. T. Trowbridge's resonantly titled *A Picture of the Desolated States* (1868)—or, somewhat more optimistically, on the regeneration of Southern societies from old order into new.[10] Indeed, the first Southern sketches commissioned by Holland for *Scribner's Monthly* partook of the latter variety of conventional postwar reportage: focused on Virginia, the Southern state usually seen as most iconically national, those articles archetypally chronicled "New Ways in the Old Dominion."[11]

With *The Great South*, Holland was up to something fundamentally different. As he presented the series with a transatlantic appropriation of British imperial travel-writing modes, Holland registered the extent to which secession, conquest, and occupation had transformed the internal relationship of the nation to its Southern states. In implicitly packaging the Southern states for his readers as a sort of domestic Africa—an imaginatively parallel field for the projection of imperial power *within* the United States—Holland built upon at least a decade of attempts by writers North and South to understand the domestic sectionalist crisis by global analogy to the relationships between European nations and their colonies. Indeed, at least since 1861, the antagonism between North and South had been posited, in the pages of the *Atlantic Monthly* and elsewhere, as a struggle for supremacy between "New England [and] New Africa."[12] To represent the Southern states under Reconstruction as a colonized region of the United States, parallel to colonized regions of the European powers around the globe, was, fundamentally, to assert a new stature of equality for the United States among the imperial nations of the world.

I mean to suggest that it was this global reframing of the relationship between the nation and its defeated, occupied Southern states that made *The Great South* series a revelation—and an education—for U.S. readers of the day. Even Holland's selection of his correspondent for the series telegraphed to his readers the connection that he was making between British imperial writing about Africa and U.S. postwar writing about the Southern states. Stanley himself might have been Holland's first choice, but the editor secured the next best possibility: Edward King, a little-known, 26-year-old aspiring journalist, whose sole claim to fame was having been Stanley's last press corps companion before the latter's secret departure for Africa and Livingstone. King had first appeared in *Scribner's Monthly* in late 1872 with the articles "An Expedition with Stanley" and "How Stanley Found Livingstone," both of which sought to capitalize on his casual acquaintance with Stanley in Spain as the two covered the Carlist insurrection for different U.S. newspapers in late 1869.[13] In the first of these pieces, King wrote of his close associations with his "brother of the craft" in the tropical clime of southern Spain: "We slept; we waked; we ate pomegranates: and meantime the lusty sun poured down unrelentingly, waking the fair land into tropical fervor and voluptuousness. . . . We had at last got beyond Europe." After lingering on the "haughty ancient Moorish look" of "these tall, voluptuously formed dark women, who . . . were not Europeans," King left *Scribner's* readers with the image of himself and Stanley standing side by side on the Mediterranean coast, "point[ing] carelessly beyond the throbbing rim of the purple sea" and breathing: "Africa!"[14] By the time those words appeared in the magazine, King was on his way to the stateside version of the dark continent as the "enterprising man" in charge of Holland's "unprecedented" Southern expedition (248).

Global Color

King's last dispatch to *Scribner's* from Europe left him standing with his readers on the southernmost edge of Spain, gazing across the Mediterranean with eroticized longing toward the Africa his British-American companion soon would penetrate. The first installment of *The Great South* found King in a transatlantically transported but arrestingly analogous position: at the port of New Orleans, with illustrations and text calculated to direct the longing gaze of his readers across the Gulf of Mexico.[15] In moving from the rim of the Mediterranean to the rim of the Gulf, King transposed a surrogate experience of European empire into a more immediate projection of U.S. empire to come. The southward gaze from Spain toward Africa became the southward gaze from domestic Africa toward Spanish America.

Just so, the Reconstruction South entered U.S. literature as an imaginative geographic nexus for conceptualizing U.S. empire in the 1870s, the decade when, as Amy Kaplan has put it, the United States increasingly was "turning outward after the Civil War."[16] As I already have proposed, federal administration of the underdeveloped and war-ravaged Southern states allowed U.S. writers to draw certain parallels to European exertions in Africa, and thereby to assert, through transatlantic comparison, the legitimacy and power of the United States on the world stage. Insofar as U.S. writers viewed the former Confederacy as a conquered possession of the nation, they facilitated a transatlantic appropriation of European imperial discourse; like King, they situated the Reconstruction South in a global context—as both the U.S. (*The Great South*) and London (*The Southern States of North America*) titles of his series attest—and they vaunted the imperatives of capitalist development and the trials of the "Civilizing Mission."[17]

But as much as a site for analogy, the Reconstruction South served as a site for exception to the cultural forms of European empire, as a ground for asserting a fundamental American divergence from those forms. In this sense, the Southern states rendered abject before U.S. rule easily appeared as a point of privileged and intimate access to Spanish America, for as Jon Smith and

Deborah Cohn recently have remarked, "[i]f we define 'America' hemispherically . . . the experience of defeat, occupation, and reconstruction—particularly
if this historical trauma is broadened to include the African American experience of defeat under slavery—is something the South shares with *every* part of
America [other than the United States]."[18] To the extent that U.S. writers and
readers saw the region being reconstructed as an inherent part of the nation,
they claimed as national heritage the shared inter-American experiences of
colonization, slavery, defeat, occupation, and—improbably—resistance to Yankee (Yanqui) imperialism. From King's travel series to the so-called local color
fiction that closely followed it, writing about the Reconstruction South fostered
the development of stories about a projected U.S. hemispheric dominance
exceptional for its self-critical capacity, its empathy born of shared experience
with those being dominated.

The travel writing led to the fiction in more ways than one. Holland's
series did indeed secure the place of *Scribner's Monthly* (later *Century Magazine*)
on the late nineteenth-century U.S. literary scene, and the series has been
credited with developing the national audience for regional fictions of the U.S.
South that continued to grow well into the twentieth century.[19] As well, King,
during his stay in New Orleans, "discovered" the aspiring fiction writer George
Washington Cable, whose popular 1870s stories are the subject of the second
half of this article.[20] (Like Holland and King, Cable understood the Reconstruction South to be a culturally—as well as materially—exploitable resource; even
as Holland was plotting the *Scribner's* "expedition" in early 1872, Cable was
encouraging readers of the *New Orleans Picayune* to capitalize on Louisiana's
history as a literary subject: "Here lie the gems, like those new diamonds in
Africa, right on top of the ground. The mines are virgin."[21]) Cable's meteoric
rise to national fame, in turn, often is seen—along with the slightly earlier
and equally explosive appearance of Bret Harte's stories from the far west—as
the inauguration of so-called local color fiction as a major (if not *the* major)
literary form in the later nineteenth-century United States.[22] Re-placing these
most significant of 1870s writings about the Reconstruction South in the rising global consciousness of their U.S. readers helps to explain why this writing
that seems strictly insular and resolutely backward-looking so perfectly spoke
to the expansionist and forward-marching temper of the times.[23]

The story that I am telling about the King-Cable episode varies substantially from how its significance normally is construed in nation-centric U.S.
literary history. *The Great South* usually is seen as doing the cultural work of
postwar sectional reconciliation—even, it has been claimed, helping to turn
national public opinion against Reconstruction.[24] "[T]he North was made
acquainted with the vast resources of the South, and the South was pleased
and flattered by the attention," recollected publisher William Ellsworth more
than eighty years ago, in an assessment that has not substantially altered since.
"The result was most helpful in creating good feeling between the sections."[25]

But everything about Holland's presentation of the series belies the idea that reconciliation was its primary intent: his initial projection of an international English-speaking audience for *The Great South* undermines the notion that re-educating Northerners was his goal, just as his snippy editorial admonishment to "fault-finders" in the Southern states at the close of the series raises doubt that appeasing Southerners was his aim.[26]

If the long-serviceable reconciliationist thesis is discarded, though, attempting to account for the national popularity of either King's series or Cable's fiction exposes the difficulties inherent in conceptualizing postbellum "local color" writing as a genre. For the genre by definition explodes the notion of the "local" that is its ostensible subject; in producing the "local" for consumption by a supra-local audience, local color writing necessarily exceeds its geographical designation.[27] Its national, or indeed metropolitan, audience has led critics to claim that the genre speaks foremost to national or metropolitan concerns—that the "gesture toward the local" simply "ratifies the hegemony of the 'national' as a standard," or that the "archeological" impulse of local color writing evidences a cultural reaction to "an era of industrial progress and heightened materialism."[28] Increasingly, critics have surmounted the local/national symbolic dyad to identify a nascent global consciousness in local color writing: attention by Kaplan and Richard H. Brodhead to the ethnographic dimensions of the genre has highlighted the connections between intra-national regional and extra-national imperial exoticisms, whereas Hsuan L. Hsu recently has marshaled cultural geographer Neil Smith's concept of "jumping scales" to map interchanges between the local and the transnational in turn-of-the-century regional fiction.[29]

To recover the purchase of local color writing for U.S. readers in the 1870s and 1880s, it is important to go even farther in this reassessment: to acknowledge that the term *local color* itself—as it originated in postbellum literary terminology—participated from its coining in a broader Western imperial discourse invested in maintaining and relating hierarchies based upon geographical location (locality) and racial categorization (color). When the term emerged in the late 1870s, it denoted what we might now discern as a mutually constitutive narrative process of peripheralization and racialization, as in this early usage in the *Atlantic*: "What gives an oddly contrasting local color to this dignified speech [of "the Southern ladies"] is the pronunciation of certain words,—a pronunciation probably caught in childhood from negro nurses."[30] Here, a description of regional peculiarity in matters of dialect, labor organization, and population shades easily into an account of racial intermixing or indeterminacy; local deviance from a metropolitan norm is also, inextricably, a deviance in color from an Anglo-Saxon norm.[31] Returning to the initial conceptualization of the category of local color warns us that this fiction cannot be taken as a comfortably domestic constant against which we may measure the hemispheric entanglements of other U.S. and comparative American literary forms.

As "local color" writing in its original formulation constructed geographical peripherality and supposed biological inferiority in tandem, the genre—like its close relative, European imperial travel writing—created narratives that explained the underdevelopment of a region as the product of the inferiority of its native inhabitants. Such is the explanatory paradigm for a proper U.S. Reconstruction of the occupied Southern states that King develops over the course of *The Great South*, a text that he describes in his authorial introduction to the book as "an exhaustive catalogue of the material resources of the South and the social condition of its people" (n.p.). These two elements—exuberant detail of Southern natural resources, coupled with copious evidence of the degeneracy of Southern people, white and black—organize almost every one of the ninety descriptive installments of the book.

In his geographical descriptions, King unquestionably situates *The Great South* in the context of underdeveloped regions around the globe. Compared with any other desirable territorial possession in the world, the Southern states are "inexhaustibly rich" (330) in natural resources: King claims that mineral deposits, timber, and fertile soil are present in every nook of the region to a degree presumably incomprehensible to readers foreign and domestic, whose "wildest ideas" about Southern wealth "can be none too exaggerated for the reality" (240). Bolstered by more than 100 site-specific engravings of unmined rock formations and uninhabited landscapes, King catalogues Southern raw materials ranging from a mythical "gold belt" (491) stretching from North Carolina to Georgia—a story that gestures back to the earliest European designs on the American hemisphere—to a more up-to-date, industrial-age coal field in the Appalachians, which "considerably" exceeds "the entire coal area of Great Britain" (532). Assessing the potential aids and impediments to extraction and improvement of the "riches" (331 and passim) he details, King again echoes much earlier European colonialist promotions of America as "neu-gefundenes Eden": Southern raw materials are unparalleled in their ease of access, as the soil requires "but little attention" (78, 348), the ore little smelting, and the coal—like those diamonds in Africa—is located conveniently "at the surface" (682) of the earth.

Yet despite the ready availability of these sources of vast wealth, King repeatedly informs his readers, all had lain fallow until U.S. occupation of the Southern states, for "the natives of the poorer class, who might make fortunes by turning their attention to it, are too idle to develop the country" (403). Thus, King's figuring of the unequaled yet undeveloped riches of the peripheral South unfolds in tandem with his extensive proofs of the degeneracy of its local population, white and black. His late account of "the old town of Alexandria [Va.]" is typical:

> It occupies a position admirably fitted for large industrial activity . . .
> and yet it languishes. Its inhabitants seem to lack the vigor and the

enterprise needed to seize upon and improve their fine advantages.
They are in the attitude of waiting for something to turn up. . . . The
streets were not paved until a Northern officer, during the occupation in
war times, insisted upon having a pavement of cobble stones laid down,
and met the expense by fines levied upon whiskey-selling. . . . One sees
nerveless unthrift in many small Virginian towns. It seems graven in
the nature of whites and blacks. An occasional conversation with the
negroes led me to believe that they offer as many hindrances to the
advent of capital as their ex-masters do. Both seem suspicious that some
improper and undue advantage is to be taken of them. (797)

According to King's diagnosis, this incapability for improvement "graven in
the nature" of Southern "inhabitants" may be blamed at least partially upon
climatic and historical determinants. "The aboriginal [white] Texan . . . is a
child of the sun; he dislikes effort; it gives him no gratification to labor" (177);
whereas "the tough moral fibre of the Anglo-Saxon . . . is not perceptible in the
negro; neither could it be expected, considering that he was brought from the
jungles of Africa into a comparatively wild region in America" (780). Such characterizations, in turn, easily progress into biological determinism: King reiterates that "the rural Caucasian" (372) is "lean and scrawny, without animation"
(346), "all [with] the same dead, pallid complexion" (774), while "the negro . . .
lets the African in him run riot" (452–453).[32] What sometimes reads as King's
bi-racialization of Southern incapacity for self-rule is, again, bolstered by
visual evidence; the *Scribner's* engravers also produced more than 100 "wayside
sketches" (473) of "Southern Types" (771 and passim): physiognomic caricatures
of slack-jawed Southerners white and black that often exhibit distorted facial
features (such as low foreheads and exaggerated noses and lips) and assume
more or less bestial postures (such as slouching, crouching, and begging).

   Taken together, the two organizing elements of King's "exhaustive" text
create a moral imperative for the U.S. occupation and administration of a
populated and resistant territory—an imperative ideally suited to the postbellum needs of a national audience beginning to imagine the United States as
a modern imperial power on the European model yet ambivalent about the
prospect. The overarching claim of *The Great South* is that the most vital natural stores of the North American continent have until now been in the possession of "inhabitants" (797) devoid of the productive capabilities that would
allow them to make use of those resources. The fledgling imperative of U.S.
empire proposed in King's catalog of the Reconstruction South might best be
described as an imperative of improvement: unless progress is imposed from
outside of the region, its "riches" (689 and passim) will continue to "languish"
(797) unused, its "natives" (106 and passim) living "the very rudest and most
incult life imaginable" (542). By contrast, with "proper investment" (239) of
"Northern capital" (403 and passim) trained on the harvesting of Southern

riches, King programatically concludes again and again, the nation "will find one of its most profitable fields" (110) and will place itself "at that pinnacle of commercial glory" (239) equivalent to the European nations that similarly harvest the riches of the globe. And while uplift of the "native" population is a priority clearly secondary to the attainment of national "commercial glory," King optimistically speculates that U.S. administration may even in the course of time civilize the degenerate Southern peoples into worthy laborers in the modern order: "We may expect in a few years, as . . . the persistent idlers are crowded to the wall, to see [the negro and] the Southern poor white transformed into industrious and valuable members of society" (776).

Perceptible in the moral imperative for Reconstruction King formulates is the utility of the new "local color" writing for developing a popular hemispheric expansionist imaginary in the postbellum United States. For even as King presents his readers with a region of simultaneously peripherialized and racialized "color" analogous to colonial territories abroad, he uses precisely the claim of the "local"—the domestic, the intimate—to differentiate U.S. administration of the American South from other forms of global empire.

Hemispheric Louisiana

King establishes this distinctiveness of the U.S. role in *The Great South* in the first seven chapters of his book, which pointedly diverge from his derivative appropriation of Victorian imperial travel-writing modes to focus on the colonial history of Louisiana. "For a century-and-a-half," he writes on the first page, Louisiana "was coveted by all nations; sought by those great colonizers of America,—the French, the English, the Spaniards. It has been in turn the plaything of monarchs and the bait of adventurers. Its history and tradition are leagued with all that was romantic in Europe and on the Western continent in the eighteenth century (17)."

By beginning with American colonial history and with the archetypal global opposition of "Europe" to "the Western continent," King situates the United States as itself part of a colonized hemisphere that is unevenly throwing off the historical yoke of European empire. Thus, he carefully distinguishes both the current federal occupation of Louisiana (in 1873–1875), and the original U.S. acquisition of the territory, from the long prior history of Louisiana's changing imperial masters. For instance, "each building" in New Orleans "which confesses to an hundred years has memories of foreign domination hovering about it" (37), implying that U.S. control of the territory since 1803 has involved the opposite of "foreign domination"—rather, has involved Louisiana's domestic American liberation.

Most important, the American-colonial-to-U.S.-liberated trajectory that King recounts provides a template for further U.S. expansion southward. As he sums up:

To-day a tract of country which, two years ago, was comparatively as unknown to the masses of our citizens as Central Africa, is now easily accessible . . . and in a few years the outside world will suddenly discover that a journey to Mexico is no more difficult than the present journey to New Orleans, and that new lands and territories have been opened up to speculation and profit as if by magic. (187–188)

King's "expedition" plays a central role in this inexorable southward expansion: "discovering" the global context of the nation's domestic possession of Louisiana becomes the first step in conceptualizing a hemispheric expansion of the United States that may be signally distinguished from competing European designs on Spanish America. King's intensive focus on Louisiana and its past allows for a rehearsal of U.S. acquisition and administration of a previously colonial, semitropical American territory, and the Gulf Coast location of New Orleans easily directs the acquisitive gaze of his readers yet farther south—which perhaps explains why Louisiana and southern (or "Spanish") Florida so quickly became the most popular sites for writing about the Reconstruction South in the 1870s, replacing the focus of antebellum writers on the upper Southern states.

In giving this particular version of Louisiana pride of place in the book version of *The Great South*, King almost certainly was influenced by Cable's early stories, which he was reading and helping to place in *Scribner's* as he wrote his own dispatches. Cable's paradigmatic "local color" stories became by far the most popular and celebrated treatment of the Southern states published during Reconstruction, so it is worth thinking about what could have constituted their intense appeal to U.S. literary critics and readers alike. Unlike King's encyclopedic work of Southern travel writing, these stories all operated within an extremely limited setting: a markedly liminal version of New Orleans in which Cable stresses the geographical in-betweenness of the city—at the southernmost limit of the United States, but the center of the American hemisphere—as well as a particular moment of historical in-betweenness—the early nineteenth-century transition from European imperial rule to U.S. acquisition. The opening sentence of "Jean-Ah Poquelin" (1875) demonstrates Cable's typical historical orientation of the reader:

In the first decade of the present century, when the newly established American Government was the most hateful thing in Louisiana—when the Creoles were still kicking at such vile innovations as the trial by jury, American dances, anti-smuggling laws, and the printing of the Governor's proclamation in English—when the Anglo-American flood that was presently to burst in a crevasse of immigration upon the delta had thus far been felt only as slippery seepage which made the Creole tremble for his footing—there stood . . . an old colonial plantation-house half in ruin.[33]

The generic "local color" reading of Cable's fiction sees his historical setting as isolated in time and space, designed principally to produce nostalgia by documenting a regionally specific way of life already lost to the standardizations of modernity at the poignant moment of its imminent demise. Twentieth-century critics of Cable also, and more compellingly, have identified his setting as not only a paean to the past, but also an analog for his present and the conflicts between white Louisianans and the "newly established American Government" of the state under Reconstruction.[34]

Cable's historical setting is surely forward-looking as well. This opening sentence of "Jean-Ah Poquelin" alone implies a narrative trajectory strongly reminiscent of King's moral imperative for Reconstruction as a template for future U.S. expansion. As requisite background for the plot is the "old colonial plantation-house half in ruin": a reminder that the colonial system of plantation production, for which tropical America was valued during the first centuries of European New World empire, has become outmoded, no longer profitable or competitive in the modernizing world economy.[35] Hand in hand with this note of economic exigency comes Cable's certainty that the "Creole" locals of tropical America are not able to transform their own colonial way of life in order to participate in historical progress and develop their own territory:

> The indigo fields and vats of Louisiana had been generally abandoned as unremunerative. Certain enterprising men had substituted the culture of sugar; but while [his brother] was too apathetic to take so active a course, [Jean Poquelin] saw larger, and, at that time, equally respectable profits, first in smuggling, and later in the African slave trade. What harm could he see in it? (91)

Unlike "[c]ertain enterprising men"—the vanguard of the coming "Anglo-American flood" of U.S. immigration—who transform the defunct colonial means of production to render local resources again profitable under changing economic conditions, Cable's Creoles "lack the vigor and the enterprise needed to seize upon and improve their fine advantages" (King 797). While his brother does nothing at all, Cable's title character perversely invests himself even more fully in the passing colonial order by outfitting himself for the last days of the Atlantic slave trade. More disturbing than his colonial lack of economic foresight here is his colonial lack of metropolitan ethics: his degenerate inability, diagnosed by Cable's rhetorical question, to "see harm in" his course of (re)action.

Precisely because of this perverse inability or unwillingness to evolve with the changing times, Cable's colorful local characters have become in his stories mired in a nonproductive way of life marked by repetitive compulsions, mental and physical disease, and decay. On Jean Poquelin's last voyage to Africa, his brother contracts leprosy; when the two return to their rotting plantation, Jean seals off his land and allows it to revert to swamp, to hide the fact that his brother—now equally rotting—is illegally concealed there rather than banished to the "*Terre aux Lépreux*" (100). Thus are the two Poquelin brothers rendered one a social outcast and the other a walking corpse by their attempt at slave trading; by the second page of the story, they have come to embody and perpetually live out the evil excesses of the colonial order that produced them. Cable's Creole characters achieve no expiation or redemption from their infernal colonial stasis, though; it is only the U.S. takeover of Louisiana that advances the plot of the story, interrupting what threatens to become a repetitive, nonproductive narrative cycle. In "Jean-Ah Poquelin," the "newly established American government" intervenes in Jean's willful neglect of his land by building a new municipal street through his plantation, draining his swamp, and filling in the canal that cuts his plantation off from the growing New Orleans suburbs that surround it. Despite Poquelin's colorful "curses upon the United States, the President, the Territory of Orleans, Congress, the Governor and all his subordinates" (94), this development forced by the U.S. government finally exposes the secret of his brother's whereabouts and his own strange behavior, and brings the narrative to its resolution.

Cable's stories seem in many ways designed to assure readers that this sort of U.S. intervention in the name of progress for the underdeveloped American South—even when vehemently opposed by the "native inhabitants"—is both inexorable and morally for the best. In terms of inexorability, outside control of Louisiana is a narrative inevitability in Cable's stories given the characterological stasis of his local Creoles; without it, there would be no plot. In terms of the moral rectitude of the U.S. takeover, Cable generally subordinates thorny conflicts over political control and property ownership to cultural clashes between his Creoles and their U.S. occupiers. The material dispossession of his Creoles by "les Américains"—"the fertile birthright arpents . . . tricked away from dull colonial Esaus by their blue-eyed brethren of the North"[36]—remains a dimly comprehended, schematic background element for the stories, often metaphorized as a suprahuman force of nature: to go back to the first sentence of "Jean-Ah Poquelin," as "the Anglo-American flood that was presently to burst in a crevasse of immigration upon the delta." Cable instead confines the fierce objections of his Creole characters to the new U.S. order to matters of culture, ranging from their comedic over-investment in matters of trivia ("kicking at . . . American dances . . . and the printing of the Governor's proclamation in English") to their more seriously flawed opposition to basic tenets of "Anglo-American" civilization ("the vile innovations of the trial by jury . . . [and] anti-smuggling laws").

In the case of "Jean-Ah Poquelin," Cable represents the expropriation of the Poquelin *marais* by bureaucratic U.S. administrators as primarily a cultural, rather than material, loss to the native Creoles. As the "new American government" takes control of Jean Poquelin's land, its enforced improvements crowd out the colorful local tales about ghosts, haunting, witchery, and murder that have arisen to explain Poquelin's reclusion and his brother's disappearance. These endangered tales, themselves artifacts of "local color," are, of course, precisely what Cable's story purports to mine, preserve, and deliver to its U.S. readers—and, indeed, it is the destruction of the mystery undergirding the local lore that provides the rewarding resolution of Cable's plot. "Jean-Ah Poquelin" finally leaves Cable's readers in the rather comfortable position of both tacitly claiming and emotively disavowing U.S. domination of his Southern Creoles and their territory. The only substantial U.S. character, a minor development official called "little White," takes over the narration of the story as the title character expires along with the tales and rumors that have sheltered him. "Little White"—nonthreatening though morally and racially superior to the Creoles, as his name suggests—creates an ad hoc funeral for Poquelin and becomes the author of the exposé of his secret, affectionately declaiming the seeming moral of the story: "'Gentlemen . . . here come the last remains of Jean Marie Poquelin, a better man, I'm afraid, with all his sins—yes a better—a kinder man to his blood—a man of more self-forgetful goodness—than all of you put together will ever dare to be" (100). This stagy valedictory to an anachronistic native, whose human value can be recognized only after his demise, becomes quite typical of later "local color" fiction, and it functions in Cable's early story to invite U.S. readers simultaneously to remember and to forget the material basis of the Creole's cultural displacement—to remember and to forget that the demise of the Poquelin legend enables the takeover of the Poquelin land by "little White's" own "Building and Improvement Company" (95).[37]

The extent to which Cable's stories worked to engage and to validate U.S. intervention in Southern America was perceived by the many laudatory critics of his own day, who found the applicability of the stories to extend quite beyond the borders of the Reconstruction districts. The author of a *Harper's* lead essay on "The Recent Movement in Southern Literature" found a proto-imperial pedagogical function in the stories comparable to King's moral imperative for Reconstruction: Cable was "the recognized master over the enchanted, semitropical realm, beautiful with flowers, yet marked by the trail of the serpent"; in other words, his stories taught not only the Edenic promise of underdeveloped, fertile lands but also their fallen stature—the original sin of their coloniality and, implicitly, the possibility of their redemption with proper management by the United States.[38] In another vein, Lafcadio Hearn, the essayist who would become the pre-eminent U.S. orientalist of the later nineteenth century, attributed to his reading of "Jean-Ah Poquelin" a wholesale awakening of his desire for the global exotic; in an 1883 essay, he claimed that "that strange little tale . . . and its exotic picturesqueness had considerably influenced my anticipations . . . and prepared me to idealize everything peculiar and semi-tropical that I might see."[39]

This assurance of contemporary critics that Cable's "local color" stories were hemispherically or indeed globally exportable may be linked to his pitching of the conflict between Southern natives and their U.S. administrators as one between "Creoles" and national citizens. As he focuses on the passing of the "Old Creole Days" (the title of the first collection of his stories) of pre-1803 colonial Louisiana life, Cable draws sharp oppositions between the coloniality of his Creole characters and the national stature of their interloping U.S. antagonists. Creolized by definition, Cable's Louisianans share in common only their colonial American nativity; according to other markers of cultural belonging, they are wildly indeterminate, of no extricable linguistic, national, or racial origin. Cable's Creoles are always multilingual—though, significantly, never fluent speakers of standard English—and they are of hopelessly tangled genealogies.[40] French and Spanish, African and Choctaw heritages intermingle inseparably, as in the story "Belles Demoiselles Plantation" (1874), in which the lineal descendants of a seventeenth-century French nobleman have assumed, after a century of colonial American life, the various names De Charleu, De Carlos, and "Injun Charlie." Most infuriating to Cable's fellow New Orleanians in the 1870s was his insinuation that Creoles are racially as well as nationally indeterminate: for instance, the De Charleu descendant referred to as "half-caste" on one page becomes "plainly a dark white man" on the next;[41] the title character of "'Tite Poulette" (1874) is at the beginning of the story the daughter of a woman "[y]ou would hardly have thought of . . . as being 'colored,'" at the end of the story instead the "Spaniards' daughter," and throughout an epitome of Creole beauty, "her great black eyes made tender by their sweeping lashes, the faintest tint of color in her Southern cheek."[42] Cable's characterization of the Louisiana Creoles finally obviates the notion that a local class of identifiable elites exists to be dispossessed by U.S. rule. While he records local preoccupations with caste, Cable implies that caste distinctions are simply another form of colorful local folklore, that a master class cannot be extricated from a slave class in Louisiana, nor a "white" (by Anglo-Saxonist standards) group of Creoles cordoned off from the heterogeneous colonial population.

Cable's U.S. characters, by contrast, evince a cultural homogeneity opposite to the hybridity of his Creoles: they are monolingual English speakers to the point of comedy, and they are rigidly Anglo in cultural and racial origin. Perhaps for this reason, the legitimacy of the many markers of U.S. political and military might in the stories is never questioned, even by the Creoles who resent that power: Jean Poquelin himself concedes, at the height of his protest against U.S. incursion on his land, "*Mais*, I know; we billong to *Monsieur le Président*" (93). Cable's Creoles possess no competing affiliation to recognized (European) nations; their extra-Louisianan connections are limited to other (mostly American) colonial sites: they are "Creoles, Cubans, [colonial] Spaniards, St. Domingo refugees, and other loungers"; they are "*amigos . . .* Creoles, [Irishmen], and lovers."[43] The U.S. takeover of this abandoned colonial

site thus violates no competing claims of legitimate possession, and Cable's
primary opposition of Creoles to U.S. citizens finally serves to validate U.S.
nationalism as the only legitimate and recognizable American nationalism,
measuring the distance between the nationality of the United States and the
coloniality of the rest of the Americas.

Cable's creolized and historically liminal Louisiana thus illuminates what
Sandhya Shukla and Heidi Tinsman recently have called the "transnational processes of domination" that are exposed to analysis by a hemispheric American
studies paradigm—and it shows one way that U.S. writers in this pivotal period
of expansionist energy used the odd status of the South during Reconstruction
to imagine the nation as both participating in and aloof from those processes
of domination.[44] Cable's focus on the early nineteenth-century transition
from European to U.S. rule in Louisiana locates the United States as a middle
term in the archetypal global divide that King denominated between "Europe"
and "the Western continent." When Louisiana is understood by readers as a
colonized territory—in the parlance of Reconstruction politics, a "conquered
province"—the switch from French to "*Américain*" masters in the stories affirms
the commensurate stature of the United States vis-à-vis the European imperial
nations, and the U.S. occupation of Louisiana appears a process of continued
imperial domination. When Louisiana is regarded as a constituent member-
state of the United States, however, the United States appears on the American
side of "Europe's colonization and nation-building in its 'New World'" (3), and
the U.S. occupation of Louisiana appears a process of colonial liberation. This
dual signification makes Reconstruction a central metaphor for postbellum
expansionist ambitions. As writers detail the nation's process of civilizing
its own creolized, slaveholding, underdeveloped, morally recalcitrant, and
violently resistant domestic Southern reaches, the U.S. increasingly appears
poised to redeem the rest of the ostensibly subnational, non-English-speaking,
"semitropical" American South from its long colonial history.

The South as a Field of Expansion

For Albion Tourgée, author of the most successful novel about Reconstruction
published in the 1870s, the move from Reconstruction to neocolonial intervention farther south appears to have been an obvious and natural progression.
A Fool's Errand (1879) follows Tourgée's Michigan-born protagonist, Comfort
Servosse, through the various indignities he encounters while seeking both
to develop "the subjugated territory" and to uplift "the African population"
of the Reconstruction South.[45] In the last chapter, the frustrated Servosse
finally moves *farther* south to find a "struggle suited [to] his adventurous
nature" and an "enterprise afford[ing] scope for his powers of projection and
organization":

He had been engaged by a company of capitalists to take charge of their interests in one of the republics of Central America. The work was of the most important character, not only to the parties having a pecuniary interest therein, but also as having a weighty bearing upon that strange contest between civilization and semi-barbarism which is constantly being waged in that wonderfully strange region, where Nature seems to have set her subtlest forces in battle-array against what, in these modern times, is denominated "progress." While the earth produces in an abundance unknown to other regions, the mind seems stricken with irresistible lassitude, and only the monitions of sense seem able to awaken the body from lethargic slumber. (348)

Tourgée's paragraph reads as a plain, if distilled, exportation of the modes developed to represent Reconstruction in both King's and Cable's local color writings. Following King's moral imperative for Reconstruction, Tourgée locates the "wonderful strangeness" of the underdeveloped Southern territory Servosse is managing—its exoticism, its "color"—in the formulaic combination of its unparalleled natural resources ("the earth produces in an abundance unknown to other regions"), with its degenerate and nonproductive local population ("the mind seems stricken with irresistible lassitude"). And echoing Cable's subordination of material dispossession to descriptions of cultural conflicts, Tourgée introduces and simultaneously dismisses in a subordinate clause the notion that to work for a Northern "company of capitalists" is to work in the *dis*-"comfort"ing service (Servosse) of "pecuniary interest"; instead, Tourgée highlights the cause of "civilization" against "semi-barbarism" as the true "character" of Servosse's management. Even in this short passage, Tourgée telegraphs that Servosse, like Cable's "little White," is no doctrinaire imperial functionary; instead, he possesses an admirable sense of the relativity of his position and a powerful empathy with the inhabitants he is forcibly civilizing. Tourgée styles him an administrator of "what, in these modern times, is denominated 'progress,'" who can mourn, even as he condemns and destroys, the colorful local "semi-barbarism" that his ironically soi-disant "progress" replaces.

A decade later, Tourgée remained convinced that the Reconstruction South was the key literary setting for a United States becoming ever more invested in the hemispheric expansion of its "interests." But his idea of the proper hero in this now-historical setting had changed diametrically. In the much-remarked 1888 essay, "The South as a Field for Fiction," Tourgée claimed that U.S. literature had "become not only southern in type, but distinctly Confederate in sympathy," and he proposed that this shift unexpected by most Northerners was actually a boon for national culture.[46] Although the hero of his novel had been the Northern agent of "progress," Tourgée now proposed that the hero of the Reconstruction saga was the dispossessed Southerner, white or black;

and rather than a chronicle of the travails of the civilizing process, he argued, the story of the conquest and reconstruction of its South should figure in U.S. fiction as the formative tragedy of national history. This tragic story could be told equally well from the vantage of either the ex-slaves or the ex-masters of the South, Tourgée postulated ecumenically. On the one hand, because "[t]o the American Negro the past is only darkness replete with unimaginable horrors," his life "as a slave, freeman, and racial outcast offers undoubtedly the richest mine of romantic material that has opened to the English-speaking novelist since the Wizard of the North discovered and depicted the common life of Scotland" (410).[47] On the other hand, because "[t]he level of Caucasian life at the South must hereafter be run from the benchline of the poor white, and there cannot be any leveling upward . . . the dominant class itself presents the accumulated pathos of a million abdications" around whom "will cluster the halo of romantic glory" (412).[48] Tourgée hypothesized that this focus on the Reconstruction South as the ground for national tragedy was becoming essential to U.S. culture not only because tragedy is the stuff of great literature ("The ills of fate, irreparable misfortune, untoward but unavoidable destiny: these are the things that make for enduring fame" [411]), but also, and more important, because a tragic past ennobles a nation: "The brave but unfortunate reap always the richest measure of immortality" (412). A U.S. national mythology that claimed its defeat and occupation of its South as its own would stake out a place for the nation in "the epoch of romance," canonizing its people as "glorified by disaster" (411).

Thus, twelve years after the official end of Reconstruction, Tourgée argued that the most valuable resource still to be extracted by the United States from its Southern states was not King's gold and coal, not Cable's local history and legend, but instead the distinctive Southern experience of being reconstructed by a perhaps unjustly powerful, but nonetheless intimately related, neighbor to the north. George Handley recently has proposed that "[t]he Union's attempt to integrate the New South after the Civil War fortified on an international scale the very plantation structures the North had decried, structures it had depended on for its economic growth," and Comfort Servosse's Central American idyll would seem to support the idea that the Reconstruction South served as a rehearsal or a training ground for the hemispheric expansion of U.S. power.[49] But with his language of mines, fields, discovery, development, and "the almost unparalleled richness of Southern life" (406), Tourgée exhorted his 1888 U.S. readers, poised on the threshold of pursuing hemispheric empire, instead to expropriate imaginatively *the defeat and occupation* of the former Confederate states as a tragic experience of their national life. "[A] vigorous people," Tourgée wrote, channeling the language of Anglo-Saxonist expansionism, "demand a vigorous literature" (411). Placing the humiliated Reconstruction South at the center of that literature would enable the nation's southward projection of coercion and force—precisely by allowing U.S. readers to feel themselves the empathetic, self-critical, and righteous founding victims of their own nation's power.

NOTES

1. On Holland's ambitions for the new magazine and his proposal to Scribner, see Harry Houston Peckham, *Josiah Gilbert Holland in Relation to His Times* (Philadelphia: University of Pennsylvania Press, 1940), 168–189.

2. Mrs. H. M. Plunkett, *Josiah Gilbert Holland* (New York: Charles Scribner's Sons, 1897), 77–84; Peckham, *Holland*, 174.

3. Stanley, who emigrated from Wales at around age sixteen, claimed to have fought with both Confederate and Union armies. Some of his Civil War reminiscences recently have been republished as *Sir Henry Morton Stanley, Confederate*, ed. Nathaniel Cheairs Hughes, Jr. (Baton Rouge: Louisiana State University Press, 2000).

4. For the vocabulary used to characterize the Livingstone venture, see Stanley's "Introductory" in *How I Found Livingstone: Travels, Adventures and Discoveries in Central Africa . . . [etc.]* (New York: Scribner, Armstrong & Co., 1872), xv–xxiii. Subsequent page references will be cited parenthetically in the text. *In Darkest Africa* (1891) is a later title from Stanley. Stanley's African correspondence for the *Herald* throughout the 1870s can be seen as creating an audience for Bennett's European edition, forerunner of the *International Herald Tribune*. See Charles Robertson, *The International Herald Tribune: The First Hundred Years* (New York: Columbia University Press, 1987), 14–16.

5. Edward King, "An Expedition with Stanley," *Scribner's Monthly* 5:2 (Dec. 1872): 105.

6. Josiah Gilbert Holland, "Topics of the Time: 'The Great South' Series of Papers," *Scribner's Monthly* 9 (1874): 248. Subsequent page references will be cited parenthetically in the text.

7. Edward King, *The Great South: A Record of Journeys in Louisiana, Texas, the Indian Territory . . . [etc.]*, illus. J. Wells Champney. (Hartford: American Publishing Company, 1875), 493. Subsequent page references will be cited parenthetically in the text.

8. Edward King, *The Southern States of North America: A Record of Journeys . . . [etc.]* (London: Blackie & Son, 1875), n.p.

9. Plunkett, *Holland*, 27.

10. Fletcher M. Green's bibliography of travel accounts of the states undergoing Reconstruction published between 1865 and 1880 lists 245 titles; see Green's "The South in Reconstruction" in *Travels in the New South: A Bibliography*, ed. Thomas D. Clark (Norman: University of Oklahoma Press, 1962), 11–125.

11. Jed. Hotchkiss, "New Ways in the Old Dominion," *Scribner's Monthly* 5:2 (Dec. 1872): 137–160; 5:3 (Jan. 1873): 273–294. The illustrations for this article, as well as some of Hotchkiss's descriptions, were eventually incorporated into the book versions of *The Great South*.

12. Charles Eliot Norton, "Reviews and Literary Notices," *Atlantic Monthly* (February 1861): 253.

13. King, "Expedition"; "How Stanley Found Livingstone," *Scribner's Monthly* 5:3 (Jan. 1873): 298–315. Stanley had done King the favor of mentioning him in the preface to *How I Found Livingstone* as "young Edward King, who is making such a name in New England" (xix).

14. King, "Expedition," 106–109.

15. Engraver J. Wells Champney presented the original series title as words that had been

half-submerged, then pulled dripping from the Gulf; this imagery implies that only half of *The Great South* to be examined by the series lies above the Gulf of Mexico; in *Scribner's Monthly* 7 (Nov. 1873): 1.

16. Amy Kaplan, *The Anarchy of Empire in the Making of U.S. Culture* (Cambridge, Mass.: Harvard University Press, 2002), 58.

17. Mary Louise Pratt usefully relates the discourse produced by British Victorian travel writers in Africa, commonly referred to under the rubric of the "Civilizing Mission," to that produced by in the same years by Britons in South America, whom she terms the "capitalist vanguard" for neocolonial relations between the empire and the newly independent American states (*Imperial Eyes: Travel Writing and Transculturation* [New York and London: Routledge, 1993], 144–155). Both discourses Pratt cites, as well as the imaginative geographical links between Africa and South America she uncovers, are important for my reading of King.

18. Jon Smith and Deborah Cohn, "Introduction: Uncanny Hybridities" in *Look Away! The U.S. South in New World Studies*, ed. Smith and Cohn (Durham: Duke University Press, 2004), 2.

19. W. Magruder Drake and Robert R. Jones provide an excellent overview of twentieth-century literary-historical interpretation of the significance of the series; see their "Editor's Introduction" to *The Great South* (Baton Rouge: Louisiana State University Press, 1972), xxxiii–xxxv.

20. Biographers and critics of Cable have continued to use the language of King's "discovery" of the author—language very much invested in the "expedition" enterprise of *The Great South*. Both King and Cable commented in the 1890s on the widespread usage of the "discovery" language to describe their relationship in the 1870s; see Lucy L. Cable Biklé, *George W. Cable: His Life and Letters* (New York and London: C. Scribner's Sons, 1928), 43–45.

21. This quote is taken from Cable's "Drop Shot," *New Orleans Picayune* (25 Feb. 1872), quoted in Louis B. Rubin, *George Washington Cable: The Life and Times of a Southern Heretic* (New York: Pegasus, 1969), 35.

22. The relationship between postbellum "local color" writing of the South and of the Far West is worthy of further study, because both bodies of writing triangulate into fantasies of hemispheric or Pacific expansion for the United States. Amy Kaplan's reading of the "imperialist routes" of Twain's regional fiction draws generative connections between these cultural fields (*Anarchy*, 51–91).

23. Richard H. Brodhead eloquently has provided the classic account of the significance of the genre often termed "local color" as "the principal place of literary access in America in the postbellum decades"; he also posed, over a decade ago, the question I am asking here: "what gave this of all genres such appeal at this time?" (*Cultures of Letters: Scenes of Reading and Writing in Nineteenth-Century America* [Chicago: University of Chicago Press, 1993], 116–117).

24. The classic and still-cited account of *The Great South* as a tool of reconciliation is Paul S. Buck, *The Road to Reunion, 1865–1900* (Boston: Little, Brown, and Co., 1938), 130–132.

25. William Webster Ellsworth, *A Golden Age of Authors: A Publisher's Recollection* (Boston: Houghton Mifflin Co., 1919), 50–51.

26. The last lines Holland wrote in *Scribner's Monthly* in regard to the series read: "[I]f there are any fault-finders [in the region represented], they must remember the difficulties of the task, in the immense area attempted to be covered, and the wide

variety of reports and opinions to be culled, often with the impossibility of verification" (249).

27. Although it arises from their evaluation of present conditions, compare Hardt and Negri's recent call for attention to "precisely the *production of locality*, that is, the social machines that create and recreate the identities and differences that are understood as the local," and their interrogation of the notion that "we can (re)establish local identities that are in some sense *outside* and protected against the global flows of capital and Empire" (Michael Hardt and Antonio Negri, *Empire* (Cambridge, Mass.: Harvard University Press, 2000), 44–46.

28. Judith Fetterley, "'Not in the Least American': Nineteenth-Century Literary Regionalism as Un-American Literature," in *Nineteenth-Century American Women Writers: A Critical Reader*, ed. Karen L. Kilcup (Oxford: Blackwell, 1998), 27; Eric J. Sundquist, "Realism and Regionalism" in *The Columbia Literary History of the United States*, Emory Elliott, Gen. Ed. (New York: Columbia University Press, 1988), 501.

29. Kaplan, "Nation, Region, and Empire," in *The Columbia History of the American Novel*, ed. Emory Elliott et al. (New York: Columbia University Press, 1991), 252–253; Brodhead, 121–133; Hsuan L. Hsu, "Literature and Regional Production," *American Literary History* 17:1 (2005): 62.

30. Anon., "The Contributors' Club," *Atlantic Monthly* 42 (1878): 244.

31. Barbara Ladd cites another interesting early definition of "local color," from Cable's later *Century* editor Robert Underwood Johnson, as "a historical tendency"—which is very much related to the process I am describing here of creating an explanatory narrative for underdevelopment (*Nationalism and the Color Line in George W. Cable, Mark Twain, and William Faulkner* [Baton Rouge: Louisiana State University Press, 1996], 43).

32. See Matthew Jacobson's *Whiteness of a Different Color: European Immigrants and the Alchemy of Race* (Cambridge, Mass.: Harvard University Press, 1998), 43–68, for the distinction between the categories "Anglo-Saxon" and "Caucasian" in the 1870s—a distinction King carefully maintains throughout *The Great South*, never assigning white "natives" the designator "Anglo-Saxon," while using that term as the default race for (non-Southern) "Americans."

33. G. W. Cable, "Jean-Ah Pouquelin." *Scribner's Monthly* 10 (1875): 91. Subsequent page references will be cited parenthetically in the text.

34. Arlin Turner, *George W. Cable, a Biography* (Durham: Duke University Press, 1956), 93–95; and Ladd, *Nationalism*, xv.

35. I take the term "tropical America" from D. W. Meinig, who proposes that American hemispheric geography in the colonial era be understood according to climatic and economic function factors that would group together the southern seaboard North American states, the Caribbean islands, and Central and South America as far south as the northern coast of Brazil. See Meinig, *The Shaping of America: A Geographical Perspective on 500 Years of History. Vol. 1: Atlantic America, 1492–1800* (New Haven: Yale University Press, 1986).

36. G. W. Cable, "'Sieur George." *Scribner's Monthly* 6 (1873): 745.

37. With this locution, I mean to reference Benedict Anderson's thoughts in *Imagined Communities: Reflections on the Origin and Spread of Nationalism* (London and New York: Verso, 1991) about the "reassurance of fratricide" in nineteenth-century nationalism, which, he claims, following Ernest Renan, requires citizens of a nation simultaneously to remember and to "already have had to forget" past conflicts between peoples who have been subsumed under the national aegis (199–203).

38. Charles W. Coleman, Jr., "The Recent Movement in Southern Literature," *Harper's New Monthly Magazine* 74 (1887): 840. The fallen-Eden motif is a commonplace in 1870s writings about the Reconstruction South; for instance, the much-quoted first lines of *The Great South* read, "Louisiana today is Paradise Lost. In twenty years it may be Paradise Regained" (17).

39. Hearn, "The Scenes of Cable's Romances," *Century Illustrated Monthly Magazine* 5 (1883): 40.

40. Gavin Jones argues that "dialect writing was, in part, a confirmation of cultural hegemony" because it served as a deviation against which a homogenized "American English" could be asserted, at a time when the English language was for many U.S. cultural commentators an indicator of the Anglo-Saxon racialist "quality of national culture" (*Strange Talk: The Politics of Dialect Literature in Gilded Age America* [Berkeley: University of California Press, 1999], 9–10).

41. G. W. Cable, "Belles Demoiselles Plantation," *Scribner's Monthly* 7 (1873): 739–740.

42. G. W. Cable, "'Tite Poulette." *Scribner's Monthly* 8 (1874): 674, 684, 675. On the postbellum debates about what "Creole" signified racially, Ladd usefully notes: "[T]he white southerner's insistence that 'Creoles' are 'white'—and only 'creoles' (lowercase) are mixed—is intended to protect the southerner from being aligned too closely with former slaves or with colonialism in the New World" (xv). It is precisely this subsumption of "white southerner" under the aegis of "Creole," that, I am proposing, made Cable's stories so apt for formulating a popular version of the Reconstruction South that allowed for projections of U.S. hemispheric expansion.

43. G. W. Cable, "Posson Jone'," *Old Creole Days* (New York: Heritage Press, 1943), 45–46; "Café des Exiles," *Scribner's Monthly* 11 (1875): 735. "Posson Jone' " is the only one of the stories collected in *Old Creole Days* (1879) that was not published in *Scribner's Monthly*; it appeared in *Appleton's*.

44. Sandhya Shukla and Heidi Tinsman, "Editors' Introduction: Our Americas: Political and Cultural Imaginings," *Radical History Review* 89 (Spring 2004): 5. A subsequent reference will be cited parenthetically in the text.

45. [Albion W. Tourgée], *A Fool's Errand. By One of the Fools* (New York: Fords, Howard, & Hulbert, 1879), 154, 117. Subsequent references will be cited parenthetically in the text.

46. Albion W. Tourgée, "The South as a Field for Fiction," *Forum* 6 (1888): 405. Subsequent references will be cited parenthetically in the text. "As evidence" for this claim, Tourgée noted that "a few months ago every one of our great popular monthlies presented a 'Southern story' as one of its most prominent features; and during the past year nearly two-thirds of the stories and sketches furnished to newspapers by various syndicates have been of this character" (407).

47. Given that Tourgée was, following his years of work in the Reconstruction government of North Carolina as a judge and Republican party official, one of the foremost Northern authorities on the Ku Klux Klan, his choice of moniker for Sir Walter Scott in this particular context indicates, I hope, his recognition of the gap between the experiences of black and white Southerners that he seemingly registers ("the past is only darkness replete with imaginable horrors" versus "the accumulated pathos of a million abdications") even as he elides it.

48. It is important to acknowledge how greatly all of the representations of Reconstruction considered in this essay differ from later novelistic treatments, in that the existence of a class of white Southern elites is either elided or denied outright, and *all*

Southerners, white and black, are presented as properly the subjects of U.S. administration. Compare the overtly Southern-partisan, white-supremacist turn-of-the-century novels of Thomas Nelson Page and Thomas Dixon—which usefully have been read in the context of nascent turn-of-the-century U.S. imperialism by Walter Benn Michaels (*Our America: Nativism, Modernism, and Pluralism* [Durham: Duke University Press, 1995] and Scott Romine ("Things Falling Apart: The Postcolonial Condition of *Red Rock* and *The Leopard's Spots*," in *Look Away! The U.S. South in New World Studies*, ed. Cohn and Smith, 175–200)—that instead focus their energies on presenting the legitimacy of "home rule" by precisely such a class.

49. George B. Handley, *Family Portraits in Black and White: Postslavery Literatures of the Americas* (Charlottesville: University of Virginia Press, 2000), 20.

7

The Mercurial Space of "Central" America

New Orleans, Honduras, and the Writing of the Banana Republic

KIRSTEN SILVA GRUESZ

The poet-provocateur Guillermo Gómez-Peña offers this "turn-of-the-century geography lesson" in "The Last Migration: A Spanglish Opera":

> dear reader/ dear audience
> repeat with me out loud:
> México es California . . .
> Puerto Rico es New York
> Centroamérica es Los Angeles
> Honduras es New Orleans . . .[1]

This equation of New Orleans with Honduras, placed as it is in the midst of more prominent U.S. sites undergoing "Latinization," may have escaped notice at the moment when "The Last Migration" was first published in 1996. But in the wake of Hurricane Katrina and the much-remarked transformation of traditional ethonoracial communities along the U.S. Gulf Coast with the influx of Spanish-speaking migrant workers, it may seem positively prophetic—indeed doubly prophetic, since the few media commentators who have recognized that there was a Latino population in greater New Orleans before Katrina date its presence to 1998, when the devastation of another hurricane, Mitch, sent tens of thousands of displaced Hondurans to the city. Gómez-Peña's poem predates even this migration milestone, reminding us that the post-Mitch diaspora that made New Orleans home to the second-largest urban concentration of Hondurans in the world could only have taken place because of already existing circuits of migration and cultural exchange dating back nearly a century. The Latinization of the U.S. Gulf Coast does indeed disrupt more traditional spatializations of the Anglo-Latino border zone that cling to the path of the Rio Grande, but the *temporal* coordinates of that border require some rethinking as well.

Exactly fifty years before the "The Last Migration" was published, the Honduran writer Guillermo Bustillo Reina included a poem titled "Viaje a Nueva Orleans" (Voyage to New Orleans) in his collection of nostalgic national "romances." The poem begins by comparing the speaker's travels to those of Hernando de Soto, whose celebrated expedition up the Mississippi had preceded him by some four hundred years. Ironically mimicking de Soto's "explorations," he and his companions traipse from one French Quarter barroom to the next, then boldly venture by streetcar to City Park (where they learn to "conjugate the verb *amar*" with the local women), before they turn around again to head home. The poem concludes with this stanza:

El viejo Misisipí,	Old man Mississippi,
centenario y paternal,	centenarian and fatherly,
nos torna al Golfo de México,	directs us toward the Gulf of Mexico,
deseándonos Bon Voyage.	wishing us Bon Voyage.
En la cubierta del barco	On the deck of the boat
nos ponemos a ruminar	we set to ruminating on
los indelebles recuerdos	the indelible memories
de la alegre Nueva Orleans	of gay New Orleans
que es una prolongación	which is an extension
de nuestro nativo lar,	of our native home,
con una mitad latina	with one half Latin
y sajona otra mitad,	and the other half Saxon,
cóctel de razas rotundas	a cocktail of sonorous races
en lírico bacarat.	in a lyrical crystal glass.[2]

Co-opting the trope of embodied geographical expansion so central to the discourse of Manifest Destiny, this thoroughly modern explorer reclaims New Orleans as his *own* territory to explore, as an "extension" of "our" native home (the term he uses, *lar*, is an archaic Latin adaptation that suggests the hearth to which the epic hero returns). *Prolongación*, which I have rendered as "extension," contains the same temporal as well as spatial resonance it has in English, so this phrase also reverses the temporal priority that has governed Anglo-American apprehensions of Central America at least since the primitivist fixations of nineteenth-century Mayanists like John Lloyd Stephens and Ephraim Squier: that is, the idea that Central America nations are even later arrivals than the rest of Latin America to the table of modernity. From Stephens and Squier to the 1971 Woody Allen film *Bananas* and the computer-simulation game "Tropico," they have been characterized with reference to the atavistic political formation of the "banana republic" and the neocolonial economic formation of the touristic "retreat into paradise."[3] At the same time, however, Bustillo's poem ends by representing New Orleans as a harbinger of a potential *future*, adapting one of the city's own favorite symbols of pleasurable excess, the cocktail glass. With "one half Latin and the other half Saxon," New Orleans mixes a "cocktail of sonorous races" like two kinds of liquor; and the adjective describing this Baccarat crystal glass, "lírico," carries the sense of "utopian" and "fantastical," as well as "poetic."

As a Honduran born in the imperial year of 1898, who came to adulthood during the general wave of political leftism and anti-imperialism that peaked during Sandino's revolution in Nicaragua and the Faribundo Martí movement in El Salvador, Bustillo was very aware of the unusually close political and economic ties that bound his country to Louisiana. His personal history there augurs for a reading of this poem as a deliberate mockery of the very touristic clichés it seems to spout: during his youth, Bustillo had founded an expatriate cultural journal, *Revista Continente*, in New Orleans with the tragic and gifted Arturo Martínez Galindo. Some of Martinez Galindo's short stories, collected in a slender posthumous volume called *Sombra*, are set in the alien spaces of New Orleans and Washington, D.C. One begins on a steamship of the Great White Fleet (*La Flota Blanca*) on the Gulf of Mexico en route to New Orleans, where (says the narrator) "almost all the passengers were originally from those beloved lands that extend, so blue, so blue, from the Rio Grande to the Panama Canal. It was in the good old days, when the steamers weren't completely overwhelmed with flocks of Yankee tourists."[4] Although Bustillo's poem does not state this explicitly, it is almost certain that his meditation on deck, his "goodbye" to Old Man Mississippi and the ghost of de Soto, also takes place on a fruit steamer, with passengers above, and bananas (along with, perhaps, a few laborers) below. Thus both Bustillo's and Martinez Galindo's work—and, I will argue here, a whole set of English-language texts that reference the link between New Orleans and Central America—demands to be read with reference to a single commodity, the banana, and the intricate web of economic and social relations that it created.

Inspired by Sidney Mintz's classic work on sugar, John Soluri's recent study *Banana Cultures* attempts to trace the historical processes by which an organic object, a plant, becomes an export commodity whose circulation profoundly shapes geopolitics—focusing precisely on the way that twentieth-century cultures in Honduras and the United States evolved in tandem. The banana, he writes, is an exemplary case of "the dynamic relationship between mass production and mass consumption": when bananas became popular as a Midwestern breakfast food during the early twentieth century, the pressure to innovate new agricultural technologies and newly intensified economies of production increased, resulting in the vertically integrated, monopolistic plantation model of companies like United Fruit Company (UFC) and Standard Fruit in their heyday. As with sugar, the banana's ascendance into commodity status also generated new migration patterns among black laborers, and is thus associated with racialization processes as well.[5] The tropical fruit industry, justly vilified for its role in maintaining neocolonial conditions along much of the Central and South American coast for much of the century, is associated with an extreme form of negative critique in Latin American cultural production: the venerable "banana novel" subgenre that begins with the Costa Rican Carlos Luis Fallas's 1941 novel, *Mamita Yunai*, moves through the Honduran Ramón Amaya Amador's *La prisión verde* and Nobel laureate Miguel Angel Asturias' "banana trilogy" in the 1950s, and culminates with its most famous avatar, *Cien años de soledad* and its climactic massacre in the banana-growing town of Macondo. These works share a Marxist-influenced vision of the *frutero* as a kind of corporate octopus (the UFC's nickname was *el pulpo*), and the U.S. government as a cynical imperial power supporting the company's stranglehold on the transportation, communications, and (at least by implication) electoral and military infrastructures in many smaller nations.[6]

That form of critique seems virtually absent in U.S. literary treatments which, according to Stephen Benz's seminal article on the "tropicalizing" logic of Anglo-American representations of Central America, tend to describe the spaces where the fruit industry took hold as dreamy, timeless "Lotus-lands" that enchant hapless Northerners, who are unmindful of their real dangers. Benz indicts O. Henry's 1904 *Cabbages and Kings*, in which the term "banana republic" first appears, for adding a specific regional trope of comic ineptitude and political corruption to these standard symbols of the tropics.[7] The two literary modes of identifying the banana trade as the crucial mediator between the United States and Central America, then, could not appear more diametrically opposed in modality—tragic versus comic—or in their corresponding political intentions. Taking my inspiration from Bustillo's identification of New Orleans as the imaginative "pivot" on which he swings his reversal of traditional hemispheric hierarchies of modern/primitive, I want to challenge that apparent opposition. During the half-century of its dominion as the banana's main port of entry to, and dissemination within, the United States, New Orleans itself registered and made canny use of this vision of the city as a transit point between the "Latin" and "Saxon" worlds in order to further economic development agendas that frequently turned on increased trade with Latin America. I will revisit this representational and actual economy with particular reference to an important but largely forgotten Spanish-language literary and cultural review, *El Mercurio*, published between 1911 and 1927 in the same building as, and partially funded by advertisements from, the New Orleans Progressive Union, the forerunner of the Chamber of Commerce. Although it carried advertisements for the fruit companies and their subsidiaries like the Great White Fleet, *El Mercurio* also published some of the most visionary anti-imperialist Spanish-language writers of the period. A reading of *El Mercurio* insists on a more complex modality for representations of the banana—one rooted in the particular identity of New Orleans as a city that attracted exiles, tourists, and entrepreneurs from Central America.

King Cotton Is Dead, Long Live Señor Banana

Once the undisputed center of Southern commerce, the "Queen of the South," the port of New Orleans suffered tremendous reversals after the Civil War. One of the themes of the World's Industrial and Cotton Centennial Exposition, which ran from December 1884 through May 1885, was that New Orleans could restore its former glory by becoming the "central point" for future trade with Latin America: its most popular exhibit by far was the Mexican Pavilion, where legions of Northern visitors heard mariachi music for the first time. Ironically, as the exposition began, cotton was already a leveled-off sector, and shipping oranges and grain to and from the Midwest was the only area of trade growth; Eugene Smalley's two-part account of the Cotton Exposition for *The Century Magazine* closes with a cartoon of two sign painters crossing out the slogan "Cotton Is King" and lettering the decidedly less poetic "Corn Is King" above it.[8] Smalley finds New Orleans generally dismal and devastated, and its exposition a mere shadow of the Centennial Exposition in Philadelphia eight years earlier (though built, he admits, with a fraction of the capital). Yet he also associates the Cotton Exposition with the future project of Southern redemption, a redemption to be found in

> the rise of a new national idea,—namely, that there are vast and inviting fields to the south of us waiting to be conquered for our industries and our commerce. This idea . . . has taken strong hold of the manufacturers of the North. They have sent their fabrics and machinery to New Orleans because it is the natural mart of all the regions bordering upon the Gulf of Mexico, in which they hope to find a new outlet for their goods, and because they expect to meet here the people of those regions.[9]

As Robert Rydell writes, the Cotton Exposition, like later world's fairs in Atlanta, Tennessee, South Carolina, and Virginia, touted a progressive vision of the "New" South to belie Northern accusations about the region's persistent racial oppression (accusations that were themselves couched in racialized terms about "degenerate" Southern whites).[10] Smalley's discussion of the potential for expanding U.S. trade with Latin America through connections made at the Exposition must, then, be framed within his general assumption that the Southern populace was morally vitiated, and so lacking in "national feeling" that the raising of the Stars and Stripes in the opening ceremonies provoked more hisses than cheers. What is needed, he surmises, is a shot of "fresh Northern blood and capital to the business circles of the Crescent City. . . . New blood is needed, because the old stock becomes lethargic."[11] But if "new blood"—understood as an analogy for both persons and capital—were to come from the North, it must have freer, more extensive places to circulate, which meant looking south of the South. Smalley saves his only unreserved praise for the Mexican Pavilion, where he observes—in contrast to the decay and morbid nostalgia of New Orleans—"the new life that is stirring in Mexico since the building of railways from the United States, and of the ambition of the educated element to put their country in line with the forward march of civilization." He adds in the sequel, "One marvels that a people who can produce all these things should make so small a figure in the sum-total of the world's civilizing forces."[12] The discourse of world's fairs always circulated around visions of the "city of the future," but New Orleans can only enter this future, this "forward march of civilization," by drawing from the examples that lie to the north *and to the south* of it. New Orleans can earn its way back into the affective national compact, then, by helping to consolidate U.S. economic dominance over the hemisphere.

Some New Orleanians seized upon Smalley's identification of the Mexican Pavilion as the great success of their exposition, the novelty for which it would be remembered. A local consortium of investors purchased most of the exposition grounds, and redesigned and reopened it as the "North, Central, and South American Exposition, Promotive of the Commercial and Industrial Unity of the Three Americas" from November 1885 through April 1886. A notice of the projected Three Americas Exposition (as it came to be known) also published in *The Century* claimed that it "has for its object the solution of the industrial problem of the United States," that is to say, the problem of surplus products and the need for new markets. "Up to the present moment the South has been the market for this oversupply," writes the author, but with that market near saturation, "There is but one direction in which the necessary relief from this inevitable over-supply can be found, and that is in the countries of Central and South America," an export market now controlled by Europe. "The deflection of this Central and South American trade from Europe to the United States is the highest international problem with which our country has at present to deal; and nothing will tend to solve it sooner than the [new] Exposition at New Orleans, where a hemispherical commercial policy can be inaugurated."[13]

In contrast to the instrumentality of this argument to Northerners about the value of the Three Americas Exposition, the organizers adopted a loftier rhetoric of familial relation during the fair itself. In his opening speech the exposition's president, S.B. M'Connico, addressed the Latin American and Caribbean trade representatives with this remarkably Whitmanian injunction: "If we desire closer and more intimate reciprocal relations with the countries you represent, your interests lie as strongly in the same direction . . . we recognize and rejoice in the kinship of our nations, and greet them as Americans should greet Americans." His deliberate use of "American" as a marker for the whole hemisphere anticipates the rhetorical revival of Bolivarism in the Pan-American Congresses that were to come later in the decade. But the common "interest" between New Orleanian and Latin American fairgoers, the grounds of their "intimacy" as fellow Americans, is described within a more specifically *regional* imaginary of the Gulf of Mexico as well. January 22, 1886, was named

"American Mediterranean Day," celebrating that "great central Sea" that, in this new partnership of "the commercial union of the Three Americas will so revolutionize the commerce of the world that the prestige of the American will soon rival if not eclipse that of the European-Mediterranean."[14]

Most importantly, the Exposition of the Three Americas further disseminated a visual and verbal set of representations of New Orleans as the center, both literal and figurative, of the modern geopolitical order, as is evident in the cover of the official exposition program (see Figure 1). The program boasts, "There is no point in the Western Hemisphere so suitable and appropriate . . . as the city of New Orleans. It is not only a geographical center, but . . . [as] the deepest and safest harbour on the continent and covering the ports of Mexico, Central and South America and the West Indies, it becomes the commercial center, the meeting or exchange point, where the inhabitants of the three Americas can most conveniently gather. The cosmopolitan characteristics and large admixture of the Latin race in the Crescent City make it specially

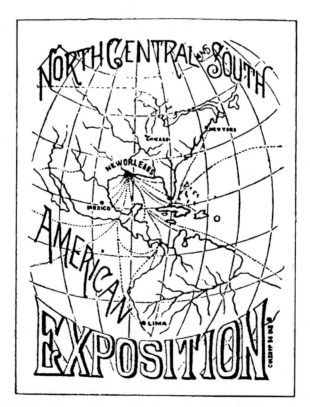

FIGURE 1. Cover of "The North, Central and South American Exposition, Promotive of the Commercial and Industrial Unity of the Three Americas: Statement, Prospectus, and Description." New Orleans, 1885. Courtesy University of Texas Library.

attractive to the inhabitants of Spanish America."[15] Trade relations are built upon the hybridization of culture, and location itself becomes a commodity—both a site for exchange and the embodied *principle* of exchange.

Northern periodicals largely ignored the Three Americas Exposition, perhaps because they assumed that the Latin American and Caribbean exhibits were the same as they had been for the Cotton Exposition, even though the fair's organizers tried to emphasize their new tactic of attracting Latin American *buyers* for U.S. products rather than simply showcasing the import wares and resources of those exotic locales. However, it did not go unnoticed by that patriarch of Latino letters, José Martí, who plugged the fair to his readers in Buenos Aires and elsewhere in the circulation zone of *La Verdad*. A *crónica* titled "La Próxima Exposición de New Orleans" in 1885 praises the plan to reshape the Cotton Exposition grounds into a specifically hemispheric place of mutual exchange, and strongly urges Latin American producers, landowners and policy-makers to attend. Suggestively, the piece includes a cautionary note that too *much* travel in the United States can be dangerous, alluding to the potential to become disoriented by the sheer size of the country, the bewildering diversity of the *yanquis* and their "hostile, insuperable" language, and to inadvertently sell pieces of their land instead of its produce. The Exposition of the Three Americas, Martí proposes, offers the perfect solution: travelers can go just as far as the familiar city of New Orleans to see assembled the best U.S. products and technologies. New Orleans, he writes, "summons us with tenderness and there is no risk in coming, only benefit." He then gives a New Orleans address to which one can send for a brochure in Spanish.[16]

Martí's fears about Latin Americans being swindled or seduced into selling their territory were, of course, based in fact. Would-be concessionaires for various railroad and canal projects had been acquiring land in Central America for decades. And while the tropical fruit companies would eventually consolidate their power through their stranglehold on the transportation and communications infrastructures in these nations, in the early days (as Soluri points out) the banana trade was characterized by its diversity, with dozens of small native producers testing their entrepreneurial skills.[17] Likewise, before the advent of refrigerated shipping, when importers had to be fast and agile in order to get the crop to market before it spoiled, there were dozens of competing importers as well, spread out from Galveston to Charleston. Nonetheless, the port of New Orleans completely dominated the import of bananas to the United States by 1905, and the story of the city's second flowering as an economic power before World War II is powerfully bound up with that of the industry.[18] Two rival import concerns begun by Sicilian immigrants, Salvador d'Antoni and the three Vaccaro Brothers, joined forces when d'Antoni married a Vaccaro daughter, and their company eventually grew into Standard Fruit, which remained a family-owned New Orleans business until its 1964 buyout by Castle & Cook (now Dole). The Vaccaro-Antoni's chief competition came from another immigrant, Samuel Zemurray, who started the Cuyamel Fruit Company. Both companies had major landholdings on the north coast of Honduras; the Vaccaros sold half their land in 1906 to Minor Keith's United Fruit Company. United Fruit, though based in Boston (like the "banana king" in Dorothy West's 1948 *The Living Is Easy*), kept a secondary branch office in New Orleans to handle their southern fleet and finally merged with Cuyamel Fruit in 1929. Zemurray himself took over the new powerhouse, eventually to be reorganized as Chiquita Brands. Zemurray would retire to Honduras after a few notorious stunts that involved refitting his retired fruit steamers as gunboats in support of three different military coups.[19] Keeping in mind this powerful set of associations between New Orleans and the specific political-economic formation described as a "banana republic," let us now turn to how representations of that formation describe the city during the decades of its emergence from Reconstruction-era abjection into a self-proclaimed modernity.

Cabbages and Critics: The Literary Invention of the Banana Republic

The strong identification between the *fruteros* and New Orleans is rarely ever remarked upon in the thin body of criticism that exists on O. Henry's *Cabbages and Kings*, the collection of interlinked stories that played such a seminal role in the formation of representations of the "banana republic" that it described for the first time. When, in July of 1896, William Sidney Porter made the questionable decision to flee indictment in Houston after an accounting discrepancy at the bank where he worked became public, he fled to New Orleans and found there both his pen name and his passage to asylum. Though he had originally planned to go to Mexico, Porter caught a fruit steamer underway to Honduras, where he settled in the small North Coast port of Trujillo (rendered as "Anchuria" and "Coralio" in the book) for most of a year before returning to face trial. *Cabbages and Kings*, a novel told in loosely connected chapters, was published in 1904, after his release from prison, and made his reputation.[20] Even after moving to New York, the setting of most of his better-known stories, he continued to fictionalize both New Orleans and Central America. These works portray New Orleans not as the site of quaint Creole customs and dialect, à la George Washington Cable or Grace King, but as the anchor of the Northland that it represents for the characters of his Anchuria/Honduras. In other words, he adopts the view from South, as inflected by the banana trade.

New Orleans and New York are the major offstage sites for *Cabbages and Kings*, the shadowy seats of power where governmental and capitalistic interests cynically collude to foment mock revolutions. But it also represents the most proximate site of culture to the residents of Anchuria. The cast of characters in *Cabbages and Kings*, which ranges across a broad spectrum of social classes, includes a few North American émigrés like the U.S. consul Willard Geddie who ultimately choose to stay there, requiring—according to the laws of comic romance—an alliance with "native" women. Geddie, fresh from a heartbreaking rejection by a New York society girl, falls for the half-Irish, half-Indian Paula Brannigan, with her "tinge of Indian brown," who "had attended a convent school in New Orleans for two years; and when she chose to display her accomplishments no one could detect any difference between her and the girls of Norfolk and Manhattan."[21] Likewise, the expatriate Frank Goodwin eventually marries the Anchurian president's former paramour, the New Orleans-born Isabel Guilbert, who has a "mingled French and Spanish creole nature that tinctured her life with such turbulence and warmth" (6). While New Orleans has often signaled racial indeterminacy of a suspect sort in U.S. literature, as the home of tragic mulatoes and mulatas from Stowe's Cassy to Faulkner's Charles Bon, here a New Orleans upbringing or education seems to perform a *positive* kind of whitening function for mixed-race characters.

Just the opposite occurs on the docks of New Orleans, where the constant traffic between the States and Anchuria threatens to level distinctions of race and national origin among the working people, outcasts and con men who gather there. New Orleans is the transit point for itinerants of all nationalities, always on the alert for opportunities, hitching rides on "tramp" steamers like the *Karlesfin* that are unaffiliated with any particular nation or company. In the chapter titled "The Shamrock and the Palm," for instance, an Irishman named Clancy is standing on the levee looking at the ships on the Mississippi one morning when he is approached by a "brown man" (165) calling himself General De Vega, who recruits Clancy for a "filibusterin'" expedition in Guatemala (168). But rather than finding military glory and the promised rewards, Clancy has to work along with other New Orleanians—"Dagoes, nigger-men, Spanish-men and Swedes" (173)—on a railroad in the tropical interior. He escapes on a banana boat, where he runs into the same general, now "black-faced and ragged" (180) and hungrily stuffing bananas into his mouth. When they reach New Orleans again, Clancy cannily returns the dirty trick on the general by turning him in to O'Hara the cop as an escaped fugitive, and the general's limited English does not permit protest. The story ends with Clancy taunting "the little man filibusterin' with a rake and shovel" as he sets to scrubbing down Ursulines Street with a prison labor gang, "and he'd look at me black" (187–188). Like Twain's King and Duke tarred and feathered by the mob in *Huckleberry Finn*, Porter's "general" gets a taste of his own con, and in a way that affiliates him with an abject racial darkening. Here the New Orleans waterfront stands for both a total lack of law and order (with its subterranean economy, shady get-rich-quick schemes, and smuggling) and for the *restoration* of the Right (ironically identified with a Irish cop, who is not so fully assimilated into "Americanness" that he fails to come to the aid of his countryman). Ironically, this inversion of the usual migrant-labor exploitation fable is distantly linked to the new hemispheric strategy begun at the Cotton Exposition: over a thousand U.S. workers were recruited there to work on a railroad on the north coast of Guatemala, subjected to harsh conditions and then dissuaded by force from leaving; David McCreery suggests that Porter heard stories of this affair both in New Orleans and in Honduras.[22]

This seriocomic turn on "filibustering" as the occasion for small-scale deception mirrors the behind-the-scenes machinations occurring on a larger scale in Anchuria, as the Vesuvius Fruit Company prepares to replace an unfriendly regime with one of its own choosing. Porter alludes throughout to the Italian roots of Standard Fruit's immigrant owners: the Vesuvius Fruit Company's local representative is "Mr. Franzoni," and another player is "Mr. Vincenti"; the name "Vesuvius" itself suggests the old country. Porter writes, "It was rumoured that the revolution was aided by the Vesuvius Fruit Company, the power that forever stood with chiding smile and uplifted finger to keep Anchuria in its class of good children. Two of its steamers, the *Traveler* and the *Salvador*, were known to have conveyed insurgent troops from point to point along the coast" (145). At points like this, the tone of the narrative seems to slide out of arch satire and into something more like muckraking journalism, the profession Porter had tried before accounting. The dark humor—but also the site of potential readerly outrage—occurs in *Cabbages and Kings* when its characters confuse the language of markets with that of politics. "Reasonably," says a corrupt consul, "an established concern like the Vesuvius would become irritated at having *a small, retail republic* with no rating at all attempt to squeeze it. So, when the government proxies applied for a subsidy [to build the railroad the VFC demands] they encountered a polite refusal" (279, emphasis mine). Although Frank Goodwin espouses his commonsensical feeling that "a business firm does not go to war with a nation," after the successful coup, the company agent Vincenti disabuses him of this naïve notion: "Oh, it is only a matter of business . . . and that is what moves the world of to-day. That extra *real* on the price of bananas had to go. We took the shortest way of removing it" (292), that is, by removing the government that made the tax—a curious sort of efficiency. Although he is prepared to see Anchuria as a vestigial, primitive kind of paradise, Geddie finds the country in the grip of a particular *modernity* associated with "the world of to-day," in which markets drive politics rather than the other way around.

If we ceased to identify *Cabbages and Kings* with its most generative phrase— "banana republic"—and substituted instead Vincenti's characterization here, "a small retail republic," what new comparisons and analogues would come into view?[23] Porter's depiction of the Vesuvius Fruit Company as an example of monopoly capitalism that is benignly tolerated by "republican" forms of government echoes the far better-known representations of unchecked corporate power that are central to the work of Frank Norris, Sinclair Lewis, and the younger Jack London, but Porter—characterized as a minor satirist—falls far outside the canon of American Naturalism, and *Cabbages and Kings* goes in and out of print.[24] Like *The Octopus* or *The Iron Heel*, the book bluntly sizes up the relative power of capital and labor, as well as the general ineffectualness of "reformist" proposals. But its offshore setting and Porter's depiction of the Trust as a *global* rather than a national problem suggest that the better point of comparison might be with the anti-imperialist writings of Twain, with his caustic comments on "the Blessings-of-Civilization Trust" and on international diplomacy as a crassly motivated "game" in "To the Person Sitting in Darkness" (*viz.* Porter's "the game still goes on" [8]).

Cabbages and Kings does not engage with social realism by any of the usual definitions, but its attention to economics is obsessive. The situation in Anchuria implicates all of us, New Orleanians and New Yorkers, in something new and distinctly modern: the transnational political-economic formation of the "small retail republic." The book may be seen as struggling to find a generic mode adequate to its representation. Is it "mock seriousness," the mode Porter attributes to the self-made Anchurian admiral, or tragicomedy? Or is it pure burlesque—a "show" put on to distract the mark while the con is being worked? The final chapter, "The Vitagraphoscope," rejects the comic ending of a vaudeville romance ("Therefore let us have no lifting of the curtain upon a tableau of the united lovers" [307]) in favor of the fragmented gaze offered by the "vitagraphoscope," or "moving pictures." Only these fleeting, filmic glimpses of the fate of the novel's principal characters, Porter seems to be suggesting, are appropriate to describe what has happened in Anchuria. Rather than initiating a representational apparatus of Central America as a timeless or primitive "Lotus-Land," then, *Cabbages and Kings* uses Anchuria to suggest to U.S. readers how they, too, are linked with it in a new world order.

Mercurial Time: Writing New Orleans in Spanish

If *Cabbages and Kings* reiterates, but also problematizes, the Exposition-fueled vision of New Orleans as the center of the hemisphere, so too does the ambitious publishing project that took shape as *El Mercurio* beginning in 1911. A sixty-page monthly review featuring original color covers, photographic news dispatches from Europe and the Americas, and as much original literary and cultural material as it could solicit, *El Mercurio* lasted for sixteen years: one of the longest runs of any U.S.-based Spanish-language review up to the present moment. Despite the fact that it published some of the most important Modernist writers from Spain and Latin America, its presence has gone virtually unremarked by literary historians in that field, much less in Latino studies. Yet the magazine's editors clearly saw themselves as part of the modern internationalization of culture so sacred to its interwar moment, and appear to have chosen New Orleans for its strategic location between northern and southern, western and eastern hemispheres (its cover price was listed in Mexican pesos and Spanish pesetas, as well as U.S. dollars). While it does not make a point of translating English-language texts, or U.S. culture in general, for that global

Hispanophone audience, *El Mercurio* does recognize its placement within local and national Spanish-speaking communities: the opening issue's editorial statement remarks, "To the whole of the Spanish-language press, *but especially that of the United States*, Mercurio sends its warm greetings as it appears on the flowering field of Latino journalism."[25] While the magazine aspired to high-cultural seriousness, foregrounding poetry, book reviews, and the visual arts (the editors made much of their page decorations, original fonts, and original Art Nouveau illustrations on their color covers), the advertisements in its front and back matter reflect a promotional agenda of a very different origin. *El Mercurio* established its offices in the building owned by, and contained advertisements from, the New Orleans Progressive Union, a forerunner of the Chamber of Commerce.

Mercurio carried on the "progressive" post-Reconstruction work of representing the hemispheric centrality of New Orleans visually, as these ads for the Merchants' and Manufacturers' Bureau and for a local exporter suggest (see Figures 2 and 3). Some of the texts that the review published also reiterate the earlier discourses of the city's proximity to the "Latin" world in the same language of familiarity that we saw in Martí's chronicle on the Three Americas Exposition. One early piece blurring the distinction between article and advertisement rhapsodizes,

> the geographical location of New Orleans has made it the logical Latin market of the North . . . the Latin traveler [*viajero latino*] will also find many attractions in New Orleans. It is of the United States and of the tropical countries at the same time. Without the architectural grandiosity that envelops the tops of buildings in fog, New Orleans offers the picturesque spectacle of a cosmopolitan city, that leads one *without any brusque transition* from the tropics to the frozen regions [*regiones heladas*] of America. Its broad streets, its parks and gardens, appear like a breath of air. You could say of them that they have Saxon size and Latin color.[26]

Note here how the instrumental language of the Exposition and the Progressive Union ("the logical Latin market") gives way, in this passage, to the assertion of simultaneity ("of the United States and of the tropical countries at the same time") and continuity of vision: the traveler arrives from the south "without any brusque transition" to a place with "Latin color." Given the magazine's insistence on harmonizing cutting-edge literary content with modern artwork, this dwelling on New Orleans as a site of a particularly Latin way of seeing is very suggestive. A back-cover ad for their engraver shows books and pictures, rather than boats and trade goods, spilling out from New Orleans toward the rest of the hemisphere—emblematizing the very work of cultural dissemination that *El Mercurio* claimed to be doing (see Figure 4).

FIGURE 2. "New Orleans, Axis of the Western Hemisphere." *El Mercurio*, no. 29 (March 1914), xxii. The strings that the allegorical female figure appears to be pulling represent shipping lines. Courtesy California State Library.

FIGURE 3. Advertisement for Louis Goldstein & Sons Co., New Orleans. *El Mercurio*, no. 39 (Jan. 1915), iv. New Orleans is figured as the mouth, not just of the Mississippi, but of Uncle Sam in general. Courtesy California State Library.

While its involvement with the Progressive Union and its promotional work—ads for the Great White Fleet and the Standard Fruit Steamship Line appear as well—might lead us to think that *Mercurio* would be unwilling to print anything politically sensitive, that was in fact not the case. The Salvadoran-born Máximo Soto Hall, whose short novel *El problema* is justly considered the first anti-imperialist fiction in Latin America, was a frequent contributor to the first two volumes of *El Mercurio* while he lived there, in his early forties, at the peak of his fame as a poet and diplomat. In his dozen or more contributions dated from New Orleans, Soto Hall penned everything from a fluff piece on the history of the Napoleon House bar, to an investigation on the state of tropical medicine, to a poem on the sinking of the Titanic. The Peruvian José Santos Chocano, whose *Alma América* inspired Rubén Darío's turn toward anti-imperialist writing, first published a number of his poems here—including one titled "Pasajera" (In Passing or Passenger), written and dated aboard a United

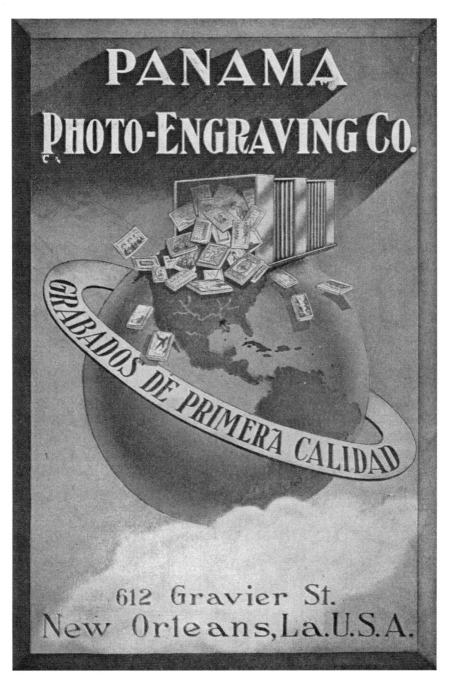

FIGURE 4. Advertisement for Panama Photo-Engraving Co. *El Mercurio*, no. 39 (Jan. 1915), back cover. Courtesy California State Library.

Fruit boat in the Gulf of Mexico. Moreover, extant copies of *El Mercurio* contain some very suggestive depictions of Latino life in the city that merit recovery and republication, including one short story that helps mediate between those apparently opposed traditions of the socially conscious *novela bananera* in the Latin American tradition and the U.S. representational tradition beginning with *Cabbages and Kings* whose relationship to the comic mode I have been trying to complicate.

Published under the pseudonym of "Lapis Lázuli," this story is titled "El regenerador de Centro-América: Historia cómico-trágica para llorar cinco minutos" (The Regenerator of Central America: A Tragicomic Story to Cry about for Five Minutes). It opens with a scene of storytelling in New Orleans.[27] One night at the foot of St. Louis Street, the narrator bumps into an old acquaintance of his named Eladio Pérez. Pérez recalls how, on just such a night a few years ago, he had met a wealthy Central American, Sagastumes, who had decided to spend his considerable fortune bringing modernity and progress to his unnamed native land. Eladio, who is perfectly fluent in English and in Spanish, becomes the man's private secretary, as he plans an electoral campaign and seeks the aid of the State Department. He receives a cabled directive to go to Washington to see the Secretary of State, and when they arrive, a functionary addresses Sagastumes as "General." The candidate responds, "I'm not a general, but I could be if it was necessary." The staffer responds, "What? a Central American presidential candidate who's not a general yet?" But the State Department pretends to know nothing about the appointment, and after a week of waiting, Sagastumes and Pérez go back to New Orleans disappointed. They are contacted by the mysterious Central American Revolutionary Trust Company, which starts to dictate to Sagastumes how these things are done. Send us $100,000, they instruct him, to get an appointment with the Secretary of State; then write another check of the same size to buy arms. Sagastumes starts to go gray. They request another $100,000 check to outfit the gunboat for the insurrection. Sagastumes begins to waste away. "How many people do you have ready to undertake this revolution?" they ask, to which our good reformer responds, "Just me and my secretary—but we're counting on the will of the people." Not good enough: another $100,000 for mercenaries. Sagastumes and Pérez head for San Diego, where they are to meet the ship, the *Conqueror*, disguised as "cow-boys" (hair bleached, clean-shaven, looking like "a son of Roosevelt," as Pérez says).

When they finally arrive on the Central American coast, Sagastumes and Pérez place the national flag on the beach, read their liberatory proclamation to the townspeople, and start to unpack the crates of munitions to outfit their would-be followers. But instead of guns they find "sardines, salmon, whiskey, crackers, catsup, oysters, shrimp, pickles, etc., etc., but arms—not even painted ones!" [¡ni pintadas!]. The Yankee captain of their ship, having grown fond of Eladio Pérez, saves him from the local police by claiming that the two "revolutionaries" are just mental cases; he takes Pérez back to New Orleans, making him peel potatoes to cover his fare. Sagastumes is not so fortunate: he is shot by a firing squad. As Pérez reaches the end of his story, the narrator sees that his friend is crying, and gently ventures that he must have come to love his employer. "I'm crying because they executed six months of my unpaid salary along with him," Pérez sobs, leaving the reader with a final laugh—though a dark one. The naïve Sagastumes, who falls from would-be democratic reformer to "General—if you need me to be," is an easy mark for the con artists of the Revolutionary Trust Company, who presumably also brought home the profits from those crates of oysters and whiskey. But the secretary of state's refusal to see Sagastumes, although his functionaries clearly know who he is, strongly suggests that the "Trust" had help from on high in stacking the deck against him. One can only conjecture whether "Lapis Lazuli" had read the famous book about Anchuria by "O. Henry," although the subtitle of the story—"A tragicomic history to cry about for five minutes"—seems in tune with the modality of *Cabbages and Kings*. The unnamed country in "The Regenerator of Central America" may or may not be Honduras, which had just undergone two turbulent years of regime change under Zemurray's direction involving a U.S. Marine force—events that would of course have been widely covered in other New Orleans newspapers, if only alluded to in this cultural review. What's interesting about Eladio Pérez as a character is that he is not identified with any homeland. Sagastumes approaches him in New Orleans because he is a fellow Spanish speaker who can translate English for him: an Americanized Latino. As with "Anchuria," the unnamed country is meant to be fungible, a small retail republic in a wholesale geopolitical order.

While *El Mercurio* was not exclusively affiliated with Honduras, the next Spanish-language magazine to appear in New Orleans after its demise was. In an interesting, though short-lived, joint publishing experiment, the monthly magazine *Lucero Latino* was edited in Tegucigalpa but published in New Orleans from 1933 to 1934. The pages of *Lucero Latino* offer a window into the thriving relationship between Central American elites and New Orleanian businesses: its advertisers included not only the Great White Fleet and its rival, the "Standard Fruit & Steamship Co., Vaccaro Line," but U.S. export products from furniture and facial whitening creams to Listerine and Kellogg's All-Bran. Four pages at the front of each issue were devoted to boarding-school ads, promising "especial atención a alumnos de países Hispano-Americanos." A personal shopper advertised to women readers that she would send the season's latest fashions from New Orleans, and traffic discreetly in such things as undergarments. This cultivation of two-way traffic between New Orleans and Central America peaked under the mayoral administration of deLesseps "Chep" Morrison from 1946 to 1961, when Morrison made regular junkets to the city's favored trading partners, effectively conducting diplomacy from a municipal level.[28]

"Your Mama's Got Change Coming':
Accordion Crimes and Hurricane Katrina

As the century wore on, the Honduran elite and professional classes continued to visit New Orleans frequently to purchase consumer goods, to send their children to school, or to imagine and enact forms of political organization not possible in the constricted air of home. The original *barrio lempira* in the Lower Garden District, where Honduran restaurants and dance halls served as community centers, dates from the 1930s, when *Lucero Latino* flourished. The fruit companies ceased their passenger service in the 1950s, a time of moderately successful strikes against both United and Standard Fruit across Central America. Honduras became the source of a major stream of migrant labor after 1963, when a U.S.-backed military coup unseated the moderate government of Ramón Villeda Morales; and again after 1998, when Hurricane Mitch devastated the northern Honduran coast.[29] The post-Mitch diaspora, in particular, included a higher concentration than ever before of *garífunas* of African origin (there are now nearly as many Garífunas living in the United States as in Honduras; Los Angeles, New York and New Orleans are the primary sites in which they congregate). Why, then, have representations of New Orleans in the wake of Katrina so insistently labeled the influx of Mexican and Central American migrant laborers as "sudden" and "new"?

To get at an answer we might turn to the related suppression of national memory around New Orleans as a port of entry for immigrants in general[30]—a role that is, as we recall, taken for granted in *Cabbages and Kings* but that is absent in more recent fictions of migration, with one significant exception: Annie Proulx's 1996 *Accordion Crimes*, which provides my final example. This fictional micro-history of immigration in the twentieth century begins just before it, on the docks of New Orleans. Accompanied by his young son and his newest creation, a beautiful green button accordion, a Sicilian accordion-maker gets off the boat with dreams of saving to buy a music store. A paisano promises: "The fruit boat gives work at once! . . . You get off the ship, walk down the dock and get a job in two minutes carrying boxes of oranges! The man hiring you speaks Sicilian, he understands you!"[31] The accordion-maker is soon crushed by the weight of the banana poles on his back, and finds himself in debt to the Sicilian boss, a man named Archivi who is known as "Signor Banana." Proulx writes of the boss: "Archivi is bananas and fruits from Latin America . . . Archivi is deals and ingenuity, and that hard work that makes a fortune, a fortune that grows and swells . . . he owns ships, warehouses, thousands work for him, he moves in the high circles of New Orleans society . . . he shook the hand of John D. Rockefeller" (31). (Salvador d'Antoni, on whom this character was likely modeled, was able to hold out against competitors because he had the foresight to buy all the ice companies in New Orleans.) Rather than emulating Archivi's providential path to success, the accordion-maker has the bad luck to walk right into the midst of one of the worst anti-immigrant riots in U.S. history, which resulted in the lynching of ten Sicilians thought to have conspired to kill the city's chief of police in 1891.[32] After the accordion-maker meets his violent end, the book follows the fate of his green button accordion as it is bought, bartered, and stolen by musicians who over the years play on it the sounds of various ethnic cultural traditions. In its hundred-year history, though the accordion changes hands many times, nothing changes fundamentally in the everyday struggles of its owners; it is as if time folds back in on itself, accordion-style, in a relentless repetition of the same patterns of impoverishment, racialization, and segregation.

But before this initial chapter ends, readers also follow, uncomfortably, the story of a middle-class striver named Pinse as he decides to join the vigilante mob and to do something about the "greasy dago Archivi." Pinse, out of work, projects his frustration onto the newest waves of immigrants: "All out of a depraved greed for the banana trade, the banana trade! . . . ridiculous . . . a festering foreign corruption was rotting Louisiana's heart" (43). When Pinse, trembling at his own power, staggers triumphantly from the scene of the hanging, a colleague who had previously doubted Pinse's worth offers him a business opportunity: "We are setting up a new company to handle the trade . . . we think of calling it Hemisphere Fruit" (49). Proulx's allusion to the internal struggles of the fruit industry—its efforts to take over production in Central America while driving out competition in the United States—ironizes the whole discourse of hemispheric centrality that New Orleanian trade boosters, as well as pan-Latinists like the editors of El Mercurio, had vigorously promoted. (It might serve as a sobering check, as well, on the current revival of this language of hemispherism.) The character of Pinse suggests that anti-immigrant sentiment, this fear of "festering foreign corruption," draws from the same well as neocolonial economic opportunism, and that both find an outlet in violence. His dismissal of the banana itself as "ridiculous" echoes the nativist representation of Central American politics by way of a comic modality that, as I have been arguing here, Porter's novel itself problematizes. Proulx's choice of the accordion—the musical equivalent of the banana—as the vehicle for her fictional history of the making of the modern United States likewise insists on preserving a place for satirical outrage even (or especially) when linked to an object that has come to signify low comedy.

Accordion Crimes resembles Cabbages and Kings in other suggestive regards as well: both are shaped as episodic narratives that compound many stories into novelistic format, and both capitalize on the surprise ending. In the final section, titled "Your mama's got change coming," the accordion comes nearly full circle, back to rural Mississippi in the present day. Broken down and discarded as worthless, it falls out of a junk dealer's truck and gets smashed on the road. None of its owners, in all those years, had discovered its secret: a Mexican conjunto player in Texas in the 1940s had secreted several thousand-dollar bills between its boards. When the accordion is flattened, three dirt-poor African-American boys find one of the bills flapping along the roadside and realize, with excitement, that they can now buy sodas: it's a hot day. The woman who runs the corner store takes the thousand-dollar bill, tremblingly hands them the sodas, and asks them to relay a message to their teenaged mother: "Tell her come to the store. She got change comin'" (380). With perfect comic timing, this line comes as close as the novel will allow to articulating a tiny sliver of hope about the generational cycle of poverty, and it hinges on the double meaning of "change." Is there *really* change comin'? the reader must ask. And if so, how long, O Lord, how long? The novel reminds us here that African-Americans have historically been excluded from the celebratory memorialization of Americanization-as-assimilation; their presence resists insertion into such a teleology. The immigrant story and the African-American story are not often enough linked the way they are in this novel—both at the micro-narrative level (many of the new arrivals in the various chapters, for instance, find themselves living in historically black neighborhoods) and in the broader structural conception of the book, with its circular return to a setting very close to that of its opening.

It is highly suggestive that Proulx initiates her historical investigation of the "crimes" of anti-immigrant sentiment in New Orleans, not in some better-known port of entry. Archivi's very name recalls the archives that she, in Howard Zinn-like fashion, has mined for violent moments that have been selectively repressed in the national memory in the interest of maintaining a cohesive myth of immigrant assimilation. Proulx may or may not have read Martí's *other* major *crónica* (a genre of essayistic reportage) about New Orleans, one written in response to the 1891 Sicilian lynchings she describes in the first chapter. Martí's text begins memorably, "And from today forth, no one with the least bit of piety will set foot in New Orleans without horror." The city that, in the piece on the Exposition of the Three Americas, had previously seemed to Martí a "safe," sororial space, now strikes him—as he imaginatively surveys its palm trees and Creole architecture, so reminiscent to him of Havana—as a scene of terrible betrayal.[33] If Martí did not ask the further question about whether such anti-immigrant violence shares some common sources with the anti-black violence he also noted soberly in his *crónicas*, Proulx picks it up a century later.

Now let's imagine a further chapter that Proulx did *not* write in 1996—one in which the Sicilian's green button accordion bobs above the detritus of the floodwaters unleashed by Hurricane Katrina, then comes to land, as the waters recede, under one of the rust-colored bathtub-rings that mark the surviving homes of the Lower Ninth Ward, of Lakeview and Chalmette, leveling the distinctions of race and class that the names of these neighborhoods formerly marked. Imagine that accordion being called to testify about the many Spanish-speaking victims of the flooding who were afraid to seek the various forms of relief for which they were entitled.[34] Imagine how the conversation following Mayor Ray Nagin's statement, during the first influx of Latino migrant laborers engaged in demolition and cleanup, that New Orleans "has been and must continue to be a chocolate city," might have been different if Gómez-Peña had stood in the background in one of his postmodern–folkloric costumes chanting, "Honduras es New Orleans." Surely the current impoverishment of ways to imagine this "new" Latino population in the thicket of existing mythic-historic constructions of New Orleans has something to do with the persistence of an outdated racial binarism, as well as the nation's general unwillingness to understand immigration as a function of geopolitical circumstances that are created *onshore* as well as off.

NOTES

1. Guillermo Gómez-Peña, *The New World Border* (San Francisco: City Lights, 1996), 211–212.

2. Guillermo Bustillo Reina, "Viaje a Nueva Orleans," in *Romances de la tierruca y otros poemas* (Tegucigalpa: Imprenta Calderón, 1950), 25–28. Several other poems in this collection are signed with a composition date and place of 1928–1929 in New Orleans. I have translated "bacarat" as a reference to the venerable brand name, but it resonates as well with the card game—gambling, liquor, and conspicuous consumption of luxury goods all being long linked to the touristic experience in New Orleans.

3. See especially Stephen Benz, "Through the Tropical Looking Glass: The Motif of Resistance in U.S. Literature on Central America," in *Tropicalizations: Transcultural Representations of Latinidad*, ed. Frances Aparicio and Susan Chávez-Silverman (Hanover: University Press of New England, 1997), 51–66; and, for the Latin Americanist perspective, see Ileana Rodriguez, *Transatlantic Topographies: Islands, Highlands, Jungles* (Minneapolis: University of Minnesota Press, 2004), chaps. 4–5. On the persistence of banana-republic stereotypes in "Tropico," see Shoshana Magnet, "Playing at Colonization: Interpreting Imaginary Landscapes in the Video Game Tropico," *Journal of Communication Inquiry* 30 (2006): 142–162. Thanks to Maritza Stanchich for bringing this game to my attention.

4. Arturo Martínez Galindo, "Aurelia San Martín," *Sombra* (Tegucigalpa: Imprenta Calderón, 1940), 57 (translation mine). Martínez Galindo's existentialist short stories have recently been the object of renewed critical attention, but like Bustillo, he was principally known as a journalist and political agitator during his short lifetime: he was likely murdered for political reasons at the age of forty. The steamship line of the "Great White Fleet" was a marketing moniker of United Fruit, playing on (but not to be confused with) the armed fleet sent on a triumphant tour of the Pacific under President Theodore Roosevelt.

5. John Soluri, *Banana Cultures: Agriculture, Consumption, and Environmental Change in Honduras in the United States* (Austin: University of Texas Press, 2005), 3. Soluri's work builds on a considerable number of recent micro-histories of the tropical fruit industry in Latin America such as Darío Euraque's *Reinterpreting the Banana Republic: Region and State in Honduras, 1870–1972* (University of North Carolina Press, 1996), and the essays collected in *Banana Wars: Power, Production and History in the Americas*, ed. Steve Striffler and Mark Moberg (Durham: Duke University Press, 2003).

6. On the flourishing of the "banana novel" in Latin America, roughly between 1930 and

1960, see Ana Patricia Rodriguez, *Dividing the Isthmus: Central American Transnational Literatures and Cultures* (University of Texas Press, 2007), chap. 1.

7. Virginia Jenkins, in *Bananas: An American History* (Washington, D.C.: Smithsonian, 2000), discusses the association between the banana and comedy, from the first appearance of jokes about slipping on banana peels in turn-of-the-century New York to the phallic overtones of vaudeville comedy (20–29).

8. See Joy J. Jackson, *New Orleans in the Gilded Age* (Baton Rouge: Louisiana State University Press, 1969), who notes that, having lost so much primacy in the regional economy to Atlanta, the Panic of 1873 "hit New Orleans harder than any other city" (209), so it retooled itself away from exports and toward greater imports in the growth areas of tropical fruit, sugar, and coffee; the storied Cotton Exchange was joined in the 1880s by the Produce Exchange and the South American and Mexican Exchange.

9. Eugene V. Smalley, "The New Orleans Exposition," *Century* 30:1 (May 1885): 3–14. On the geographical destiny implied by the term "natural mart," see my essay, "The Gulf of Mexico System and the 'Latinness' of New Orleans," *American Literary History* 18 (2006): 468–496.

10. Robert Rydell's classic *All the World's a Fair: Visions of Empire at American International Expositions, 1876–1916* (Chicago: University of Chicago Press, 1984), argues that these Southern expositions represented "not a nostalgic retreat into myth, but a powerful explanatory ideology that shaped the national and world outlook of untold numbers of Southerners and other Americans . . . [and] succeeded in reintroducing antebellum imperial dreams to millions of fairgoers" (104). See also Paul F. Stahls, *A Century of World's Fairs in Old New Orleans, 1884–1984* (Baton Rouge: Louisiana State University Press, 1984).

11. Smalley, "In and Out of the New Orleans Exposition: Second Paper," *Century* 30:2 (June 1885): 187.

12. Smalley, "The New Orleans Exposition," 11–12; and Smalley, "In and Out," 190.

13. Richard Nixon, "An Exposition of the Three Americas," *Century* 31:1 (November 1885): 153.

14. Press release from the fair's Commissioner of Special Days dated Dec. 9, 1885 (Historic New Orleans Collection, MS Box 215). The fair's opening day was designated American Peace Day as "a tribute to Peace as a preliminary step toward the inauguration of an American Hemispherical policy, based upon more intimate commercial, social, and political relations between the various nations of North and South America." *The North, Central and South American Exposition Gazette*, Nov. 1885, p. 1.

15. "The North, Central and South American Exposition, Promotive of the Commercial and Industrial Unity of the Three Americas: Statement, Prospectus, and Description," New Orleans, July 13, 1885, 42–43. Virtually the same language would later be reiterated by boosters seeking, unsuccessfully, to locate the 1915 Panama Pacific Exposition in New Orleans.

16. "La próxima exposición de New Orleans," *Obras Completas* (La Habana: Editorial Nacional de Cuba, 1963–1973), 6:369–370. New Orleanians "beckon us affectionately and there is no risk in coming, only good fortune" ("Nos llaman con cariño y no hay riesgo de venir, sino provecho") (371). Martí had previously written on the Cotton Exposition (November 1883; *Obras*, 8:364–365). His many writings on Central America, to which he had a strong biographical connection, include a piece on the new demand for bananas and its disturbing tendency toward monoculture ("Plátanos," June 1883; *Obras*, 7:187–189), and a strongly worded denunciation of Secretary of State

James G. Blaine's Latin American policy as directed toward "the peaceful and deci-sive occupation of Central America and the adjacent islands by the [United States]." ("América Central," February 1885).

17. See Soluri, *Banana Cultures*, 18–27, 77–80.

18. On New Orleans as "a kind of Latin foothold on the American shore" in this era, see Peirce Lewis, *New Orleans: The Making of an Urban Landscape* (Charlottesville: University of Virginia Press, 2003), 56–58; and the 2000 New Orleans Public Library exhibit curated by Wayne Everard: "New Orleans, Gateway to the Americas," available at http:nutrias.org/~nopl/exhibits/gateway/gateway.htm (accessed December 14, 2001).

19. See Lester Langley and Thomas Schoonover, *The Banana Men: American Mercenaries and Entrepreneurs in Central America, 1880–1930* (Lexington: University Press of Kentucky, 1995), 115–166.

20. According to Gerald Langford, in *Alias O. Henry* (New York: Macmillan, 1957), Porter wanted to settle in Honduras and wrote his wife, Athol, asking that she join him there (103–105). He returned to the United States in January 1897 (again via New Orleans) only upon receiving word that she was gravely ill. Athol died shortly afterward as he faced criminal prosecution, was found guilty and sentenced; he served time in the Ohio State Prison from May 1898 to July 1901. Several of the chapters of *Cabbages and Kings* were previously published in magazines, leading critics to disagree about whether to characterize it as a novel or a sequence of stories with thin glue holding them together; see Paul S. Clarkson, "A Decomposition of *Cabbages and Kings*," *American Literature* 7 (1935): 195–202. The major contemporary study is Eugene Current-Garcia, *O. Henry: A Study of the Short Fiction* (New York: Twayne, 1993).

21. O. Henry (William Sydney Porter), *Cabbages and Kings* (Garden City, N.Y.: Doubleday, 1915), 33–34. Subsequent page references given in the text. Although the Vesuvius Fruit Company's money seems to come from New York, its agents all come from New Orleans. Vincenti bets "ten dollars to a dinner at the Saint Charles [Hotel]" on a card game (290). The hundred thousand dollars embezzled by the departing president of Anchuria is ultimately recovered—minus a big chunk claimed by the New Orleans lawyers.

22. David McCreery, "Imitating Life: O. Henry's *The Shamrock and the Palm*," *Mississippi Quarterly* 34 (1981): 113–121.

23. The term "banana republic" actually appears only once in the book, in connection to the Anchurian war minister's plan, proposed with "delightful mock seriousness," to create a navy.

24. Current-Garcia notes of the eight post-*Cabbages* stories set in Latin America that they are characterized by "wish fulfillment and romantic escape" (48–49), but says nothing about their considerable element of political commentary. Brady Harrison, in chapter 4 of *Agent of Empire: William Walker and the Imperial Self in American Literature* (University of Georgia Press, 2004), argues for *Cabbages and Kings* as a satire of the "imperial self," using Quentin Anderson's formulation and suggestively linking both Porter and his characters to post-1898 imperial masculinity as epitomized by Richard Harding Davis. The key text here is "A Ruler of Men" (1906), another satire of filibustering.

25. "Página personal del editor," *El Mercurio* 1:1 (Sept. 1911): 2, translation and emphasis mine.

26. M. B. Trevezant, "New Orleans and Panama: La gran vía del tráfico," *El Mercurio* 1:2 (Oct. 1911): 32–33, translation and emphasis mine.

27. *El Mercurio* 2:2 (March 1912): 13–14. Who was Lapis Lázuli? Given the traditional asso-ciation of editorial work with the blue pencil [*lápiz*], we might suspect one of the editors.

28. It is suggestive that *El Mercurio* ceased publication at the very time when the intense competition between Cuyamel and United Fruit provoked federal intervention over predatory competitive practices, which resulted in their merger. On the continua-tion of New Orleanian efforts to cultivate the Latin American trade in the 1940s and 1950s through such vehicles as the building of the International Trade Mart, see Arthur E. Carpenter, "Gateway to the Americas: New Orleans' Quest for Latin Ameri-can Trade, 1900–1970" (dissertation, Tulane University, 1987). On "Chep" Morrison's self-identification as a "spiritual Latin," see his *Latin American Mission: An Adventure in Hemispheric Diplomacy* (New York: Simon and Schuster, 1965), 6. Barbara Epstein, in *Sustaining New Orleans: Literature, Local Memory, and the Fate of a City* (New York: Routledge, 2006), discusses the "Latin Roots" movement in city politics in the late 1970s with reference to the city's "vampiric" trading on its own history during the popularity of Anne Rice's novels (167–171).

29. Samantha Euraque, "'Honduran Memories': Identity, Race, Place and Memory in New Orleans, Louisiana" (B.A. thesis, Louisiana State University, 2004), documents the Honduran diaspora through oral histories and neighborhood studies. In every census since 1960, Honduras has been either the first or second nation contributing to the foreign-born population of New Orleans (Katherine Donato and Shirin Hakimzadeh, "The Changing Face of the Gulf Coast: Immigration to Louisiana, Mississippi, and Alabama," *Migration Information Source*, January 2006). Although the 2000 census recorded only about 50,000 Hispanics in Orleans Parish, the Honduran Consulate has estimated that there were between 125,000 and 150,000 Hondurans in Greater New Orleans prior to the hurricane (Eduardo Castillo, "Latin America Searches for Word of Missing in Aftermath of Hurricane Katrina," *San Diego Union-Tribune* [AP], Sept. 3, 2005).

30. See Joseph Logsdon, "Immigration through the Port of New Orleans," and the response by Randall Miller, 105–124 and 127–137 in *Forgotten Doors: The Other Ports of Entry to the U.S.*, ed. M. Mark Stolarik (Philadelphia: Balch Institute Press, 1988). Through the nineteenth century, writes Logsdon, New Orleans was either the first or second most common port of entry for Latin American and Spanish immigrants, and continues to be the major one for Nicaraguans, Hondurans, Guatemalans, and Belizeans.

31. E. Annie Proulx, *Accordion Crimes* (New York: Scribner, 1996), 23. Subsequent refer-ences given in the text.

32. During this episode nineteen Italians, some of them recent immigrants who did not speak English and some assimilated citizens, were tried for conspiracy to kill the city's chief of police, Hennessey. When a jury failed to convict based on the extremely thin evidence, a group of vigilantes met in Congo Square, stormed the jail, and murdered ten of the suspects, displaying their distorted bodies in the streets and hoisting the vigilante leader, a lawyer and newspaperman named Wyckliffe, on their shoulders to loud hurrahs. See Jerre Mangione and Ben Morreale, *La Storia: Five Centuries of the Italian American Experience* (New York: HarperCollins, 1992), 200–213, for the ensuing diplomatic standoff with Italy. Randall Miller comments on the twentieth-century usage of "Dagoes" to mean the "'mixed-blood' fruiters and fisherman in Orleans, Jefferson and Plaquemines Parishes," who were considered effectively "Negro" (136).

33. Martí, *Obra* 12:494; my translation.

34. See Brenda Muñiz, "In the Eye of the Storm: How the Government and Private Response to Hurricane Katrina Failed Latinos," report by National Council of La Raza, 2006. On the Nagin controversy, see James Varney, "Nuevo Orleans?" *Times-Picayune*, October 18, 2005. On the demographic shifts that have occurred since the hurricane, see Donato and Hakimzadeh, "Changing Face"; and Elizabeth Fussell, "Latino Immigrants in Post-Katrina New Orleans," paper presented to the Regional Seminar on Labor Rights, Oct. 19–22, 2006.

8

"I'm the Everybody Who's Nobody"

Genealogies of the New World Slave in Paul Robeson's Performances of the 1930s

MICHELLE A. STEPHENS

> The Negro has not become a master. When there are no longer slaves, there are no longer masters.
>
> —Frantz Fanon, *Black Skin, White Masks*[1]

In 1939, after traveling for a number of years throughout Europe and Africa, the African American actor and singer Paul Robeson returned home with his family to Harlem. Almost immediately he was asked to perform the song "Ballad for Americans" in a radio broadcast that aired later that year. In his biography of Robeson, Martin Duberman describes the broadcast as "an instant sensation," bringing Robeson a level of acclaim that mirrored his earlier rise as a concert singer of the spirituals.[2] In the 1920s, however, both black and white American audiences understood Robeson to be conveying in the spirituals the racial music of the black slave. The audience's reception of the radio performance was markedly different because now the black singer seemed able to represent the entire national community, the very embodiment of the country's cherished political ideals.

By the mid-1940s, Paul Robeson's status as a national cultural hero would be tainted by his avowed socialism and support for the Soviet regime. However, in debates concerning Robeson's "Americanism" and the extent of his patriotism in relationship to his commitments to internationalist ideology, few discuss the specifically *hemispheric* dimensions of his popularity for black audiences during the first third of the twentieth century. In his signature first novel published in England in 1953, for example, the Anglophone Caribbean author George Lamming describes a Robeson performance as the very vehicle that enables two characters, the young island boys Trumper and the narrator G., to a deeper apprehension of race as a source of identity alongside other possible utopian and imagined notions of community.[3] In the words of Lamming's Caribbean character Trumper, Robeson reminded the black man that, unlike the "Englishman, an' the Frenchman, an' the . . . man of America," black identity "ain't have nothin' to do with where you born."[4]

In a recent interview Lamming described Robeson's continued importance in the Caribbean throughout the 1940s as a figure of black male identity that transcended country and nation.[5] His popularity in the islands was unchanged even as he was understood in more negative terms as a subversive in the United States. If one traces the various paths taken by this African American performer throughout the 1920s and 1930s, one finds alongside the typical debate between nationalism and internationalism, which shapes the writing of radical histories in the United States during this period, evidence of an alternative form of race radicalism that also questioned the specifically *national* dimensions of liberatory politics. In the Lamming novel, freedom and the "rights o' the *Negro*" are detached from the sense that one's political identity is grounded in nationality, or nativity. The specifically hemispheric dimensions of black identity bring into focus instead the intimate and contested relationship between discourses of race and nation, *as* discourses of political freedom, from the very onset and creation of the Atlantic New World.

This essay explores the competing political genealogies Robeson represented as an embodiment of the New World slave throughout the 1930s, one whose various performances—whether in song, in the press, onstage, or onscreen—resonated both nationally for white and black American audiences and hemispherically in the surrounding black communities throughout the diaspora. His performance of the "Ballad for Americans" came at the end of a decades-long struggle in which the singer tried to understand the various meanings his blackness evoked in both national and transatlantic spaces. As we explore Robeson's own efforts to gain control of the meaning of his performances, we discover the contradictory understandings of freedom he generated among the two racial audiences he addressed throughout much of his career: whites across transatlantic and imperial spaces and blacks across diasporic and colonial worlds.

Our understanding of the historical influence of this cultural figure for many different "American" communities needs to move beyond the accounts of his later reputation as a socialist. We need to travel backward to the 1920s and 1930s, the formative decades in Robeson's development of a narrative of race that would later guide his internationalist class politics. In addition, Robeson's multiple geographies of influence—the meanings generated from his performances as they traveled nationally, hemispherically, and globally— reveal the role of the figure of the New World slave in popular and political discourses of freedom during this period.

Transatlantic Discourses and the Figure of the New World Slave

Despite the elision of the Haitian Revolution in continental political theory, the protagonist whom we most immediately associate with the struggle for freedom in modernity is the American slave.[6] Feminist scholars in African diaspora studies have argued that the masculinism of much black and colonial nationalist discourse depends on the elision of slavery through its projection onto the body of the female slave.[7] But the slave on the plantation, a figure for the oppressed, colonized, and conquered, is not the same figure as the fugitive slave imagined in flight from the plantation, and a notion of the slave's quest toward a future freedom involves a slightly different, and more universalizing, rhetoric than the language of struggles for national independence. In his auto-biographical writings Paul Robeson linked his own fate to that of the fugitive slave, defending his right to travel after the denial of a U.S. passport in the 1950s by proclaiming: "From the very beginning of Negro history in our land, Negroes have asserted their right to freedom of movement. Tens of thousands of Negro slaves, like my own father, [ran away, some] to foreign countries not to secure their own freedom but to gain liberation for their kinsmen in chains."[8]

The discourse of freedom projected in the racialized voice of the black slave uncannily mirrors certain aspects of the revolutionary political discourse of the slaves' masters. As Michel Foucault argues, in Europe alongside the reframing of monarchical sovereignty in revolutionary republicanism, a form of anti-sovereign political discourse also emerged that drew from a racial language. Modernity represents precisely the moment when political struggle, the defense of the rights of both the individual and the nation-state, were evoked not in the name of *the* people but in the name of *a* people, a special, chosen people in world history. During the revolutionary era, in the hands of those newly in power, the struggle against sovereignty became one of protecting this chosen race from conquest, tyranny, oppression, and slavery.[9] Foucault's argument helps us to broaden our understanding of discourses of racial and cultural nationalism in the Americas. While this mode of understanding history through a racial lens lay submerged in European discourses of sovereignty, it gained much more ground in the New World as a way of recounting various struggles for freedom against the colonial empires.[10]

We find forms of this mode of history telling in the revolutionary languages of liberty developed by colonial elites in the Americas—the vernaculars of "creole pioneer" nationalisms Benedict Anderson describes as originating in Latin America and the United States and traveling back across the Atlantic to the metropoles. Simultaneously we find this discourse of freedom in the alternative ideological formation taking shape under the broader rubric of anti-slavery radicalism.[11] Both of these modes of historical speech, borrowing from metropolitan discourses of race and liberation, have had a purchase within black diasporic narrative traditions as a way of recounting the linked histories of African-descended New World subjects. They appear in the form of the "revolutionary romance," whose "fairly recognizable structure," David Scott notes, "typically begins with a dark age of oppression and domination . . . followed by the emergence of the great struggle against that oppression and domination, and the gradual building of that struggle as it goes through ups and downs, temporary breakthroughs and setbacks, but moving steadily and assuredly toward the final overcoming, the final emancipation."[12]

Classic anti-colonial texts such as C. L. R. James's *The Black Jacobins* and Frantz Fanon's *The Wretched of the Earth* rely on this narrative structure to tell a history of the race that legitimates black revolutionary action.[13] For both Afro-Caribbean and African American writers, the slave's flight from the plantation provides a key narrative scenario for this parallel discourse of racial freedom, a source for ideologies of black struggle and statehood in the twentieth century. So, for example, in his Appendix to the 1962 reprinting of *The Black Jacobins*, C. L. R. James states, "Wherever the sugar plantation and slavery existed, they imposed a pattern. . . . an original pattern, not European, not African, not a part of the American main."[14] For James, this uniquely West Indian pattern linked the Haitian and Cuban revolutions across their respective centuries. Later, James would add the figure of the North American fugitive slave to his narrative account of historical, black, revolutionary action in the New World, arguing that the runaway slave served as a fundamental catalyst in U.S. political history.[15] James's Caribbean and American discourses reflect, respectively, the symbolic importance of the figure of the slave in intersecting diasporic and national histories.[16]

Later in his life Paul Robeson would recall how his father's tales of slavery "haunted his memory and infused his singing of the slave spirituals with a special knowledge and poignancy."[17] However, when Robeson evoked the oratorical legacy he inherited as the proud "son of an ex-slave," not even he was aware of the full extent of contradictory historical meanings such a figure already represented in the New World imaginary. As the primary performative space for his early portrayal of and construction as the New World slave, the spirituals would become the site for his restaging of broader legacies of oppression and discourses of freedom in United States national political discourse.

At his successful first concert on April 19th of 1925, which "propelled [him] into a stratosphere of acclaim," Robeson performed slave songs that established an indissoluble link between the singer and the American past. This link led simultaneously to his appeal among white audiences and his disfavor among the New Negro intelligentsia in Harlem during the 1920s and 1930s. For members of the black cultural elite, the spirituals signified a racial performance that brought them "'down' to the level of 'the slave people' among whom the songs had originated." But the songs resonated for a national audience precisely because their racialism was perceived to be of the soul rather than of the black body.[18]

Robeson's slave in the spirituals was a noble soul, and in his singing he enabled national audiences to project their own universally held investments in the political meaning of suffering and oppression onto the black male body. Hazel Carby has argued that Robeson's performances of the spirituals "enabled the public to appreciate a cultural form that had its source in the history of slavery without the uncomfortable associations with exploitation and oppression that the nation would prefer to forget."[19] She continues, "Negroes, the people whose 'sorrow and hopes' Robeson is said to express and to embody, are the cultural vessels which contain liberal amounts of spiritual and religious experience upon which the [national] audience can draw." However, while it is true that the popularity of Robeson's spirituals among white audiences relied on a certain historical evasion of black slavery, it is also true that his performances fit within a desired narrative of freedom in American political and popular culture. To the degree that Robeson represented the displaced voice of the slave past, the American people as a "race" could find in blackness a way of understanding the nation's disavowed past of conquest and slavery.

The special poignancy of the spirituals as both Negro and American music reflects and parallels Robeson's dual role as a racial and national cultural hero. In his performance of the slave Robeson acted as a surrogate, allowing a national, white audience not so much to forget slavery as to reclaim it as a part of their redemptive inheritance in the nation's journey toward freedom and political liberty. The simultaneous effect of this act of reclamation was the disavowal of the real historical subjects most recently to inherit that history as a racial narrative. Robeson's surrogated performance did not allow the disavowing of slavery and oppression per se. On the contrary, it provided a way of integrating slavery into the rhetorical and discursive inheritance of the nation, while simultaneously evading the black bodies that still bore the burdens of that enslavement in the racially segregated world of the early twentieth century.

Robeson's cultural politics throughout the 1930s represented precisely an effort to disconnect his art from the rhetorical boundaries of the slave as trope in American national discourse. If the spirituals were at first his pathway to a sphere of performative influence within the nation, by the early 1930s Robeson sought to establish a deeper genealogy for black music outside the nation, in the transatlantic past. His increasing politicization can be tracked in public statements in which he paired an indictment of American culture with a certain kind of racial speech, one that located the source of the spirituals beyond the specificity of his own New World history and in a broader genealogy of the cultural origins of the race. As Robeson would state for the press in 1933: "We [blacks] are a great race, greater in tradition and culture than the American race. . . . I am going to produce plays, make films, sing chants and prayers, all with one view in mind—to show my poor people that their culture traces back directly to the great civilizations of Persia, China, and the Jews."[20]

Robeson's Developing Politics and
the Racial Genealogy of Cultural Forms

In his understanding of the spirituals throughout the 1930s as reflections of universal patterns in human culture, Robeson's approach to the slave songs resembled that of his contemporary, W. E. B. Du Bois. In *The Souls of Black Folk*, Du Bois represented the spirituals as indigenous folk songs in order to locate them as products of American history and society.[21] As Carby argues, the spirituals became in Du Bois's hands "the very means for imagining black people as integral to the national political community and for imagining black culture as a form of national culture."[22] However, Robeson took his belief in the form's indigeneity in a very different direction, seeking to reconnect black American history to older cultural patterns embedded in folk music, political patterns in which one could find the racial outcry against forgotten acts of oppression and conquest.

Initially, and somewhat predictably, Robeson's study of the spirituals led him to a focus on African origins. As his biographer writes, "As if *one* dam within him had burst, and overflowing with new ideas, Robeson started to jot down notes—a gauge of his excitement, since he rarely committed thoughts to paper. In the Western world, he wrote, in North and South America, the West Indies and the Caribbean, the black man [contributes primarily] to American culture," and "the culture of his respective milieu" in the various nations of the New World. Hence, the "Westernized black" was "decadent, cut off from his source," and Africa alone could provide the key to the future of black cultures in the Americas—"From there will come his real contribution to [the] culture of the world."[23] But soon Robeson would develop an even broader understanding of the genealogy of race discourse itself as a universal cultural form, one deeply and inextricably embedded in a political narrative.

During a tour of Central Europe, Robeson described "Slav peasant music" as having "a great deal in common with ours," proclaiming that "in the countries which have for centuries suffered under an alien yoke, I found a more instinctive response . . . than in countries like England, who have forgotten what it is like to be conquered."[24] Underlying the cultural connections Robeson was making lay a forgotten, racial and political etymology of slavery, as Srinivas Aravamudan has also described. Aravamudan asserts: "the etymology of *slavery* refers back to the particular servitude of Slavs rather than the later history of the commodification and enforced transportation of Africans, [which] may be suggested by some, is the proper and natural signification of slavery. In this case, the proper and natural signification is itself the result of having forgotten an earlier ethnography."[25] In his own ethnographic journey,

Robeson discovered in the spirituals not just a notion of culture as the carrier of specific racial content; he also excavated a deeper politics of form in which the very desire to express a counter-narrative of racial and political oppression was part of the very structure of human cultures. In his notes Robeson wrote: "I, however, am more profoundly impressed by likenesses in cultural forms which seem to transcend the boundaries of Nationality. Whatever be the Social and Economic content of the culture—Archaic, Clan and Tribal organization, Feudalism, Capitalism, or Socialism—this cultural Form seems to persist, and to be of vital importance to the people concerned."[26]

A closer reading of the ways in which Robeson's race discourse was moving him into more complex territory than the search for racial origins is crucial to understanding the sophisticated ways in which race would later serve as the foundation for his internationalist class politics. Robeson was making distinctions that went far beyond the mere observation that race is a social construction. Racial discourse is also the result of a shared, intercultural, performance in which peoples construct meaning, and their own culture, out of their political interactions with each other. Robeson wrote in his notes: "all races, all Peoples are not nearly as different one from the other as textbooks would have it. . . . Most differences [are] only superficial. History of Mankind proves this. No pure race. No pure culture. No people has lived by itself." These insights would lead Robeson to take explicitly anti-nationalist cultural positions: "I am not a Nationalist. . . . To me, the time seems long past when people can afford to think exclusively in terms of national units. The field of activity is far wider." Robeson called instead for something very similar to Joseph Roach's notion of intercultural performance: "'if the world is to prosper [it must be] broadened to transcend national boundaries,' toward the 'possible synthesis of, and on the other hand, constant interplay between related cultural forms.'"[27]

Understanding race diachronically, as an intercultural and discursive form present throughout human cultures, did not prevent Robeson from arguing for the specific relevance of racial discourse, the language of an oppressed group spoken from the shadows of a suppressed history, in synchronic political contexts. In this way, Robeson traced the genealogy of race back to the future, from Old World contexts of empire and serfdom back to New World futures of race and nation. In his paralleling of the history of the Russian peasant with that of the African slave, Duberman explains, "Robeson was not trying to postulate a common origin among these varied cultures and races but, rather, to pinpoint 'a common element of centuries of serfdom [and therefore a] common way of looking at life.'"[28] Robeson argued that one could see in the racial discourse of the American slave a newly emergent political narrative, born in the colonial hemisphere and now aligning itself against modernity's national "way of looking at life." "[Blacks] are a race . . . but not a people," Robeson would assert, "as disharmonious as the white race is."[29] His distinction between race and peoplehood represented his unwillingness to ascribe the racial group's unity to black nationalist discourses of imagined community. Rather, New World black subjects participated together across various territorial borders in creating a hemispheric discourse of race as a counter-narrative to nationalist narratives of Western modernity. Even if not identical, the overlapping political worldviews of members of a diasporic interculture were generated from their shared histories of colonial conquest, slavery, and oppression across Caribbean, Latin American, and African American geographies.

In his singing Robeson tried to reconfigure the historical meanings attached to the voice of the New World slave, to see his national story in light of the hemispheric, transatlantic, and global histories that surrounded it. In his acting Robeson would also represent, consciously and unconsciously, the synchronic political implications of blackness as a modern discourse of racial resistance. As Duberman describes, "At the same time that Robeson was trying to formulate a theoretical position, he was trying on a practical level to incorporate his new values into his work as an actor."[30] Yet, at the kinesthetic level where meaning is expressed by and mapped onto the body, the actor was also forced to struggle with a range of visual connotations that affixed blackness to his male body in racialized and gendered ways specific to a segregated society. Simultaneous with his attempt to infuse his vocal performances with a broader sense of the race narrative as a human, intercultural, political possession, Robeson was also determined to fit the black male body onto the American stage in a natural way, and to find in film a narrative scenario that the black actor could control. Amid the color lines of contemporary North American society, Robeson would attempt to limn on stage the bodylines of a free black male subjectivity, delineating through his physical movements and acting choices the kinds of environments within which his performances could be meaningful for a diasporic and resistant racial politics.[31]

Acts of Blackness: Robeson and the Semiotics of Black Masculinity Onstage and Onscreen

As Robeson learned to manipulate the boundaries within which he could represent black freedom in the American theater, he also envisioned using film to take his message to a broader diasporic community. The more he explored the genealogy of the New World slave, the more he looked for a hero to serve as the narrative vehicle for the story of the race. This was the quest he communicated in a 1932 interview for the Jamaican newspaper *The Daily Gleaner*, where Robeson is quoted saying, "If the real great man of the Negro race will be born, he will spring from North America. The Negro Gandhi or Mussolini cannot be begotten but in the land of ancient oppression and revolutionary emancipation."[32] If the cultural narrative of the race lay in a genealogy of folk forms that retold not just the story of Africa but also of the slave's New World diaspora and scattering, for Robeson, the descendant of African American fugitive slaves, the political narrative of the race would begin on the stage of American national discourse. Together his stage and screen performances in the 1930s reveal the different prescriptions and possibilities shaping his portrayals of black masculinity during the decade and his reception by multiracial and multinational audiences.

Throughout the 1930s Robeson would struggle with the realization that, in his performance of black masculinity onstage for national audiences in the United States, racial physiognomy outweighed historical narrative, and the color line threatened to subsume the heroic storyline and racial genealogy he hoped to convey. David Scott has pointed out that in the narrative of revolutionary romance, the racial hero functions as a literary vehicle that "embodies the forward historical movement and drives the narrative out of the dark and into the light."[33] This is also the figure that speaks from the shadows declaiming, as Foucault describes, "we had no rights, and that is why we are beginning to speak and to tell of our history."[34] Robeson's quest for such a racial hero was taking place in a national culture and social environment in which the black male actor was praised not for his skill in translating narratives of freedom theatrically, but for the supposed instinctive nature of his dramatic performance. The gendered meanings imposed upon Robeson's body in a national American context—the Negro's supposedly natural and emotive expressiveness; the hypervisibility of black masculine appearance, color, size, and shape—posed a challenge to his deep desire to place the history of the New World Negro, and of race discourse itself, in the much broader hemispheric context of African transplantation, slavery and revolution.

Robeson's physique and appearance would become central features of reviewers' evaluations of his talents as an actor, his physical attributes interpreted and described as naturally dramatic features of his body. Even C. L. R. James took this tack, recalling that in his performance in *Black Majesty*, "Robeson's power onstage was primarily due not to his acting skills *per se* but to the immensity of his personality. . . . It's not a question of acting," James would continue, but rather, "The physique and the voice, the *spirit* behind him—you could see it when he was on stage." In rehearsals for his stage performance as Jim Harris in *All God's Chillun*, the play's director, André Van Gyseghem, felt Robeson was "not a finished actor," because of certain "technical deficiencies—awkward body movement, a tendency to declaim." Then, as Robeson refined the more kinesthetic features of his performance, another critic doubted whether Robeson even understood "how he created the 'beautiful' effects he did with his voice, hands, and 'somewhat ungainly body.'"[35]

Robeson was very aware of the regulatory environment in which he worked, a knowledge reflected in the self-conscious ways he carried his body in the early stages of his career. The challenges he faced in this regard were visible in his early rehearsals for O'Neill's play *The Emperor Jones*—Robeson's portrayal of the title character, Brutus Jones, was one of his first popular stage performances. As observed by his wife, Essie Robeson, the black actor was awkward "in moving his six-foot-two-inch frame around a small stage . . . without seeming to mince," forcing his director to continually coach him by saying, "Don't hold yourself in; you look as though you're afraid to move." "I am," Paul answered, continuing, "I'm so big I feel if I take a few steps I'll be off this tiny stage." Robeson had to be encouraged by the director's instruction: "You must have complete freedom and control over your body and your voice, if you are to control your audience." Essie Robeson also recounted the lengthy process by which Robeson trained both his voice and his body to "act natural" in the role of the black emperor. During rehearsals Robeson "fell to work in earnest . . . memorizing his part,'" and if "sometimes the lines came out too much like an oration or a declamation . . . Paul went back to work, phrase by phrase, word by word, 'digging down to the meaning of every single comma'—until the speech came out sounding natural." Far from not knowing how he created the "beautiful" effects he did with his voice, hands, and "somewhat ungainly body," Robeson worked hard to learn precisely how best to fit himself, literally and figuratively, onto the American stage. He handled his body so well that one reviewer would exclaim after seeing Robeson in *The Emperor Jones*: "Physically this full-blooded negro fitted the role."[36]

If the Negro was a born actor, then essentially there was no actor, no black interiority, only the surface—epidermis—of the display of blackness itself. For the Negro actor, the role of the noble American slave was often prescribed as an instinctive act, a role the black actor could master naturally in performance but not with any conscious control over the narrative within which that performance gained meaning. Onstage, Robeson would attempt to counter this national cultural discourse of a natural blackness with a self-conscious attention to the actual movements and semiotic meanings of his body. The high level of kinesthetic awareness Robeson brought to his performances reflected his wish to change the parameters within which his physicality could be perceived, and thus reconfigure the potentials for meaning making represented by the black male body in American culture.

However, increasingly throughout the 1930s the actor felt the need to go beyond bodylines to the racial storylines that lay within black male subjectivity. In his film projects and choice of roles, Robeson hoped to offer his own rendition of a natural, masculine blackness, embodied not in the national figure of the American slave but in a figure more resonant for diasporic and hemispheric audiences—the figure of the black sovereign. The film industry became a key site for Robeson as he struggled to locate roles that would allow him to elaborate further onscreen the politics of representation he had started to develop in his study and later performances of the spirituals. Comparing the two dramatic mediums of the stage and the screen, Robeson appreciatively described the latter's ability to bring the actor's performance, if not the actor himself, closer to his audience than was possible on stage.

As early as 1930, Robeson was both aware of and actively avoiding the kinds of roles that awaited him in Hollywood, declaring to one British reporter, for example: "I'm afraid of Hollywood. . . . Hollywood can only realize the plantation type of Negro." The actor hoped instead to use the cinema to tell a much broader story of the New World slave, looking for films with "a fine romantic story and an excellent Negro part, [such as] stories of the great Negro emperors—Menelik, Chaka." In so doing he knew he was going against national type; as he told members of the British press, "America . . . would hardly believe that there had ever been such a person as great as a Negro emperor, but in England you know it. You have had to conquer one or two."[37] Robeson thought he had succeeded in finding such a cinematic vehicle when the renowned Soviet filmmaker Sergei Eisenstein approached him to play Toussaint L'Ouverture onscreen. When this project fell through, Robeson persisted to "cast around for a film role that might foster the ideals he had come to espouse."[38] Two films in particular would provide Robeson with this opportunity—*Song of Freedom* (1936) and *Jericho* (1937). In their narratives and plots, each film offered the actor a cinematic scenario in which he could reclaim both the voice of the slave and the body of the black male sovereign.

In *Song of Freedom* Robeson played a concert singer who abandons his stage career in the United States to assume his own genealogy as an African king (see Figure I). The plot of the film provided an almost direct analogy with Robeson's own efforts to understand the genealogy of the music of the American slave. As Duberman describes the plot further:

> Based on Claude Williams and Dorothy Holloway's *The Kingdom of the Zinga*, the film . . . tells the story of John Zinga (played by Robeson), a London dockworker whose glorious bass voice is accidentally discovered, launching him into international success as a concert singer. . . . Zinga learns that [he is also] the King of Casanga. Abandoning his concert career to return to his people, he is met with scorn . . . until he bursts into sacred song, thus persuading them of his royal heritage.[39]

Many of these plot elements replicated details and events in Robeson's own artistic biography—the rise to national and international fame as a concert singer (of the spirituals rather than the opera); the "discovery" of an African past (ideologically rather than biographically); the locating of the roots of black music in a Continental past (Robeson's own tracing of the spirituals back to Old World cultures and political forms versus John Zinga's sacred song). Consciously or not, the film allowed Robeson to communicate his own individual journey as a broader metaphor for the race's quest for self-knowledge and cultural liberation. Proof that this storyline addressed a communal need among black audiences was evidenced by the fact that, of all his films, this was one of the few to find favor in Harlem. Duberman recounts, "the *Pittsburgh Courier* welcomed *Song of Freedom* as the 'finest story of colored folks

FIGURE I. Paul Robeson in *Song of Freedom* (1936). Courtesy of the Douris Corporation (www.classicmovies.com).

yet brought to the screen' [and] Langston Hughes wrote Essie, 'Harlem liked *Song of Freedom*.'"[40]

Jericho, on the other hand, was set in Cairo and afforded Robeson access to a much broader geographic and historical landscape with which to tell the New World Negro's story than was available to him on the American stage. In Cairo, Robeson and his costars would encounter aspects of the Old World that were part of the cultural legacy of the human race. One costar tells of Robeson's impromptu singing performance in "the King's chamber at the geometric center" of the Great Pyramid of Giza: "The first note . . . almost crumbled the place . . . and [when] the last reverberation had gone away . . . I was crying, the dragoman was crying . . . and Paul was crying. . . . There were tears going down our faces. And we almost daren't breathe to break the spell of the thing."[41] The story captures a particularly moving moment of New World subjects finding themselves in the presence of a monument to the shared human past, now rendered apprehensible through their intimate communion in Robeson's song. Here the voice of the slave takes the group away from their respective nationalities to a very different narrative of their racial past, one in which the dark sands of history have preserved African sovereignty as a testament to the intercultural history of the species, rather than as the possession of peoples and nationalities in power.

Jericho, which also played in New York under the title *Dark Sands*, created a further diasporic connection between Robeson and North African culture. His female lead and counterpart, the Princess Kouka, was not an actress but a member of a Sudanese royal family, acting for the first time as the female counterpart to Robeson's character, Jericho Jackson, a fugitive soldier who escapes the United States to lead a North African tribe (see Figure 2). While

FIGURE 2. Paul Robeson and Princess Kouka in *Jericho* (1937). Courtesy of the Douris Corporation (www.classicmovies.com).

Jericho, like *Song of Freedom*, appeared at first to rely on a straightforward back-to-Africa narrative, cinematic techniques such as the switchback shot (enabling a film, after editing, to tell a story that can switch back and forth between different scenes, shots, and locations) kept the storylines in the present, moving back and forth between America, Europe, and Africa. In so doing, both films established genealogical connections between these three spaces as a context for the New World black subject's self-transformation. The narrative of linear descent proved to be a mere backdrop for an intersecting story of intimacy and communication between African Americans and Africans situated coevally in space and time. This cultural intimacy, metaphorically reflected in the romance between Princess Kouka and Jericho Jackson, was taking place not only in the racial past but also in the geopolitical present of the early twentieth century.

Robeson was proud of his roles in both of these films, describing *Song of Freedom* as providing "a *real* part for the first time," and stating even more enthusiastically about *Jericho*, "It's the best part I have ever had for a picture."[42] *Jericho* also added another dimension to Robeson's efforts to achieve verisimilitude in his acting. Robeson felt the film was a particularly good vehicle for his voice—"He felt he could use it in a 'perfectly natural' way while filmmaking, without having to strain for volume and projection, as he sometimes had to onstage or in concert." The declaiming and awkward movements that had so hampered his ability to act blackness naturally onstage for white audiences now became secondary to elements of plot and characterization in the films in which he chose to participate. In these movies he hoped to find the means to represent black political power as a natural feature of hemispheric and transatlantic modernity, but one separate from the American discourses of freedom embodied by the slave.

Hemispheric Scenarios: Reading the National Against the Grain

As we move across several disciplinary boundaries, borrowing methodologies from performance studies and race and gender studies and developing readings of various kinds of texts—film, song, narrative, biography—our goal here is to trace around the borders of the nation alternative ways of organizing transnational, cultural, and political histories in the Americas. The close reading of narrative in dialogue with performance, archive in relationship to repertoire, is crucial for understanding the hemispheric scenarios within which national discourses are constructed and staged.[43] When both U.S. and black literary studies limit themselves to reading narratives and cultural figures strictly within national parameters, they miss the moments when a text or a performance attempts to qualify and subvert the discourse of the nation by revealing new or alternative racial and gendered genealogies.[44] In the geographies charted by Paul Robeson and his cultural choices during the 1930s, we learn that we need

not shift our focus from the American national subject to a more global, internationalist stage. Rather, we need to see this subject through the lens of other
discourses of race and subjectivity that lie just outside his country's shadow.

For too long Robeson's political significance in American studies has
remained wholly set within the narrative of his national alienation as a socialist, with little recognition or understanding of how a politics of race, shaped
by his attentiveness to circumatlantic hemispheric histories, may have had an
impact on his radicalism and subsequent incompatibility with U.S. cultural
politics. Similarly, when scholars in African American and Caribbean studies
define their fields along strictly national lines, they miss an opportunity to
explore the various intersecting meanings of gender and blackness uniting
black male subjects in conversation across diasporic spaces. Since Robeson
spent much of the decade traveling away from the United States, both literally
and figuratively, it is a central irony of his 1930s career that upon his return
to the country he should have been asked, serendipitously, to sing the "Ballad
for Americans." This performance immediately reinstated him as a national
cultural hero, the figure for a freedom now embodied by *both* the slave *and* the
American state. This profound irony serves here as a useful point of closure,
for it offers the opportunity to read the ballad both as a textual artifact of an
unambiguously national performance and simultaneously as a transcript of
the hemispheric, racial geography within which that performance accumulated its various meanings.

While we do not have access to the immediacy and resonance of Robeson's
performance in 1939, by reading the lyrics of the ballad against the grain we
can reimagine how he embodied the nation's song by reconstructing the textual role of the slave. On the surface of the text, "Ballad for Americans" is an
account of a national people's evolving faith, their belief that their country
represents the very essence of political liberty.[45] Beginning "in seventy-six
[when] the sky was red," the ballad proceeds over the course of seventeen
stanzas to describe the nation-building project—("Building a nation is awful
tough. / The people found the going rough")—as one that involves winning the
hearts and minds of different types of people in the national community. The
stanzas are organized not just as a conversation but as a dialogue with a persuasive intent—to convince the listener that America stands for "a mighty fine
idea," that of "Liberty or death." Belief is the central issue at stake throughout
the song—"Did they all believe in liberty those days? / Nobody who was anybody believed it. / Ev'rybody who was anybody doubted it. / Nobody had faith."
Furthermore, this (New World) belief in liberty is set defiantly against (Old
World) sovereignty in the ballad's opening lines: "In seventy-six the sky was
red / thunder rumbling overhead / Bad King George couldn't sleep in his bed /
And on that stormy morn, Ol' Uncle Sam was born."

Despite the opening focus on the nation's political values, the "Ballad for
Americans" is often remembered for its later verses that retell the typically

American story of different peoples' cultural and social assimilation. In this land of social equality and cultural diversity, various figures for the people continually morph into each other as we follow along the country's history. Over time and stanzas the song moves from the founding fathers, to the miners and pioneers, to Abe Lincoln, to the rich and the poor, and then finally to the verse often cited as the crescendo of the song's multicultural and multiclass message:

Well, I'm an
Engineer, musician, street cleaner, carpenter, teacher,
How about a farmer? Also. Office clerk? Yes sir!
That's right. Certainly!
Factory worker? You said it. Yes ma'am.
Absotively! Posolutely!
Truck driver? Definitely!
Miner, seamstress, ditchdigger, all of them.
I am the "etceteras" and the "and so forths" that do the work.
Now hold on here, what are you trying to give us?
Are you an American?
Am I an American?

I'm just an Irish, Jewish, Italian,
French and English, Spanish, Russian, Chinese, Polish,
Scotch, Hungarian, Swedish, Finnish, Greek and Turk and Czech.

In later installments, revisions of the ballad's lyrics have added new types of immigrants to this list, all of them (tellingly) members of groups we now describe as people of color. The ballad itself, however, is democratically free of such racial distinctions; included through their ethnic designation these people make up merely more of the diverse cultures that interact to make a multicultural America. They also blend in nicely with the array of people from other types of categories, for example of religion and employment, all of a mix in this more progressive vision of the culture (or cultures) of the United States:

Well, I'm an
Engineer, musician, street cleaner, carpenter, teacher,
How about a farmer? Also. Office clerk? Yes sir!
That's right. (Homemaker?) Certainly!
Factory worker? You said it. (Mail carrier?) Yes ma'am.
(Hospital worker?) Absotively! (Social worker?) Posolutely!
Truck driver? Definitely!
Miner, seamstress, ditchdigger, all of them.
I am the "etceteras" and the "and so forths" that do the work.
Now hold on here, what are you trying to give us?
Are you an American?
Am I an American?

I'm just an Irish, (African,) Jewish, Italian,
French and English, Spanish, Russian, Chinese, Polish,
Scotch, Hungarian, (Jamaican,) Swedish, Finnish, (Dominican,) Greek
        and Turk and Czech
(and Native American.)
[additions in parentheses]

The focus on this narrative of cultural diversity, whether in celebration or in critique, misses the ways in which that narrative continues to overshadow the *political form* of the nation described in the ballad's beginning stanzas. In other words, the question of who deserves citizenship in the nation is a separate and very different question from who can represent it, and it is in answering this latter question, both in the positive and in the negative, that the racial dimensions of the tale assert themselves. These dimensions also map the ballad's hemispheric inheritance, a political discourse of race that relies on particular narrative modes to define a people as worthy of freedom, democracy and national self-determination.

Despite the theme of racial, cultural, gender, and class democracy in "Ballad for Americans," the *political* narrative the ballad tells is one where certain hierarchies and structures of the *race* narrative emerge. The song's language clearly mirrors the anti-sovereign discourse Foucault describes, and the sense that the country and the "nobodies" who are its people speak from the shadows: "Our country's strong, our country's young, / And her greatest songs are still unsung / From her plains and mountains we have sprung, / To keep the faith with those who went before. / . . . We nobodies who are anybody believe it. / We anybodies who are everybody have no doubts." The narrative rhythm David Scott describes, of trials and tribulations that will be overcome, shapes the ballad's tone of uplift: "As America grew in peace and war / And a million wheels went around and 'round. / The cities reached into the sky, / And dug down deep into the ground. And some got rich and some got poor. / But the people carried through, / So our country grew." When the struggle against slavery enters the narrative, it comes with a well-defined national hero to drive this people's history from darkness into light—"Let my people go. That's the idea! / Old Abe Lincoln was thin and long, / His heart was high and his faith was strong. / But he hated oppression, he hated wrong, / And he went down to his grave to free the slave."

One line in the ballad tellingly reveals the slave's position in relationship to this larger story. In the nation's song, one man is freed for the redemption of another—"A man in white skin can never be free while his black brother is in slavery." As the ballad describes the process by which *a* people go from being nobodies to becoming Americans, the political meaning of the nation is founded on the need to believe in (white) freedom, while the cultural becomes the space to incorporate ethnic others into that idea of racial freedom. Politically, however, there is still a nobody—the (black) slave as the racial nobody—who defines non-freedom and exists in a space simultaneously present within and invisible to the national community. This is a figure that also slides in and out of view in the song, hovering in the shadows, somewhat outside of the community created in and by the ballad's chronicle.

While Robeson sang this song to the thrilling amazement of national audiences, he remained uninvited to the various social occasions honoring the song's composers. His own present but invisible status was also evident in the many occasions he was asked to eat in his room after a performance so that the white patrons of his hotel would not see him publicly. This disavowal of the racial subject was knit into the very text of the ballad itself, in the voice of the balladeer reciting the song. The text is narrated in the first person by someone who keeps trying to name himself, but as the story of the nation takes over, by the end he is told who he is supposed to be. This narrator first appears in the fifth stanza when he defines his own political will to believe in the nation as the very source of his identity. He soon gains a respondent and we realize that the discussion is a three-way conversation, with multiple players representing multiple layers of persuasion, each dependent on the other's performance of belief and faith. A third voice in the ballad represents a chorus of the nation's believers, who then vie with the narrator for the telling of the story. As the balladeer begins a line, the (national) chorus ends it, continuing on to recount many of the important political stories the song contains. When the narrator finally names himself as the entirety of the long list of peoples who constitute the nation, the ballad closes with his assertion—"For I have always believed it, and I believe it now, / And now you know who I am. / Who are you? / America! America!"

Just before this moment, however, the balladeer reflects in more rueful tones on his representative role in the song:

> Still nobody who was anybody believed it.
> Everybody who was anybody they doubted it.
> And they are doubting still,
> And I guess they always will . . .
>
> Say, will you please tell us who you are?
> What's your name, Buddy? Where you goin'? Who are you?
> Well, I'm the everybody who's nobody,
> I'm the nobody who's everybody.

The balladeer's willingness to perform his identity as the "nobody who's everybody" is crucial to this conversation about the meaning of the nation-state and its continued existence through the faith of its people.

When we imagine Paul Robeson as this rueful balladeer, the racial subject standing in the shadows of the national hero he is supposed to represent, the black male performer also becomes a figure for the nation's disavowed racial and historical character. In his 1939 performance of the "Ballad for Americans," Robeson, the proud descendant of the ever-present New World slave, ended the decade still on the outskirts of the imagined national community. Yet, he was also given the role of assuring that community of its distance from a much less noble racial past. It is only within the context of Robeson's embodied performance that the ballad can be read against the national grain, as part of a larger hemispheric scenario in which the national and the racial coexist.

Some years later, Robeson's Francophone Caribbean counterpart, Frantz Fanon, would assert in his own genealogy of race, *Black Skin, White Masks*, "I am not the slave of the Slavery that dehumanized my ancestors."[46] Here Fanon took himself, and his readers, away from the resonant power of narratives of racial oppression in which the struggle for freedom is projected onto the black male body. "Was my freedom not given to me then in order to build the world of the *You?*" Fanon asked, interrogating the process by which the black body becomes the cipher or metonym for a reduced sense of racial meaning. The trope of the New World slave slips easily into a discourse where race becomes representative of the body of a people, rather than the signifier for various forms of intercultural address in which "peoples" come to understand themselves in relation to others. In contrast, Fanon held out the vision of a more deconstructive and intersectional process by which he, as a black man, could consciously assess the genealogies of power shaping his own performance of black masculinity: "My final prayer: O my body, make of me always a man who questions!"

Fanon asks us to explore the forms of agency we achieve when we perceive ourselves as subjects constructed within and against certain constraints. It is in this sense that his words evoke Paul Robeson, given the great importance the actor placed on studying the forms of racial narrative constructing his own sense of self. As in Fanon's call, Robeson's body became the ground from which he attempted to use his freedom to address his audiences as they recreated their own racial identity through his. Our ability to read his gendered body and performance of blackness in these complex ways depends on our willingness to understand racial discourse dialogically, as constituted in national spaces constantly crosscut by and reacting to transnational, intercultural processes.

NOTES

1. Frantz Fanon, *Black Skin, White Masks* (1952), trans. Constance Farrington (New York: Grove Weidenfeld, 1967), 219.

2. Martin Duberman, *Paul Robeson: A Biography* (New York: New Press, 1989), 236.

3. George Lamming, *In the Castle of My Skin* (Ann Arbor: University of Michigan Press, 1991). As they listen to Robeson singing the words, "Let my people go," the following dialogue ensues between the two characters:

[G.:] "I like it. . . . That was really beautiful."

"You know the voice?" Trumper asked. . . . "Paul Robeson," he said. "One o' the greatest o' my people."

"What people?" I asked. I was a bit puzzled. . . .

"My people," he said again, "or better, my race. . . . None o' you here on this islan' know what it mean to fin' race." (294–295)

4. Ibid., 297.

5. David Scott, "The Sovereignty of the Imagination: An Interview with George Lamming," *Small Axe*, no. 12 (September 2002).

6. See Sibylle Fischer's excellent discussion of the Haitian Revolution as a silenced text, in her introduction to *Modernity Disavowed: Haiti and the Cultures of Slavery in the Age of Revolution* (Durham: Duke University Press, 2004).

7. Two works in particular that explore this representative elision of the female slave in both African American and Caribbean revolutionary contexts are Hazel Carby's *Race Men* (Cambridge, Mass.: Harvard University Press, 1998) and Belinda Edmondson's *Making Men: Gender, Literary Authority, and Women's Writing in Caribbean Narrative* (Durham: Duke University Press, 1999).

8. Paul Robeson, *Here I Stand* (Boston: Beacon Press, 1958), 63, 66–67.

9. Michel Foucault, *"Society Must Be Defended": Lectures at the College de France, 1975–1976*, trans. David Macey (New York: Picador, 2003), 59, 61.

10. Ibid., 70.

11. For more on the "creole pioneers," see Chapter 4 in Anderson's *Imagined Communities: Reflections on the Origin and Spread of Nationalism* (rev. ed., New York: Verso, 1992). On anti-slavery radicalism as a hemispheric political alternative to Creole nationalisms in the region, see Fischer, *Modernity Disavowed*.

12. See Stuart Hall's interview with David Scott, online in *BOMB Magazine*, no. 90 (Winter 2004–2005).

13. C. L. R. James, *The Black Jacobins: Toussaint L'Ouverture and the San Domingo Revolution* (London: Allison & Busby, 1989); Frantz Fanon, *The Wretched of the Earth* (New York: Grove Weidenfeld, 1963).

14. C. L. R. James, "From Toussaint L'Ouverture to Fidel Castro," in Anna Grimshaw, ed., *The C. L. R. James Reader* (Cambridge: Blackwell Publishers, 1992), 296.

15. C. L. R. James, *American Civilization* (Cambridge: Blackwell Publishers, 1993).

16. While in James's narrative of a "Caribbean quest for national identity" the slave is a transnational figure whose political movement from one island to another shifts the entire hemisphere historically away from slavery and diaspora and toward revolution, in the context of U.S. history the fugitive slave's actions bring the individual nation-state closer to fulfilling its emancipatory ideals. James discusses the Caribbean quest in "From Toussaint L'Ouverture to Fidel Castro" (Grimshaw, 296) and the role of the fugitive slave in essays such as "The Revolutionary Answer to the Negro Problem in the USA" (Grimshaw, 182).

17. Duberman, *Paul Robeson*, 10.

18. Ibid., 81, 33.

19. Carby, *Race Men*, 92–93, 97.

20. Duberman, *Paul Robeson*, 169.

21. W. E. B. Du Bois, *The Souls of Black Folk* (reprint; New York: Penguin Books, 1969).

22. Carby, *Race Men*, 89, 91.

23. Duberman, *Paul Robeson*, 169–173.

24. Ibid., 129.

25. Srinivas Aravamudan, *Tropicopolitans: Colonialism and Agency, 1688–1804* (Durham: Duke University Press, 1999), 5.

26. Duberman, *Paul Robeson*, 201–202.

27. Ibid. In *Cities of the Dead: Circum-Atlantic Performance* (New York: Columbia University Press, 1996), Joseph Roach argues for an understanding of hemispheric culture as an *inter*-cultural formation, where relationships and interactions *between* peoples defined what then became central to each culture's values and sets of meaning.

28. Duberman, *Paul Robeson*, 175.

29. Ibid.

30. Ibid., 202.

31. In *Race Men* Carby coins the term "bodylines" to describe a performative world in which the black male body can be seen and portrayed as "both autonomous and inspirational" (3). Her discussion of Toussaint L'Ouverture's distinctive role in C. L. R. James's writings (113) provides a context for Robeson's portrayal of the Haitian liberator in James's 1936 play, *Black Majesty*.

32. Duberman, *Paul Robeson*, 133. His 1932 interview in Jamaica's *Daily Gleaner* was ultimately titled, "Paul Robeson Looks for a Negro Mussolini" (Duberman, *Paul Robeson*, 610).

33. Hall, "David Scott" interview, in Duberman, *Paul Robeson*.

34. Foucault, *"Society Must Be Defended,"* 70.

35. Duberman, *Paul Robeson*, 197, 167, 64–65.

36. Ibid., 59–60.

37. Ibid., 169.

38. Ibid., 178.

39. Ibid., 204.

40. Ibid., 204.

41. Ibid., 210.

42. Ibid., 204, 209.

43. For further discussion of the scenario as the basic meaning-making unit of a performance, see Diana Taylor, *The Archive and the Repertoire: Performing Cultural Memory in the Americas* (Durham: Duke University Press, 2003), 28.

44. Also see Roach's notion of circumatlantic "genealogies of performance" in *Cities of the Dead*, 189.

45. All lyrics from "The Ballad for Americas," both in the original and the revised, are taken from the online website, International Lyrics Playground, at http://lyrics playground.com/alpha/songs/b/balladforamericans.shtml.

46. Fanon, *Black Skin, White Masks*, 230–232.

9

The Promises and Perils of U.S. African American Hemispherism

Latin America in Martin Delany's *Blake* and Gayl Jones's *Mosquito*

IFEOMA C. K. NWANKWO

Central and South America, are evidently the ultimate destination and future home of the colored race on this continent . . . the advantages to the colored people of the United States, to be derived from emigration to Central, South America, and the West Indies, are incomparably greater than that of any other parts of the world at present.

> —Martin R. Delany, *Condition, Elevation, Emigration and Destiny of the Colored People of the United States. Politically Considered* (1852)

We should be international. Not just provincial. We shouldn't just be a provincial people. That's what they want, just to keep us thinking we're a provincial people, and they're the universalists. That their perspective is the universal perspective. They claim for their provincial perspective universality. We're a universal people. We're more universal. 'Cause we don't think everybody's supposed to be like us.

> —Gayl Jones, *Mosquito* (1999)

Both Martin Delany, in his advocacy of U.S. African American emigration to Latin America, and Gayl Jones, in her call for U.S. African Americans to be "international" and "not just provincial," argue that engaging the world beyond the United States is crucial to their community's struggle to be acknowledged as equal to European Americans.[1] They are voices in long-standing debates over whether this battle is most effectively fought by U.S. African Americans embracing a supra-national conceptualization of community that negates the salience of national boundaries, or by emphasizing their connection to the United States and demanding what Rebecca Scott describes as "public rights." Engagements with Latin America and Latin Americans have constituted a crucial element of U.S. African American attempts to gain access to and recognition within mainstream U.S. literary, intellectual, and political discourses. Historical and recent trends in American literary studies, however, have made grappling with these representational and ideological interactions a particular challenge.

In their introduction to the special issue of *Modern Fiction Studies* dedicated to the "Trans-American Imaginary," Paula M. L. Moya and Ramón Saldivar rightly declare "that unless we make more visible the unequal relations of domination that exist in this hemisphere, our conception of American literary history will remain both incomplete and inadequate." Those unequal relations, whether in terms of economic capital, cultural capital, or political power, have determined the construction of the canons, conventions, and courses of U.S. literary history, and, as such, must be foregrounded in our attempts to depict that story. Not doing so, Moya and Saldivar go on to contend, "has the effect, finally, of devaluing . . . literatures that look south and west instead of north and east."[2] The increasing attentiveness in literary scholarship toward hemispheric perspectives, evidenced by José David Saldivar's *The Dialectics of Our America* (1991) and more recently by Kirsten Silva Gruesz's *Ambassadors of Culture* (2001), is indeed demanded by historical realities. Copiously documented by scholars such as Louis Pérez, the stubborn presence of the U.S. state in Latin American histories, particularly in the independence movements that created Cuba and Panama, in the governance of Chile and Nicaragua, and in the agricultural labor markets of Costa Rica and Colombia has shaped not only lives and literatures in the United States and Latin America, but also the ways in which the histories of those lives and literatures are told.[3]

As a consequence, recent hemispherist scholarship has often focused primarily (and appropriately) on the "unequal relations" between the United States and the Latin American nations and states, especially with respect to what Michael Mann has called "financial transnationalism,"[4] and on the genealogical links between white mainstream and Latin American writers that have hitherto been obscured by the transference of those inequalities onto the processes of constructing literary canons and histories. Such an orientation, however, has led to a dearth of critical scholarship on relations between U.S. African Americans and the rest of the Americas.[5] Unsurprisingly, the fact that the most vocal proponents of the "new" hemispherist American studies have been primarily Latino/Latina studies and Latin American studies scholars has left the place of U.S. African American studies in the hemispheric Americanist movement unclear.

This essay, while informed by a cognizance of the U.S. nation's dominance, posits a model for including U.S. African American life and thought in the new hemispherist American studies that arises out of U.S. African American literary texts themselves. This framework eschews the assumed oppositions between "real" (read national) African American literary studies and the "new" transnational approach, while illuminating the limits of hemispherist approaches modeled on now canonical concepts such as José Martí's "Our Euro-Indigenous America" (*nuestra mestiza América*). Through readings of Delany's *Blake* (1859–1862) and Jones's *Mosquito* (1999), I hope to show that these writers' textual encounters with Latin America simultaneously serve as weapons in their battle to claim subjectivity as defined by Enlightenment and U.S. nationalist discourse, and as bases for their strident calls for collective action against the beneficiaries of the "unequal relations" created by the hemisphere's hegemons.

In the nineteenth century, debates about the usefulness of associations (textual, material, or otherwise) with Latin America to U.S. African Americans' struggles at "home" surfaced especially clearly in public figures' positions on emigration, Manifest Destiny, and the Haitian Revolution.[6] Latin America functioned as a mid-point between Africa and the United States—a space through which U.S. African American thinkers could make clear that they were Americans, while also calling attention to the fact that they, too, had an international network. Martin Delany, for example, was simultaneously an active proponent of emigration and of a broad notion of community that linked U.S. African Americans with other oppressed American populations. He thus describes the populations of Latin America as "our brethren—because they are precisely the same people as ourselves and share the same fate with us."[7]

Delany's novel, *Blake; Or, the Huts of America*, provides a highly detailed literary representation of the hemispheric connections he posited and valued in *Condition*. The text dramatizes the planning of a hemispheric version of the Haitian Revolution. The leader of the revolution is Henry, a slave represented as being both U.S. African American and Cuban, and as having a talent for moving easily within and among various "American" communities. Through an emphasis on Henry's in-depth knowledge of and ability to bond with disparate cultures both within the United States and throughout the rest of the hemisphere, Delany fights for Black men's access to the range of models of public manhood available to white men.[8] In *Blake*, the hemisphere becomes both the means and locus of this battle's realization. The novel posits a way of thinking that runs counter to the aforementioned tendency among Americanist scholars to think of work by or about U.S. African Americans as falling neatly into one of the two categories—as part of the "new" hemispherist American studies, or as holding firm to academic versions of the national political commitments that undergirded the creation of African American studies in the first place.

Blake is supra-national, in that nation-state borders are repeatedly transgressed, blurred, and negated and differences between individuals and groups residing in disparate countries are frequently represented as nonexistent, minor, or irrelevant. At the same time, *Blake* is a profoundly nationally oriented text.[9] Even as Henry Blake moves easily into, out of, within, and among multiple communities, the goal of his revolution is to create a new nation, specifically a new Black nation. In addition, Delany spends considerable time and effort attempting to capture and/or represent particular worldviews, cultural traditions, and histories of communities. The text itself is torn between grasping the sociopolitical value of taking a hemispherist stance, particularly during this era in which the U.S. state sought to execute its own "Manifest Destiny" in Latin America, and acknowledging the continuing reification of the nation in mainstream U.S. intellectual and political discourse.

In the later twentieth century (and into the twenty-first century), the question of the relevance of the rest of the Americas to U.S. African Americans' struggles has underpinned tensions and perspectives on the possibility of coalition building between foreigners and U.S. African American workers. Recent public debates in Detroit, Michigan, over the city council's approval of a proposal for an "Africantown" business zone to compete with the vibrant Mexicantown, Greektown, and Arab American business districts in the city illustrate the extent to which these tensions are escalating. Of the city council's report on the plan, journalist Marisol Bello notes that it "complains that immigrants . . . are stealing resources, jobs, and other opportunities from blacks" and "call[s] on the city to level the playing field between blacks and the newcomers who it says are economically surpassing them."[10]

Displaying a cognizance of both the longer history of debate over U.S. African Americans' attitudes toward the other oppressed populations in the hemisphere, and of these particular twentieth- (and twenty-first-) century manifestations, Gayl Jones explicitly links her novel *Mosquito*—a work that tells the story of a U.S. African American woman who helps Mexican immigrants across the border—to Delany's *Blake*. Jones has her main character note, "I remember [my friend] be reading one of them books called Blakes, or the Huts of America . . . she say it were an interesting book, as a historical book and the types of ideas it contained."[11]

Foremost among the "types of ideas" that link the two novels are positions on which forms of hemispherism are most useful for U.S. African Americans. Jones's intervention lies primarily, and more explicitly than Delany's, in the realm of epistemology. She is clearing space, so to speak, to allow for a more expansive understanding of the range of knowledge and ways of knowing and expressing knowledge within and across the U.S. nation and the hemisphere. *Mosquito* is not invested in "national manhood," "heroic manhood," or any other established form of manhood depicted by Delany and others as the magic key that will open the door to their being recognized as equal in U.S. society.

In fact, Jones expressly discards that framework because it is too limiting: "I'm thinking what it would be like if Martin Delany put a character like you in a book with a man like Blake. I know one thing, you'd be freer to express yourself, 'cause you don't have the burden of being an exemplary woman" (546). *Mosquito*'s goal is not to imagine or effect the creation of a nation-state, whether Black or otherwise. It is concerned, rather, with uncovering the fundamental, almost spiritual, connections between the peoples of the hemisphere, an approach that could be productively described as universalist or humanist. At the same time, *Mosquito* delves into the particulars of various locations and communities. In valuing both commonality and distinctiveness, it lays bare the falsity of the perceived opposition between hemispheric (or universalist) and national (or particular) orientations.

The epigraph from *Mosquito* at the beginning of this essay highlights that much more is at stake in U.S. African Americans' decisions about whether to "be international" than an individual's own choices about identity. Those decisions are also part of a long-standing battle with the dominant discourses over access to universality. U.S. African Americans, *Mosquito* argues, should "be international . . . not just provincial" because "[those in power] want to keep us thinking we're a provincial people, and they're the universalists" (277). Jones makes a point of undercutting prevailing definitions of universality as a benign quality that one (or a community) either inherently has or does not have. She calls attention to the hegemony implicit in "their" claiming to have "the universal perspective," and posits a new conception of universality that contradicts it: "we're more universal. 'Cause we don't think everybody's supposed to be like us." The universal as traditionally understood, Jones argues, is actually "a provincial perspective" that has been widely imposed.

Caren Kaplan has made a similar argument, decrying the ways in which literary critics construct canons by detaching "exiled" thinkers from the displaced masses of which they are, in fact, part. Kaplan asks: "can the mystified universalism of such representations be countered by strategies of localization or placement or by expanding the subject from singular to plural?"[12] Jones defies such "mystified" and value-laden deployments of universalism by emphasizing the hemispheric epistemology of an individual from a supposedly provincial population.

In *Blake* and *Mosquito*, hemispherism functions as a localized (almost nationalist) cosmopolitanism—one that allows U.S. African Americans to claim a connection to a specific terrain and history, while also proving that they too can craft notions of self and community that cross or negate national borders. Cosmopolitanism is a crucial element of universalism, particularly in the construction of literary and intellectual canons.[13] Prevailing modes of anointing canon-worthy intellectuals (such as the detachment from the masses criticized by Kaplan) are based not just on a "mystified universalism," but also specifically on the extent to which that universalism is seen as being manifested through the embrace of a particularly circumscribed cosmopolitanism. Delany's and Jones's hemispherist approaches recall and revise Simon Bolivar's dream of "consolidating the New World into a single nation," while recognizing that "America is separated by . . . conflicting interests, and dissimilar characteristics."[14] They want to view the hemisphere in terms of a potential for collectivity, while also highlighting the differences among oppressed peoples, thus demonstrating that U.S. African Americans are not provincial—that they, too, can recognize, comprehend, and embrace that which is different or unfamiliar.

Delany's Manifested Destinies

Delany contemplates Latin America in his nonfiction political writing as well as in his fiction. In *Condition, Elevation, Emigration and Destiny of the Colored People of the United States (1852)*, he goes so far as to specify the Latin American countries to which he thinks U.S. African Americans should emigrate: "we consequently . . . select NICARAGUA, in Central America, North, and NEW GRANADA, the Northern part of South America, South of Nicaragua, as the most favorable point at present, in every particular, for us to emigrate to." Tellingly, he attributes his advocacy of emigration to this region to his belief that this is a place where U.S. African Americans can "rise to the full stature of manhood," telling his brothers and sisters, "the moment your foot touches the soil, you have all the opportunities for elevating yourselves as the highest, according to your industry and merits."[15] The bulk of *Condition* actually consists of his delineation of the special contributions that U.S. African Americans have already made and could continue to make to the United States, should it choose to accept them, and his identification of the barriers to their doing so. This exhortation, then, simultaneously seeks to inspire hope in U.S. African Americans as well as to stoke the fires of fear and jealousy among the powerful in the United States who see Latin America as theirs (and theirs alone) for the taking, and U.S. African Americans as subhuman barbarians who contribute nothing to the advancement of the U.S. nation. Delany essentially retorts, "[F]ine, if you don't want us, we'll take our talents to that neighbor you think is so weak and make her stronger than you could ever imagine."

The first half of *Blake* takes place in the U.S. South and features Henry, infuriated by the selling away of his wife to Havana, instigating revolt across the region by detailing for slaves the range of reasons that rebellion, although risky, is a much better option than continuing to endure enslavement: "From plantation to plantation did he go, sowing the seeds of future devastation and ruin to the master and redemption to the slave." He works to convince slaves like Mammy Judy, who encourages him to "put yeh trus' in de Laud" instead of fomenting "mischief," that his plan is worthwhile.[16] The section ends with

Mammy Judy and others escaping to Canada. Henry, however, has still not found his wife so he decides to book himself as a sailor onto a ship heading for Cuba.

The second half of the novel is set in Cuba. By having his novel extend into Cuba, Delany elbows his way into the raging debate about the annexation of Cuba to the United States. Cuban Creole elite support for annexation was strong, for economic as well as political reasons. These Cuban-born white elites had already begun to increase their trade with the United States in the immediate wake of the Haitian Revolution, and saw great economic advantages to strengthening that relationship. They believed that becoming part of the U.S. union would save them from the tyranny of Spain, tyranny that included what they saw as unbearable commercial taxes. Pivotal to the annexation debate was the concern that Cuba was undergoing a process of Africanization because of the large numbers of enslaved Africans who were being brought to the island to keep the sugar mills running. The threat of a mass uprising of those Africans struck fear in the hearts of many U.S. and Cuban government officials and members of the elite. That threat, some said, could be minimized by U.S. annexation and the concomitant preservation of the system of slavery. Others, however, believed that should the United States decide to annex Cuba, it would be annexing a country with a very high probability of a Haitian Revolution–like uprising. Consequently, the Spanish crown directly threatened the Creole elites with the emancipation of the slaves, should they continue to push for annexation to the United States.[17] Delany craftily appropriates these discourses and debates to unsettle the nerves of proslavery advocates everywhere.

In a move that highlights his insight into the forces driving hemispherism from "above," Delany explores the tensions and anger central to the uneasy alliance among American planters, Creole elites, U.S. merchants, U.S. governmental forces, and peninsular powers in Cuba. But just as central to Delany's hemispherism is his desire to delineate the diversity and complexity of those in nineteenth-century Cuba who sought to challenge this tenuous ruling class. *Blake*'s Cuban world is populated by individuals of a wide variety of skin tones, occupations, classes, and origins, ranging from slaves like Henry and his wife Lotty/Maggie, who came from the U.S. South, to Cuban Creole slaves like Dominico, newly captured Africans like Mendi and Abyssa, and "educated, wealthy ladies" like Madame Cordora and her daughter. Importantly, these very different individuals unite in the service of the freedom of all with any African blood (Delany's terminology). The point that Delany makes through his depiction of Cuba is that people of African descent in this hemisphere, regardless of their status, color, or national location, should share in a collective desire for freedom.

The Cuban part of the novel is distinguished by Delany's inclusion of a Cuban version of Henry: Plácido. The two are bound together not only by blood—Plácido is depicted as Henry's cousin—but also by their commitment to "the common cause of our race" (*Blake*, 195); they also mirror each other in their radical and racial politics. Each of the characters represents one of Delany's arguments about the best way for Black men in the hemisphere to counter the dehumanization imposed on their race. They embody the tug-of-war in Delany's mind between hemispheric and national approaches to imagining a Black revolution.

Like the novel itself, Henry Blake skillfully crosses national, cultural, and linguistic boundaries. Henry bonds with the Cubans of color before either he or they realize that he is "the lost boy of Cuba." He expresses interest in hearing their tales of mistreatment and abuse, and empathizes with them. At one point, a slave mistress "compelled [the mother] to scourge her own child till he fell motionless and bleeding at her feet." We are told, "to all this Henry was a serious spectator, having twice detected himself in an involuntary determination to rush forward and snatch the infernal thing of torture from the hand of the heart-crushed mother" (170). He meets with Native American leaders in Arkansas to find out "whether in case that the blacks should rise, they may have hope or fear from the Indian" (87). Upon hearing a satisfactory answer that emphasized the historical ties between Native Americans and Blacks, Henry decides to "impart" to the chief the details of his revolutionary plan. Delany never portrays Blake as having any difficulty speaking with any group in its native language.

Delany ascribes a less expansive form of this capacity for bonding with multiple cultures to Plácido, who is very knowledgeable about the history of and happenings across the Atlantic world, but does not have Henry's facility for moving into, among, and across multiple cultures. He is portrayed for the most part as being epistemologically, culturally, and physically rooted in Cuba, even though he does feel an affinity for other African Americans. By presenting Plácido in this fashion, Delany explores an alternative mode of envisaging the possible ways that African Americans can manifest their sense of connection to one another—specifically, by suggesting that individuals need not physically travel across geographical or national borders to do so, and by making it clear that different communities may have different struggles, even if they do share a larger political vision.

For example, when a fellow revolutionary asks Plácido whether the Blacks on Cuba's Caribbean "sister islands" will be able to help their cause, Plácido remarks that those in the British Caribbean, although free, cannot help because their current goals are different from those of the Cubans: "What they [Blacks of the British Caribbean] most desire is freedom and equality politically, practically carried out, having no objection to being an elementary part of the British body politic" (288). Plácido contrasts the British Caribbean situation to the Cuban one in which "here in Cuba we are the political and social inferiors of the whites, existing as freemen only by suffrance, and subject to enslavement at any time" (288). In addition, he points out that in Cuba they have a two-headed pro-slavery Hydra (pro-slavery Spain and pro-slavery Cuban Creole elites) that they must fight to gain their freedom. While he would like the two groups to join hands in the revolutionary struggle, he recognizes that each has its own particular circumstances and histories that will also govern their immediate actions. As long as slavery exists in Cuba, none of the people of color in Cuba can truly be free. In the British Caribbean, by contrast, the people "have all been fully enfranchised" (289), but they must continue to push for the practical carrying out of the promise implied in enfranchisement. Freedom in the novel, whether in Cuba or the British Caribbean, is explicitly linked to enfranchisement, thus underscoring the extent to which Blacks' desire to be recognized as equals drives political and revolutionary action in the novel.

Through his representations of Henry, Delany argues that the ideal revolutionary Black leader is pure Black, manly, and able to move easily between and among cultures (albeit in the service of revolutionary and violent ends), and further that those who do not have those qualities can only be truly revolutionary by association with the "exemplary man." Through Plácido, however, Delany experiments with an alternative notion of a racial revolutionary—one who is less Black ("the yellow gentleman," 193), and less manly ("sinewy," 192), and who, though tied to one location, crosses national borders intellectually rather than physically in his multiple commitments to Black community. Inspired by *Blake*, while also dissenting from key aspects of Delany's novel, Gayl Jones, in *Mosquito*, undertakes her own experiment in representing the possibilities of a Black internationalism in the American hemisphere.

Mosquito's Epistemology

Jones, as I have said, explicitly links *Mosquito* to *Blake*. Mosquito is a "king sized" (as she describes herself) U.S. African American truck driver who, somewhat in the manner of Blake, travels from place to place, making connections with Native Americans, Chicanos, and other inhabitants of "*nuestra América*" (as Jose Martí described Latin America). She works on "the New Underground Railroad" transporting Mexicans across the U.S. border, at first unknowingly (when a pregnant Mexican woman sneaks aboard her truck), then quite consciously. Mosquito observes and relates the many histories and (often disparate) realities that characterize life in America, in addition to holding forth on such things as socio-cultural theory, Oprah Winfrey, the nuances of Puerto Rican curse words, Dante, and "blond rappers." Her closest friend is a Chicana intellectual and bartender, Delgadina, who introduces the ironically named Mosquito to the histories, languages, and cultures of the borderlands.

Since the publication of *Corregidora* (1975) and *Eva's Man* (1976), Gayl Jones's work has garnered substantial critical attention from scholars, particularly those reconsidering the painful histories and legacies of slavery and the Black female body.[18] The scholarly discourse on *Mosquito*, however, has been sparse, even though the novel directly treats one of the most prominent threads in current scholarship on the African Diaspora—Black internationalism.[19] Jones's novel develops a detailed account of a U.S. African American internationalism that interrogates and goes beyond recent discourse by positioning an individual who is not only Black, but who is also both female and working class, as the agent of this border crossing. What Jones's main character and novel display is not simply border crossing, though. Jones consciously and powerfully articulates a new type of hemispherism, one that differs from Delany's because it does not have as a goal the building of a specific "nation" (Black or otherwise) and therefore does not require the downplaying of differences, whether national, cultural, or linguistic. Jones constructs Mosquito as an individual who explicitly claims knowledge of the U.S. Southwest, in particular, and the world, in general, for herself and for other "cosmopolitan Negroes," to employ Mosquito's term.

No other U.S. African American novel since *Blake* has posited such a materially, ideologically, and geographically ambitious international vision, particularly one of the interconnectedness of U.S. African Americans and people of Latin American descent.[20] The implications of this intervention for American literary history are significant. *Mosquito* provides a paradigm for incorporating U.S. African Americans into hemispherist American Studies while also calling attention to the existence of a genealogy of U.S. African American hemispherism and locating itself within it. At the same time, Jones distinguishes her text in noteworthy ways, including making her protagonist significantly different from the exemplary man, a figure so definitively embodied in Delany's *Blake*.

Four other aspects of Jones's model stand out. First, Mosquito gains and expresses knowledge about communities beyond her own (racial and national). She works to decipher various local ways of thinking, seeing, and speaking instead of simply being aware of their existence. Mosquito goes beyond basic references to nations and cultures from all over the globe, to employing them in her effort to fathom the vast dimensions of human consciousness. Second, her movements across borders do not replace her link to her *patria* and cultural/racial community. Mosquito names and claims her U.S.-ness and her U.S. African Americanness even as she creates and/or names connections with the non-U.S. and the non-U.S. African American. Third, Jones critically analyzes philosophical discourses on the historical, contemporary, and future makeup and import of continental America. In particular, *Mosquito* confronts the meanings of the U.S.-Mexican border and the concept of "*la raza cosmica*" (the cosmic race). Fourth, she makes us aware of the consistent presence of the voice of Mosquito's Chicana intellectual friend, Delgadina, and the periodic but substantive presence of the voice of her U.S. African-American friend Monkey Bread. By positioning these women as narrative voices at key points, Jones creates a community of speaking cosmopolites who are women of color, and who also represent disparate elements of the American community and consciousness. Mosquito the character, because of this sharing of the narrative voice, avoids the burden of having to be the exemplary one, a burden that Jones suggests weighed down Blake. Mosquito is able to escape the trap because epistemology is at the heart of Jones's intervention.

Mosquito knows the world, particularly the world created and linked by the aforementioned "unequal relations." At one point, she both sings and contextualizes one of the hottest (Trinidad) carnival songs of 1999—"Big Truck." She even recalls the name of the group that sings the song. She compares her truck to the "Big Truck" in the song and the carnival celebrants milling around the truck to those who are fascinated by her truck: "it's just like in that Caribbean rap video where the people is following this big truck . . . lots of Caribbean peoples . . . I remember when I first heard that video I be in my truck sometimes and I just starts singing that song my ownself" (92). The dialectic of foreign versus familiar drives this moment. The "Big Truck" goes from being foreign to Mosquito, to being familiar, to ultimately being part of her cultural toolbox. At first the emphasis is on its Caribbeanness. Familiarity enters briefly as she tries to find the language to recognize it, and she ultimately makes sense of it using her own cultural referent—a rap video. Then she reiterates its distance from her by referencing the "Caribbean peoples" in the video. She again hints at its familiarity by indicating that she is able to remember when she first heard it. Eventually, she embraces it as part of her own repertoire and sings it herself.

In this transforming of the foreign into the familiar, Mosquito parallels Henry Blake, who was able to move so easily into communities that, at times, even the natives did not recognize him as a "foreigner." Crucially, though, in contrast to Blake's, Mosquito's epistemological interactions with the world are not explicitly marked as being in the service of a predetermined political mission.

For example, whereas Plácido's discussion of the British Caribbean was directly driven by a concern about whether the Blacks on the islands could help in "the mission," Mosquito and Delgadina's conversation about the British Caribbean is motivated by a desire to emphasize the epistemological links between the Caribbean and the United States. She connects the two histories through the story of a white U.S. woman who discovers that the story of the other America is also her story. After viewing *Roots*, "she decided that she'd trace her roots and traced them back to Jamaica. Well . . . when she goes to the little village she finds out the patriarch of her family is a little Black man (536). The woman went insane upon discovering that she was now Black according to her own—that is to say, the U.S.—racial classification system. As Mosquito points out, though, she need not have worried about the matter because "she coulda still played white in Jamaica" (536). She bases this notion on the fact that when Delgadina went to Jamaica, Jamaicans "thought she was white"

(536). She goes on to add that the woman could have chosen to continue to play white in the United States. In that additional insight she reveals the fundamental connection between the racial taxonomies of the United States and Jamaica—both have major holes. In one fell swoop, Jones dramatizes the fact that a working-class U.S. African American woman has this broad-based knowledge of the racial infrastructures of her continent and is able to mock their perpetual leakiness. Jones also calls attention to an interchangeability that she contends typifies the American condition. As Americans (broadly speaking), both Delgadina and the white woman who goes insane are heir to both the racial classification systems and the racial mixtures that distinguish the Americas and, more generally, the world created by the Atlantic slave trade.

Mosquito also identifies Brazil and the Cape Verde islands as part of her epistemological world. She intimates that the two countries exemplify the cultural contact and mixture that intrigue her: "They's a reddish tint to his brown complexion. Actually he one of them type of men of color. . . . Like a lot of them mens in Brazil. And I even seen Africans his complexion . . . I guess some of them Cape Verde Africans that color, though, on account of them Portuguese. Just like them Brazilians. But they's still natural Africans" (124). She connects and compares Brazil, Cape Verde, and Hawaii, retracing the geography of the Atlantic slave trade and U.S. imperialism, and connecting the peoples located along those routes. Here Jones at once invokes and subtly critiques the notion of people of color. She uses this notion to emphasize a connection between Brazilians, Cape Verdeans, and Hawaiians, but also undermines the concept by taking it literally and suggesting that the term *people of color* obfuscates the fact that the Brazilians and Cape Verdeans are "still natural Africans" with a definite African heritage. Mosquito's statement, therefore, troubles the notion that the only "natural Africans" are the dark ones. This statement is part of the broader interrogation of the belief in racial and cultural purity undertaken in the novel. At the same time, it indexes her desire to "find a center," to echo Antillean theorist Edouard Glissant.[21] Her statements here reinforce the fact that the hemispheric perspective put forward in *Mosquito* cannot and should not be read as being absolutely opposed to a desire for some sense of fixedness, whether of racial community or nation.

The novel actually begins with Mosquito claiming epistemological possession of U.S. terrain. She not only shows herself to be firmly connected to the United States, but also more connected to it than most others. She challenges the reader with her knowledge:

> Who amongst y'all knows the name of every tree? . . . I might not
> know the names of them trees, but I knows them by better than they
> names. . . . Now if you tries to play me for a fool and tell me that the
> tree you's planted is a South Florida tree. I knows that you might have

planted it in South Florida, but that its origins is in the Pacific Southwest or even South Central. (3)

Mosquito knows the length and breadth of the U.S. terrain, including the history of each tree, and strongly articulates that knowledge. She highlights her inherent instinctive knowledge of the fundamental building blocks of America. She rejects the mode of knowing that would focus on the memorization of the names of the trees in favor or a more instinctive way of knowing, one that she marks as "better." Crucially, her way of knowing is not disrupted by the movement of the trees from one site to another. In this way, Jones subtly links her discourse on the terrain with her arguments about the roots and routes of the people of the Americas. Routes do not negate roots. At the same time, she once again reveals a profound desire to identify a single root.

Mosquito goes on to claim a specific region of that U.S. terrain, the U.S. Southwest. She declares, "I knows the Southwest" (3), and emphasizes the fact that her claiming of the Southwest for herself (and other U.S. African Americans), Native Americans, and Mexicans is a rejoinder to European American claims: "You know that pueblo architecture. I guess that the Mexican influence, or the Native American aesthetic, it ain't neoclassicism. Though I guess them cowboys claims it like they claims the Southwest for theyself. There's them real cowboys . . . Mexicans and Navajos . . . and 'Oklahoma Africans'" (5).

The "real cowboys"—the Mexicans, Native Americans, and Africans—have been displaced by "them cowboys." Mosquito links the groups by calling attention to their common erasure by the "unequal relations" of epistemological power. The statement recalls Delany's reference to Latin Americans of color as "our brethren" in the pro-emigration text *Condition*, especially in its highlighting of terrain as a battleground for the oppressed peoples of the hemisphere.

Blackness and the Border

In fact, Mosquito uses the language of borders to explain the legal and material privileges that allow those in power to appear to be universal or cosmopolitan. They are privileged, not cosmopolitan, she argues, and the two should not be confused. Conversely, Blacks are oppressed, not provincial:

> The rich don't have borders, all the borders are open for them. Do you think the rich are respectors of borders? The rich don't have borders. They talk that patriotism shit for the common man so's they can keep him in their control. . . . The people who are really in power have no allegiance to any country. . . . They are above the law of any one country. There is no such thing as that, not when you're talking about people. I mean it's all a question of power. (297)

This point is made within the context of a novel that includes both her own travels and the migration of Mexicans to the United States (through the "new Underground Railroad"—a terminology that links the history of Blacks with that of Mexicans), thus denaturalizing the border. It is a site created, policed, and determined by those in power and one that only operates against those who are disempowered. U.S. African Americans and Mexicans are linked by the fact that they are both subject to borders. In addition, Mosquito's statement identifies patriotism as a tool of those in power, and national allegiance as a sentiment held only by the disempowered. She therefore encourages a connectedness that centers on the common condition of disempowerment and marginalization and consequently discards a focus on borders or national affinities, echoing Delany's stance in *Condition* but without the racialist energy of *Blake*.

Mosquito's drive to grapple with border discourse is intensified by her conversations with Delgadina. In one of those conversations the novel is implicitly identified as "border art." Delgadina defines border art in response to Mosquito's questioning:

> You know . . . border art can be anything. . . . You can even write a novel and call that border art. Anything that uses the real border or the border as metaphor is border art. But the concept of border art don't just have to be the Mexican-American border, though, it can be any country that has a border with another country. (284)

The border here is presented as metaphorical as well as material (as it is at several other points in the text). She calls attention to the universality of the concept of "the border," again illustrating the tug-of-war between the drives toward expansiveness and toward particularity evident throughout both *Mosquito* and *Blake*. Further, the border as defined here produces a border way of knowing ("border gnosis" in Walter Mignolo's words) that can then be represented in art.[22] The specific reference to a novel, and specifically to a novel that presents borders as both metaphorical and real, suggests that Jones intends this novel to be viewed as border art, thereby expanding the definition to include art produced by U.S. African Americans. Jones highlights the fact that aesthetic knowledge can be the basis of connections between Americans while also calling attention to the workings of power in the determination of which aesthetics and which aesthetic knowledge will be valued.

Jones also mines conceptualizations of race for their potential contributions to a hemispheric notion of community. She breaks from Delany by distancing *Mosquito* from the overt and purist racialism of *Blake*, and by extension from the text in which he most clearly delineated his purist notions of race—*The Origin of Races and Color* (1879). In the latter he states that a "general intermarriage of any two distinct races would eventually result simply in the destruction . . . of the less numerous of the two," and further that the "mixed race" offspring of an intermarriage is "an abnormal race," and will eventually, with continued crossings, once again become "one of the pure races."[23] In her exploration of possible alternatives, Jones directly takes up the concept of "*la raza cosmica*" (the cosmic race), first put forward by Mexican activist and philosopher José Vasconcelos, who argued that the cultural and racial *mestizaje* of Latin American people gave them the potential to be the cosmic race, the universal race that would bring peace and happiness and unite the different races of the world in harmony. He prophesied, "the world's races [will] tend to mix more and more, until they form a new human being, composed of a bit of all of the existing nations."[24] Jones chooses to foreground Vasconcelos in order to carve out a space for exchange, dialogue, and interaction between Latin Americans and U.S. African Americans, a move that is particularly instructive for hemispheric American studies. She explicates the concept and the way it speaks to the complexities within various Latin American and U.S. Latin American communities, but does not stop there. She critiques it and uses it to lay bare the, at times, ugly realities and underpinnings of the relations between U.S. African Americans and Mexican Americans.

For example, Mosquito speaks of a waitress whom she describes as "one of the brown skin Mexican Americans . . . the kind that you would mistake for African American till they tell you that they Mexican American or speak with they brand of English. . . . But they got Mexicans and Chicanos of all kindsa colors and people like Delgadina that why they call theyself the cosmic race" (189). Here she interrogates the notion that U.S. African Americans and Mexican Americans can easily be distinguished based solely on color, and in so doing questions the notion of an absolute separation between these two American ethnicities. Read within that context, then, her reference to the cosmic race is meant as an acknowledgement of the multiplicities that characterize Mexican American as well as U.S. African American histories and lives.

Mosquito also criticizes the racist and racial silences implicit in "*la raza cosmica*." After noting the multiplicity within Mexican American communities, she muses, "I ain't never heard nobody talk about African Mexicans, though, but I know that they had slavery in Mexico same as the U.S. . . . But most Mexicans she be telling me is mestizos which is a combination of Spanish and Indian. That the closest she come to admitting she got any African in her own ancestry" (189–190). She uses her knowledge of history to accomplish her goal of questioning the absence of Africans from this ideal of America as the home of the new universal human, "*la raza cosmica*." When Delgadina first introduces Mosquito to the concept, Delgadina encapsulates it by saying that Mexicans can look like a wide range of stars from Sean Young to Kim Basinger. Mosquito reflects, "only person she don't say she kinda look like is when we go to see one them Whoopi Goldberg movie. But the truth is, she kinda look like that

Whoopi Goldberg too, except she more yam-colored than that Whoopi" (121). Delgadina's rejection of the possibility that she might bear a resemblance to Whoopi Goldberg exemplifies a history and present of the erasure and negation of the Africanness within—a history that is a key reason, Jones suggests, that the utopian romantic hemispherism Bolivar, Delany, and others dreamed of cannot be fully realized.[25] This critique is a key part of Jones's hemispherist methodology, especially because it foregrounds not just the variation within specific groups, but also areas of potential friction between groups. She goes beyond simply creating a novel in which there are seamless, happy connections among resistant American communities.

Jones's refusal to represent hemispheric connections as seamless is further illustrated by the fact that Mosquito does mention conflict between U.S. African Americans and Mexicans at several points: "a lot of African Americans they be treating Mexicans and Chicanos just like them gringos like they's second-class or even third-class citizens" (183). It is important to note, though, that Mosquito is quoting Delgadina in this statement. Delgadina was able to identify her as not being from the Southwest because she treated Delgadina like a first-class citizen from the very beginning. The inclusion of substantial portions of Delgadina's notebook as well as her lengthy discourses work to reiterate Jones's commitment to having the text speak from multiple American perspectives. Delgadina's meditations on her identity, in particular, are included and appear to be aimed at providing insight into Mexican American experiences. Delgadina speaks of feeling lost because she is a creature of two worlds. She wonders, "Should I be in Latin America? Would I find my true self there?" (202); she speaks of the difficulty of writing in a language that is not her own; and she explicitly names the pain of being a child of the border: "I am exiled in this America" (204). She embodies the border between "this America" (the United States) and "*nuestra América*," not feeling wholly comfortable in either. She does not share Mosquito's comfort (whether epistemological, cultural, or otherwise) with the U.S. terrain.

For Jones, however, neither this sharing of the narrative voice nor the conflicting perspectives articulated in that process precludes *Mosquito* from being a truly U.S. African American text. Her dedication to both multiplicity and specificity is encapsulated in her 1994 article written in the voice of the U.S. African American novel: "I am a multicultural, multilinguistic, multivernacular novel and at the same time, I am a self-defined African American novel, that is *la verdadera historia*."[26] Jones blazes a trail—dramatizing the overlapping yet distinctive and sometimes contradictory elements of "the real story" of America in all its voices, while reminding us of those in whose footsteps she treads, expanding our notions of the presumed loci of hemispherist epistemology, and warning of the perils of overvaluing or imposing similitude in our drive toward a hemispheric perspective. It is all in the epistemology.

This essay has contextualized Jones's work, charting a genealogy of U.S. African American authorship that illustrates U.S. African American writers' cognizance and theorization of a hemispheric consciousness that does not oppose nation to hemisphere but shows the two to be mutually enforcing concepts. That *Blake* and *Mosquito* cover a range of themes, gender perspectives, chronological and geographical settings, historical events, and narrative voices and strategies points to the expansiveness of this generally unrecognized genealogy. If we are to honor this genealogy and truly reap the benefits of nuance and complexity promised by the hemispherist turn in American literary studies, we would do well to go beyond reifying reductive thinking that posits U.S. African American studies as either needing to be protected from the encroachment of approaches focused on Latin America (or Canada or the Caribbean, for that matter) or as a separate (nationally bound) entity altogether. The hemispheric engagements of U.S. African American writers did not begin or end with Langston Hughes. They are not always manifested in the figure of the cosmopolitan (male) intellectual traveling across national boundaries. The extent to which the full potential of the new hemispherism is realized depends on our commitment to listening to a range of American voices, to seeing America, the continents, through the eyes of all our Americas. As *Mosquito* reminds us, "we're more universal" when "we don't think everybody's supposed to be like us" (277).

NOTES

1. *U.S. African American* here refers to people of African descent from the United States. *African American* is a general term more appropriate for describing all people of African descent in the Americas. *Black* here is intended as a general term to index people of African descent more broadly.

2. Paul M. L. Moya and Ramón Saldivar, "Fictions of the Trans-American Imaginary," *Modern Fiction Studies* 49 (2003): 2.

3. See Jose David Saldivar, *The Dialectics of Our America: Genealogy: Cultural Critique, Literary History* (Durham: Duke University Press, 1991); Kirsten Silva Gruesz, *Ambassadors of Culture: The Transamerican Origins of Latino Writing* (Princeton: Princeton University Press, 2001); and Louis A. Pérez, *Cuba and the United States: Ties of Singular Intimacy* (Athens: University of Georgia Press, 1997).

4. Quoted in Bruce Robbins, *Feeling Global: Internationalism in Distress* (New York: New York University Press, 1999), 34.

5. Richard Jackson has been a pioneer in an effort to change this trend; see his *Black Writers and Latin America: Cross-Cultural Affinities* (Washington, D.C.: Howard University Press, 1998).

6. In my analysis of the nineteenth-century debates in this essay, I will focus on the first two arenas. I have explicated the third in much greater depth in *Black Cosmopolitanism: Racial Cosmopolitanism and Transnational Identity in the Nineteenth-Century Americas* (Philadelphia: University of Pennsylvania Press, 2005).

7. Martin Robison Delany, *The Condition, Elevation, Emigration, and Destiny of the Colored*

People of the United States. Politically Considered (1852; Baltimore: Black Classic Press, 1993), 180.

8. Among these is the "national manhood" identified by Dana Nelson in her analysis of the texts of white male public figures from the eighteenth- and nineteenth-century United States; see her *National Manhood: Capitalist Citizenship and the Imagined Fraternity of White Men* (Durham: Duke University Press, 1998).

9. The definitions of nation I am invoking here are: nation as the term to describe what results when a state structure defines itself through a particular territory—the nation-state; nation as "imagined community"; nation as a grouping identified by outsiders (Delany/Blake in this case) as a nation; and nation as "imagined community" with a desire to have a specific territory.

10. See Marisol Bello, "Detroit Council OKs Plan That Touts Racial Separation," *Detroit Free Press*, September 21, 2004, at *http://www.freep.com/news/locway/detplan21e_20040921.htm* (accessed July 21, 2005).

11. Gayl Jones, *Mosquito* (Boston: Beacon Press, 1999), 545. Future page references will be cited parenthetically in the text.

12. Caren Kaplan, *Questions of Travel: Postmodern Discourses of Displacement* (Durham: Duke University Press, 1996), 4.

13. See Thomas Schlereth, *The Cosmopolitan Ideal in Enlightenment Thought: Its Form and Function in the Ideas of Franklin, Hume, and Voltaire 1694–1790* (Notre Dame: University of Notre Dame Press, 1977).

14. See *Selected Writings of Bolivar*, ed. Lewis Bertrand (New York: Colonial Press, 1951), 38.

15. Delany, *Condition*, 188, 189.

16. Delany, *Blake; or, The Huts of America* (Boston: Beacon Press, 1970), 188, 189. Future page references will be cited parenthetically in the text.

17. See Pérez, *Cuba and the United States*, 39, 48.

18. Foundational texts in this scholarly discourse include: Claudia Tate, "Corregidora: Ursa's Blues Medley," *Black Literature Forum* 13 (1979): 139–141; and a special issue of *Callaloo* on "Gayle Jones: Poet and Fictionist," 5 (1982): 31–111.

19. See, for example, Paul Gilroy's *Black Atlantic: Modernity and Double Consciousness* (Cambridge, Mass.: Harvard University Press, 1993), Brent Edwards's *The Practice of Diaspora: Literature, Translation, and the Rise of Black Internationalism* (Cambridge, Mass.: Harvard University Press, 2003), Michelle Wright's *Becoming Black: Creating Identity in the African Diaspora* (Durham: Duke University Press, 2004), and my *Black Cosmopolitanism*. One of the few critical articles written on *Mosquito* is Carrie Tirado Bramen, "Speaking in Typeface: Characterizing Stereotypes in Gayl Jones's *Mosquito*," *Modern Fiction Studies* 49 (2003): 124–155.

20. That is not to say that other novels have not seriously engaged the international or that they have not been cosmopolitan. James Baldwin's *Another Country* (1960) and Claude McKay's *Banjo* (1929) are only two of the better-known works that have done so. They do not, however, deal with the Hispanophone Americas.

21. See Edouard Glissant, *Caribbean Discourse*, ed. J. Michael Dash (Charlottesville: University of Virginia Press, 1994).

22. See Walter Mignolo, *Local Histories/Global Designs: Coloniality, Subaltern Knowledges, and Border Thinking* (Princeton: Princeton University Press, 2000).

23. Delany, *The Origin of Races and Color* (1879; Baltimore: Black Class Press, 1991), 92–93.

24. José Vasconcelos, "La raza cósmico" (1925), in *Obras Completas* (México: Libreros Mexicanos, 1958), 2:901 (my translation); see also 909, 942.

25. For a recent scholarly discussion of this absence in Mexican historical discourse see Patrick J. Carroll, "Los mexicanos negros, el mestizaje y los fundamentos olvidados de la 'Raza Cosmica': Una perspectiva regional," *Historia Mexicana* 44 (1995): 403–437.

26. Jones, "From the Quest for Wholeness: Re-Imagining the African-American Novel: An Essay on Third Word Aesthetics," *Callaloo* 17 (1994): 509.

10

PEN and the Sword

U.S.–Latin American Cultural Diplomacy and the 1966 PEN Club Congress

DEBORAH COHN

In June of 1966, the International PEN[1] Club held its annual conference in New York City. This was the first time in forty-two years that the United States had hosted the meeting. Arthur Miller had just been elected president of the organization and the week-long congress, which drew more than 600 people from 56 countries, marked a moment of international prestige for PEN. Committed to promoting understanding and defending free expression, conference organizers sought to provide authors from all ideological backgrounds with an opportunity to communicate with one another and to create an environment in which Cold War politics were ostensibly put aside in favor of cultural exchange and interchange. In 1966, PEN had 76 centers in 55 countries.[2] It had always had a strong base in Europe, where most of its congresses had been held since it was founded in 1921. PEN officials were keenly aware of the significance of holding the conference in the United States at a time when Cold War tensions were high. Thus they did their best to facilitate the participation of delegates from centers in Eastern Europe and Cuba. Officials also reached out to so-called "Peripheral Writers" from Africa, Asia, and Latin America, where there were few established PEN centers. These efforts were motivated by a sincere desire to make the event a success and to use it as a means of stimulating PEN activity worldwide. At the same time, the outreach was a strategic move that reflected the contemporary surge of public interest in the United States concerning developing nations that were vulnerable to communist advances.

This essay studies the conference as a site of competing and conflicting interests between the hemispheric agenda of U.S. Cold War nationalism and aspirations for Western acclaim that were shared by a group of Latin American writers who were initially united in support of the Cuban Revolution (1959), which they regarded as bringing the possibility of political and cultural autonomy to Latin America. The conference marked a moment of extreme visibility for Latin American literature and is mentioned in almost every literary history that studies this period. I identify the many ways in which, following Pierre Bourdieu, the literary activity that the conference enabled took place within and was made possible by the U.S. field of power. Thus we can see how even the most avowedly non-political of organizations was not only caught up in a web of hemispheric cultural diplomacy but deliberately played to it, framing its bids for support from the U.S. State Department and philanthropic organizations in terms of the conference's contributions to the national interest. And yet it would be misleading to study the conference solely as an official hemispheric outreach program that served the U.S. national interest by extending its political reach and improving its image through the Americas—even if it was framed by organizers and approved by government officials as precisely this. Such an approach would only tell part of the story and would overlook a key aspect of the event's significance: the fact that Latin American writers viewed the conference as a platform for extending through the hemisphere and beyond the reach of a literary movement that was deeply interwoven with aspirations of regional sovereignty and solidarity. In order to understand the political and cultural forces at play in the conference, then, it must be studied from a vantage point that draws on both U.S. and Latin American studies. The conference's importance and legacy, I argue, lie in its status as a tug-of-war between U.S. national politics and hemispheric policies on the one hand and regional goals that transcended the interests of individual Latin American nations on the other.

In the 1950s and 1960s, Cold War politics played a determining role in molding U.S. cultural policy at home and abroad. This was a period of government-funded outreach and exchange programs such as the clandestinely Central Intelligence Agency–funded Congress for Cultural Freedom (CCF), the National Defense Education Act of 1958, and the U.S. Information Agency (USIA). Department of State and USIA funding for international tours of *Porgy and Bess* and jazz legends such as Louis Armstrong and Duke Ellington, for example, reflected the belief of many U.S. political leaders that cultural programs were a Cold War necessity. These programs operated on the principle that the promotion of U.S. art abroad was a testament to U.S. cultural achievements and artistic freedom and would bring prestige to the nation. In the long run, advocates of these programs expected that greater understanding of the nation's cultural production would benefit national security. In recent years, scholars such as David Caute, Walter Hixson, Michael Krenn, Frances Saunders, Lawrence Schwartz, Penny von Eschen, and others have made significant contributions to documenting the Cold War dimension of such outreach programs, focusing primarily on U.S. cultural diplomacy efforts with Europe and Africa and within the United States. Relatively little work has been done on the cultural politics at play in U.S.-Latin American relations, though,[3] and the 1966 PEN Congress has not been studied as an outreach program that similarly courted foreign intellectuals in the service of the national interest.

I have chosen to focus on the conference's intervention into U.S.-Latin American cultural diplomacy because of the tremendous opening that it provided for Carlos Fuentes and Mario Vargas Llosa, as well as other Latin American writers, who were at this moment rising to prominence throughout the West as part of a movement known as the "Boom" in Spanish American literature. Boom fiction was innovative and experimental. At the same time, the movement was a marketing phenomenon that was characterized by a dramatic increase in the publication, translation, and distribution of Latin American literature. As Lois Parkinson Zamora has observed, Boom writers participated in "an unprecedented literary conversation" in which they read and responded to one another's works, "emphasiz[ing] the communal nature of their literary project."[4] This "conversation" was an outgrowth of the writers' support for the Cuban Revolution: authors considered themselves to be part of a group whose agenda included constructing and promoting a pan-Spanish American cultural identity. At the time of the PEN Club meeting, the Boom was a major phenomenon in Spanish America and its star was on the rise in the United States. The U.S. academy recognized this ferment and began opening its doors to Latin American writers: from 1965 to 1967, Chilean novelist José Donoso was at the Writers' Workshop at the University of Iowa; Nicanor Parra, a Chilean poet, held a Fulbright at Louisiana State University from 1965 to 1966; and Mexican writer Octavio Paz was a visiting professor at Cornell in the spring of 1966, during the institution's "Latin American Year." The translation of Latin American literature was also receiving a great deal of critical and public attention. For example, since 1964, the Inter-American Foundation for the Arts (IAFA) had been promoting and subsidizing the translation of Latin American literature into English and helping to put Latin American writers in touch with U.S. writers and publishers. And in 1967, Gregory Rabassa received the first National Book Award for Translation for his translation of Julio Cortázar's *Hopscotch* (*Rayuela*).

The increasing interest in literature from Latin America was an outgrowth of the growing public interest in the region itself. The Cuban Revolution was deemed a "clear and present danger" that took the threat of communism to the United States' doorstep. The spread of Leftist activism throughout Latin America only heightened the interest in the region. National security, in the government's eyes, depended on the security of the hemisphere, and the United States worked to bring Latin America under its sway through political and cultural programs. Presidents Kennedy and Johnson used the Alliance for Progress as a means of gaining goodwill in the region, while private organizations with anti-communist inclinations such as the Ford and Rockefeller philanthropies joined forces with government agencies, directing funds at Latin American studies programs in the university, as well as at efforts to counter Cuba's influence on Latin American intellectuals by making U.S. cultural activity attractive to them. The timing of the conference was auspicious in terms of providing the United States with a public relations opportunity. Opposition to the Vietnam War was mounting both domestically and internationally and anti-Americanism was on the rise, fueled in Latin America by U.S. interventions in Cuba and the Dominican Republic. The conference also gave Latin American writers a timely opening that allowed them to position themselves as equals on a stage occupied by some of the world's most renowned and influential authors even as they cemented their bonds with one another. Thus the meeting served as a vector that simultaneously enabled U.S. policy interests in Latin America and Latin American writers' designs on the U.S. and Western literary and political scenes. It also brought to the foreground the dialogic nature of the relationship between North and South during the Cold War, and the polyvalent nature of the Cold War for both regions.

Conference Organization: Invitations, Funding, and Visas

PEN officials were aware of the political and cultural fervor in Latin America and set out to draw both established and up-and-coming writers from the region. In addition to delegates from existing PEN Centers, the PEN American Center invited Pablo Neruda, who had been a major attraction at the 1965 congress in Bled, Yugoslavia, as a headliner. It also worked to attract talented writers from countries where there were no PEN Centers. In late 1965, Lewis Galantière, a playwright, translator of French literature, and newly minted president of the PEN American Center, contacted experts on Latin America for the names of writers who best represented contemporary currents in literary activity; he ultimately invited more than forty of the writers who had been suggested to him.

PEN Club officials walked an extremely fine line in their preparation of the conference. Although they were insistent that the organization was "nonpolitical," it was virtually impossible to separate cultural activity from the political sphere at this time. Organizers faced two key hurdles: ensuring U.S. visas for international participants and raising funds for the conference itself. Both of these were determined by Cold War interests and pressures, and it was imperative to have government support in order to overcome them. At this time, there was very little public support for the arts, so PEN sought contributions from members, U.S. publishers, and various organizations. Most of the conference's funds came from philanthropies. The Ford Foundation was the largest benefactor, giving $75,000.[5] As Kathleen McCarthy has observed, during this period, the foundation's "international arts and humanities grants were cast in ideological terms, weapons in the Cold War quest for the hearts and minds of men."[6] This was evident in Galantière's framing of his application for funds from the foundation: "Your interest in the Congress, we suggest, may be viewed under these several aspects: world understanding; the American national interest in exposing to the American scene influential men and

women from thirty or more countries; and the preservation and encourage-
ment of literary values."[7] The commitment of these funds was directly tied to
the State Department's endorsement of the conference: the foundation asked
for, and received, an official letter indicating that the State Department supported the conference and its goals.

PEN was also in touch with the department because it needed to find out
how to facilitate the process of getting visas for conference participants. It was
emblematic of the times that Galantière's invitations to writers included an
urgent query as to whether the recipient could get a visa to enter the United
States. The question of visas had a direct bearing on the congress. Organizers
knew that the conference's success—and PEN's reputation—depended on their
being able to circumvent the Immigration and Naturalization Act of 1952, otherwise known as the McCarran-Walter Act. Section 212(a)(28) of this law authorized the denial of visas to foreigners who believed in, wrote about, or were
affiliated with organizations that promoted communism. With few exceptions,
McCarran-Walter automatically denied U.S. visas to communists or individuals
from communist countries, though the Department of State could authorize a
waiver of ineligibility if it chose. Visas for visitors from Cuba and East Germany
were more difficult to arrange.[8] So, too, were visas for individuals from non-
communist countries who had been blacklisted for communist affiliations or
anti-American statements.

Some of the experts whom Galantière consulted argued that the participation of Latin American writers in the congress could benefit the national interest. Robert Wool, the director of the IAFA, felt that it was important for political
reasons to invite Alejo Carpentier, a renowned writer and outspoken supporter
of the Cuban Revolution who was president of the Cuban PEN Center. He was
even more interested in having Neruda attend, for he was one of the most
widely read poets in the United States, as well as a communist with numerous
followers. According to Wool, his "influence and connections were so wide that
the gesture of inviting him (with assurance of a U.S. visa) was itself *politically*
useful. It would itself constitute an excellent way of dissuading others from
thinking of boycotting the Congress" (emphasis in original).[9] But, like several
others, Wool also expressed concern that some of the authors might have difficulty entering the United States under McCarran-Walter. This concern was well
founded, for Neruda, as well as several other prominent writers, had, in fact,
previously been denied U.S. visas. PEN officials were extremely concerned that
a State Department refusal to grant visas to delegates would not just be damag-
ing to the organization's reputation but could also prove embarrassing to the
United States. Thus they played up the congress's importance in meetings with
State Department officers, framing it as an event that would be in the national
interest because it would provide foreign intellectuals with a positive experience in the United States. Hence, John Farrar, head of Farrar, Straus, & Co. and
Galantière's predecessor as president of the PEN American Center, wrote to

Secretary of State Dean Rusk that writers abroad were "powerful moulders of public opinion and of government cultural policy," that literature was one of "this country's strongest moral forces in its international relations," and that the conference would therefore "be of special significance for the advancement of the American national interest."[10]

Conference organizers struggled to navigate the conflicting movements in U.S. Cold War policy. On the one hand, they needed to work around a "containment policy" that, among other things, tried to prevent communism from spreading to the United States by barring from the country foreign intellectuals with communist ties (however broadly defined), which would have kept many potential participants from the conference. On the other, the organization actively courted foreign writers in the hope that their presence at the conference would be "in the national interest," that is, that any goodwill that they bore toward the United States could be used to sway the attitudes of their compatriots toward the nation. In the year leading up to the conference, Galantière was in close touch with State Department officials. He pressed the case of PEN as a non-political organization that "nevertheless possessed a high degree of moral authority which had political consequences." He noted that Miller, the first American president of PEN International, had been elected unanimously over the objections of the French PEN Center, which had put forth a candidate "whose own attitude was inimical to the United States and whose friendly relations with communist circles were well-known." Miller was respected in both the United States and Eastern Europe, and Galantière claimed that his election was evidence of the respect of international writers for the U.S. literary community and "the service which, by its very existence, [this community] rendered the American national interest." Echoing Farrar, Galantière argued that the conference would attract writers from Africa, Asia, and Latin America who were "influential molders of opinion" and whose "exposure to the American scene was deemed desirable by the Department of State."[11]

Galantière was eager to demonstrate how the participation of Latin American writers would be of particular benefit to the national interest. As he wrote to Charles Frankel, assistant secretary of state for Educational and Cultural Affairs, "I believe it cannot be gainsaid that the most sensitive area today of anti-Americanism . . . among intellectuals is Latin America. . . . [The experts on Latin America that Galantière consulted] are in agreement about the political sensitiveness and influence of the literary and intellectual circles in these countries." Galantière paid special attention to getting a visa for Neruda, who had visited the United States in 1943 but repeatedly had visa requests denied since then, turning him into an even more vocal critic of the United States. He wrote to Frankel that

> strong cards would be taken out of anti-American hands, the climate
> in intellectual circles would change . . . if the Chilean Communist poet,

Pablo Neruda ... agreed to come and [was] granted [a visa. Neruda] would no longer be able to go about the world proclaiming that "They are afraid of me, a poet. Where else does this happen except in a fascist state?" To disarm the most widely read of all living poets in this manner, and to let him see for himself that Americans are not ogres would, I think, be in the American national interest.[12]

State Department officials agreed that the success of the congress and the cultural exchanges that it would enable were "in the national interest." Assistant secretary of state Harlan Cleveland wrote Galantière that he agreed "with Mr. Farrar's remarks on the influence exerted by writers and on the mutual benefits to be derived from discussions between writers from countries of widely varying political and social backgrounds."[13] Officials in the offices for Eastern Europe and Cuba agreed to assist with the arrangement of visas, including removing obstacles to approval and hastening the consideration of waivers when necessary. In the end, the challenge was greatly simplified when in May of 1966 the State Department conceded that the delays and humiliation entailed by the denial of visas had "marred this country's image as a free and open society" and announced "improved administrative machinery to expedite granting visas to guests of international conferences held in the United States." The new policy, which could only be applied to individuals traveling to international conferences or sports events, authorized the secretary of state to recommend that "the national interest requires a group waiver of the provision of law which would otherwise automatically exclude all persons invited to the conference who had at any time been associated with a Communist party."[14] The first group waiver was granted to the PEN Congress.

For conference organizers and most participants, the group waiver was the end of the story: there is no record of conference participants being denied visas under the new policy. The State and Justice Departments, however, remained interested in several of the participants, viewing their presence as potentially "contrary" or "prejudicial to the public interest." In particular, the Federal Bureau of Investigation (FBI) carefully monitored Neruda's U.S. visit. Weeks before the group waiver policy was approved, the U.S. Embassy in Chile recommended an advance waiver of Neruda's inadmissibility "so that the Communists would not be able to capitalize again on the portrayal of Neruda as a 'persecuted progressive.'"[15] Like Galantière, State Department officials were keenly aware that a visa denial would give Neruda an opportunity to publicly denounce the United States and granted him a visa on the grounds that "his admission ... would deprive [him] of the opportunity to make a public issue of United States immigration laws."[16] Additionally, J. Edgar Hoover had been following Neruda's activities since the early 1950s at least, so the bureau kept close tabs on him during his visit. The FBI director ordered the New York office to find out the details of his itinerary, adding that "In view of the subject's

Communist Party affiliations, New York should alert appropriate Latin American and Communist Party sources in order to be advised in the event subject's activities affect the security interest of the United States."[17] The FBI also alerted the White House as to Neruda's presence, "[i]n view of his prominence in the Chilean Communist Party and his easy entry into this country."[18] From the beginning of the planning through the conference itself, then, PEN sought out and/or was shadowed by official U.S. oversight of its meeting. At the same time, the organization also reached out to experts on Latin America in order to ensure that the region's cultural activity was accurately represented. Both interest groups agreed, for the most part, that the presence of Latin American writers would serve the U.S. national interest. Their ultimate goals were radically different, though, and U.S. officials, and even conference organizers, failed to take into consideration the importance of the conference to the writers themselves.

The Conference

The conference ran from June 12 to 18, and its official theme was "The Writer as Independent Spirit." The topic had obvious political implications, which PEN officials took pains both to acknowledge and deflect. As Farrar wrote to Rusk, "this theme reflects a movement which has been gathering force for ten years in the countries under authoritarian rule. . . . But I must add that International P.E.N., though constantly active in the defense of free expression and communication, is not a political organization, and this theme has not, for P.E.N., a narrowly political connotation."[19] PEN officials worried that political issues might arise that would thwart the spirit of open exchange that they hoped to foster at the conference. They were also concerned that the conference would become a forum for decrying the Sinyavsky-Daniel show trial of early 1966, in which two Soviet dissident writers had been convicted of "anti-Soviet activity." The incident had set off international protests and, because of the restrictions on freedom of expression that it reflected, it became a stumbling block in contemporary negotiations to set up a PEN center in the USSR. In the end, the case did not come up and, despite the ideological differences among participants, only two political interventions of note seem to have taken place. First, Valery Tarsis, a Russian writer who had been stripped of his citizenship and sent into exile for anti-communist remarks, called for a "hot war" and the atom bombing of the USSR. His speech was protested by fellow participants and condemned by Miller for violating the conference's goals of encouraging diversity of beliefs.[20] Second, during a session on "The Writer as Public Figure," Neruda and Ignazio Silone, an Italian anti-communist writer, got into a heated ideological debate. Silone declared the intellectual to be "the leader against the totalitarian state," and Neruda, who felt singled out by the remark, challenged Silone's characterization of the socialist states as totalitarian and took him to task for introducing the Cold War into the discussion; he also claimed that he had met more happy writers in socialist countries than in capitalist ones. All subsequent panelists except Miller attacked Neruda for his declaration.[21]

In general, Latin American writers held a prominent place in activities throughout the week. The conference opened with an extremely successful public reading by Neruda—his first ever in the United States—at the Poetry Center of the 92nd Street YWHA-YMHA. Archibald MacLeish introduced the event by stating that Neruda should be considered "'an American poet' since the word 'American' belonged to both continents and since South America was too small to lay exclusive claim to such expansive myth-making."[22] One of Neruda's translators brought the audience to its feet by declaring the Chilean the greatest living poet anywhere. Neruda read pieces that spanned his career, including several anti-American and anti-imperial poems. During the rest of the week, Latin American writers were well-represented on the round tables that were the cornerstones of the conference: Brazilian poet Haroldo de Campos spoke on "The Writer in the Electronic Age" along with R. Buckminster Fuller, Richmond Lattimore, Marshall McLuhan, and Norman Podhoretz; Fuentes and his compatriot Ramón Parrés, as well as Ralph Ellison, participated in the session on "Literature and the Social Sciences on the Nature of Contemporary Man"; and João Guimarães Rosa of Brazil and Victoria Ocampo, an Argentine writer and vice president of PEN International, appeared with William Jovanovich and Melvin Lasky in the panel on "The Writer as Collaborator in Other Men's Purposes."[23] Neruda was originally scheduled to participate in the panel on "The Writer in the Electronic Age," but he protested that it was not an appropriate subject for him (according to one observer, some of the Latin Americans "thought that this was PEN's way of neutralizing Neruda") and he was reassigned to the aforementioned panel with Silone.[24]

But the most memorable event at the congress for the Latin American writers was one that was not in the original program. Despite the rising international prominence of Latin American literature, many writers had not yet met in person. The PEN Congress provided them with a unique opportunity to do so, which they seized by asking Miller to set up a session on Latin American literature. Miller agreed and asked Emir Rodríguez Monegal, a Uruguayan critic and editor of *Mundo Nuevo* (Paris), a new journal focusing on contemporary currents in Latin American literature, to moderate the panel. Altogether, twenty-three Latin American writers from seven countries attended the conference[25] and many of them spoke at the session, which was open to all participants. The problems that each writer identified were echoed repeatedly. Writers observed that high levels of illiteracy resulted in few publishing opportunities in the regions and small markets. Speakers addressed the problem of isolation and the difficulty of fostering the pan-Latin American literary tradition that the Boom sought to cultivate when there was little circulation of works within or between the different nations. They also spoke about underdevelopment and the writer's responsibility to challenge censorship and take up the cause of the poor. Several writers acknowledged the importance of the PEN Club in bringing them together and helping them to overcome the obstacles that they faced. Neruda called on Vargas Llosa, who had been particularly eloquent on the lack of a social role for literature in Peru, to found a PEN Center upon his return home. Manuel Balbontín, president of the Chilean PEN Club, presented several proposals to the organization: that it lobby to have Latin American and Spanish literature included in high school and university curricula; that it urge large publishers to translate and publish selected Latin American works in English; and that it set up a committee with Latin American representatives to compile a collection of key literary works from the region for translation. Miller closed the session by offering PEN's services in attempting to address these issues.[26]

Though hailing from different nations, the spirit of transnational camaraderie that characterized the Boom was evident throughout the conference. Writers seemed to view themselves not as representing their own nations, but as part of a Latin American delegation, and they were given pride of place at the conference. Miller, for example, spent quite a bit of time socializing with them during the week and later praised the impromptu round table as "the most encouraging and useful session."[27] Rodríguez Monegal wrote that the conference marked Miller's discovery of Latin American literature.[28] In fact, the Latin American writers used the congress, created in the shadow of and in many ways enabled by the United States' hemispheric Cold War agenda, to open the eyes of writers from the United States and abroad to their work, and to make connections that would serve them well as their fame grew over the next few years.

Backlash: PEN, Publicity, and More Politics

In terms of both publicity and material support for the promotion of Latin American literature in the United States, the PEN Congress was a windfall. Following the conference, Roger Stevens, chairman of the newly founded National Endowment for the Arts (NEA), heeded Balbontín's call to support the dissemination of Latin American literature in the United States by awarding a grant to the IAFA to support the foundation's fledgling translation program.[29] Such funding was critical: it helped the organization to offset the cost of translation for presses that were reluctant to assume all of the financial risks involved in publishing works by authors who were only beginning to gain reputations in the United States. The NEA funds also subsidized the foundation's 1967 conference in Puerto Azul, Venezuela, allowing several of these authors to continue their dialogues with other Latin American and U.S. authors, including Miller.

Neruda took advantage of being in the United States to visit Washington, D.C., where he recorded some of his poetry for the Library of Congress collection. He also gave a reading at the University of California at Berkeley that was attended by Allen Ginsberg and Lawrence Ferlinghetti, as well as by Vargas Llosa and Uruguayans Juan Carlos Onetti and Carlos Martínez Moreno, who were traveling together at PEN's expense in order to make connections with the U.S. literary community. Neruda and Ferlinghetti had met in Havana in 1960 and were drawn to one another by both politics and literature. (As Ferlinghetti has repeatedly commented, Neruda declared to him when they met that "I love your wide-open poetry," to which he responded, "You opened the door.") Ferlinghetti had been involved in publishing Spanish American literature for some years—City Lights released Chilean poet Nicanor Parra's *Antipoems* in 1960—and, along with Ginsberg, had traveled to Chile in 1960 to participate in a meeting of writers, where they had met Parra, Martínez Moreno, and others. After Neruda's recital, the Beat poets spent several days showing Vargas Llosa, Martínez Moreno, and Onetti around San Francisco.[30] It was a meeting of radically different movements—the counterculture of the Beats in contrast to the masculinist cosmopolitanism and aspirations of Western acclaim of the Latin Americans—that nevertheless bore witness to the growing imbrication of the lives and work of writers from different nations in the hemisphere.

The conference received widespread coverage in the *New York Times* and elsewhere; *The Nation* published an article on Neruda's activities in New York and promised to include more articles on Latin American literature in the future. Neruda deemed the conference "the best international meeting of writers to date" and congratulated the PEN Club on being "the first institution to break down the Cold War boundaries between the capitalist and socialist worlds during the postwar period."[31] The round table devoted to Latin American literature was widely publicized in U.S. media directed at Hispanic readers and in newspapers and journals throughout Latin America. Rita Guibert, a journalist for *"Life" en español*, a Spanish edition of *Life* magazine that included additional articles on Hispanic topics, covered the conference, as did Miller's wife, Inge Morath, who was a photographer with the magazine. The August 1 issue of *"Life" en español* included an interview by Guibert with Neruda and an article in which Fuentes hailed the conference as a sign of the end of the Cold War in literature. Rodríguez Monegal, in turn, published a chronicle of his experiences at the conference in *Mundo Nuevo* later that year[32] as well as a transcript of the round table on Latin American literature.[33]

Not all of the publicity for the congress was positive, however. The Cold War tensions that Fuentes identified as having been laid to rest soon resurfaced dramatically. In late July, newspapers in Havana published an open letter to Neruda in which a number of Cuban writers, including Carpentier, Roberto Fernández Retamar, and Nicolás Guillén—all of whom had declined invitations to the conference—denounced the presence of Latin American writers at the event. The Cubans declared that the United States' authorization of visas for the Latin Americans and other Leftists had been politically expedient. They viewed intellectual exchanges between the United States and Latin America as part of a concerted "castration program" and claimed that the writers' participation in the conference could be presented as a symbol of easing up of Cold War tensions and used as a means of neutralizing opposition to U.S. politics at home and in Latin America. The Cubans further criticized Neruda for, supposedly, betraying the Revolution.[34] The letter also brought Rodríguez Monegal and Fuentes into the fray. Since *Mundo Nuevo* was founded in early 1966, the former's position as editor had been extremely embattled. Even before the first issue was published, rumors that the journal received covert funds from the U.S. government began to circulate. From the beginning, many pro-Cuban intellectuals publicly denounced the journal, and several writers refused to publish in it. The last straw came in April of 1966, when the *New York Times* broke a story on covert CIA funding of several anticommunist organizations, including the CCF, which was *Mundo Nuevo*'s primary source of financial support.[35] Several widely circulating Cuban and pro-Cuban journals followed the story closely and vilified Rodríguez Monegal for his supposed complicity with a U.S.-determined political agenda—accusations that the letter from the Cubans also leveled. (Had the Cubans known the details of Neruda's trip to Washington, D.C., they would no doubt have criticized him for this, too: the poet was invited to the capital by Stephen Spender, who was then the poet laureate consultant in poetry to the Library of Congress, but who is perhaps better known as a founder and editor of the CCF's British journal, *Encounter*.) Finally, the letter excoriated Fuentes for speaking in his article in *"Life" en español*—described as an instrument of the U.S. establishment and an "organ of imperialist propaganda"—of the "end of the Cold War in any field at the same time that North American troops, that have just assaulted the Congo and Santo Domingo, savagely attack Vietnam and prepare to do it anew in Cuba."[36]

The letter from the Cubans took Neruda and Fuentes by surprise. Neruda was not accustomed to having to defend himself against other supporters of Cuba and he was profoundly shaken. He sent the Cubans a telegram in which he reiterated his commitment to the Revolution and called on them to work together with him toward "the necessary continental, antiimperialist unity among writers and all revolutionary forces."[37] Fuentes, in turn, who at this time still supported the Cuban Revolution, found himself on the one hand accused of selling out the Revolution and, on the other, repeatedly denied visas to enter the United States because of his support of Castro and other Leftist causes. He made no public response to the letter, but pulled out of writing an introduction for an edition of Carpentier's *The Lost Steps* because "I have no wish to be further assailed by the Cuban writers . . . [and because] it is obvious that my prologue would be considered by Carpentier and the Cuban writers as some sort of Fifth column activity . . . I feel personally insulted by the declarations I refer to."[38] These authors' responses reflected an incipient breakdown in the political unity that had heretofore held the Left together.

"In the National Interest"

In 1971, what became known as "the Padilla affair" brought about the final disintegration of political unity in the Left, once and for all splintering support for the Revolution among intellectuals from Latin America, the United States, and Europe. For several years, Cuban poet Heberto Padilla had written work in which dissent from the official line was evident. While there were some attempts to censor his work, he was generally held up as an example of the Revolution's ability to tolerate criticism from within. In 1971, however, Padilla was arrested as a "counterrevolutionary"; he was not released for more than a month, and only after he issued a public "confession" in which he recanted his dissident views. Writers such as Fuentes, Vargas Llosa, Simone de Beauvoir, Juan Goytisolo, Jean-Paul Sartre, and Susan Sontag, among others,[39] signed a public letter of protest to Fidel Castro, and many formally broke with Castro and the Revolution at this time. Like the Padilla affair, the Cubans' letter to Neruda in 1966 responded to the increasingly hard line that Castro was taking toward dissent. The letter came on the heels of criticism by Castro of the Chilean Communist Party, which was on a more "revisionist" and less "revolutionary" course at this time. Neruda was a member of the Chilean Party and some suspected that the letter was directed at the Party as well as at, and through, the poet.

The letter and its aftermath foreshadowed the Padilla affair and the schism that it introduced among supporters of Cuba. This incident, too, came with a price tag for the Revolution, as well as what might have been seen as side benefits for the U.S. national interest. Fuentes's support of Cuba cooled significantly after this episode. The letter also left Neruda, a longtime defender of socialist revolution, hamstrung, and his ability to support Cuba severely compromised. As his longtime friend Jorge Edwards wrote, "how could he continue as a communist militant and at the same time direct his heavy artillery, of proven efficacy, against his colleagues, who represented a young revolution, the only one on the American continent, the only one that spoke our language?"[40] On a personal level, the poet never completely forgave the Cubans. He never again interacted with Carpentier, even though the two had been friends for years, and even though this avoidance required careful choreography in later years, when Neruda, in his capacity as Chilean ambassador to France under Salvador Allende, had to visit the Cuban Embassy in Paris where Carpentier was the cultural attaché.[41] And he took his revenge on Guillén obliquely in his memoirs, where he refers to Spanish poet Jorge Guillén as "Guillén (the good one: the Spanish one)."[42]

PEN officials carefully followed the fallout from the letter. According to a post-conference report, "Cuban and other Communist Party reproaches against Neruda brought articles by other Latin Americans in his defense, and in refutation of the charges leveled against the United States in the communist press." This observation was, however, but a small part of PEN officials' efforts to spin the conference's accomplishments in terms of their benefit to the national interest. They complimented themselves on the attendance of foreign intellectuals whose role as public figures could be "seen in the newly developing countries where, because writers form a high proportion of the educated social stratum, they fill leading posts in diplomacy, ministries of education and information, institutions of learning . . . and the mass as well as the quality journals." They also stated that participants saw "The fact that delegates from the East German PEN Center could be present at the first congress they had ever attended on non-communist soil, and that the world-renowned communist Chilean poet, Pablo Neruda, was able, through our intercession, to come to the United States for the first time since 1943 . . . as confirmation that the U.S. Government, though it defrayed a part of the costs, did not intervene to lend the congress a propaganda cast." Finally, they claimed that "By arranging the presence of twenty-three prominent Latin American writers . . . American P.E.N. dissipated a cloud that had long hung over U.S.-Latin-American relations in literary and intellectual circles, at least to the extent that for those writers the United States has ceased to be symbolized exclusively by the 'big business' whipping boys of the militant anti-Yanqui."[43]

For U.S. officials, PEN officers, and Latin American writers alike, the PEN Congress had several unintended consequences. For the Latin Americans, the conference was both a beginning and an end. It marked a turning point in the visibility of the writers and their work in the United States. At the same time, even as the writers strived to create an image of a transnational movement unified by and grounded in its support for Cuba, the event brought to the foreground tensions among different types of Leftism that, in turn, precipitated political rifts that forever changed several key writers' relationships with the Revolution. Thus the aftermath of the letter from the Cubans anticipated the polarization of attitudes toward the island that became more pronounced in the 1970s. From the perspective of Cold War cultural diplomacy, the conference was a paradox, and all parties in the tug-of-war went home declaring victory. On the one hand, the congress was one of many staging grounds in the battle for "the hearts and minds" of foreign intellectuals, and it was extremely successful in its goal of generating symbolic capital for the United States throughout the hemisphere and beyond. On the other, it functioned as a venue that allowed writers from an "at risk" region, many of whom were drawn together precisely by their support for Cuba, to deepen their relationships and pursue their ideals within the political sphere of the antagonist. Official U.S. interests saw the Latin American writers as cultural diplomats whose goodwill was to be cultivated as a means of influencing public opinion in their native lands. Despite the PEN Club's final assessment of the conference's effects on the writers, though, the latter eluded the reach of the United States' hemispheric Cold War agenda. The Latin American authors instead viewed themselves as ambassadors representing their region to the West, and they did their utmost at the conference to usher Latin American literature into an international mainstream, erasing once and for all the label with which PEN had previously identified them: "Peripheral Writers (Latin-America)." It is a testament to the success of these authors' goals that Vargas Llosa, who attended the conference as an up-and-coming writer from a country that did not have its own center, became president of PEN International in 1976.

As a case study, the PEN Congress demonstrates the limitations of scholarly approaches that are confined within the national or regional boundaries set by area studies, themselves products of the Cold War. As of the 1960s, the field of cultural production for Latin American literature was truly international: many authors lived in Paris, spent time in the United States, and published in Spain. They established close, and mutually influential, friendships and collaborations with U.S. and European writers. The history of the conference underscores this process of reciprocal influence. Thus it demonstrates the necessity of redefining the parameters of study of Latin American (and U.S.) literature as hemispheric rather than regional or national by revealing the extent to which Latin American literary production at this time was tied to both Latin American and U.S. fields of power, which were themselves so tightly interwoven. Latin Americanists have traditionally emphasized the opportunities for networking and visibility that the conference afforded Latin American authors, as well as the attack on Neruda. This is important to understanding the history of the Boom, but it overlooks the considerable role that the hemispheric agenda of U.S. Cold War nationalism played in enabling the conference in general and the attendance of the Latin Americans in particular. However, a study that focused on PEN's and the State Department's courting of Latin American writers as "molders of opinion" would deny these writers the agency—and the agenda—that was clearly in evidence in their efforts to establish Latin American literature as a phenomenon worthy of international attention. In the final analysis, the conference serves as both a model and a touchstone for hemispheric American studies. The congress brought together individuals from different nations and regions in symbiotic relationships even as it laid bare both the contradictory forces at play in U.S. Cold War cultural politics and the schisms in the Latin American Left. As a discipline, hemispheric American studies must likewise find a way of acknowledging that it is more than the sum of its national and regional studies parts, an approach that allows it to recognize and accommodate the differences within the parts as well as the bridges—and contradictions—that join them.

NOTES

I want to thank the National Endowment for the Humanities and Vanderbilt University's Robert Penn Warren Center for the Humanities for fellowships that have been of tremendous assistance to my research; any views, findings, or conclusions expressed here do not necessarily reflect those of these institutions. I am also grateful to Claire Fox, Matt Guterl, George Handley, and, especially, to Caroline Levander and Robert Levine for their comments on this essay. Finally, I am indebted to Mario Vargas Llosa and Rita Guibert for interviews that provided me with insights into the conference, and to John King and Gerald Martin for their helpful responses to my many queries.

1. The acronym stands for "poets, playwrights, essayists, editors, and novelists."

2. Preliminary docket to Henry T. Heald from F. F. Hill, October 11, 1965. PA0600-0051, Ford Foundation Archives (hereafter FFA). Used with permission of the Ford Foundation.

3. The essay by Claire Fox in this volume is a key exception and an important contribution to scholarship in this field.

4. Lois Parkinson Zamora, *Writing the Apocalypse: Historical Vision in Contemporary U.S. and Latin American Fiction* (Cambridge: Cambridge University Press, 1989), 20–21.

5. Preliminary docket to Heald from Hill, October 11, 1965, PA0600-0051, FFA.

6. McCarthy, "From Cold War to Cultural Development: The International Cultural Activities of the Ford Foundation, 1950–1980," *Daedalus* 116 (Winter 1987): 93.

7. Proposal from Galantière to Ford Foundation, June 23, 1965, PA0600-0051, FFA.

8. Exchange agreements with the USSR made it easier for Russians to get U.S. visas.

9. Memorandum, Galantière to Congress File—Peripheral Writers (Latin-America), February 14, 1966, Department of Rare Books and Special Collections, Princeton University Library, PEN Archives, Box 157, Folder 12 (henceforth identified as "PEN Archives"). Used with permission of Princeton University Library.

10. Letter, Farrar to Rusk, April 12, 1965, PEN Archives, Box 160, Folder 6.

11. All citations from confidential memo from Galantière, September 20, 1965, PEN Archives, Box 160, Folder 6.

12. All citations from letter, Galantière to Frankel, March 2, 1966, PEN Archives, Box 160, Folder 6.

13. Letter, Cleveland to Galantière, April 28, 1965, PEN Archives, Box 160, Folder 6.

14. Citations from Department of State press release, Joint Statement by the Departments of State and Justice, May 3, 1966, PEN Archives, Box 160, Folder 6.

15. Biographical sketch of Ricardo Neftali Reyes Basoalto from FBI (Washington, D.C.), August 23, 1966, 100-HQ-163706, Serials 1–49, Section 1, obtained from the FBI under the Freedom of Information and Privacy Act (FOIPA).

16. Memorandum from W. R. Wannall to W. C. Sullivan, June 23, 1966, 100-HQ-163706, Serials 1–49, Section 1, FOIPA.

17. Airtel from J. Edgar Hoover to SAC, New York, June 17, 1966, 100-HQ-163706, Serials 1–49, Section 1, FOIPA.

18. Memorandum from J. Edgar Hoover to SAC, New York, August 5, 1966, 100-HQ-163706, Serials 1–49, Section 1, FOIPA.

19. Letter, Farrar to Rusk, April 12, 1965, PEN Archives, Box 160, Folder 6.

20. "Soviet Writers Denounce P.E.N," *New York Times*, 29 July 1966, <http://www.il.proquest. com/proquest/> (NYT ProQuest; accessed July 5, 2006).

21. See Harry Gilroy, "Ideologies Stir P.E.N.Delegates," *New York Times*, 18 June 1966 (NYT ProQuest; accessed June 5, 2006), and Luis Yglesias, "Pablo Neruda: The Poet in New York," *The Nation*, 1 July 1966, 52–55.

22. Selden Rodman, "All American," *New York Times*, 10 July 1966 (NYT ProQuest; accessed, 7 June 2006).

23. List of round tables and participants, PEN Archives, Box 160, folder 1.

24. Yglesias, "Pablo Neruda," 53.

25. "Some Results of the XXXIV International P.E.N. Congress," n.d., PA0600-0051, FFA.

26. For a transcription of the session, see "Papel del escritor en América Latina," *Mundo Nuevo* 5 (noviembre de 1966): 25–35.

27. Miller, *Timebends: A Life* (New York: Harper & Row, 1987), 595.

28. See Rodríguez Monegal, "Diario del P.E.N. Club," *Mundo Nuevo* 4 (octubre de 1966): 41–51, reprinted at <http://www.archivodeprensa.edu.uy/r_monegal/bibliografia/ prensa/artpren/mundo/mundo_046.htm> (accessed 7 June 2006).

29. Rodriguez Monegal, "Diario."

30. Vargas Llosa, interview by author, tape recording, 21 May 2006, Stratford, UK.

31. Quoted in Rodríguez Monegal, "El P.E.N. Club contra la guerra fría," *Mundo Nuevo* 5 (noviembre de 1966), 87. Translation mine. Unless otherwise noted, all subsequent translations are mine as well.

32. Rodríguez Monegal, "Diario del P.E.N. Club."

33. See "Papel del escritor en América Latina."

34. "Carta abierta de los intelectuales cubanos a Pablo Neruda," *Marcha* 1315 (agosto 5 de 1966), 31.

35. Rodríguez Monegal always denied that the journal's funding came from the Congress, even in the face of evidence to the contrary.

36. "Carta abierta," 30.

37. "Habla el poeta," *Marcha* 1315 (agosto 5 de 1966), 31.

38. Cited from a letter from Carlos Fuentes to Herbert Weinstock dated 16 November 1966, in the Alfred A. Knopf, Inc., records held by the Harry Ransom Humanities Research Center at the University of Texas at Austin Library, box 918, folder 13. Used with permission of the Ransom Center.

39. Gabriel García Márquez's and Cortázar's signatures also appeared on the letter, though the former subsequently claimed that he had not consented to having his name included and the latter retracted his protest and affirmed his support of Castro.

40. Edwards, *Adiós, Poeta* (Barcelona: Tusquets Editores, S.A., 1990), 149.

41. Ibid., 150

42. Neruda, *Confieso que he vivido: Memorias*, 2nd edition (Buenos Aires: Editorial Losada, 1974), 165.

43. All citations from "Some Results of the XXXIV International P.E.N. Congress," Report from PEN to the Ford Foundation, n.d., PA0600-0051, FFA.

11

The Hemispheric Routes of "El Nuevo Arte Nuestro"

The Pan American Union, Cultural Policy, and the Cold War

CLAIRE F. FOX

In 1948 the Organization of American States (OAS) became the supreme governmental body of the inter-American system, while the name of its predecessor organization, the Pan American Union (PAU), continued to refer to the Organization's General Secretariat in Washington, D.C. Undergirded by two far-reaching hemispheric security treaties, the Organization envisioned a cultural arm to round out its hemispheric profile, and in this regard, a relatively small office at the Pan American Union known as the Visual Arts Division emerged to play a singular role among U.S.-based arts institutions in the two decades following World War II. Previously, during the Good Neighbor Policy period, New York's Museum of Modern Art (MoMA) and Nelson Rockefeller's Office of the Commissioner on Inter-American Affairs had dominated hemispheric arts initiatives through large-scale traveling exhibitions and other forms of cultural exchange. After the war, these institutions passed the torch of hemispheric cultural policy to the Pan American Union, where the Visual Arts Division, under the directorship of Cuban critic and curator José Gómez Sicre, carried on the work of organizing arts programs for U.S. and Latin American publics.

Gómez Sicre's ebullient 1959 proclamation of the birth of a hemispheric arts circuit in the Americas captures the heady optimism of these postwar years:

> El artista joven de América sabe que van naciendo centros internacionales de arte en su propio continente y tiene ya como puntos obligados de recepción, a Nueva York y a Buenos Aires, a Rio de Janeiro y a Lima, a Ciudad de México y a São Paulo, a Caracas y a Washington. . . . París ha dejado de ser "el centro" para convertirse en "un centro" más.

> (The young American artist knows that international art centers are being born in his own continent and now has as obligatory reception

points New York and Buenos Aires, Rio de Janeiro and Lima, Mexico City
and São Paulo, Caracas and Washington. . . . Paris has stopped being "the
center" in order to become "another center.")[1]

This hemispheric panorama promised not only renewed cultural and intellectual exchange between the Americas and European countries following the
privations of World War II, but also, for the first time, the possibility of cultural parity with them.[2] The "young artist," a recurring protagonist of Gómez
Sicre's criticism, liberates himself from national arts institutions where stale,
official tendencies such as indigenism and muralism still flourish. He breaks
the "vicious cycle" of "academia-beca al exterior-salón nacional-premio-
profesorado" (academy–foreign grant–national salon–prize-professorship)[3]
in order to make a cosmopolitan pilgrim's journey through the hemisphere's
capitals, with an obligatory stop at the PAU in Washington, D.C.

It is likely that the prototype for this "young artist" is José Luis Cuevas, a
twenty-one-year-old draftsman from Mexico City whom Gómez Sicre recruited
for his first major solo exhibition at the Pan American Union in 1954. The
show's resounding success propelled the enfant terrible toward international
stardom. Cuevas's drawings sold out immediately, leading to a meeting with
Alfred H. Barr, Jr., director of collections at the Museum of Modern Art,
coverage in *Time* magazine, and New York gallery representation, as well as
enthusiastic critical reception in Paris and the blessing of Picasso. For Gómez
Sicre, who had struggled to get Latin American artists to exhibit at the PAU,[4]
the show marked the beginning of a long career arc, the high points of which
included organizing the Esso (Standard Oil) Salons for Young Artists throughout Latin America in 1964–1965 and the founding of the Museum of Modern
Art of Latin America at the PAU in 1976.[5]

Cuevas and Gómez Sicre maintained an enduring friendship, while Cuevas's art and celebrity went on to generate volumes of spirited polemics, many
penned by the artist himself. This essay focuses on three important moments
in the Gómez Sicre–Cuevas relationship—1954, 1958–1959, and 1967–1968—in
order to explore how Cuevas's "hemispheric" success assumed different forms
in U.S. and Mexican contexts. Cuevas's divergent profile in each country owes
something to his keen awareness of their respective cultural institutions
and policies. Toby Miller and George Yúdice observe that in Anglo-European
contexts cultural policy is traditionally aimed at transforming an "ethically
incomplete" citizen into a "well-rounded" one, through state-sponsored mass
education and arts programs.[6] The OAS adopted a similar model for its cultural policies of the postwar period; the "well-rounded" hemispheric citizen
stood at the center of ever-widening communities extending from city to
nation and continent. Given the long-standing tradition of anti-imperialism
in Mexico and that country's own strong state cultural policies dating from

the post-Revolutionary period, however, some Mexican intellectuals perceived the OAS's offer of hemispheric citizenship as an either/or proposition, one that pitted U.S.-identified hemispherism against national sovereignty. Cuevas skillfully negotiated this either/or proposition through his self-conscious presentation in the media and his canny use of allegory and citation, although I argue that the hemispheric Cuevas and the national Cuevas often seemed to address different publics and issues. In the United States, Cuevas was portrayed as an angst-ridden visionary of the postwar period, while in Mexico he was a consummate parodist and staunch critic of the national political and artistic culture. In this binational dynamic, a third country, Cuba, also played a significant role. Gómez Sicre's negative personal experiences with several members of the Cuban intellectual sector influenced his interactions with artists in Mexico and elsewhere, and Cuevas's own Cuban heritage likewise helped to cement his friendship with Gómez Sicre. And, as Cuba became a flashpoint of the Cold War in the Americas during the 1960s, the PAU cultural programs became increasingly concerned with countering American intellectuals' support for the Cuban Revolution.

Regardless of geographical or ideological perspective, a preoccupation with Cuevas's national identity pervades the existing critical work about the artist. Cuevas's petulance toward the Mexican School of Art, epitomized in the murals of "los tres grandes"—Diego Rivera, David Alfaro Siqueiros, and José Clemente Orozco—provoked some critics to position him symbolically outside of the Mexican nation. Ida Rodríguez Prampolini is not alone among critics in questioning whether Cuevas's drawings could have even been inspired by Mexican realities.[7] Cuevas's opposition to post-Revolutionary Mexican nationalism and state-supported arts led many critics to align him with a loosely configured tradition of Mexican avant-garde artists whom Octavio Paz retroactively identified as emissaries of La Ruptura (The Rupture).[8] While Cuevas's early supporters praised his art for its universality and transcendence, his detractors criticized it for being "ensimismado" ("self-absorbed") or "extranjerizante" (foreign).[9] These poles of debate can be loosely associated with the artist's U.S. and Mexican profiles outlined previously; however, the dichotomy is further complicated by the fact that contemporary debates *within* the Mexican intellectual sector also revolved around an opposition between "universalism" and "nationalism," albeit with a different ideological valence than the one circulated through the OAS. Cuevas belonged to a generation of postwar Mexico City-based intellectuals who, as Deborah Cohn has argued, crafted a fusion of internationalism, mexicanidad, and left-inflected pan-Latin Americanism that became hegemonic in the Mexican cultural arena from the late 1940s through the late 1960s, defining itself in opposition to particular strains of nationalist populism associated with the institutionalization of the Mexican Revolution from the 1920s through the mid-1940s.[10] The publication of Octavio Paz's landmark essay collection, *El laberinto de la soledad (The Laby-rinth of Solitude)*, in 1950, according to Cohn, marked the consecration of the cosmopolitanist discourse on Mexican identity and culture.[11] For the emergent intelligentsia loosely coalescing around *El laberinto*'s easy intercalation of Western and autochthonous cultural elements, she clarifies, "cosmopolitanism was never meant as a means of eluding Mexico and its problems," but rather, it was viewed as a path for Mexico to assume its place as a peer among nations in the postwar international community.[12] In matters of literary and artistic taste, nevertheless, this group shared Gómez Sicre's predilection for experimental modernist aesthetics over didactic or documentary realism, a mode perceived by both parties to be outmoded and mannerist.[13] Keeping in mind these points of formal convergence and ideological divergence throughout this essay, I underscore Cuevas's fluency in the languages of Cold War universalism at the PAU and the urban cosmopolitanism of his Mexican coterie in order to highlight the way in which Cuevas's diverging profiles expose increasing tensions between two Cold War area designations: the "third world" that fractures the Americas along a north-south axis, and the united "western hemisphere" envisioned by the OAS security framework.

Cuevas's art has been the subject of perceptive and thorough scholarly study, but his roles as a writer and public intellectual merit further attention, for they illuminate the larger question of how Latin American intellectuals attempted to reconcile the concepts of an autonomous national or local culture with a burgeoning postwar international art market, increasingly concentrated in the United States. My approach to the study of cultural policy attends not only to its purported objectives, but also to its deployment and reception in different locations. As Mary Louise Pratt has argued, metropolitan narratives of modernity rarely envision the transformations that they will undergo in the course of their own diffusion.[14] This is true of the PAU arts programs, which differed from other U.S.-based Cold War cultural diplomacy initiatives in that they were not concerned with exporting U.S. art to Latin America, or vice versa, but rather with finding and promoting Latin American cognates for particular values and ideas. The programs interacted opportunistically with existing modernist currents in many different locations in ways that sometimes challenged the metamessage of containment and resulted in unusual or unpredictable alliances. Cuevas's extensive travel along the hemispheric art circuit in the early years of his career, for example, led to an advocacy of pan-Latin American modernisms that he marshaled in an effort to reform the Mexican cultural establishment. Through this analysis, I hope to contribute to an emerging body of scholarship about the cultural Cold War in the Americas, as well as to ongoing research about twentieth-century American aesthetic movements that distinguishes intersecting modernist trajectories from generalizations about "Latin American art" that are still prevalent in U.S.-based criticism.[15]

New York Stole the Idea of Modern Art—Then What?
The PAU Visual Arts Division Under José Gómez Sicre

Gómez Sicre's egalitarian view of the hemisphere's "art centers" avoids the difficult issue of New York's emerging prominence among the art worlds of the Americas and Europe in the postwar period.[16] Scholars have noted that as the Popular Front gave way to the Cold War, cultural capital shifted from Europe to the United States, and in aesthetic terms, critical consensus tended away from various forms of social realism and toward abstraction and other avant-garde aesthetics.[17] Art historian Serge Guilbaut regards the period 1946–1951 in the United States as a formative "silent interval," when a range of critical discourses about abstraction and modern art became consolidated into an overarching narrative of the New York School's triumph over the School of Paris.[18] After that, abstract expressionist painting in the United States became a "weapon of the Cold War," conveying notions of free expression, individualism, and sanctioned dissidence in U.S.-produced propaganda for export.[19] The PAU Visual Arts programs have been described in terms that roughly follow these trends in the U.S. art world, that is, as part of a vast Cold War propaganda machine for which Gómez Sicre devised his own brand of "political apoliticism" in order to combat various tendencies of committed art in Latin America.[20] While his taste, ideas about modern art, and exhibition practices all owe something to the Good Neighbor Policy arts programs of the 1940s, Gómez Sicre gradually modified their orientation at the PAU, emptying them largely of their U.S. content and framing them instead through corporate multinational patronage and Latin Americanist discourses explicitly tied to concepts of supranational citizenship, universalism, developmentalism, and rebellious, youthful aesthetics.

The uneven power dynamic among the hemisphere's "art centers" in the postwar period paralleled the structure of the OAS more generally. The years following the establishment of a hemispheric security framework were ones of continual crisis for the newly baptized Organization, as the inter-American system took the form of "coexistence not only between a rich, powerful state and twenty small, weak ones sharing the same continent, but between different social systems and much else besides."[21] The Cold War ushered in a period of heightened U.S. interventionism in Latin American countries, at the rate of about one intervention every thirteen months during the decade of the 1960s.[22] Cuevas's 1954 exhibition at the PAU occurred at an important juncture in the OAS's early history, several weeks after the Central Intelligence Agency–organized coup of the democratically elected Jacobo Arbenz presidency in Guatemala. The coup was preceded by OAS debates in which the United States sought to censure Arbenz's regime, culminating in John Foster Dulles's "Caracas Declaration," which the Mexican delegation ultimately abstained from signing on non-interventionist principles.[23]

Within the OAS, the PAU Department of Cultural Affairs was anomalous for its preoccupation with *Latin American* cultural identity during the Cold War period, in seeming contrast to the Organization's broader concerns with *hemispheric* security and economic policy. The PAU cultural programs reflected a relatively narrow view of culture as elite arts and letters. They capitalized on an arielista disdain for U.S. philistinism, proffering a culturalist, continental version of "Nuestra América" that implicitly targeted official Latin American nationalisms as obstacles to hemispheric unity.[24] The PAU Department of Cultural Affairs' concept of cultural citizenship stressed "modernity without modernization," as it detached cultural autonomy from political and economic questions, and offered a model of Latin American belonging that preempted other potentially threatening forms of internationalism based on class or ethnicity.

The Organization's first Latin American Secretary General, former Colombian president Alberto Lleras Camargo (1947–1954), funded the PAU Department of Cultural Affairs in an effort to modernize the OAS and give it a Latin American profile.[25] The "Latin Americanization" of the PAU provided a supportive atmosphere for Gómez Sicre to develop arts programs that challenged exotic and folkloric stereotypes about Latin American culture commonly held in the United States. A native of Matanzas, Cuba, Gómez Sicre traveled to New York in the early 1940s to pursue the study of art history and criticism. He was a self-taught art critic and curator who had mounted shows in Cuba and the Dominican Republic and leveraged this background to become an advisor to Alfred H. Barr, Jr., on the Museum of Modern Art's 1944 exhibition "Cuban Painting Today." Over the course of his thirty-five years at the PAU, Gómez Sicre helped secure the international careers of a select group of Latin American artists, curated nearly four hundred exhibitions, and served as an ad hoc art dealer and consultant. His curatorial reach extended from U.S. to Latin American arts institutions, as well as to juried international competitions and biennials.[26] Gómez Sicre's critical writings are, in the charitable words of fellow critic Marta Traba, "casi franciscanos" (almost Franciscan),[27] but his talent for organizing exhibitions, administrative acumen, and taste, communicated through witty and often devastating bons mots, converted his office into a major institutional player in the hemisphere's art worlds.

Gómez Sicre acted as an informal art dealer at the PAU, where he cultivated relationships with the OAS ambassadors and undersold artists' work to them. Sometimes the artists complained about this practice, but Gómez Sicre countered that he was stimulating their careers by circulating their work throughout the hemisphere.[28] Indeed, one of his highest compliments to an artist was to declare his work "exportable."[29] Gómez Sicre's advocacy of free trade in the arts provided a partial resolution to the contradiction between Latin Americanism and pan-Americanism that separated culture from the other branches of the OAS. For him, value accrued to art through international circulation and exchange; implicit in this perspective was the idea that U.S. arts institutions were not so much a terminus for Latin American art as an export-processing zone, where aspiring artists had critical and monetary value added to their work before having it re-exported to Latin America. Gómez Sicre's general view of culture through the lens of comparative advantage rather than national patrimony presages the type of supranational arts administration that characterizes many contemporary neoliberal cultural policies.[30]

Gómez Sicre's personal background helps to account for his advocacy of a continental, as opposed to national, approach to modern art. In Havana, he had been affiliated with progressive intellectual circles associated with El Lyceum and the Galería del Prado, but he was also frustrated by the apathy he encountered toward the arts in a system that favored academicism and those with connections.[31] Although Gómez Sicre described his love of art as arising out of patriotism ("amor patrío"),[32] it is likely that his cubanía functioned as a blessing and a curse after the 1961 Punta del Este conference, which culminated in the controversial vote to expel Cuba from the OAS. Claiming to have survived a McCarthy-era witch hunt within the Organization thanks to his brother's military connections, Gómez Sicre now found himself barred from hiring his old friend, Cuban artist Mario Carreño, to work with him at the PAU,[33] while he closely monitored the political orientation of Latin American artists and maintained a Cuban artistic presence through exhibitions featuring art by Cuban exiles. Gómez Sicre perceived himself as a Cold Warrior; his pronounced anti-leftism figured prominently in his curatorial judgments well into the 1980s.[34] Yet, his status as a pre-Revolutionary Cuban immigrant also made him a complex figure who cannot be characterized as a mere spokesperson for U.S. foreign policy. He supported corporate patronage of the arts but despised "the vulgarity of the North Americans"; he opposed both Batista and Castro; and he recognized Puerto Rican art even though the OAS did not recognize Puerto Rico.[35]

Gómez Sicre, Cuevas, and Kafka

Gómez Sicre's writings of the immediate postwar period display a search for counterparts to U.S. trends. His 1946 "Credo" echoes some ideas associated with prominent U.S. critics such as his mentor at the Museum of Modern Art, Alfred H. Barr, Jr.: namely, that art and politics are "corrientes paralelas que no deben confluir" (parallel currents that should not flow together); the masses should be trained to appreciate difficult art instead of consuming facile genres; and modern art must continually nourish itself "de viejas cenizas o de frutos exóticos" (through old ashes or exotic fruit), this last point, a tacit endorsement of primitivism that resonates with Gómez Sicre's profound interest in pre-Columbian and Afro-Cuban cultures.[36] Eventually, Gómez Sicre replaced such programmatic formulations with references to his own stable of curatorial triumphs. Although José Luis Cuevas's youthful exhuberance and autodidacticism at first suggest an unlikely embodiment of Gómez Sicre's critical values, Gómez Sicre seemed immediately to grasp the young draftsman's potential to serve as an emblem of "el nuevo arte nuestro" (our new art)[37] in Latin America, while Cuevas's thematic concerns with the human condition promised marketability in the United States and Europe—in other words, Cuevas was "exportable."

The "internationalism" of the postwar era presented a double bind for Latin American artists, for often they could not gain entrée to the art market without deracinating their work and relocating to Europe or the United States.[38] Evidently, Cuevas struck the right chord between assimilation and distinction with his metropolitan critics. His drawings and lithographs evoked comparisons to classical and contemporary European masters, especially figures such as Goya, Daumier, Toulouse-Lautrec, Grosz, and Picasso; these reviews stressed the importance of tradition and craft for the artist's aesthetic project. At the same time, Cuevas's work drew enough associations with Mexican traditional and popular arts—from Nayarit sculpture to Oaxacan candy skulls—so as not to be labeled derivative. From the mid-1950s to the mid-1960s, Cuevas's supporters praised his work for transcending parochial Mexican nationalism and Cold War dichotomies; they held up Cuevas's expressive figuration as a golden mean between what they characterized as the antiseptic, mannerist abstraction favored in the United States, and the dogmatic social realism associated with the Soviet Union.

The mediating figure of famed Mexican muralist José Clemente Orozco is crucial in positioning Cuevas's aesthetic as one of "feliz mestizaje" (happy mestizaje)[39] between Europe and the Americas and between Moscow and Washington, D.C. On the occasion of Cuevas's first solo exhibitions in the United States and Europe, Gómez Sicre and French museologist Jean Cassou respectively compared Cuevas's expressive techniques to those of Orozco. Cuevas had a conflicted relation to the muralists, but his satirical impulse and unflinching gaze at the seamy side of life, conveyed through grotesquerie and exaggeration, shared affinities with Orozco, even though the latter was more explicit than Cuevas in condemning the abuse of power.[40] In any case, the generational affiliation served Cuevas well; in 1960 U.S. critic Selden Rodman dubbed Cuevas "Orozco's heir" in his influential book, *The Insiders*, which helped to consecrate Cuevas's reputation in the United States and Mexico. Rodman's paean to a new generation of figurative artists, the "insiders" of the book's title, explicitly attacked both abstract expressionism and socialist realism from the anti-Stalinist left, while promoting heightened subjectivity and expressive figuration as ethically appropriate modes of artistic production in a time of apocalyptic crisis. Cuevas's critical reputation was further bolstered by Argentine-Colombian critic Marta Traba's 1965 study, *Los cuatro monstrous cardinales (The Four Cardinal Monsters)*, the "monstrous" a sobriquet that Cuevas shared with Willem de Kooning, Francis Bacon, and Jean Dubuffet. Traba also championed expressive figuration as a third way, but unlike Rodman—who ascribed a messianic and redemptive mission to this aesthetic—Traba viewed Cuevas as an unwitting medium, channeling collective horror through his own personal solitude.[41]

Cuevas's formation as an artist, beginning with a quasi-mythical birth above the paper factory where his grandfather worked as a manager, became a recurring theme in Cuevas criticism and the artist's own writings. Cuevas had drawn since early childhood, developing his skills during a life-threatening bout of rheumatic fever at the age of ten, which put an end to his occasional lessons at Mexico City's famous art school, La Esmeralda. He resumed art lessons briefly in his teens under the direction of Lola Cueto at Mexico City College, but for the most part he was self-taught. His older brother was a psychiatrist in training at a public mental institution in Mexico City, and as an adolescent, Cuevas would accompany his brother to work, making quick sketches of the patients as his brother performed his rounds. Cuevas' drawings from the early 1950s demonstrate a fascination with Mexico City's lumpen, its prostitutes, beggars, criminals, disabled, and mentally ill, whom he observed from the window of his family apartment as a child.[42] The human body, including his own, in states of extremity—death, illness, madness, decay, sexual arousal, or deformity—and rendered monochromatically in delicate, hesitant lines punctuated by occasional explosions of ink, would come to be his signature aesthetic.

Felipe Orlando, a Cuban painter residing in Mexico, introduced Cuevas to Gómez Sicre in 1954, which in turn led to the invitation to exhibit at the PAU. Both Gómez Sicre and Cuevas shared Catalán-Cuban ancestry, and the Cuban connection helped to cement their friendship.[43] Cuevas's mother's family was Cuban by way of Mérida, Yucatán, and it appears that, for his part, Gómez Sicre brought memories of his own experiences in Cuba to bear on his interactions with Cuevas and the Mexican arts establishment. Cuevas's thematics bore a resemblance to those of Gómez Sicre's old friend Fidelio Ponce de León, a tubercular, maudit painter whose jaundiced eye contrasted with the exuberant neobaroque espoused by the Grupo Orígenes, Gómez Sicre's former intellectual antagonists.[44] As a young man, Gómez Sicre had sustained his own polemics with Siquieros. Cuevas came from the relatively small Mexican middle class that was striving for self-definition in an age of heightened developmentalism; his willingness to hold up a cracked mirror to the nascent Mexican "economic miracle," brash irreverence toward the establishment, and youthful ambition no doubt read as a sort of retributive narrative to Gómez Sicre.

Over a two-month period in summer 1954, the PAU's makeshift gallery exhibited forty-three of Cuevas's drawings and watercolors. The works, ranging in price from $15 to $40, sold out completely; several were purchased through agents on behalf of U.S. collectors and museums.[45] The drawings, culled from several different series, featured portraits from the psychiatric hospital and morgue where Cuevas's brother worked and from Mexico City's poor neighborhoods, including midwives, prostitutes, and malnourished and disabled children.[46] In terms of scale, intimacy, and subject matter, the exhibition was a dramatic contrast to the grand thematics of Mexican muralism. The PAU show was Cuevas's first major solo exhibition, and in a basic sense, it provided him with an immediate professionalization. Within days of the vernissage, Cuevas sold his work to the Museum of Modern Art and made his first lithograph.[47] More profoundly, the PAU consecrated Cuevas's self-fashioning as an "alienated visionary," a persona that he would selectively display in publicity through the ensuing decades. Clad in an overcoat, riding the subway, and leaning out of doorways on the streets of New York, Cuevas gazed provocatively from photoessays on the pages of *Cosmopolitan* and *Life en español*. This photogenic persona was explicitly tutored by Gómez Sicre and cued to referents in Anglo-European aesthetic modernism, existentialist philosophy, and the Holocaust (Figure 1). Already a budding polemicist, Cuevas began tying his art to literature after the PAU exhibition; not only did he begin to combine literary and visual elements in his work, but he started to write extensively about his influences. The *Time* coverage of the PAU exhibition captures Cuevas as a coy poseur, noting "He found [Washington, D.C.] too orderly and antiseptic for inspiration. But Cuevas managed to escape [the exhibition], spent some time at St. Elizabeth's Hospital for the mentally ill, sketching."[48] He went to the hospital in search of another modernist hero, Ezra Pound, who was interned there at the time. Cuevas later recounted bemusedly how much he enjoyed shocking his U.S. readers through the *Time* piece, in which he confessed to having discovered his artistic vocation while sketching a disembowled rabbit.[49]

As Cuevas boarded the train in Washington, D.C., bound for New York after the exhibition's opening events, Gómez Sicre gave Cuevas copies of Franz Kafka's "The Metamorphosis" and *The Trial*.[50] The inspiration that Cuevas drew from these works resulted in their next collaborative project, a suite of pen-and-ink drawings, titled *The Worlds of Kafka and Cuevas* and published in 1959 as a bilingual, limited edition artist's book by Falcon Press in Philadelphia. The book debuts a different Cuevas than the one featured in the 1954 exhibition, as Shifra Goldman notes:

> It was in the era following Cuevas' Pan American Union show that he began to withdraw from *apunte del natural* (drawings from life) and turn increasingly to his imagination, literature, and art for artistic inspiration. More and more his work featured monsters, grotesques, freaks, and aberrations—a trend that apparently began with his response to Kafka.[51]

The Worlds of Kafka and Cuevas arose through Cuevas's two-month residency at the Philadelphia Museum College of Art in the winter of 1957–1958. Its

FIGURE 1. José Luis Cuevas and José Gómez Sicre standing before Georges Braque's *Still Life: Le Jour* (1929), National Gallery of Art, Washington, D.C., 1957. Photo courtesy Biblioteca y Centro de Documentación "Octavio Paz," Museo José Luis Cuevas. © 2007 Artists Rights Society (ARS), New York/ADAGP, Paris/SOMAAP, Mexico City.

twenty-four folio pages juxtapose Cuevas's drawings to excerpts from Kafka's *Amerika* and *The Trial*, Kafka's personal letters, and select interpretations of Kafka's work by psychotherapist Rollo May and Kafka's biographer Max Brod. Gómez Sicre's introduction to *The Worlds of Kafka and Cuevas* relates Cuevas to the "Czech visionary" through their shared psychic primitivism and archetypal characters:

> Both artists . . . satirize and give vent to scorn; both suffer from inadaptability to society; both feel crushed by the burden of a humanity which to them is repulsive. The figures of Cuevas' drawings, which, though almost always based on tangible reality, never seek to present individual

characterizations, were already the equivalent of mankind as depicted
in Kafka's novels—gross, brutal and subhuman.[52]

Gómez Sicre's Kafka is a prophet of the Cold War, that "loneliness, emptiness,
and anxiety which would engulf us in the twentieth century."[53] *The Worlds
of Kafka and Cuevas* stresses personal alienation and psychoanalytical interpretations of Kafka's life and work over the author's countervailing social
criticism.[54] In years following, Gómez Sicre continued to provide similar inspirational material to Cuevas during the latter's dry spells. Cuevas recalls, for
example, that in 1971, Gómez Sicre sent him photographs of the Dachau concentration camp and Freud's Vienna office in the hope that they would ignite
the artist's inspiration, but they did not do the trick.[55]

Cuevas's longstanding fascination with Kafka, commencing with this project, however, gently resists Gómez Sicre's universalist framing in favor of a
more specific allegorical interpretation. Cuevas's mass ingestion of the emerging field of comparative literature was no doubt a gambit for placement in
the international art market, but it also opened the door to a polysemic game
of references, for in the Mexican context, Cuevas's grotesque renditions of
canonical works could also be interpreted through the lens of "critical appropriation" prevalent in many aspects of Latin American expressive culture.[56]
Just as Sander Gilman argues that Kafka's European Jewish readers possessed a
cultural formation that enabled them to perceive a darkly humorous retelling
of the Dreyfus Affair in *The Trial*, so Cuevas tied Kafka's allegorical tales to a set
of Mexican referents that described his own position with respect to cultural
nationalism.[57] The social Kafka certainly emerged in Cuevas's native country,
where he and author Carlos Fuentes transculturated *The Trial*'s boundless
bureaucracy through their derogatory nickname for Mexico, "Kafkahuamilpa,"
coined precisely when the Gustavo Díaz Ordaz administration (1964–1970) was
reviving cultural nationalism as an official discourse.[58] In Mexico, too, Gómez
Sicre's appropriation of Jewishness as a general code for alienation was tem-
pered by Cuevas's emerging consciousness of his Sephardic heritage on his
father's side, as Cuevas developed connections to prominent Ashkenazim in
the Mexican cultural industries and expressed support for Israel in the mid-
1960s. In Mexico, Kafka served as Cuevas's gateway to a new form of cultural
politics that permitted him to be politically active in Mexico while claiming a
set of affinities beyond the nation.

Meanwhile, Behind the Cactus Curtain . . .

The image of Cuevas as an alienated, solitary artist seems incongruous in
Mexico City, where he rapidly became visible among the capital's beautiful
people and identified with la Zona Rosa, the upscale commercial district that
he claims to have named. Cuevas was almost always affiliated with some arts

group, though his commitments were sometimes fleeting, and the breakups sometimes rancorous, as in the case of his relationship to the figurative artists of Nueva Presencia (New Presence).[59] Cuevas moved in and out of various circles from the mid-1950s to the mid-1960s, including the artists associated with Galería Prisse, Galería Proteo, Galería Souza, Los Interioristas (the Interiorists, precursors to Nueva Presencia), and Los Hartos (the Fed-up). His coterie extended beyond the plastic arts to the hipster intellectuals known as La Mafia,[60] and actors and directors associated with experimental film and theater, such as Alfonso Arau and Alejandro Jodorovsky. Though they differed in significant respects, these figures shared a common orientation broadly aimed at introducing new aesthetic currents and creating alternative cultural venues around nightclubs, theaters, galleries, magazines, and commercial districts. As Jean Franco has observed, Cuevas participated in a broad generational campaign waged against exclusionary cultural policies; those who rebelled were "not for 'accessibility' but rather for access."[61]

In spite of this wave of anti-establishment cultural activity, the Mexican press frequently portrayed Cuevas as a "títere del imperialismo" (puppet of imperialism), while Siqueiros accused Gómez Sicre of "destrozando al movimiento pictórico mexicano" (destroying the Mexican pictorial movement), and Gómez Sicre and Cuevas were rumored to be lovers.[62] Gómez Sicre's institutional affiliation suggested another manifestation of U.S. cultural imperialism that threatened the venerable muralist movement and its attendant values of heroic masculinity and national sovereignty. These overlapping sexual and geopolitical threats converged in a caricature by Alberto Beltrán that appeared in 1960 in the Mexico City newspaper *Excélsior*, in which Gómez Sicre appears as a feminized liberty figure before the U.S. Capitol building, cradling a fetal José Luis Cuevas in the train of his flowing gown. With one gesture, Gómez Sicre banishes the old regime (including a Revolutionary solider rendered in muralist fashion), as he ushers in the new (Figure 2).

Although powerful leftist critics in Mexico, such as Raquel Tibol, opposed Cuevas, he also had his defenders among progressive intellectuals affiliated with *México en la cultura*, the cultural supplement of the Mexico City newspaper *Novedades*, to which Cuevas also contributed. From the late 1950s through the 1960s Cuevas effectively defended himself from his detractors through the publication of polemical "open letters" in the press in which he insisted on his ideological independence and protested his exclusion from the national arts establishment. As Cuevas began to exhibit his work in Latin American countries, he forwarded reports to the Mexican press about the art scenes of cities such as Caracas, Santiago, Lima, and Buenos Aires, and he denounced Eurocentrism and unilateralism on the part of Latin American arts institutions. Cuevas's growing international profile facilitated his cultivation of a speaking position uncorrupted by state clientelism, a purity by virtue of exclusion, as it were.

FIGURE 2. Caricature of José Gómez Sicre and José Luis Cuevas by Alberto Beltrán as an accompaniment to the article by S. Mozhniagun, "La estética viciosa del abstraccionismo" ("The Vicious Aesthetic of Abstractionism"), *Excélsior*, sección dominical, año XLIV, tomo II, 27 de marzo de 1960. Courtesy of Periódico Excélsior, S.A. de C.V.

One of Cuevas's early letters published in *México en la cultura* in 1958, while Cuevas was in New York following his Philadelphia residency, utilized the phrase "La Cortina de Nopal" (the Cactus Curtain) to develop an extended analogy between Soviet socialist realism and Mexican muralism. The following year a translation titled, "The Cactus Curtain: An Open Letter on Conformity in Mexican Art" appeared in the United States in an issue of *The Evergreen Review* dedicated to Mexican culture; both versions of the letter circulated widely in the United States and Mexico.[63] Though Cuevas's critique of muralism was certainly not original by the late 1950s, "The Cactus Curtain" exceeded common bounds of decorum in terms of its irreverence and thinly veiled references to real individuals. The letter introduces an allegorical working-class boy named Juan, whose parents fail to appreciate the monumental portraits of their noble ancestors displayed prominently in murals about town, and are instead moved by movie stars, radio soap operas, popular singing idols, and other mass cultural icons. Juan displays artistic inclinations at an early age, and he enters the state art school where he learns to draw "las figuras simplificadas" (simplified figures) and hackneyed themes.[64] Juan experiences an epiphany one day when by chance he comes across some foreign art books and is moved by this work produced outside of Mexico. But, in order to gain the protection of the national arts institutions, he suppresses his decadent foreign drawings and declares himself to be a member of the "Mexican School" on a questionnaire at the Instituto Nacional de Bellas Artes (National Institute of Fine Arts). In its Orwellian conclusion, Juan becomes thoroughly incorporated into the state arts establishment. At first he believes that he can sell his derivative work to tourists while pursuing his own agenda, but instead he ends up wealthy and brainwashed, spouting slogans such as, "[E]l tequila es la mejor bebida del mundo y que 'Como México no hay dos' y que el resto del mundo debiera alimentarse de enchiladas" (Tequila is the best drink in the whole world. There is no country like Mexico. The rest of the universe ought to eat enchiladas).[65]

Fellow "mafioso" Carlos Monsiváis perceives in Cuevas's early writings a direct assault on certain shibboleths of Mexican political culture under the ruling party, the PRI: Cuevas's egotism confronts the party's opportunistic populism; his cosmopolitanism challenges the use of xenophobia as a form of censorship; and his stridence defies el ninguneo, or imposed invisibility.[66] In the United States, however, the analogy linking Mexico to the Soviet Union lends the letter to a broad Cold War interpretation, as in the case of the *Kafka and Cuevas* book. An attentive reading of "The Cactus Curtain" and other writings from this period makes it clear that Cuevas conflates myriad totalitarianisms, from Batista's Cuba to Imperial Russia, Nazi Germany, and Peronist Argentina. But in the U.S. context, Cuevas's letter made him appear to be a dissident oppressed by a communist bureaucracy.[67] From the perspective of Eisenhower-era containment policies, "The Cactus Curtain" was a fitting endorsement of Gómez Sicre's programs targeted at "rescuing" the continent's young artists.

The conclusion of "The Cactus Curtain" features another narrative shift, from allegory back to autobiography, as Cuevas defiantly proclaims his ongoing struggle against all of the "Juans" in his life.[68] Yet reading Juan's life story next to Cuevas's gives the vertiginous impression that the fictional Juan and the real Cuevas actually share much in common, for each has his share of formative experiences with unsupportive fathers, nude models, and humiliation at the Instituto Nacional de Bellas Artes. Juan, the hack, ends up selling his work to vulgar tourists, while Cuevas does sell his work in Mexico, but "casi siempre a extranjeros" (almost always to foreigners).[69] Cuevas's internationalism leads him to struggle against el ninguneo (invisibility), and Juan's nationalism alienates him from his own creativity. These parallel plotlines suggest another way of reading Cuevas's allegory, one that might be called transnational, for Cuevas's early life writings stage a rare encounter between his U.S. and Mexican personae in testimonials reflecting the PAU and the Instituto Nacional de Bellas Artes as the Scylla and Charybdis of his early career. The momentous passage in "The Cactus Curtain" in which poor Juan must declare his affiliation before the Instituto Nacional de Bellas Artes bureaucrat Víctor Reyes bears a palimpsestic relation to a similar questionnaire that Gómez Sicre submitted to Cuevas prior to the 1954 exhibition. The PAU questionnaire inquires, among other things, whether Cuevas is influenced by Orozco's expressionism (here Cuevas's answer is "no," although later both parties would claim a resounding "yes") and whether Cuevas is interested in "el mensaje político en su obra o sólo la expresión humana y los valores plásticos" (a political message in your work or only human expression and artistic values), to which Cuevas astutely replies, "No no me interesa." (No, I am not interested [in a political message]).[70] Juan's responses at the Instituto Nacional de Bellas Artes and Cuevas's own responses at the PAU reveal Cuevas to be an able code-switcher, well aware of the "correct" answers to particular questions at both institutions.

A complex and contradictory profile of the young artist thus emerges through Cuevas's polyvalent address to audiences in Mexico and the United States, respectively. While Cuevas associates the muralists' sales abroad with their mediocrity and venality, he associates his own international fame with innate talent and freedom from persecution. These contrasting forays into the international art market yield rich ironies. For example, Cuevas ridiculed Mexican painter Raúl Anguiano's prize at the 1954 Salón Nacional for his mother-and-child portrait, quipping that Anguiano's work was appropriate for use as a Coca-Cola ad, while ten years later, Gómez Sicre in fact recommended Cuevas to illustrate a quote by Nietzsche for a Container Corporation of America advertising series titled "Great Ideas of Western Man."[71] As Cuevas and Gómez Sicre's friendship moved into the 1960s, their divergent conceptions of how art related to the market became evident in Gómez Sicre's response to the Alliance for Progress and Cuevas's 1967 *Mural efímero (Ephemeral Mural)*, a project for which the artist utilized a patently commercial venue, the billboard, to address local and international publics, while also altering the manner in which he had previously engaged national and hemispheric cultural policies.

The Alliance for Progress and the *Mural Efímero*

John F. Kennedy's 1961 announcement that the OAS would have a new mission administering the Alliance for Progress obliged the PAU Department of Cultural Affairs to craft a fresh justification for its existence, in lieu of the realpolitik that had served so well through the 1950s. Suddenly the Department's relatively narrow focus on elite culture was confronted by the Alliance's emphasis on literacy, public health, and vocational training as preconditions for the creation of a stable middle class that would embrace liberal democracy and be capable of consuming high culture. In strategic opposition to the policies of the Cuban Revolution, Director of Cultural Affairs Rafael Squirru redefined the Department's claims about the importance of intellectuals to *development*, as he went to battle with the revolutionary leader Che Guevara over control of the key phrase, "El Hombre Nuevo" (The New Man), that is, the party who would emerge transformed by either revolution or liberal democracy.[72]

At the same time, Gómez Sicre's early experiments with corporate patron-age for the arts dovetailed well with the developmentalist principles of the Alliance. In 1964 and 1965, he organized the Esso (Standard Oil) Salons for Young Artists, held throughout Latin America, which rewarded artists work-ing in modernist idioms. Before the OAS diplomatic community, Gómez Sicre highlighted the profits that he had pumped into American economies through sales of art at his PAU exhibitions, but there were also signs that Gómez Sicre's inner aesthete chafed at the primacy the Alliance accorded to economic factors. In his editorials for the PAU *Boletín de Artes Visuales*, he pre-ferred to describe development in biological rather than economic terms, and he stressed that culture and the economy were of equal importance.[73] Gómez Sicre's anxiety with respect to the new economic policies intersected with his increasingly conflicted feelings about Cuevas's fame. In another *Boletín* editorial, he proffers Cuevas's Kafka book and the going prices of Cuevas's drawings in New York as examples of Latin American success in the international arena, while he simultaneously insists that art should not be viewed as a commodity and rails against the inflated art market. Only critical judgment and posterity, he argues, confer aesthetic value.[74] Even at the end of his career, it is clear that Gómez Sicre never resolved his conflicts regarding art's use value and exchange value, between his desire to make Latin American art accessible and visible throughout the hemisphere while also having it circulate accord-ing to free market principles. "Tan bueno como Cuevas" (as good as Cuevas) remained Gómez Sicre's benchmark for aesthetic achievement, while he also conceded that his old adversary Raquel Tibol was right: "[Cuevas] ha mal-gastado su talento con sus obsesiones del 'jet-set'" (Cuevas has misspent his talent on his jet-set obsessions).[75]

Cuevas, in contrast, had never observed a strict division between high and low art nor was he preoccupied about art's commodity status. His own taste formation, steeped in U.S. and Mexican movies, pulp fiction, and popular entertainment, was in fact similar to that of Juan's parents in "The Cactus Curtain." Cuevas's work in the 1960s increasingly drew on influences from mass culture, as demonstrated in his most celebrated challenge to the muralists, the *Mural efímero* (1967), a prefabricated billboard situated at a busy intersection in the Zona Rosa. The *Mural*'s most prominent feature was Cuevas's monumental signature flanked by an animated self-portrait of the artist, blurring the line between art and publicity in another gesture of self-conscious egotism. Described by journalists as Mexico City's first "happening," the public unveiling of the *Mural* was sponsored by the Galería de Arte Mis-rachi and accompanied by revelry, including a female cheering squad sport-ing miniskirts, go-go boots, and Cuevas sweatshirts. The *Mural* was actually neither an isolated event nor a first, but part of a wave of similar events held in Mexico City in the 1960s that referenced transnational youth culture and generational conflict.

The *Mural* signaled a turning point in terms of Cuevas's relation to both the PAU and Mexican cultural institutions. Ostensibly, the work summoned the techniques of Pop Art for yet another attack on officialist solemnity.[76] Preliminary publicity also made much of the fact that, at a certain point, Cuevas relinquished creative control of the project to the technicians of billboard manufacturer Calafell, much as the more self-effacing Sol Lewitt was known to do in his conceptual artworks, which also included ephemeral murals. But while the *Mural* broadly referenced the New York art scene and transnational commercial culture, it also bypassed Gómez Sicre's comparatively narrow curatorial interest in painting, drawing, and sculpture. Gómez Sicre in fact loathed Pop Art and other contemporary art movements. The former, he maintained, could only have meaning in the context of rampant U.S. consumerism; it was doomed to mannerist imitation in Latin American countries.[77] Cuevas's declaration that he would destroy his piece after thirty days to make way for an advertisement mocked the muralists' aspirations to posterity, but also implicitly challenged Gómez Sicre's ideas about aesthetic value (Figure 3).

FIGURE 3. Cuevas (middle left) at work with design team on the *Mural efímero* (*Ephemeral Mural*), 1967. Photo courtesy Biblioteca y Centro de Documentación "Octavio Paz," Museo José Luis Cuevas. © 2007 Artists Rights Society (ARS), New York/SOMAAP, Mexico City.

As in previous projects, Cuevas's *Mural* addressed multiple publics, but in this case its address extended beyond the hemisphere. In the upper part of the work, beside the artist's signature, was to be the figure of a soccer player in honor of the upcoming summer Olympic Games in Mexico City. In light of the outbreak of the Arab-Israeli War of 1967, however, Cuevas altered the composition so that the *Mural*'s lower half featured an aggressive athlete (described in some accounts as a North American football player) and other agitated figures on the left-hand side and an abstract rendering of nuclear catastrophe on the right. The upper part of the mural, meanwhile, featured a self-portrait of Cuevas alongside the artist's signature-logo. In interviews following the *Mural*'s unveiling, Cuevas compared his work to Picasso's *Guernica* and announced that, instead of destroying his work, he was contemplating auctioning pieces of it to raise money for the Israeli government or donating it to the Tel Aviv Museum of Art.[78]

The *Mural*'s dual valence, ludic in the national arena and somber in the diasporic one, arose out of Cuevas's close ties to Mexico City's Jewish community, rather than through Gómez Sicre's tutoring in universalism; moreover, it stressed internationalism on terms other than those described by OAS policies. The *Mural* was also framed by two other uncharacteristic public art projects. The previous year Cuevas had created a collage titled *Yo No Olvido (I Do Not Forget*, 1966) for Mexico City's Centro Deportivo Israelita (Jewish Sports Center), which incorporated into its composition a fragment of barbed wire recovered from the Warsaw Ghetto by Mexican news anchor Jacobo Zabludovsky, who later helped Cuevas to secure the venue for the *Mural*.[79] And in 1968, Cuevas and other well-known artists painted a collaborative mural at the campus of the Universidad Nacional Autónoma de México (National Autonomous University of Mexico) in support of the student movement for democratization.[80] Such projects challenged Gómez Sicre's persistent characterization of Cuevas as an apolitical artist, as well as those critics who continued to portray Cuevas as an errant Mexican. Turning away from traditional class- and party-based activism, Cuevas and his generation were beginning to define an alternative public sphere in Mexico City through innovative linkages between transnational mass culture and community-based movements.

Conclusion

If Cuevas's projects of the mid-1960s signaled diverging paths between himself and Gómez Sicre, the year 1968 marks a definitive watershed in their relationship. Although they remained friends, their institutional connections diminished.[81] In the second half of the decade, Gómez Sicre's cachet in the hemisphere's art worlds gradually declined due to several factors, ranging from revelations in 1966 and 1967 about covert Central Intelligence Agency funding of cultural programs abroad to an increasingly diverse range of Latin

American intellectual perspectives circulating in the United States.[82] Yet, in spite of their chronically underfunded and understaffed condition, the PAU Visual Arts programs displayed arguably greater longevity and impact than other OAS initiatives of the Cold War period. After the assassination of President John F. Kennedy, President Lyndon B. Johnson quickly withdrew major support for the Alliance for Progress, observing that the OAS "couldn't pour piss out of a boot if the instructions were written on the heel."[83] Well before then, many Latin American member states had become dissatisfied with OAS policies and instead gravitated toward Raúl Prebisch's Economic Commission for Latin America and other United Nations organizations.[84]

For Cuevas, 1968 marked the year of his symbolic "repatriation" with regard to the Mexican state and his undoubtedly orchestrated public reconciliation with David Alfaro Siqueiros, the only surviving member of "los tres grandes." Siqueiros attended Cuevas's exhibition, "Crimen" (Crime) just days after the tragic massacre of peaceful student demonstrators by Mexican government sharpshooters at the Plaza de las Tres Culturas in October 1968.[85] The massacre brought an end to the playful antics of the Mafia and effected an abrupt reconfiguration of the Mexican intellectual sector. "Mafioso" Carlos Monsiváis, registered the massacre's sobering effect in his crónica about Cuevas's *Mural efímero*, published in 1970. The piece includes a post-event epilogue, dripping with irony, in which the writer returns to the glamorous Zona Rosa and encounters a world where all is as it was before, and apparently, no one knows anything about the horrific events of 1968. Monsiváis's description of the *Mural* stresses its banality, making it, like the Zona Rosa neighborhood, seem more a sign of continuity than change.[86]

In the years following 1968, Cuevas gravitated toward the cultural policies of President Luis Echeverría, aimed at capturing center-left intellectuals. His work appeared on a Mexican postage stamp in 1971, and he held his first government-sponsored exhibition the following year. In some ways, he became the Juan of his youthful allegory, espousing the virtues not of the Mexican School but rather of the artists associated with La Ruptura from the state-funded art museum that today bears his name in Mexico City's Centro Histórico, where individual galleries are dedicated to his early supporters, including José Gómez Sicre. The stakes that Cuevas laid out in the parallel life stories of Juan and Cuevas proved eerily prophetic, for as Cuevas has taken his place in the national arts establishment, he has been increasingly less visible in U.S.-based Latin American art projects spearheaded by a new generation of curators and critics, who share Gómez Sicre's Latin Americanist vision but are critical of his political and aesthetic perspectives. Given Gómez Sicre's attempts to "contain" Mexican muralism in the postwar years, there is some irony in the fact that Cuevas, who claims to have ignited the Latin American drawing boom in the 1960s, and to have influenced a diverse range of artists throughout the Americas, from Fernando Botero to Andy Warhol, has now been so thoroughly confined to his birthplace by contemporary critics.[87]

The continued divergence between ideologically inflected concepts of hemisphere and nation suggests that the legacy of Cold War pan-Americanism is still palpable in the hemisphere's art worlds. The narrative of Cuevas and Gómez Sicre's complex ideological and geographical locations in the two postwar decades emphasizes the link between aesthetic existentialism and an emerging corporate-centered neoliberalism that contrasts sharply with Mexican state-centered cultural policies of containment and cultural nationalism. On the other hand, the framework provided by contemporary hemispheric studies offers a means of illuminating unexplored connections between the national and hemispheric registers. The Cuevas case also reveals striking similarities between the construction of "lo nuestro" (that which is ours) on the part of the Pan American Union and the Instituto Nacional de Bellas Artes. Though these institutions promoted different aesthetics, each constructed a mythical concept of freedom based on the activities of elite intellectuals, and each upheld a culturalism that stood in marked contrast to the capitalist development initiatives and suppression of popular movements simultaneously being enacted in other social arenas.

NOTES

I would like to thank the librarians and archivists who assisted me with the research for this paper: Maria Leyva, Stella Villagrán, and Beverly Wharton-Lake at the OAS, and Eduardo Cabrera Nuñez at the Museo José Luis Cuevas. I would also like to thank Leslie Judd Ahlander, Félix Angel, and Annick Sanjurjo for speaking to me about their experiences working in the PAU Visual Arts Division. Finally, I extend my thanks to Deborah Cohn, Laura Rigal, Caroline Levander, Bob Levine, and the faculty and graduate students in Romance Studies at Duke University for their helpful comments as I prepared this essay.

 1. José Gómez Sicre, "Nota editorial," *Boletín de Artes Visuales* 5 (mayo–diciembre 1959): 2. Translations are mine unless otherwise noted.

 2. On this period in Mexico, see Deborah Cohn, "The Mexican Intelligentsia, 1950–1968: Cosmopolitanism, National Identity and the State," *Mexican Studies/Estudios Mexicanos* 21 (2005): 141–182.

 3. José Gómez Sicre, "Nota editorial," *Boletín de Artes Visuales* 9 (enero–junio 1962): 1.

 4. Michael C. Marcellino, "Conversation with José Gómez Sicre," *Latin American Art* 3 (1991): 26.

 5. The museum was renamed the Art Museum of the Americas in 1991.

 6. Toby Miller and George Yúdice, *Cultural Policy* (London: Sage, 2002), 12–15.

 7. Ida Rodríguez Prampolini, *Ensayo sobre José Luis Cuevas y el dibujo* (Mexico City: Universidad Nacional Autónoma de México, 1988), 48.

 8. Octavio Paz, "Tamayo en la pintura mexicana," *Panorama* 1 (1952): 49–59.

 9. Among the critics mentioned in this essay, Jean Cassou, Selden Rodman, and Marta

Traba are Cuevas supporters, and Shifra Goldman, Ida Rodríguez Prampolini, and Raquel Tibol are detractors.

10. On these intellectual debates, see Cohn, "The Mexican Intelligentsia, 1950–1968."

11. Ibid., 150–52.

12. Ibid., 153.

13. Ibid., 156.

14. Mary Louise Pratt, "Modernity and Periphery: Toward a Global and Relational Analysis," in *Beyond Dichotomies: Histories, Identities, Cultures, and the Challenge of Globalization*, ed. Elisabeth Mudimbe-Boyi (Albany: State University of New York Press, 2002), 21–47.

15. For work on the cultural Cold War in the Americas and Latin American modernisms, see Deborah Cohn, *Creating the Boom's Reputation: The Promotion of the Boom in and by the United States.* (Nashville: Vanderbilt University Press, forthcoming); Jean Franco, *The Decline and Fall of the Lettered City: Latin America in the Cold War* (Cambridge, Mass.: Harvard University Press, 2002); Andrea Giunta, *Vanguardia, internacionalismo, y política: arte argentino en los años sesenta* (Buenos Aires: Paidos, 2001); María Eugenia Mudrovcic, *Mundo Nuevo: Cultura y Guerra Fría en la década del 60* (Rosario, Argentina: Beatriz Viterbo, 1997); and Mari Carmen Ramírez and Héctor Olea, *Inverted Utopias: Avant-garde Art in Latin America* (New Haven: Yale University Press in association with the Museum of Fine Arts, Houston, 2004).

16. Serge Guilbaut, *How New York Stole the Idea of Modern Art: Abstract Expressionism, Freedom, and the Cold War*, trans. Arthur Goldhammer (Chicago: University of Chicago Press, 1983). On the postwar Latin American arts infrastructure, see Jacqueline Barnitz, "New Museums, the São Paulo Biennial, and Abstract Art," *Twentieth-Century Art of Latin America* (Austin: University of Texas Press, 2001), 143–165.

17. In addition to Guilbaut, *How New York Stole the Idea of Modern Art*, see, for example, Lawrence Schwartz, *Creating Faulkner's Reputation: The Politics of Modern Literary Criticism* (Knoxville: University of Tennessee Press, 1988).

18. Guilbaut, *How New York Stole the Idea of Modern Art*, 11.

19. See, for example, Eva Cockcroft, "Abstract Expressionism: Weapon of the Cold War," *Art Forum* 12 (1974): 39–41.

20. Guilbaut, *How New York Stole the Idea of Modern Art*, 2–3. For discussions of the PAU Programs during the Cold War, see Eva Cockcroft, "The United States and Socially Concerned Latin American Art: 1920–1970," Luis R. Cancel et al., *The Latin American Spirit: Art and Artists in the United States, 1920–1970* (New York: The Bronx Museum of the Arts and Harry N. Abrams, 1988), 184–221; Shifra M. Goldman, *Mexican Painting in a Time of Change* (Austin; University of Texas Press, 1977), 27–40; and Orlando Suárez Suárez, *La jaula invisible: Neocolonialismo y plástica latinoamericana* (Havana: Editorial de Ciencias Sociales, 1986).

21. Gordon Connell-Smith, *The Inter-American System* (London: Oxford University Press, 1966), 329.

22. John H. Coatsworth, "Liberalism and Big Sticks: The Politics of U.S. Interventions in Latin America, 1898–2004," paper presented at "Liberalism and Its Legacies," University of Iowa, 3–4 March 2006, 11.

23. Peter H. Smith, *Talons of the Eagle: Dynamics of U.S.-Latin American Relations*, 2nd ed. (New York: Oxford University Press, 2000), 137.

24. José Enrique Rodó cast Latin American intellectuals as Ariels in contrast to the vulgar

and instrumentalist U.S. Calibans in his 1900 essay, "Ariel." José Martí's 1891 essay, "Nuestra América," opens on the figure of an allegorical national subject who comes to consciousness of his common interest with other Latin Americans in light of the U.S. imperialist threat.

25. Marcellino, "Conversation with José Gómez Sicre," 26.

26. For accounts of the Division's history, see Félix Angel, "The Latin American Presence," in Cancel et al., *The Latin American Spirit*, 222–282; Alejandro Anreus, "Ultimas conversaciones con José Gómez Sicre," *ArteFacto* 18 (canícula 2000): n.p.; and Annick Sanjurjo, *Contemporary Latin American Artists: Exhibitions at the Organization of American States*, 2 vols. (Lanham, Md.: Scarecrow, 1993 and 1997).

27. Marta Traba, "Preámbulo para una exposición," *La nueva prensa*, 27 octubre–2 noviembre 1962, n.p.

28. See, for example, letter from Constancia Calderón to José Gómez Sicre, 25 February 1965, Organization of American States, Columbus Memorial Library, Archives and Records Management Services, R. G. Visual Arts–Exhibitions, 1965.

29. See, for example, José Gómez Sicre, "Nota editorial," *Boletín de Artes Visuales* 3 (junio–septiembre 1958): 3.

30. George Yúdice, *The Expediency of Culture: Uses of Culture in the Global Era* (Durham: Duke University Press, 2003), 4.

31. Anreus, "Ultimas conversaciones con José Gómez Sicre."

32. Ibid.

33. Ibid.; Memorandum from José Gómez Sicre to Dr. Juan Marín, 28 October 1961, Organization of American States, Columbus Memorial Library, Archives and Records Management Services, R.G. Visual Arts–Memoranda, Cultural Affairs, Office of the Director, 1948–1966.

34. Efraín Barradas, "Arte latinoamericano en Estados Unidos: Al márgen de algunas exposiciones," *Visión del arte latinoamericano en la década de 1980* (Lima: PNUD/UNESCO, 1994), 74–79.

35. These facets emerge in Anreus, "Ultimas conversaciones con José Gómez Sicre"; see also Alejandro Anreus, "José Gómez Sicre and the 'Idea' of Latin American Art," *Art Journal* 64 (2005): 83–84.

36. José Gómez Sicre, "Mi credo," *El nacional*, 5 mayo 1946, 9.

37. José Luis Cuevas, *Cuevario* (Mexico City: Grijalbo, 1973), 57.

38. Cockcroft, "The United States," 199.

39. José Gómez Sicre, "José Luis Cuevas: Una década en su carrera," *La nación*, 24 junio 1965, 42.

40. Goldman, *Mexican Painting in a Time of Change*, 53.

41. Selden Rodman, *The Insiders: Rejection and Rediscovery of Man in the Arts of Our Time* (Baton Rouge: Louisiana State University Press, 1960), 3; Marta Traba, *Los cuatro monstrous cardinales* (Mexico City: Era, 1965). For a discussion of these books' reception in Mexico, see Goldman, *Mexcian Painting in a Time of Change*, 41–44, 111–112.

42. José Luis Cuevas, *Cuevas por Cuevas* (Mexico City: Era, 1965), 15–23.

43. José Luis Cuevas, *Gato macho* (Mexico City: Fondo de Cultura Económica, 1994), 111–117. See also Anreus, "Ultimas conversaciones con José Gómez Sicre," regarding interconnections between the Mexican and Cuban art worlds.

44. See Anreus "Ultimas conversaciones con José Gómez Sicre." The Grupo Orígenes was

associated with its eponymous journal which ran from 1944 to1954. Its most famous member was the poet, essayist, and novelist José Lezama Lima.

45. Cuevas exhibition file, Organization of American States, Columbus Memorial Library, Archives and Records Management Services, R. G. Visual Arts–Exhibitions, 1954.

46. Cuevas exhibition file, Organization of American States, Columbus Memorial Library, Archives and Records Management Services, R. G. Visual Arts-Exhibitions, 1954. See also "Entrevista con José Luis Cuevas," *Punto de partida* 1.2 (enero-febrero 1967): 61, Pan American Union (OAS), Archives of the Art Museum of the Americas, Individual Artists files, Cuevas.

47. Cuevas, *Gato macho*, 81.

48. "A Vision of Life," *Time* 64.7 (16 August 1954): 58.

49. Cuevas, *Gato macho*, 80–81, 236–238.

50. Cuevas, *Cuevario*, 188.

51. Goldman, *Mexican Painting in a Time of Change*, 113.

52. Louis R. Glessman and Eugene Feldman, eds., *The Worlds of Kafka and Cuevas: An Unsettling Flight to the Fantasy World of Franz Kafka by the Mexican Artist, José Luis Cuevas* (Philadelphia: Falcon Press, 1959), 4.

53. Ibid., 9.

54. Rodríguez Prampolini, *Ensayo sobre José Luis Cuevas y el dibujo*, 73.

55. Cuevas, *Gato macho*, 267–268.

56. Miller and Yúdice, *Cultural Policy*, 25–26.

57. Sander Gilman, *Franz Kafka: the Jewish Patient* (New York: Routledge, 1995), 101–168.

58. The portmanteau is a pun on "Cacahuamilpa," a tourist destination near Acapulco, and on "caca," or "shit." José Luis Cuevas, "Cuevas dice: me voy asqueado de Kafkahuamilpa," *Siempre!*, 20 abril 1966, n.p., Pan American Union (OAS), Archives of the Art Museum of the Americas, Individual Artists files, Cuevas; Carlos Fuentes, "Versiones," *La cultura en México* (23 March 1966), 2, cited in Cohn, "The Mexican Intelligentsia, 1950–1968," 177.

59. Goldman, *Mexican Painting in a Time of Change*, 51.

60. On the Mafia, see Cohn, "The Mexican Intelligentsia, 1950–1968."

61. Franco, *The Decline and Fall of the Lettered City*, 43.

62. Carlos Monsiváis, *Días de guardar* (Mexico City: Era, 1970), 79; David Alfaro Siqueiros, *Me llamaban el Coronelazo* (Mexico City: Grijalbo, 1977), 493; Anreus, "Ultimas conversaciones con José Gómez Sicre." For more on sexuality and national identity in Mexico during this period, see Robert McKee Irwin, *Mexican Masculinities* (Minneapolis: University of Minnesota Press, 2003), 187–224. On José Gómez Sicre's sexuality in relation to his Cuban identity, see José Quiroga, *Tropics of Desire: Interventions from Queer Latino America* (New York: New York University Press, 2000), 45–49.

63. José Luis Cuevas, "Cuevas, el niño terrible vs. los monstruos sagrados," *México en la cultura* 473, 4 abril 1958, 7 (the letter is dated 20 March 1958); "The Cactus Curtain: An Open Letter on Conformity in Mexican Art," *The Evergreen Review* (winter 1959): 111–120. Future references to the letter will be from the bilingual volume, *Cuevas por Cuevas*.

64. Cuevas, *Cuevas por Cuevas*, 40, 198. The dual page numbers refer to Spanish and English versions of the letter from this volume.

65. Ibid., 46, 202.

66. Carlos Monsiváis, "Prólogo: Cuevas polemista," in Cuevas, *Cuevario*, 9–35. The Partido Revolucionario Institucional (PRI) dominated twentieth-century Mexican politics for almost seven decades.

67. The 1958 *New International Year Book* describes Cuevas as having "contributed several long articles to newspapers, attacking the excessive nationalism which serves as camouflage in Mexican art for Communist influences and as a justification for poor artistic quality" (New York: Funk and Wagnalls, 1959), 261.

68. Cuevas, *Cuevas por Cuevas*, 47, 203.

69. Ibid., 62, 215.

70. Letter from José Gómez Sicre to José Luis Cuevas, 11 June 1954; letter from José Luis Cuevas to José Gómez Sicre, 13 June 1954, Cuevas, exhibition file, Organization of American States, Columbus Memorial Library, Archives and Records Management Services, R. G. Visual Arts–Exhibitions, 1954.

71. M. Luisa Mendoza, "El Cuadro de Raúl Anguiano bién podría servir para un anuncio de Coca-Cola," (1954), n.p., Pan American Union (OAS), Archives of the Art Museum of the Americas, Individual Artists files, Cuevas; Departamento de Asuntos Culturales, Informe trimestral, enero–marzo 1964, Organization of American States, Columbus Memorial Library, Archives and Records Management Services, R. G. Visual Arts–Memoranda, Cultural Affairs, Office of the Director, 1948–1966.

72. Rafael Squirru, *The Challenge of the New Man: A Cultural Approach to the Latin American Scene* (Washington, D.C.: PAU, 1964).

73. Gómez Sicre, "Nota editorial," *Boletín de Artes Visuales* 9 (enero–junio 1962): 1.

74. Gómez Sicre, "Nota editorial," *Boletín de Artes Visuales* 14 (1966): 1–4.

75. Anreus, "Ultimas conversaciones con José Gómez Sicre."

76. Carlos Monsiváis, *Días de guardar*, 82.

77. José Gómez Sicre, "Nota editorial," *Boletín de Artes Visuales* 13 (enero–diciembre 1965): 2.

78. E. Deschamps, "Cuevas en la 'Zona Rosa,'" *Excélsior*, (9 junio 1967), 17A; "Hechos y gente," *Visión*, 7 julio 1967, Pan American Union (OAS), Archives of the Art Museum of the Americas, Individual Artists files, Cuevas.

79. Víctor Sefchovich, "'Yo no olvido,' cuadro de Cuevas en el C.D.I,." *El periódico dominical*, (septiembre 1966), Pan American Union (OAS), Archives of the Art Museum of the Americas, Individual Artists files, Cuevas.

80. Museo José Luis Cuevas, *Cronología biográfica* (Mexico City: Museo José Luis Cuevas, n.d. [1997]), 20.

81. In his essay for the Museum of Modern Art of Latin America's 1978 retrospective, "A Backward Glance at Cuevas," Gómez Sicre focuses almost exclusively on the years 1954–1970; and, among the fifty-six works included in the exhibition, only five date from the 1970s. José Gómez Sicre, "A Backward Glance at Cuevas," *A Backward Glance at Cuevas* (Washington, D.C.: Museum of Modern Art of Latin America, 1978), n.p.

82. On the CIA scandals see Peter Coleman, *The Liberal Conspiracy: The Congress for Cultural Freedom and the Struggle for the Mind of Postwar Europe* (New York: Free Press, 1989); and Frances Stonor Saunders, *The Cultural Cold War: The CIA and the World of Arts and Letters* (New York: New Press, 2001). On the decline of the PAU programs, see Angel, "The Latin American Presence"; and Anreus, "José Gómez Sicre."

83. George Black, *The Good Neighbor: How the United States Wrote the History of Central America and the Caribbean* (New York: Pantheon, 1988), 114.

84. John C. Dreier, *The Organization of American States and the Hemisphere Crisis* (New York: Harper and Row, 1962), 81.

85. Esperanza Zetina de Brault, "Exposición de José Luis Cuevas," *El Sol de México*, (5 octubre 1968), n.p.; Agustín Salmón, "Por la Olimpiada, Siqueiros y Cuevas firmaron ayer una 'paz transitoria,'" *Excélsior*, 30 agosto 1968, n.p., Pan American Union (OAS), Archives of the Art Museum of the Americas, Individual Artists files, Cuevas.

86. Monsiváis, *Días de guardar*, 82.

87. On Botero, see Cuevas, *Gato macho*, 108; and Anreus, "Ultimas conversaciones con José Gómez Sicre"; on Warhol, see Cuevas, *Gato macho*, 193.

12

Memín Pinguín, Rumba, and Racism

Afro-Mexicans in Classic Comics and Film

ROBERT MCKEE IRWIN

In early summer of 2005, the Mexican government issued a series of four postage stamps commemorating the comic book antihero, Memín Pinguín, a little Afro-Mexican boy created in the 1940s by Yolanda Vargas Dulché (see Figure 1). Memín quickly became the source of a diplomatic conflict, inciting raucous cross-border bickering about the comic's alleged racism. The debate was articulated in exclusively binational terms: to critics in the United States, the popularity of Memín signaled Mexico's inherent racism, while Memín's Mexican defenders claimed that neither the *Memín Pinguín* comic nor its Mexican readers were racist, and that U.S. critics, products of a national culture well known for its racist history, were ignorant of Mexican cultural history and were thus projecting a U.S. context of racial conflict onto Mexico.

Interestingly, neither side questioned the terms of the debate. Many in the United States assumed that the visual representations of Afro-Mexican characters in the comic imitated similar images long obliterated from U.S. popular culture for their racist connotations. The response of many Mexicans was that although those images may resemble well-known U.S. racist stereotypes, such imagery signifies differently in Mexico and that in fact *Memín Pinguín* is beloved in part for its message of racial tolerance. What remained unexplored by both sides is the deeply ingrained association in Mexico of Afro-Latin American culture with Cuba. After all, Vargas Dulché was inspired to create the comic during a trip to Cuba where "se enamoró de la belleza y simpatía de los niños negros" (she fell in love with the cute and friendly black children).[1] This extranational racial link was already well established through Mexico's most powerful apparatus of nationalist propaganda of the era of *Memín*'s creation (the 1940s), its cinema industry. Afro-Cuban music and dance, which became popular throughout the hemisphere beginning in the 1920s with the rise of radio, was soon deployed in Mexican film as a means of reinforcing Mexican

FIGURE 1. Mexican commemorative stamps honoring Memín Pinguín, 2005.

national identity as *mestizo*, that is, a mix of white and indigenous, by representing Afro-Latin American culture as its exotic other. The powerful Mexican
film industry, both in its "national" films and in Cuban coproductions, strove
to locate Afro-Latin Americans outside of Mexican national culture, habitually
coding them as Cuban. In other words, neither the U.S.-centric perspective
of the *gringos*, nor the Mexico-centric perspective of the Mexicans, nor even
a mere binational view of the issue is adequate: any evaluation of racism in
Memín calls for a more hemispheric perspective that takes into account the
not always national content of Mexico's cultural production, including its
enormously popular "golden age" cinema.

This study begins by reviewing the *Memín Pinguín* debate and providing a
few illustrative examples of how race is treated in the comic. It then looks to
classic Mexican film in order to explore the context from which Vargas Dulché
created and developed *Memín* and to show the degree to which Mexican stereotypes of Afro-Latin American culture are intrinsically linked to notions of
Cuban difference. *Memín*, read from the perspective of inter-Americas studies,
demonstrates the paradoxical meanings produced when a pair of characters
who were utterly alien to the Mexican imaginary were introduced into Mexican
national culture. A debate that insists on judging *Memín Pinguín* as racist or
antiracist bypasses the complexities of meanings produced by Vargas Dulché's
Afro-Mexican comic protagonists.

Memín Pinguín

Memín Pinguín, mischievous but good-hearted, has long been one of Mexico's
most beloved comic book heroes. According to comic book historians Juan
Manuel Aurrecoechea and Armando Bartra, *Memín Pinguín* "ha sido y sigue
siendo uno de los mayores *best sellers* de la historieta mexicana" (it has been
and still is one of the biggest best sellers of Mexican comic books).[2] Conceived
in the 1940s by the prolific popular writer Yolanda Vargas Dulché (1926–1999),[3]
and drawn by illustrator Alberto Cabrera, Memín was originally the protagonist of the comic strip *Almas de Niño*, a regular feature of the popular *Pepín*

comic book.[4] Teaming with illustrator Sixto Valencia, Vargas Dulché launched Memín in his own comic book in the early 1960s;[5] it would remain enormously popular well into the 1980s,[6] and continues to be published weekly (as a serial, in 32-page episodes), making its run one of the longest in Mexican comic book history. *Memín Pinguín*—and indeed Mexico's comic book industry in general—has hardly been studied despite its enormous influence, not only in Mexico, but through Latin America, the United States, Europe, and Asia.[7]

Memín Pinguín recounts the day-to-day adventures of an elementary school-age boy and his buddies. Memín lives with his widowed mother, who makes a living by taking in laundry, in a poor *barrio* of Mexico City. His best friends include a tough kid named Carlangas (a nickname for Carlos), who also lives in poverty with his single mother, who works in a dance hall (until she is "rescued" in a later episode by the wealthy man who had been Carlangas's absentee father); Ernestillo, the poorest boy of all, who in some episodes has no shoes and whose widowed alcoholic father works as a carpenter; and Ricardo, a boy from a well-to-do family whose progressive-thinking father believes, to the chagrin of his mother, that it will be healthy for him to study in a public school with children from different social classes. The boys, classmates in elementary school, experience adventures both routine (disputes with other neighborhood kids, sports competitions, struggles with schoolwork, illnesses, punishments) and extraordinary (participation in rodeos and bullfights, travels to the United States and Africa, kidnappings), often erring in their youthful fervor, but always being guided by wise adult figures including their schoolteacher, parish priest, and parents.

Mexico itself has historically been the world's largest per capita consumer of comics,[8] but in the last few decades, the genre has lost much of its readership as television has become accessible to more households and the Internet has become an increasingly important source of cultural consumption for young people. Likewise, *Memín*, a best seller in the 1960s, 1970s, and 1980s, saw its readership diminish significantly in the 1990s. However, the release of the Memín Pinguín postage stamps on June 29, 2005, stirred up an enormous controversy in North America that revived the comic's sagging popularity.

Just weeks after Mexican president Vicente Fox made the gaffe of stating that Mexican immigrants in the United States were only doing the work that no one else, "not even blacks," wanted to do, the release of the postage stamps depicting the little bald black boy with huge lips, bug eyes, protruding ears, and his hefty mother dressed in housedress and bandana incited outrage among Afro-American political activists in the United States. The Reverends Jesse Jackson and Al Sharpton were appalled that Mexicans were celebrating what looked to them like Little Black Sambo and Aunt Jemima, racist icons that had long been anathema in visual culture in the United States. The George W. Bush White House joined in, condemning the Memín stamps as "offensive."[9] Mexicans, themselves shocked that the United States, the country, aside from

South Africa, best known worldwide for its history of overt racial discrimination against those with black skin, dared to accuse Mexicans of racism, rallied to Memín's defense. The high-pitched dialogue resembled a juvenile shouting match, much like those described by José Vasconcelos in his autobiographical *Ulises criollo*, in which he recalled his youth on the Texas-Coahuila border: "Sin motivo y sólo por el grito de *greasers* o de *gringos*, solían producirse choques sangrientos" (Without any motive and only because of someone shouting "greasers" or "gringos," bloody clashes would occur),[10] only instead of shouting racial epithets at each other, now each side stridently accused the other of racism.

Dozens of U.S. newspaper columnists and bloggers expressed their shock that Mexico was honoring the representation of what to them was a classic pickaninny. The tenor of debate on *Memín* was particularly shrill on the U.S. side; and although many critics weighing in were liberals, not Mexican-hating xenophobes, their attitude was decidedly condescending. One after another they voiced a similar sentiment: the need to bring underdeveloped Mexicans up to speed with respect to contemporary protocol on race representation. Journalist Susan Ferriss expressed her annoyance that a burgeoning Afro-Mexican "black-pride movement" had not garnered widespread attention in Mexico: "it appears that the Mexican media and public are still not listening," implying that U.S. media, in which she publishes, are savvier.[11] Mexican Americans, well versed in U.S.-based civil rights discourse, weighed in on the side of the *gringos*. Renowned Chicano scholar Rodolfo Acuña complained of "the gap between civil rights conscious Mexicans in the United States and Mexican officials who defend" *Memín*, and charged that "Mexicans just don't know their own history."[12] Chicana activist Elizabeth (Betita) Martínez agreed: "We would do well, then, to talk to Mexicans about their racism," adding "with a certain effort not to sound superior."[13]

Mexicans responded with outrage, accusing U.S. critics of jumping to conclusions without even seeing a copy of a *Memín* comic book; indeed some U.S. sources got details wrong. One source, for example, erroneously claimed that Memín's white friends were all middle-class kids.[14] Historian Enrique Krauze dusted off Mexican icons José María Morelos (an independence-era hero) and Vicente Guerrero (an early Mexican president), both of African descent: "Si los reverendos Jesse Jackson o Al Sharpton conocieran los rudimentos de la historia de los negros en México, se morirían de envidia retrospectiva" (If Reverends Jesse Jackson and Al Sharpton knew the rudiments of the history of blacks in Mexico, they would die of retrospective envy).[15] One of Mexico's best known public intellectuals, Elena Poniatowska chimed in:

> En nuestro país la imagen de los negros despierta una simpatía enorme, que se refleja no sólo en personajes como Memín Pinguín, sino en canciones populares. Hasta Cri Cri creó su negrito sandía. En México, a

diferencia de lo que sucede en Estados Unidos, nuestro trato hacia los negros ha sido más cariñoso.

[In our country the image of blacks awakens an enormous sympathy, which is reflected not only in characters like Memín Pinguín, but also in popular songs. Even Cri Cri created his little watermelon boy. In Mexico, unlike the United States, our treatment of blacks has been fond].[16]

In the end both sides were right, on their own terms. Mexicans were right that *Memín*'s author, Vargas Dulché, clearly used the comic to teach racial tolerance on multiple occasions, and that many U.S.-based critics were clearly not familiar with *Memín*'s plot lines, or with Mexican history. U.S. critics were also right that many Mexican defenders of *Memín* exhibited little knowledge about antiracist discourse in the United States, and did not appear to be interested in incorporating African Mexicans into the mainstream of national culture. And *Memín Pinguín* does exhibit some undeniably racist characteristics.

Colombian critic Eusebio Camacho Hurtado notes in a study of anti-black racism in Latin America that both Memín (with his big head, exaggeratedly thick lips, odd body shape, wide eyes, and typically gawky facial expression) and Eufrosina (who also has thick lips and various irregularities with her body shape: ears, toes, etc.) "se distinguen por la deformidad de su fisonomía" (are distinguished by the deformity of their physiognomy).[17] His study cites dozens of examples from the comic in which blackness is judged as ugly, Memín is described as monkey-like, and Memín and Eufrosina behave in an awkward, uncultured manner. U.S.-based critic of Mexican popular culture Marco Polo Hernández Cuevas likewise concludes his analysis of *Memín Pinguín* by asserting: "*Memín* . . . enseñaba al mestizo a burlarse del negro como si fuera el Otro. *Memín* fue un medio más para enseñar al mestizo a renegar a todo aquéllo, dentro y fuera de él, que no fuera blanco" (*Memín* . . . taught *mestizos* to mock blacks as if they were Other. *Memín* was another means of teaching *mestizos* to deny everything within or outside of themselves that was not white).[18]

A couple of examples from *Memín Pinguín* will illustrate. In an early episode, when Memín visits his wealthy blond friend Ricardo's house for the first time, the latter boy's snooty mother faints from fright when she sees him, thinking he is a monkey.[19] The woman is later made to look foolish—Memín consoles her (in his typically ingenuously impertinent way), "¿Me perdona señora? Yo no tengo la culpa de ser negrito y de que usted sea ridícula" (Can you forgive me, ma'am? It's not my fault that I am black and that you are ridiculous);[20] however Memín's difference is clearly marked (and mocked). The same theme recurs in an exaggerated form when Memín and his buddies go on an adventure trip to Africa and Memín is kidnapped by a gorilla who mistakes him for her son.[21]

On the other hand, the comic preaches time after time that racism is wrong. For example, when on a trip for a soccer competition in Texas, a nasty looking blonde waitress refuses to serve Memín because "in this place we don't give service to negroes,"[22] leading to incredulity and then protest on the part of Memín's friends. On another occasion, this time in Mexico, while visiting a friend of Carlangas's father, the host's son arrives with his blonde girlfriend and exclaims irately, "¿Quién permitió a este negro, sentarse a nuestra mesa? . . . ¡Lárgate! . . . Los negros no deben mezclarse con nosotros" (Who let this black boy sit at our table? . . . Get out of here! . . . Blacks should not mix with us).[23] However, justice is served when later on, at a bullfight, Memín so charms the blonde girlfriend that she gives him a big kiss, right in front of her livid boyfriend.[24] The oft-reiterated lesson is that racial discrimination is wrong and must be combated.

Vargas Dulché's plots, then, in fact do coincide with antiracist thinking in the United States. However, the argument made, explicitly or implicitly, by U.S. critics that *Memín*'s racist imagery reproduces popular racist archetypes of the late nineteenth and early twentieth centuries is not without basis. *Memín* does look a lot like a pickaninny and the comic itself may have its roots in the *Our Gang* series (of both films and comics), with Memín being modeled after one of its Afro-American protagonists, such as Farina or Buckwheat,[25] and his Ma'Linda, as he calls Doña Eufrosina, certainly looks a lot like a stereotypical mammy. However, this visual resemblance is not proof that Mexicans simply copied U.S. racist imagery of the 1940s, then never bothered to correct it even as it has been largely purged from U.S. cultural production. Nor does it mean that there is no possible source of inspiration for representations of Afro-Mexicans other than U.S. popular culture. An overlooked comment by one Mexican journalist/blogger, Hache (Heriberto Vizcarra) of Tijuana, in fact, points in another direction: "Memín Pinguín is . . . an archetype . . . that is based more on the images of black Central Americans than the now-called African Americans. Memín's mother is a classic Mamá Iné."[26]

Mamá Inés is in fact not well known as a Central American, but as a Cuban icon. She is the protagonist of the classic Bola de Nieve rumba song "Ay, Mamá Inés," and her image, that of a hefty Afro-Cuban woman who wears a typical *bata cubana* and a kerchief on her head, drinks coffee, and smokes cigars, has been appropriated by coffee companies in Puerto Rico and the Dominican Republic, which continue to feature her likeness on their products. Indeed Doña Eufrosina tends to speak with a notably Cuban accent.[27] Vargas Dulché herself once remarked, Memín Pinguín "es un niño cubano con corazón mexicano" (is a Cuban boy with a Mexican heart),[28] highlighting the context—not national, but transamerican—from which the comic emerged. Eufrosina and her son are not national icons, but transnational icons: Mexican-produced (and undoubtedly U.S.-influenced) archetypes of Afro-Cuba.

Cuban popular culture, particularly music, much of it of African origin, had become a hot commodity by the 1940s. "Ay, Mamá Inés" and other popular rumbas, congas, and *cha-cha-chás* transmitted a new image of Afro-Cuban culture throughout the Americas. As Cuban writer and critic Reynaldo González notes:

> [Vargas Dulché h]abía llegado a Cuba en un momento peculiar, con la consagración de ritmos de origen africano, la defensa de los ancestros llegados en condición de esclavos, como parte del variado un mosaico cultural cuya exaltación se apreciaba en la asimilación del mestizaje y de la *poesía negrista* donde reinó Nicolás Guillén. . . . Yolanda Vargas vio, aprendió y tuvo suerte: llevó a *Memín Pinguín* a los expendios de periódicos y revistas, convertido en ídolo de niños y adultos.

> [Vargas Dulché had arrived in Cuba at a peculiar moment, that of the consecration of rhythms originating in Africa, the defense of ancestors who had arrived as slaves, as an element of diversity, a cultural mosaic whose exaltation was appreciated through the assimilation of racial mixing and in the *negrista* poetry promoted by Nicolás Guillén. . . . Yolanda Vargas saw, learned and was lucky: she took *Memín Pinguín* to the newspaper and magazine retailers, turning him into an idol of both children and adults.][29]

While the *negrista* poetry to which González refers was born from antiracist motives, generally speaking, the incorporation of Afro-Cuban culture into the Cuban national imaginary was not purely benevolent. As ethnomusicologist Robin Moore has shown, the cooptation of Afro-Cuban culture, especially its music (e.g., rumba), into Cuban national culture in the 1920s and 30s often involved a fundamental disdain for Afro-Cubans. Regarding the song "Ay, Mamá Inés," Moore writes, "[Its] lyrics . . . simultaneously reference and ridicule the verbal expression of the black Cuban underclasses. Not only is the aesthetic validity of Afro-Cuban street music implicitly belittled in this piece . . ., but the perceived childishness of the parodied dialect is heightened through its contrast with European-style musical accompaniment."[30]

Mexico was closely in touch with the Cuban popular music that promoted once excluded Afro-Cuban culture as an essential element of a newly reformulated national culture. As Afro-Cuban culture gained most attention through the conversion of popular cultural forms into mass cultural products with the rise of the radio industry in the second quarter of the century, Mexico, too, in its own burgeoning mass cultural industries, particularly its so-called golden age cinema—which lasted from approximately 1936 to 1955—gave Afro-Latin Americans greater attention than ever seen before or since in Mexican cultural production. In fact, some of the most well known representations of Afro-Latin American culture in Mexico are from classic films such as *Angelitos negros*.[31] And while most of these representations do not predate the creation of *Memín Pinguín* and therefore cannot be claimed as an influence on the creation of

Memín or Eufrosina, this cinema promoted and has come to reflect a dominant Mexican attitude toward Afro-Latin American culture that certainly bore on the development of these characters over the years, as well as their interpretation by Mexican readers.

Indeed, Mexican classic cinema made a great show of using race (blackness) to differentiate Mexican culture from Cuban culture, striving to promote a national imaginary that excluded the African diaspora by constructing an Afro-Cuban Other. Mexican golden age cinema's influence cannot be underestimated: as Mexico's leading cultural critic, Carlos Monsiváis observes, "Between 1935 and 1955 . . . this cinema, more than any other cultural form, modernised tastes and prejudices and refashioned the idea of the nation by transforming nationalism into a big spectacle."[32] Just as it promoted a variety of national stereotypes (the selfless mother, the self-assured *charro*, the tragic fallen women, etc.), golden age film exoticized Afro-Cuban music and dance, particularly the wildly erotic rumba, by contrasting them with more mellow and less sexualized Mexican counterparts. *Memín Pinguín*, one of the few contemporary representations of Afro-Mexican culture, cannot be read without taking into account the cultural milieu of the second quarter of the twentieth century when Mexican film defined Afro-Latin America's relationship to Mexico—as foreign.

Afro-Latin Americans in Classic Mexican Cinema

Mexico's "national school of cinema" took shape in the early 1940s. This nickname was assigned to a production team that won Mexico's first international cinema prize at Cannes in 1946 for the film *María Candelaria* (1943) and that together made some of Mexico's greatest classic films, including *Flor silvestre* (1943), *Enamorada* (1946), and *Maclovia* (1948). Director Emilio "el Indio" Fernández teamed with cinematographer Gabriel Figueroa, screenwriter Mauricio Magdaleno, and editor Gloria Schoemann to make a series of critically successful films that strove to express and promote Mexican national culture, although it should be noted that the powerful Mexican film industry, whose films were popular through all of Latin America, often took part in inter-American coproductions, particularly with Cuban partners. Cuba, like all other Spanish American countries with the exceptions of Mexico and Argentina, lacked the infrastructure of a film industry and thus was able to produce films only sporadically, and very often in collaboration with foreign (usually Mexican or Spanish) production companies and crews. Just as Figueroa is acclaimed for his aesthetic vision of the Mexico's landscapes, cityscapes and people, in Mexican Cuban coproductions like *María la O* (1948), he exerted an important visual influence on the Cuban national imaginary.[33] Figueroa is another figure whose work has principally been evaluated in national terms, despite his more hemispheric trajectory, which additionally includes several notable collaborations with U.S.-based directors such as John Huston (e.g., *The Night of the Iguana*, *Under the Volcano*).

One of Fernández's production team's biggest hits was *Salón México* (1949),[34] a film about a young orphaned woman, Mercedes (Marga López), who works as a dancer (and, by implication, a prostitute) in the legendary Mexico City cabaret, Salón México, and who hides her shameful livelihood from her younger sister, Beatriz, whom she is putting through boarding school in the suburbs. Mercedes gets mixed up with gangsters and suffers through a variety of melodramatic adventures set to the tune of classic dance hall music of the 1940s. There are no Afro-Latin American characters with speaking roles in the film; however they are there in the background, and their presence is striking.

The opening scene is emblematic of their treatment in this and other films of the era. Mercedes and Paco (Rodolfo Acosta), her pimp, have entered in a *danzón* contest. As they dance, the camera pans the nightclub. It is a smoky and somewhat seedy but very Mexican scene, full of men and women of recognizable racial types and fashions typical of the era in Mexico City. The music has a Caribbean flavor, but is low key and elegant, played by the club's house orchestra (mainly European style strings and woodwinds). *Danzón* is a music and dance style that came to Mexico from Cuba (although it is clearly derived from nineteenth-century European ballroom dance styles), but was embraced by the Mexican mainstream. Its rhythm is a little bit sensual, and its dancers, always couples, move together. However, the dance is quite formal, with the dancers poised in rigid postures, their bodies nearly in an embrace, but kept separate, save for the man's left and woman's right hand, which are clasped together to the side of their shoulders; the man's right hand, which rests gently upon the woman's lower back; and the woman's left hand, which touches the man's right shoulder. Film critic Dolores Tierney comments that *danzón* is "uno de los más obsesivamente rígidos ... y menos explícito[s bailes latinoamericanos] en cuanto a la sexualidad" (one of the most obsessively rigid and least sexually explicit Latin American dances).[35] The mixed-race couples who dance in the *danzón* contest, including the very white López, and the swarthier Acosta, are recognizably Mexican.

However, once the contest is over (won by Mercedes and Paco), another musical ensemble begins playing music that contrasts dramatically with the opening *danzón*. Now most of the musicians are black or mulatto, exclusively conga drummers and players of other rhythm instruments, and the beat is wild and frenetic, nothing like the romantic and melodramatic ballads typical of Mexican popular music, much less the elegant *danzón*. This rumba is danced by a lone black woman whose erotic and frenzied movements make her the center of attention, with a crowd forming around her, shouting and sweating. Mexican film critic Emilio García Riera argues that Mercedes's world, Salón México and the urban ghetto that surrounds it, is an "antro de vicio" (den of vice) that represents "el México que no debe ser" (the Mexico that should not exist), while the world of Beatriz, the pastoral beauty of her school, the national landmarks she enjoys visiting, the patriotic hero with whom she falls in love, together comprise an idealized Mexico as it should be.[36] Similar Afro-Cuban–flavored musical interludes peppered throughout the film make the contrast between the two Mexicos more pronounced and emphasize that much of the Mexico that should not exist, in fact is not really Mexican at all. There is no doubt to the Mexican filmgoing audience of the 1940s that these *rumberos* are Cuban, the rumba being an Afro-Cuban genre that had not been absorbed into Mexican high culture, but instead maintained the status of exotic import.

When rumba appeared in golden age films in Mexican contexts, it was in a watered-down form: with less African-sounding rhythms, greater orchestration, and, usually, light-skinned dancers. In the 1949 remake of *La mujer del puerto*,[37] starring the Cuban *rumbera*, María Antonieta Pons, the rumba is introduced in a *carnaval* scene, which opens with the traditional Mexican *son jarocho*, "La bamba." It is a beautiful traditional dance, but again a formal one in which stiff-backed men maintain a respectful distance from their modest female dancing partners, whose legs remain hidden beneath fluffy multilayered skirts. When light-skinned Pons, who, as is customary, plays a Mexican, breaks singing and dancing into a rumba, it is not in its "pure" Cuban form, but instead is blended into "La bamba" in a song entitled "Rumbamba." Mexican rumba is not blatantly erotic, but titillating, and its white dancers and Mexicanized rhythms are neither foreign sounding nor threatening—particularly when contrasted with the heavily Afro-Cuban–flavored rumbas of *Salón México*.

This latter, most nationalist of classic Mexican films includes an Independence Eve sequence in which the protagonist and her younger sister tour Mexico City's most glorious patriotic attractions, from the National Museum of Anthropology to the city's great Metropolitan Cathedral. The highlight of the excursion is the fireworks display held in the huge public plaza of the Zócalo, with the National Palace, the Cathedral, and other nearby buildings lit up in festive lights. Nationalist propaganda weighs heavily in Fernandez's films; *Salón México*, a famous Mexico City dance hall, already immortalized internationally in a symphony by Aaron Copland ("El Salón México," 1936), is coded as a national landmark, just as *danzón* is reified as a Mexican popular dance genre. The Afro-Latin American rumba music, however, as popular as it may have been in Mexico's nightclubs, was decidedly Cuban. Produced and promoted through Mexico's undeniably nationalist golden age film, this idea of Afro-Latin America as wild and uncultivated, erotic and wicked, and most decidedly foreign, much more than any stereotypes of English-speaking Afro-Americans imported from the United States, was and is an inescapable point of reference for Mexican readers of *Memín Pinguín*.

This is not to say that Afro-Mexicans do not appear in classic Mexican cinema. Another model for Memín is said to have been Toño el Negro, a little-known boy actor from a handful of second-tier movies from the 1930s who played roles of impoverished urban Afro-Mexican kids like Memín.[38] And one of Mexico's biggest music and film stars of the era was Maria Antonia Peregrino Álvarez, better known as Toña la Negra. Toña la Negra is best remembered for her interpretations of boleros and other romantic ballads, often mildly injected with a Caribbean flavor, and her film appearances in uncontroversial supporting (usually mainly singing) roles. For example, in Alberto Gout's *Humo en los ojos* (1946),[39] Toña is a cabaret singer in Veracruz, but her gentle stage persona, unlike that of the Cubans from *Salón México*, is overshadowed by the sexy dancing (though it is never frenetic, like that of the rumba dancers in *Salón México*) of the very Mexican (and blonde) protagonist, Meche Barba.

Afro-Mexicans, always distinct from Afro-Cubans, did exist, but only in the background of the dramas of the lives of mainstream white and *mestizo* Mexicans.[40] Likewise, they were not wild and eroticized as were their Cuban counterparts, but rather innocuous. Toño el Negro—much like Memín—was something of a lovable picaresque street urchin, and Toña la Negra—much like Eufrosina—often portrayed mild-mannered and morally upright women, even if they were often cabaret singers. As uncontroversial supporting players, Afro-Mexican actors were not a challenge to nationalist stereotypes that excluded them from the national imaginary.

Afro-Cubans, however, did stand out in Mexican golden age film. In another memorable melodrama of the era, *Angelitos negros*, based on Fannie Hurst's *Imitation of Life*, Afro-Latin American characters once again are cast in supporting roles as singers, dancers, and musicians in a Mexico City nightclub. Protagonist José Carlos Ruiz (Pedro Infante) also sings there: in blackface. Just as in *Salón México*, the sensual, tropical music of the Caribbean is marked by its Afro-Cubanness; it is not Mexican, and Mexico is simultaneously distanced from blackness.

Also appearing in blackface in this movie in the role of the female protagonist's nanny, Mercé, is Cuban actress Rita Montaner, who, despite actually being of mixed race, the real-life daughter of a *mulata*, needs to mark her difference by cosmetically accentuating her blackness. The use of black-face is striking in Mexican cinema in that it is prominent through the 1950s, employed usually for actors playing Afro-Cuban roles. What is particularly ironic about its usage is that neither Montaner nor any other Cuban actor ever appears in blackface in a Cuban film—except in the case of Mexican Cuban coproductions.[41] García Riera comments sarcastically, "El intercambio cinematográfico entre Cuba y México consistiría en que la primera daría al segundo la oportunidad de compartir la pena ante el dolor y la fatalidad de sus negros" (The cinematographic exchange between Cuba and Mexico would consist in the former giving the latter the opportunity to share in the sorrow caused by the suffering and misfortune of their blacks).[42]

In the Mexican film *Angelitos negros*, protagonist José Carlos marries Ana Luisa de la Fuente (Emilia Guiú), and it goes without saying that the affection shown him by his *mulata* cabaret costar, Isabel (Chela Castro), goes unrequited. When they have a child, the haughty, blonde Ana Luisa is shocked and disgusted to see that the baby is black. She assumes that José Carlos, whose parentage is uncertain, must also be part black, which explains why he is so at home with his black costars from his cabaret show. The twist is that Ana Luisa is the one with black blood. Her light skin and blonde hair mask the fact that she is actually the mixed-race daughter of Mercé, who had been the lover of Ana Luisa's father. Ana Luisa enacts the shock that black difference signifies to mainstream Mexico. Blackness is exotic: it may be fun for the cabaret, where Cuban music represents all kinds of forbidden and decidedly non-Mexican pleasures, but it is not Mexican and is not meant for the Mexican home.

The same pattern is played out in Gilberto Martínez Solares's scandalous *Mulata* (1954),[43] a Mexican Cuban coproduction starring Cuban actress Ninón Sevilla, teamed with Mexican leading man Pedro Armendáriz. Once again, light-skinned Sevilla, well known for playing Mexican women in films such as the classic cabaret melodrama *Aventurera*, is made up to look Cuban. In the opening scenes, she appears in full blackface, opening her mouth wide to show her teeth, and bugging out her eyes to emphasize their whites, exaggerating her blackness in the role of a washerwoman named María. For the rest of the film, she plays Caridad, the *mulata* daughter of this character, her skin darkened only to a bronze brown. Meanwhile Armendáriz plays the Mexican who tries to save her from her "savage" instincts.

Caridad finds herself drawn irresistibly to the ritual dancing of Afro-Cubans in a *bembé* ceremony on the beach near the restaurant where she works as a waitress. This syncretic celebration is more African than Christian, according to the authoritative Mexican voice of Martín (Armendáriz), who narrates the scene: "Cada paso es un eco de África conservando a través de generaciones, una mezcla de los ritmos paganos con las creencias cristianas" (Each step is an echo of Africa, preserving across generations a mix of pagan rhythms and Christian beliefs). His voice assumes the role of ethnographer as the film takes on a documentary quality. In fact, the film opens with a warning that runs across the screen during the opening credits and establishes this ethnographic effect:

> Por primera vez se presentan en una película escenas de un *bembé* auténtico. Su terrible audacia no tiene nada de inmoral. Los que ejecutan sus ritmos están haciendo una ofrenda de orden religioso y, ajenos al mundo, ofrecen todo lo que tienen, el alma y el cuerpo, al llamado mágico de las antiguas divinidades africanas. Cualquier sugestión de

impureza, en consecuencia, estará en nuestros ojos civilizados, jamás en la embriaguez purísima de frenesí.

[For the first time a movie presents scenes of authentic *bembé*. Their terrible audacity is not immoral at all. Those who execute their rhythms are making a religious offering, and disconnected from the world, offer everything they have, body and soul, to the so-called magic of the ancient African divinities. Any suggestion of impurity, in consequence, will reflect our civilized perspective, but never the utterly pure raptures of their frenzy.]

Caridad falls into this frenzied dancing—which Martín's narration describes as "sensual" and "barbaric"—in honor of the Yoruba god Changó, worshiped among Afro-Cubans through the guise of Santa Bárbara. The energy gradually heightens in the lengthy scene to the point where Caridad falls to the ground and begins writhing in the sand and a male dancer, grasping a live rooster, shakes it over her repeatedly. The scene reaches its shocking climax when other women drop and begin rolling around in the sand, several of them ripping open their blouses, baring and shaking their breasts, a soft-core pornographic element absolutely unheard of in Mexican film of the era. This sexualized "pagan" rite pretends to give Mexicans insight into the utterly exotic Afro-Cuban culture that sea captain Martín encountered in his travels. If Mexicans thought they knew something about Cuba from what they had seen and heard in nightclubs or on the radio, this film, set in Cuba and with some scenes actually filmed there, revealed to them how shockingly different Cuba was from anything they knew.

By the 1950s, there was no doubt to Mexican filmgoers that whatever connections existed between Mexico and Cuba due to their geographic proximity and easy back-and-forth access via the Gulf of Mexico, connections that brought a sanitized, stylized version of Cuban music to mainstream Mexico through radio, film, and nightclubs, were superficial. Mexico and Cuba were inherently different cultures, and the difference that separated them, as was made clear again and again in Mexican film, was racial. Yet simultaneous with this filmic construction of Mexican national culture as not black, another powerful cultural industry introduced a pair of Afro-Mexican protagonists into the national imaginary.

Memín and Afro-Mexico

Memín Pinguín and his beloved Ma'Linda were utterly unfamiliar characters to Mexican readers of the 1940s, and they remain uncanny to this day. There are so few antecedents in Mexican cultural production of Afro-Mexicans that most Mexican readers likely see these Afro-Mexican residents of an urban Mexican ghetto as anomalies, a conclusion supported by the fact that they are not part of any Afro-Mexican community: virtually no other characters in the comic are Afro-Mexican. It is not surprising to note that in the very first episode of *Memín*, when his Mexican classmates meet him on the first day of school, they are shocked to see someone like him; one comments: "Creí que sólo en las películas los habría!" (I thought they only existed in the movies!)[44]

Mexican film, the only genre of Mexican cultural production that regularly featured Afro-Latin Americans, actively excluded Afro-Latin American culture from the Mexican national imaginary, while essentializing it as Cuban. Yolanda Vargas Dulché radically altered this perspective by making a pair of Afro-Mexicans protagonists in a much-read comic melodrama. Afro-Mexicans, through *Memín*, gained a foothold into the Mexican national imaginary, but only as an isolated phenomenon, one that promoted both racial tolerance and racist stereotypes.

Memín and Eufrosina, then, are exotic curiosities who signify, above all, difference. There is no doubt of Vargas Dulché's motives in making them sympathetic protagonists of a comic book: *Memín Pinguín* teaches tolerance of difference. Yet, as exoticized figures, their difference from recognizable Mexican characters—such as the teacher, the priest, Carlangas and his Mom, or Ernesto and his Dad—is exaggerated, stereotypical, and undeniably racist.

The dynamic of this racism toward Afro-Latin Americans in Mexico, however, cannot be understood simply by recalling civil rights battles in the United States, or seeking out histories of racist representation of Afro-Mexicans in Mexican cultural production. Eufrosina is neither Aunt Jemima nor Toña la Negra; as for Memín being a pickaninny, this term has no translation to Spanish, and there is no corresponding figure available in Mexican cultural production for audiences to reference. While Vargas Dulché's characters are in many ways coded as Mexican, incorporating many recognizably Mexican idiosyncrasies in terms of how they live their everyday life—for example, Doña Eufrosina habitually serves Mexican style *garnachas* at breakfast time[45]—Memín and Eufrosina are markedly different from Memín's friends and their families: they dress differently, their physical features are distinct, and they stand out no matter where they go. Although Eufrosina is by no means the wildly sexual *mulata* well known to Mexican filmgoers, the association of these characters with golden age film's stereotypes of Afro-Cubans is inevitable—as is evidenced in Memín's tendency to break out into delirious song-and-dance numbers. The most important lesson for readers of *Memín* is that Mexico, then, like the recognizably Mexican fictional world created by Vargas Dulché, is racially diverse: not all Mexicans look like popular national archetypes such as the brave, light-skinned *charro*, the self-sacrificing *mestiza* mother, or the stoic Indian. No longer foreigners (Cubans), Vargas Dulché's boldly invented pair of protagonists are Afro-Mexicans.

In the end, as I have been arguing, *Memín* is much more than a celebration of diversity. While readers may consciously learn lessons of racial tolerance, they may unconsciously assimilate the comic's racist stereotypes. Just as Robin Moore's analysis of the incorporation of Afro-Cuban popular musical forms into Cuban national culture in the early age of radio shows elite Cuban nationalism to have exhibited its own anti-black racism, the analysis here shows that this racism was both mimicked and intensified in Mexican golden age film, a racism that could not help but echo in Vargas Dulché's comic.

This back story, as it were, to the cross-border debates of the summer of 2005 makes clear the importance of a broadly hemispheric approach to cultural analysis that does not assume any nation's cultural production to be absolutely autonomous or dependent upon only the cultural force of wealthy nations such as the United States. My triangular (Mexico–United States–Cuba) reading of this story, in fact, is only a first step to understanding the popularity of *Memín Pinguín* and its complex cultural meanings. It leaves unanswered the question of what the comic communicates to readers in countries to which it has been exported, including nations such as Colombia with a much more visible Afro-Latin American population than that of Mexico, or more distant lands such as the Philippines, where *Memín* has been endorsed by the Ministry of Education to promote reading in Spanish.[46] In other words, just as Mexico's attitudes toward blackness were influenced by those of Cuban cultural production, Mexican cultural production (including especially its golden age film and comics—and more recently, television) has exerted its own transnational influence, oftentimes in smaller, poorer countries whose own meager cultural production cannot compete with it in terms of quantity or quality, and as a result, popularity. A hemispheric approach to Mexico's cultural industries will give us clues to their role in shaping ideas of race—among many other themes—throughout the Americas.

NOTES

1. Rómulo S. Vela, "Memín Pinguín va a Washington, o el fracaso de una expedición punitiva de cómic," in *Flama: suplemento cultural* (2:23), *de Vida Universitaria: Periódico de la Universidad Autónoma de Nuevo León* 9:154, 1 Aug. 2005, 11.

2. *Puros cuentos III: historia de la historieta en México, 1934–1950* (Mexico City: Consejo Nacional para la Cultura y las Artes/Grijalbo, 1994): 373. This and all subsequent translations from the Spanish are mine, unless otherwise indicated.

3. Best known for her long-running and hugely successful comic book of melodramatic romantic adventures, *Lágrimas, risas y amor* (Harold E. Hinds, Jr., and Charles M. Tatum, *Not Just for Children: The Mexican Comic Book in the Late 1960s and 1970s* (Westport, Conn.: Greenwood Press, 1992), 53–68, she also wrote scripts for films and several popular *telenovelas* (Beth Miller and Alfonso González, "Yolanda Vargas Dulché," in *26 autoras del México actual* (Mexico City: B. Costa-Amic, 1978), 377–384.

4. Cabrera stopped illustrating comics by the early 1950s; Vargas Dulché was never able

to relocate him, and his disappearance remains "an enigma" (Aurrecoechea and Bartra, *Puros cuentos*, 391).

5. Editorial Vid, which has published *Memín* since the 1960s, was founded by Vargas Dulché's husband Guillermo de la Parra (after whom Memín, a nickname for Guill-ermo, was named).

6. Although Vargas Dulché eventually tired of writing new episodes by the early 1980s, the editors began recycling old adventures; the series was given new life in 1987 when it was released in color for the first time (Aurrecoechea and Bartra, *Puros cuentos*, 393).

7. Sixto Valencia, the cartoonist who has illustrated *Memín* since the 1960s, mentions distribution to such diverse places as Colombia, the United States, Italy, Japan, Iran, and the Philippines ("*Memín Pinguín*: Un anecdotario" in *Etcéter@*, Oct. 2003, online at http://www.etcetera.com/mx/pag12ne36.asp).

8. Hinds and Tatum, *Not Just for Children*, 6.

9. "Califica la Casa Blanca de racista estampilla de *Memín*," *El Universal Online*, 30 June 2005, at http://www2.eluniversal.com.mx/pls/impreso/noticia.html?id_nota= 291260&tabla=notas (accessed 12 Feb. 2006).

10. "José Vasconcelos," in Emmanuel Carballo, ed., *¿Qué país es éste?: Los Estados Unidos y los gringos vistos por escritores mexicanos de los siglos XIX y XX* (Mexico City: Consejo Nacional para la Cultura y las Artes, 1996), 226.

11. "Blinded by Indignation, Mexicans Ignore Black Opinion at Home," *Cox News Service*, 29 Aug. 2005, at http://www.coxwashington.com/reporters/content/reporters/stories/ Mexico_Journal28_Cox.html (accessed 9 Jan. 2006).

12. "Memín Pinguín—Stupidity Is Stupidity," *Hispanicvista.com*, 11 July 2005, at http://www. hispanicvista.com/HVC/Opinion/Guest_Columns/071105Acuna.htm (accessed 1 Oct. 2005).

13. "Looking at the Mexican Postage Stamp and Beyond," *Portside*, 19 July 2005, at http:// www.portside.org/showpost.php?postid=2361 (accessed 1 Oct. 2005).

14. Kenneth Brooks, "Memin Pinguin Comic Character is Offensive," *Ethicalego* 11 July 2005, at http://www.ethicalego.com/memin pinguin.htm (accessed 1 Oct. 2005).

15. "Los ancestros de Memín," *Reforma*, 3 July 2005, reprinted in SalvadorLeal.com, at http: www.salvadorleal.com/piensa.htm (accessed 9 Jan. 2006).

16. Quoted in Fabiola Palapa, Ericka Montaño and Mónica Mateos, "Memín Pinguín 'no es el icono popular del racismo en México,'" *La Jornada*. 1 July 2005, at http://www. jornada.unam.mx/2005/jul05/050701/a04n1cul.php?partner=rss (accessed 24 Aug. 2005).

17. *El negro en el contexto social* (Cali, Columbia: Bejerano Impresores, 1999), 91.

18. "*Memín Pinguín*: uno de los *comics* mexicanos más populares como instrumento para codificar al negro," *AfroHispanic Review* 22:1 (2003): 57.

19. Yolanda Vargas Dulché and Sixto Valencia, *Memín Pinguín* 3 (6 May 2002).

20. Vargas Dulché and Valencia, *Memín Pinguín* 4 (13 May 2002): 4.

21. Vargas Dulché and Valencia, *Memín Pinguín* 208–209 (10–17 Apr. 2006).

22. Vargas Dulché and Valencia, *Memín Pinguín* 128 (27 Sept. 2004): 9.

23. Vargas Dulché and Valencia, *Memín* 299 (1984): 21. Note that this example is from an earlier edition of the serial, published in Colombia. While minor details may change from one edition to the next, Valencia, who continues to perform occasional updates to his illustrations, does not make major changes to Vargas Dulché's plots.

24. Vargas Dulché and Valencia, *Memín* 299 (1984): 29

25. Aurrecoechea and Bartra, *Puros cuentos*, 373.

26. Quoted in "Cross Border Conversation on Race," *Global Voices Online* 7/8/2005: http://www.globalvoicesonline.org/2005/07/08/cross-border-conversation-on-race/ (accessed 24 Aug, 2005).

27. Claudio Lomnitz, "Mexico's Race Problem: And the Real Story behind Fox's Faux Pas," *Boston Review, Nov.–Dec.* 2005, online at http://www.bostonreview.net/BR30.6/lomnitz.html (accessed 14 Apr. 2006).

28. Vela, "Memín Penguín," 11.

29. Reynaldo González. "*Memín Pinguín* provoca un incidente diplomático," *La Jiribilla* 218 (Jul. 2005), online at http://www.lajiribilla.cu/2005/n218 03.html (accessed 9 Jan. 2006).

30. "The Commercial Rumba: Afrocuban Arts as International Popular Culture," *Latin American Music Review/Revista de Música Latinoamericana* 16:2 (1995): 177.

31. Joselito Rodríguez, *Angelitos negros* (Mexico City: Producciones Rodríguez Hermanos, 1948).

32. "Mythologies," in Paulo Antonio Paranaguá, ed., *Mexican Cinema*, Ana López, trans. (London: British Film Institute, 1995), 127.

33. Laura Podalsky, "Guajiras, mulatas y puros cubanos: identidades nacionales en el cine pre-revolucionario," *Archivos de la Filmoteca* 31, 1999: 156–71.

34. Emilio Fernández, *Salón México* (Mexico City: Clasa Films Mundiales, 1949).

35. "Tacones plateados y melodrama mexicano: *Salón México y Danzón*," *Archivos de la Filmoteca* 31 (1999): 223.

36. *Historia documental del cine mexicano: Época sonora, Vol. 3: 1945–1948* (Mexico City: Era, 1971), 307.

37. Emilio Gómez Muriel, *La mujer del puerto* (Mexico City: Producciones Brooks, 1949).

38. Aurrecoechea and Bartra, *Puros cuentos*, 376.

39. *Humo en los ojos* (Mexico City: Producciones Rosas Priego, 1946).

40. An exception would be the Mulata de Córdoba legend, about which Xavier Villaurrutia wrote both a film script and an opera libretto, and the story of la Negra Angustias, protagonist of Matilde Landeta's 1948 film about an Afro-Mexican woman who becomes a general in the Mexican Revolution. For more information, see Elissa Rashkin, *Women Filmmakers in Mexico: The Country of Which We Dream* (Austin: University of Texas Press, 2001); Robert McKee Irwin, "La homosexualidad cósmica mexicana: espejos de diferencia racial en Xavier Villaurrutia," *Revista Iberoamericana* 187 (1999): 293–304.

41. Laura Podalsky, "Guajiras, mulatas y puros cubanos: identidades nacionales en el cine pre-revolucionario," *Archivos de la Filmoteca* 31 (1999): 171.

42. Emilio García Riera, *Historia documental*, 230.

43. Gilberto Martínez Solares, *Mulata* (Mexico City/Havana: Mier y Brooks, 1953).

44. Vargas Dulché and Valencia, *Memín Pinguín* 1 (22 Apr. 2002): 4.

45. For example, Vargas Dulché and Valencia, *Memín Pinguín* 61 (16 June 2003): 22.

46. Valencia, "*Memín Pinguín*."

13

"Out of This World"

Islamic Irruptions in the Literary Americas

TIMOTHY MARR

The poem, through candor, brings back a power again
That gives a candid kind to everything.
We say: At night an Arabian* in my room,
With his damned hoobla-hoobla-hoobla-how,
Inscribes a primitive astronomy
Across the unscrawled fores the future casts
And throws his stars around the floor. By day
The wood-dove used to chant his hoobla-hoo
And still the grossest iridescence of ocean
Howls hoo and rises and howls hoo and falls.
Life's nonsense pierces us with strange relation.

—Wallace Stevens, from "Notes Toward a Supreme Fiction"

* "the fact that the Arabian is the moon is something that the reader could not possibly know. However, I did not think it was necessary for him to know."

—Wallace Stevens, Letters[1]

Wallace Stevens's poem represents the enigmatic impact of the moon's light moving across the floor of his room as the ethnic necromancy of a mysterious Arabian. Stevens figures poetry itself as an unearthly source of light that illuminates most fully when the hemisphere is shrouded in the darkness of night. The errant orbit of the crescent, symbolic of Islam, provides an outlying vantage point freed from the earth's terracentric singularity. Such strangeness casts an indecipherable pall over continental complacencies while still influencing the ebb and flow of oceans. Other instances of Islamic irruptions explored in this essay share some of these crepuscular aspects of the moon's present yet otherworldly power. The unsettling luminescence of the moon that is voiced by the inscrutable "hoobla-how . . . hoobla-hoo" ultimately comprises for Stevens the empowering gift of poetry that promises expansive access to a more "candid kind." This essay argues that the appearance of Islam in American situations, intimated here by Stevens's lunar "Arabian," has been a dynamic and variable intercultural process since the earliest days of European settlement in the continents that came to be called the "New World." The exotopic resources that such a presence provides have disrupted the geographical insularity of hemispheric literary studies and supplied broader planetary latitudes from which diverse critical and creative projects have been launched and enriched.

The violent attacks of Arabian hijackers on 9/11 revealed the hemisphere's vulnerability to an "overseas" menace that pierced the boundaries of the Americas in ways that have been said to have "changed everything." As the strange privacy of Stevens's moon and the stunning surprise of the terrorist attacks attest, such irruptions occur in a range of aesthetic and political registers in the post-contact history of the hemisphere. Similar to the historical communities of Muslim maroons who rejected assimilation and formed communities of resistance throughout the territories of the Americas, literary writers have evoked the spectral elusiveness of Islamic difference to imagine a variety of unincorporated spaces that lie beyond the full control of continental systems of cultural power.

The best work of the new hemispheric approaches to American studies has dislocated the United States from its metonymic centrality by tracing cross-cultural ramifications throughout the broader expanse of the Americas. Such innovative approaches as "New World studies" (Roland Greene), "inter-Americas studies" (Claudia Sadowski-Smith and Claire F. Fox), "trans-American literary relations" (Anna Brickhouse), the "trans-American imaginary" (Paula Moya and Ramon Saldivar), and "an Americas paradigm" (Sandhya Shukla and Heidi Tinsman) have bridged the boundaries that have long confined cultural inquiry within narrow frameworks of nation, ethnicity, and language.[2] This emergent enterprise has illuminated subaltern indigeneities, heterogeneous circuits, and hybrid conjunctures long obscured by established genealogies and canons. The chapters in this volume contribute to this burgeoning intercultural dialogue by demonstrating anew the fresh comparative lineages revealed by situating the local intricacies of creolization within the trajectories of a greater regionalism. By transgressively expanding the nodes of American literary studies along the longer axis afforded by north-south transcontinentalism, the critical enterprise of the new hemispherism is generating American studies that are more responsive to the complex routes of transcultural exchange.

While the new hemispheric studies have effectively countered national exclusivities and other essentializing insularities, the hemispheric bounded-ness of the enterprise, however expansive, can privilege another form of geo-graphical exceptionalism. The same epistemological limitations that required scholars to move beyond the limits of the nation and consider creolized per-spectives within the broader Americas also exist within the new paradigm of trans-American studies. The longitudinal interculturalism that charts a greater geometry within the radius of American studies (that, for example, associates Canada and the Caribbean or links Latin America with Los Angeles) also has necessary limits to the arc of its enterprise. Elena Glasberg's work on Antarc-tica powerfully dramatizes how the geographical space of that unpopulated and uncolonized continent, whose pole is one ground zero of all longitudes and latitudes, confounds national and hemispheric imaginaries.[3] When seen from a planetary perspective, continents become the largest islands on earth and hemispheric approaches devolve into a new bipolarity that can impede the imperative for planetary thinking by leaving the other side of the planet out of focus and in the dark. The longitudinal strengths of a hemispheric para-digm for literary studies thus need to be supplemented with the latitudinal linkages that characterize transoceanic systems of exchange that crisscross both the Atlantic and the Pacific. Because the oceans leave no traces of these multifarious passages, it takes a great leap to chart the rhizomatic routes that connect the Americas with the hemisphere where the other half lives.

The denotative grammar of the exception presumes an absent other within its missing clause. Any determination of what is exceptional, therefore, is dependent upon an effaced passage that haunts the sentence with the pos-sible reappearance of its unspoken enigma. Islam stands as one of the primary exclusions upon which both national and hemispheric exceptionalisms in the Americas have been constructed. The diverse world of Islam (*dar-ul-Islam*) is the most formidable frontier of alien difference embracing the breadth of the continents that are not American. Since before the settlement of the Americas by Europeans, the Islamic world has encircled its intertropical African and Asian rims, ranging on the Atlantic shore from the Arab Moors of the Maghreb (ironically a word that means "west," referring to the North African territories of Islam west of Arabia) to the Muslim groups farther south in the Senegam-bian region of West Africa (Mandes, Fulbes, Wolofs) and on the Pacific shore to the Moros of Mindanao, the easternmost extreme of the Malay diaspora from the East Indies into the Pacific. Islam thus embraces lands that geographically define the outermost edges of the Americas both in the east and in the west without having a political presence within the hemisphere other than Muslim populations residing in its countries. Despite being politically relegated to the fringes of the hemisphere, the history of Islam's displaced yet looming absence has nevertheless frequently taken form as a spectral presence throughout the Americas since their first "discovery."

Since then, Islam has provided transcultural resources for improvising different kinds of cosmopolitan literary intervention. American writers drew in divergent ways upon these liminal latitudes of Islamic difference to negotiate and contest the confining binaries of national and hemispheric racial invention. This essay explores a selection of expressive moments, like Stevens's evocation of his Arabian, where people and performances marked with Muslim signs irrupted into literary expressions in the Americas as transnational critical spaces. What I call islamicism—the transcultural orientalism ascribed to Islam by those uninformed by its actual ethos—has served peculiarly well as a mediating third dimension because its heterogeneity confounds the continental categories of race and religion that have constituted hegemonic definitions of nation and hemisphere.[4]

Authors have imaginatively embodied this deterritorialized Muslim otherness in fugitive literary characters whose alien agencies have both defined the contours and punctured the complacencies of disparate New-World projects. The specific examples analyzed in this essay are predominately drawn from my own situation as an Anglophone American studies scholar whose specialty is U.S. literature and culture. Such a traditional focus nevertheless demonstrates my argument that examining the presence of Islam in the Americas also requires turning the longitudinal comparativism of the hemisphere on its axis to reveal its eclipsed transoceanic genealogies. Such an angle of analysis also comprises a largely unexamined element of emergent comparative work in transamerican studies. Even in the literature by canonized U.S. authors from the nineteenth century such as Mark Twain, Joel Chandler Harris, Harriet Beecher Stowe, and Herman Melville, the creative latitudes and niches that islamicist approaches provided to their artistic negotiations of racial difference are revealed. The essay also explores how African Americans in the United States found new transnational freedoms in their association with Islamic faith and cultural difference ranging from the Arabic literacy of enslaved antebellum Muslims to the transnational empowerment that reversion to Islam provided to jazz musicians and members of the Nation of Islam in the middle of the twentieth century. This study concludes in the same post-World War II moment by briefly examining a powerful short story by Paul Bowles, a U.S. expatriate in Morocco, which dramatizes how African Islamic difference frustrates the capacity of American intercultural understanding. Bringing transoceanic perspectives from the Islamic world into a variety of American literary situations offers insights into more worldly modes through which hybrid racial positions were imagined in the Americas.

Islam and the Perspective of Transhemispheric Studies

From the onset of exploration, Europeans had associated the appearance of the Americas within their geographical imaginaries with the fantasy of displacing the Muslim world. The year of Columbus's journey, 1492, coincided with the *reconquista* that aimed to expel the Muslim Moors from Spain. Columbus's belief that he had landed in Asia, rather than locating the intervening continents of the Americas, is registered by the designation of Native Americans as Indians. The chief admiral of the ocean sea's first speech to the Spanish king and queen upon his return from his first voyage began with a 323-word sentence that surprisingly focused on Islam rather than on America. Islam had long been viewed by Europeans as a divine scandal whose claims of a post-Christian dispensation provoked millennial desires to subdue and supplant its despotic usurpation. Columbus spoke of the banners of Spain being placed on the towers of the Alhambra and of the Moorish king kissing their royal hands as he departed the gates of Granada into exile. Columbus's royal benefactors had sent him westward that same month with letters of instruction and an Arabic interpreter to effect further victories over "the sect of Mahoma and to all idolatries and heresies."[5] By circumventing the Islamic world and bringing the Christian gospel directly to the potentates of Asia, Columbus's detour aimed to enlist new converts to serve as eastern allies in the mission of ousting Islam from its hegemonic hold over the Holy Land since the times of the Crusades.

The eschatological project of overcoming the contentious challenge of Islam was interrupted by the surprising appearance of the Americas as an intervening field for conversion and colonization. Enrique Dussel has argued that Europe's "discovery" of America gave birth to the possibility of Eurocentric modernity because, by so doing, its "status altered from being a *particularity placed in brackets* . . . by the Muslim world to being a new *discovering universality*."[6] The rhetorical heritage of interethnic imagination that pitted Muslims (in such varied ethnicities as Moors, Arabs, Turks, Tartars, and Malays) as oppositional threats to visions of Christian victory was applied to the new territories in an attempt to comprehend its unincorporated difference. This transposition of Moorish prototypes onto American actualities persisted during the years of the Spanish American empire. For example, the Spaniards of the Coronado Expedition of 1540–1542 to the territories that later formed part of the land that Mexico was forced to cede to the United States were deceived by a native slave whom they named "Turk" because of his tawny skin color. The Turk made up tall tales of the immense wealth in gold to be found further inland and was strangled when his deceptions were discovered.[7] Such a figuration also marked the broader literary imagination of the Americas as shown in Christopher Marlowe's *Doctor Faustus*, first published in 1588, which spoke of the "Indian Moors who obeyed their Spanish Lords."[8] Max Harris has analyzed how Iberian street festivals called *moros y cristianos*, featuring mock battles in which Spanish Catholicism celebrated its triumph over Moorish subjects, were adapted to the American empire to dramatize their defeat of indigenous Aztecs. Such performances eventually evolved into sites from which native peoples could fashion their own "hidden transcripts" for resistance and revenge.[9]

Muslim Moors comprised some of the earliest settlers in the Americas and, augmented by the enslaved Africans transported from Muslim West Africa, formed a significant part of the population of the early Americas.[10] (Almost 20 percent of the present citizens of Suriname are Muslims, the highest percentage in the hemisphere.) Nevertheless, Islam has remained for the most part an exiled or excluded outsider to the different Christian cultures that controlled the colonization of the Americas. Whether relegated beyond the pale of the Atlantic and Pacific frontiers of the hemisphere or buried within the hybrid abyss of the creolized Americas, the oppositional alterity of Islam has nevertheless provided an outside challenge that writers have deployed in different ways to perform diverse and contrasting forms of ideological commentary.

Latin American literature is especially welcoming to this critical enterprise of transculturalism because of the way that the Islamic moorings of the Spanish past have been submerged within its imagined genealogies. The foundational literary example of the imposition of Islam onto South American situations is Domingo Faustino Sarmiento's *Facundo: Civilización o Barbarie* (1845), which frequently figures the Argentine gauchos—the nomadic outlaws of the inland pampas—as barbarous Bedouins or Tartars, and its caudillos as Muslim despots in an American mould.[11] Christina Civantos's *Between Argentines and Arabs: Argentine Orientalism, Arab Immigrants, and the Writing of Self and Other* (2005) explores how Arab difference is negotiated as a transoceanic field of national formation by Argentines of European descent such as Sarmiento as well as Arab immigrant writers in Argentina.[12] In the mid-twentieth century, another Argentine, Jorge Luis Borges, wrote a series of short stories and sketches in which rich references to the Islamic world offered access to a variety of alien cultural multiplicities, sometimes (as in the fascinating story "Averroës' Search") as a means of confounding the expressive limits of intercultural imagination itself.[13] More recently, the Brazilian-Lebanese author Milton Hatoum fictionally dramatized Ana Castillo's contention in *The Massacre of the Dreamers: Essays on Xicanisma* (1994) that machismo has Arab roots by figuring the patriarchal progenitors of his Portuguese-speaking characters in his novels *The Tree of the Seventh Heaven* (1989) and *The Brothers* (2000) as migrant Muslims adapting to the frontier city of Manaus in the Amazonian outback.[14] Latin American studies could benefit from examining more deeply the many ways that the Islamic contributions to Iberian and Latin American cultures, however effaced, have nevertheless informed the hybridity of identities, practices, and expressions in the Spanish-speaking "Nuevo Mundo." Even the exclamation "Olé!" is a hispanicized form of "Allah!"

The Detour of the Moor: Arab Surrogacy and Racial Performance

There are transnational moments in the most canonical literary works in which the orientalist appearance of Islam is used to confound conventional customs. An example from nineteenth-century U.S. literature dramatizing how such a process can be accomplished by the use of a single word can be seen in Louisa May Alcott's *Little Women* (1868), in which Amy March, in her "Last Will and Testament," writes about bequeathing a "turkquoise" ring she hopes to inherit, thereby humorously marking her avarice with an islamicist misspelling that announces its moral impropriety.[15] Samuel Clemens's *The Adventures of Huckleberry Finn* (1884), located at the center of the national canon both temporally and geographically, more fully exemplifies how irruptive instances from the Islamic world, even in the most burlesque of ways, can lay out literary latitudes of cosmopolitan critique useful for commenting on the racial complexity of the United States.

Halfway through *Huckleberry Finn*, Jim complains to the Duke—who is plotting another episode of deception on the shore of the Mississippi River—that their practice of roping him alone in his wigwam to prevent others from capturing him as a "runaway nigger" was "mighty heavy and tiresome" and caused him to "trembl[e] all over every time there was a sound." The Duke ciphers out a solution that temporarily liberates Jim by dressing him in a theater costume, painting his face a "dead dull solid blue," and posting a sign that reads "*Sick Arab—but harmless when not out of his head.*"[16] Jim is "satisfied" and the Duke encourages him to "make himself free and easy" while they are away, and if anybody approaches, to "hop out . . . and carry on a little, and fetch a howl or two like a wild beast." Huck notes that the average man wouldn't wait for the howl because Jim was the "horriblest looking outrage" who looked like a dead man "drownded nine days" and "considerable more than that" (210). When Huck returns to the raft at night four chapters later, he falls over backwards into the river in fear when he catches a glimpse of Jim's shocking disguise in the flash of the lightning.

Critical interpreters of the "considerable more" of this disguise have centered their analysis on the minstrel excesses that reconfine Jim within a different regime of racialized distortion. For example, E. W. Kemble's illustrations of Jim in these trappings from the first edition of the work demonstrate Henry B. Wonham's contention that such an extravagant masquerade merely absorbs Jim's identity within the degenerate burlesque of "coon caricature."[17] (See Figure 1.) To be sure, Clemens draws upon cultural stereotypes of both minstrelsy and orientalism in globalizing the specter of Jim's fearsome difference and his ludicrous subalternity. Popular Near Eastern travel narratives looked askance at the tolerance of Muslims for "santons"—madmen in their midst who were viewed as both harmless and holy—and viewed them as representative examples of how Islam infected the promise of healthy Christian

FIGURE 1. "Harmless." E. W. Kemble's illustration of Jim dressed as an "Arab" in theater clothes in *The Adventures of Huckleberry Finn* (1885) by Samuel Clemens. The sign reads "Sick Arab—but harmless when not out of his head." From the Rare Book Collection, University of North Carolina at Chapel Hill.

democracy with the vectors of despotism, disease, and delusion. Clemens's own *Innocents Abroad* (1869) depicted Arabs not as "free sons of the desert" with "picturesque costumes," but satirically as "a pack of hopeless lunatics."[18] That this scenario does inscribe Jim with a new set of ethnic fetters is symbolized by his ironic journey downstream deeper into the land of slavery. Jim is still in his costume when the Duke recaptures him for the reward money, ostensibly by being able to explain why he is dressed as such a "strange nigger" (268).

In another light, however, the metamorphosis of Jim into an outlandish oriental in the midst of the Mississippi effectively, if only temporarily, thwarts the ability of others to capitalize upon his political subjugation. Samuel Clemens's absurd expansion of Jim's ethnicity into that of an alien Arab bewilders racial binaries ("blue" skin) and frustrates the very possibility of comprehensibility ("out of his head"; "howl"). Fashioning a blue race through the circuitous evasions of Jim's hideous Arabness, Clemens creates what Édouard Glissant has called a "detour" that allows him to preserve Jim's liberty from those interested in seizing his black body. Marooning Jim away from the catastrophic categories of the racist legalisms of the land, indeed outside his plot into the very margins of his text, Clemens—as he does with his invented pseudonym—craftily creates a riverine ruse of quarantine that offers Jim a certain circumference of freedom, even from the machinations of "Mark Twain's" own masterful authority. The Duke's clever contrivance exemplifies the nomadic privileges of Samuel Clemens's own strategic creativity. *A Tramp Abroad* (1899) included an illustration of the author smoking a long pipe, dressed up in Turkish clothes with a fringed fez and pointed slippers, while "Painting my Great Picture." These islamicist moments demonstrate how Moorish positioning produced a liminal space of transnationalism in which writers could locate liberties not allowed to them through localized figuration alone. Escaping continental conventions served also as a strategy of globalizing the authority of their imaginative resources.

Seventeen years after Clemens published *Huckleberry Finn*, Booker T. Washington also deployed the detour of the Moor to illustrate the "curious workings of caste in America" that grant privileges to one person of color that are deprived to others. In his autobiography *Up from Slavery* (1901) he tells an anecdote about a near lynching in a small town when a dark-skinned man enraged the residents by visiting the local hotel. Further investigation revealed that the imperiled transgressor was a visitor from Morocco who spoke good English. "As soon as it was learned that he was not an American Negro, all the signs of indignation disappeared," Washington explained, adding: "The man who was the innocent cause of the excitement, though, found it prudent after that not to speak English."[19] That the indignities heaped on American blacks could be converted to innocence and liberty if dark skins were seen as a sign of cosmopolitan worldliness dramatized an important lesson to African

Americans. They came to understand that the strategy of inhabiting the Moor produced an emancipating detour from the path of racial violence that tragically was often the destination of resistance. Embodying the social self as foreign was a resource for freeing oneself from the hegemony of continental conventions, one whose critical latitudes licensed a resistance to localized racial norms not permitted to those confined by its dictates. Polyracial groups in the eastern United States such as the Melungeons and the communities of "Moors" in Delaware and South Carolina are sociological examples of the liminal freedoms of the maroon communities that survived in many locations in the hemisphere. The rise of the Moorish Science Temple after 1913 in northern U.S. cities attracted African American followers by reminding them that by becoming "Moors" they were part of a great "Asiatic" race that should not submit to the domestic indignities of race-based subordination. The Moorish explorer Estevanico, who explored the North American continent from Florida to New Mexico during 1528–1539, has been celebrated by generations of Africans and African Americans as an original black discoverer; his story is the first example in Kareem Abdul-Jabbar's *Black Profiles in Courage: A Legacy of African American Achievement*.[20]

The larger cultural strategy dramatized by this process of transoceanic positioning exemplifies the racial performance that Joseph Roach has called the process of "surrogation" in which restored substitutes are made to fill "a vacancy caused by the absence of an original." Despite the cultural effacement of Islam in the Americas, its alterity was never fully repressed and returned within the intercultural repertoire of "circum-Atlantic performance."[21] Although literary characterization is a performance on a different type of social stage, Clemens's "sick Arab" circulates as a textual "effigy" through which he is able to improvise a multiplicity of perspectives via the strange surrogacy of its alien mediumship.

While the Moroccan whom Booker T. Washington mentions disguises himself behind his foreign tongue, the Duke reinvents Jim as an Arab by investing him with the trappings of Shakespeare's King Lear. This signifies that Clemens was not merely engaging in the liberties of Middle Eastern minstrelsy but also parodying the pretenses of aristocracy, as the King and Duke's Royal Nonesuch episode on land reveals. A more specific historical context for Clemens was the career and reputation of a man who, along with Frederick Douglass, was the most globally prominent African American of the mid-nineteenth century. Ira Aldridge was born to free blacks in 1807 in New York City, where he trained in the theater, but he soon sought freedom from American racial restrictions by emigrating to Europe to pursue his ambitions as a professional actor. Aldridge established his fame by acting vengeful roles such as Zanga the Moor in Edward Young's *The Revenge* and Hassan the Moor in Monk Lewis's *The Castle Spectre*, as well as playing the role of rebellious slaves in abolitionist New World dramas. His most famous performance was in Shakespeare's *Othello, The Moor*, in which he began starring in the leading role during 1833. At the age of forty-two, he revived Shakespeare's *Titus Andronicus*, which hadn't been performed for over a century, and played Aaron the Moor as a hero rather than a villain.[22] (See Figure 2.)

Part of Aldridge's public persona was the invention of his genealogy as a son of a converted prince from the Fulbe people of Senegal, a region of French West Africa populated primarily by Muslims. Playbills and his published

FIGURE 2. Ira Aldrich as Shakespeare's Aaron from *Titus Andronicus. The Anglo-American Magazine* 2 (January 1860): frontispiece. Courtesy of the American Anti-quarian Society, Worcester, Mass.

Memoir of 1849 featured a biography that told of how Aldridge's father had been transported by a missionary to New York after his own father and family were butchered by a political foe. The father trained as a minister, married an American, and returned to Senegal, where Aldridge was born. Frustrated in his desire to lead his people to Christianity, the story goes that Aldridge's father went into hiding and eventually returned with his family to the United States to serve the religious needs of African Americans.[23] This imagined story of a regal African birthright cemented Aldridge's renown as an "African Roscius," leading one historian to claim that he developed an "adroit theatrical strategy" of "making a career out of playing a Moor playing a Moor."[24]

Aldridge's dramatic genius, evident in the invention of this biographical detour which like Othello pointed back to Muslim Africa, was broadly celebrated on the European continent, especially in Germany and Russia, more than it ever was in Britain. During 1852–1855, 1858–1859, and frequently after 1862, Aldridge made extended Continental tours in which he delivered his lines in English regardless of the language spoken by the rest of the company. "Princes and people vied in distinguishing him," theater critic Dutton Cook noted in 1881, "crowded houses witnessed his performances, and honors, orders, and medals were showered upon him."[25] It was during these tours later in life that Aldridge expanded beyond the Shakespearean roles of Othello, Aaron, and Shylock and began to act Macbeth and King Lear in whiteface. The French novelist and critic Théophile Gautier saw one of his early performances as King Lear in St. Petersburg in 1858. He commented on Aldridge's costume, which included "a flesh-coloured headpiece of papier mâché, from which hung some silvery locks of hair" as well as wax that "filled in the curves of his flat nose," a "thick coat of grease paint," and a "great white beard," and remarked as well (in words that were excised from the American translation): "That Aldridge had not whitened his hands was a caprice which is easily comprehensible, and they showed below the sleeves of his tunic, brown as monkey's paws."[26] But when Aldridge wished to visit the United States that same year, his wife—a white Englishwoman—refused to brave the contumely that they would encounter on the other side of the Atlantic. He died in 1867 in Poland and was buried in Lodz.

Aldridge's career dramatizes how the racial performance of a Moorish past, assembled symbolically from the high culture of Shakespearean drama and the invented romance of African royalty, constituted part of the grounds for a global celebrity that transcended the limitations of hemispheric racial norms. Frances Ellen Watkins Harper in *Iola Leroy*, for example, recalled the pride experienced by African Americans while traveling in Europe when they learned about the "princely honors" Aldridge had achieved as a "success-ful tragedian."[27] His celebrated capacity to play infidel Moors and a king in whiteface illustrates the transgressive freedoms he gained by abandoning the restricted social roles faced by African Americans in the United States to perform more creative registers of racial fashioning on the stages of the Old

World. Burlesquing Aldridge's example in the figure of Jim, Clemens conscripts his legendary liberty by appropriating his strategic performance of an African ethnicity. In both cases, a Moorish difference provides a transhemispheric stage upon which more cosmopolitan racial roles could be rehearsed.

Arabic Freedom in the Slave Community

The most extended treatment of an Arab in nineteenth-century U.S. fiction was the character of Aaron in novelist and folklorist Joel Chandler Harris's *The Story of Aaron (So Named) The Son of Ben Ali* (1896) and its prequel, *Aaron in the Wildwoods* (1897).[28] Although Harris's Aaron tales have been almost completely ignored by literary critics, partly because they have been classified as children's literature, they exemplify how islamicism was deployed by writers to negotiate the cultural politics of racist backlash at a time when the United States was unifying around legalized disenfranchisement and segregation. In the 1890s, Harris abandoned the African American storytellers Uncle Remus and African Jack in favor of an Arab slave whose cultural power was both more globally resonant and less politically threatening. Aaron allowed Harris to negotiate the ambivalence of racial identity by exoticizing its difference as a resource for social stability at the same time that he dramatized the hidden and supernatural sources of an underappreciated African power.

As the "foreman of the field-hands" (*Story of Aaron*, 4) who "was very busy during the day, and sometimes at night, managing the affairs of the planta-tion" (69), Aaron acts as an agent to preserve the system of white power on the Abercrombie plantation in "Middle Georgia," even finding time to kindly instruct the children of his "White-Haired Master." At the end of the book, when Union army foragers on Sherman's march proceed to confiscate the plantation's livestock and free its slaves, Aaron—"dressed in his Sunday best" (188)—not only tries to hide the horses and mules but chooses to stay even after granted his freedom. His final act is to consecrate the actions of another Union soldier, sent by Abraham Lincoln to protect the plantation from being ransacked, by bowing his head over their handshake "as if giving silent utterance to a prayer" (198). Harris fantasizes a post-bellum order in which Northern whites protect the property of noble Southerners with the assistance of freedmen who remain loyal to a white social system which maintains its authority even after emancipation. By enlisting Aaron in support of this order, Harris converts the alien difference of both Islam and Judaism into support for a revived Abrahamic patriarchy in which Christians retain their hegemonic authority. Oliver Herford's illustrations in the first edition emphasize Aaron's Semitic physiognomy and light skin color to disassociate him from the other African slaves (Figure 3).

Harris's choice of an Arab slave, like Clemens's figuration of Jim as an Arab, also demonstrates his attempts to locate latitudes from which he can

DE SQUINCH OWL LIGHTED ON A'ON'S HAND

FIGURE 3. "De Squinch Owl Lighted on A'on's Hand." Illustration by Oliver Herford in Joel Chandler Harris, *Aaron in the Wildwoods* (1897), 184. From the Rare Book Collection, University of North Carolina at Chapel Hill.

criticize social injustices without compromising the racial codes of some of his
readers. The transgressive power of Harris's character consistently perplexes
those with the purported authority to enslave him. Aaron's legendary reputation as the "most remarkable slave in all the country round" (5) stems from
the fact that he is seen as "no nigger" (13). In his younger days, Aaron was an
"unmanageable" runaway (36) who was "very dangerous" (37) and "too tricky
to travel with" (56). Harris locates the source of this renegade freedom in the
strangeness of Aaron's African genealogy. His Arab parents were forcibly transported from Senegambia and passed on to him his "thin lips" and "prominent
nose" and his capacity to read Arabic. Aaron's facility with Arabic is linked
with his ability to understand "the language of the animals," with whom he
is in league against the malignity of bad masters. The White Pig, for example,
exhorts him to "Return to the swamp, Son of Ben Ali, where we have no such
names [as Aaron]. The paths are all there. I have kept them hard and firm"
(135). The congressman who sends the Union squad to protect the plantation—a former teacher there whom Aaron had saved from being lynched—calls
the Son of Ben Ali in his official orders "the fugitive, who was and who remains
a mystery" (197). It is this elusive freedom that renders Aaron into a cipher
for the power and dignity of Africans who have hidden cultural resources that
cannot be subdued, such as his unique ability to tame the wild energies of the
black Arabian stallion Timoleon, whom Aaron acknowledges as the "grandson
of Abdallah" (21).

    This fugitive power of Aaron's earlier years as a slave, when he was
forced to actively resist the authority of a mean master, is accentuated in the
next book, *Aaron in the Wildwoods.* Aaron's Arab alterity possesses the "key"
that unlocks the mysteries and secrets of the swamp, transforming it from a
"treacherous quagmire" (6) into a sustaining refuge that preserves his freedom
from his owner, patrollers, hunters, and "nigger dogs." Aaron's mysterious
audacity and craftiness enable him to harness supernatural forces to preserve
his independence and attend to the crippled boy Little Crotchet on the Abercrombie plantation whenever he wishes. White masters and black slaves alike,
as well as the book's readers, are bewildered by Aaron's capacity to survive on
the margins, his ability to move through the wind and see "prophecies in the
constellations." This incomprehensible power leads his master to call him a
"yaller rapscallion" (67) and an "imp of Satan" (83), and another white man
to compare him to a picture he saw in the *Arabian Nights* of a man who had
the power to "call the elements" to help him. Many of the blacks on nearby
plantations believe him to be a conjuror because of his intimate kinship with
nature, his alien physical characteristics, and the fact that he has a "thang to
his tongue" (198) and "don't do like a nigger" (97).

    In an article in *Scribner's Magazine* two years before *The Story of Aaron*
was published, Harris commented on where he derived the cultural power he
embodied in the figure of the Son of Ben Ali.

In Georgia, the prevailing type—not the most numerous, but the most noticeable—is the Arabian. Old Ben Ali (pronounced by the Negroes Benally), who left a diary in one of the desert dialects of Arabic, was blessed with an astonishing prepotency, and his descendents after him, so that it is always easy to discover the "favor" of the old Arab in a Georgia negro who is especially intelligent or enterprising.[29]

"Favoring" the hybrid Arabian with such "astonishing prepotency," Harris elevated ("blessed") the African without having to empower blacks in ways that would undermine the national reconciliation of white supremacy being contemporaneously enacted in the *Plessy v. Ferguson* decision of 1896. According to Harris, the historical Ben Ali "never was a slave in the ordinary meaning of that term" and, as a foreman, was as "fierce a taskmaster as a negro ever had" ("Sea Island," 274). Harris here enlists the extrahemispheric exoticism of the Arab to intimate the latent potential for restoring African freedom and authority. Featuring an actual Arab slave as the progenitor of his own narrative power enabled Harris to negotiate Muslim alterity as a supernatural means of controlling slavery as well as overseeing his own creative license.

Invoking Ben Ali as the father of Aaron, Harris drew upon the heritage of an actual Muslim overseer on a large plantation on Sapelo Island in Georgia named Bilali Muhammad, whose name was derived from the Ethiopian Muslim to whom the Prophet had granted the privilege of calling the faithful to prayer. The antebellum presence of Muslims in African American communities in the coastal areas of Georgia and South Carolina, according to historian Michael A. Gomez, was "active, vibrant, and compelling."[30] Agronomist Thomas Spaulding, who developed one of the largest systems of cotton agriculture in the U.S. South, purchased Bilali and his family member from the Bahamas because he possessed skills in planting the high-quality long-staple seed that came to be known as Sea Island cotton.[31] Bilali Muhammad was a Fulbe originally from the Senegambia region of Muslim West Africa whose writing in Arabic was for a long time called the Ben Ali Diary and considered to be autobiographical, until translators over eighty years later revealed it to be part of an Islamic legal text.[32] Ronald A. T. Judy extensively analyzed the "heterography" of Ben Ali's enigmatic writing, finding it to be "a text whose polyvalence refuses to be comprehended by western literary criticism's unadulterated paradigms."[33] William McFeely called it "an icon, in the true sense—a holy object connecting Africa to America in the hand of a deeply religious man."[34] Harris's translation of the talismanic Ben Ali Diary into his own fictional expression symbolizes the resources of Arab agency that remain resistant to American control. Aaron—whose only Arabic name is the Son of Ben Ali—reveals this genealogy by unwrapping a leather "memorandum book" containing written Arabic words that appear to the children like "pothooks." Aaron responds, "Ain't a word in it I can't read," and proceeds to speak its accents, prompting the black nurse to claims that it is "no creetur talk" (*Story of Aaron*, 12). Aaron's Arabic literacy symbolizes the resources of a mysterious African past that empowers his escape from the clutches of the demeaning system of slavery. Harris in this way transforms the illegibility of Ben Ali's "Diary" into an exotic genealogy for the power of his own literary invention.

That the alterity of Arabic writing was a resource for slaves as well as for enterprising white writers such as Harris is revealed by the rediscovery of the 1831 autobiography of Omar ibn Said, a Fulbe Muslim from Senegambia who had made the pilgrimage to Mecca before being enslaved and transported to Charleston in 1807. This unique narrative has been acknowledged as the earliest piece of Arabic writing to be found in the United States, and the only slave narrative to be written in Arabic.[35] Omar identified English as the "Christian language" (77–78) and his Arabic script signified the passport of his literacy and his religion as well as a transoceanic resource preventing others from accurately interpreting the meaning of his words. His willingness to write verses from the Bible in Arabic led many to view him as an exemplar of how a literate Muslim was not a threatening black African but an avuncular Arab ("Uncle Moreau") willing to convert to Christianity and accept his status as a superior slave in America. A deeper look under the disguise of his Arabic expression, now revealed by scholars freed from the desire to interject a Christian bias, reveals that ibn Said was able to maintain and even to celebrate his faith in Islam through invocations in Qur'anic literary style as well as transcend earthly enslavement by asserting that God is ultimately "our Owner" (87). That his Arabic literacy has had different connotations for African Americans is demonstrated by the fact that one of his Arabic writings was honored as part of the cultural wealth of blacks displayed in Boston's Faneuil Hall during a 1858 commemoration of the Boston Massacre that served also as a protest against the Dred Scott decision.[36] Centering himself within a Maghrebi center of gravity, ibn Said was able to challenge the hemispheric power of both slavery and Christianity to absorb his identity and thereby to maintain a certain latitude of freedom even while remaining physically in bondage. Such liberty was accomplished through the expressive power and resistant inscrutability of his own words, words that themselves have since come to be viewed not as a threat to or resource for the intellectual hegemony of whites but rather respected as a multilingual part of the African heritage in the Americas.

Muslims, Maroons, and Transcultural Rebellion

Jim's masquerade as a Blue Arab on a raft in the midst of the Mississippi and the Son of Ben Ali's fugitive freedom in the swamps of Georgia both posit temporary spaces of maroonage that create imaginative alternatives for African freedom in the late nineteenth century. Latin America has a rich history of Muslim rebels resisting their treatment in the Americas, the most important being the 1835 revolts in Bahia, Brazil, and the most recent the 1990 Jamaat al Muslimeen attempt at a coup d'état in Trinidad and Tobago.[37] Such a rebellious presence also found expression in antebellum literature written by North American writers. Harriet Beecher Stowe (as well as the lesser known David Hunter Strother) drew upon the liminal freedoms of the swamp well before Harris to evoke a militant Muslim liberty committed to resisting the confining rigidities and injustices of enslavement. By contrast, Herman Melville constructed a transpacific horizon of islamicized difference in his fictional treatment of the Senegalese mutineer Babo off the west coast of Chile and his evocation of the malign machinations of his Asian characters. In these instances, the global horizons of Islamic difference provided transcultural resources for representing the rebellion against race-based systems of American slavery.

After resigning her title character to his grave at the hands of Simon Legree in *Uncle Tom's Cabin* (1852), Harriet Beecher Stowe undertook a more dramatically militant critique of slavery. Stowe features a black man who refuses to be a slave in her creation of the creolized rebel in *Dred: A Tale of the Great Dismal Swamp* (1856). The swamp symbolizes the resources of Dred's resistance and is portrayed as a heathen geography: "regions of hopeless disorder" on the fringes of "civilized life."[38] In concocting the multiplicity of Dred's character, Stowe combines an extravagant mixture from her own cultural archive to multiply the holy vengeance of his power. She makes him the colossal son of Denmark Vesey destined to extend his abortive rebellion against civilized hypocrisy, alluding to her belief that Nat Turner was carrying on the legacy of the revolutionary spirit. Taking his father's Bible with him, Dred rejects the teaching of the New Testament, holding the ethic of meekness to be a doctrine of enslavement and dwelling instead on the righteous wrath of Old Testament vengeance. In so doing, Stowe exoticizes the Bible by calling it an "oriental seed" rich with "endless vitality and stimulating force" (1:256). However, Stowe also signifies an African source for Dred's dissent through his mother's polycultural Mandingo heritage, which gave him his name and a legacy of intelligence, beauty, pride, and capacity that enables him to oppose oppression. Mandingos were predominately Muslim, one possible reason for Dred's adoption of a "fantastic sort of turban, apparently of an old scarlet shawl, which added to the outlandish effect of his appearance" (1:241). Dred's avenging enthusiasm thus not only borrows from Nat Turner's woeful tirades but also from the martial spirit of Muslim resistance, a transgression that Stowe minimizes both by trying to contain his jihad within the spatial and temporal limits of the Bible and by killing him off well before the end of the novel.

William Tynes Cowan's book *The Slave in the Swamp: Disrupting the Plantation Narrative* (2005) explores the cultural threat symbolized by maroons such as Stowe's Dred who could maintain their independence on the margins of settled society in the U.S. South.[39] Cowan's archetypical maroon is a "sable outlaw" named Osman who is glimpsed hiding like Dred in the Great Dismal Swamp of Virginia in a *Harper's Monthly* travelogue by the popular illustrator David Hunter Strother. At the climax of the author's exploration into the intricate and isolated swamp, Strother uncovers "a gigantic negro, with a tattered blanket wrapped around his shoulders and a gun in his hand" whose "purely African features were cast in a mould betokening, in the highest degree, strength and energy."[40] Osman functions in Cowan's analysis as a startling inscrutable racial Other who disrupts the racial complacencies of both narrator and reader with the gothic mystery of his fugitive freedom. Cowan does not analyze the ramifications of Osman's Islamic name, but like the "briery screen" that Strother portrays surrounding Osman in his visual illustration, these roots lead back across the routes of transatlantic migration to the moorings of African Islam and the inability of the Americas to absorb its contentious alterity (4–10, 14). (See Figure 4.)

The hidden islamicist power subtly suggested by Stowe and Strother in their fictional renegades from the 1850s is traced more fully in the critical cosmopolitanism of their contemporary Melville. Melville deterritorializes much of his fiction by setting it upon the fluid currents of the oceans that, as Melville says of the Pacific, "makes all coasts one bay to it."[41] Melville islamicizes characters—such as Babo in "Benito Cereno," Aleema in *Mardi*, as well as Fedallah, his crew, and even the white whale of *Moby-Dick*—so that they perform an overruling and excessive fatalism that mysteriously controls events within his literary regimes.

Babo and the dozen other rebels in "Benito Cereno," as noted in the depositions included in Amasa Delano's original travel narrative, are "all raw and born on the coast of Senegal."[42] Melville locates the sources of the revolt within the mind of Babo himself whose literacy, leadership, and name signify his Muslim heritage. Keith Cartwright has explored the significance of Babo's Senegalese ethnicity and notes that his name was "rendered from the common Fulbe name Baaba . . . as were Muri (Mory) and Atufal (Artu Faal)" (185). Melville allies Babo's plotting intelligence, which lives on in his story, with his own critical and creative authorship. Babo's "dusky comment of silence" and mute destiny bequeath the specter of his agency as an unhomely reminder of a primal freedom that refuses to be conscripted by the hegemonic codes of Continental law, even when thousands of miles and an ocean away from the African home to which he knew not how to return.[43]

The inscrutability of Melville's Pacific islamicism gains a more oriental and disembodied extreme with the dark despotism that possesses Aleema, the priest of *Mardi*, and Fedallah, the shady genie of *Moby-Dick*. Melville's naming of the "dusky" and despotic Aleema, who intends to sacrifice the angelic maiden Yillah but is instead killed by Melville's narrator Taji, is linked with the *ulema*, the name of the Persian Shiite clergy.[44] The "swart" Fedallah (*Moby-Dick*, 217), whose name in Arabic means "the sacrifice of God," runs the gamut of

OSMAN,

FIGURE 4. "Osman." Illustration of maroon in the Great Dismal Swamp by "Porté Crayon" (David Hunter Strother) in *Harper's New Monthly Magazine* (1856), 452. From the Rare Book Collection, University of North Carolina at Chapel Hill.

types of the weird and cunning Asian: he is called a Parsee (or orthodox Zoro-astrian) and worships fire; he possesses a Muslim name and wears a turban; he wears a black Chinese jacket and coils his hair in braids on his head; and he is compared, like his "tiger-yellow" crew (217), with "the like of whom now and then glide among the unchanging Asiatic communities, especially the Oriental isles to the east of the continent" (231). When the *Pequod* is waylaid by Malays after it sails through the straits of Sunda between Java and Sumatra, Ahab applauds the "inhuman atheistical devils" for encouraging him to quicken his own pursuit of the whale (383). Melville links the piracy of these "rascally Asiatics" with the savagery of Ahab's own monomaniacal revenge, replicated in the phantom crew that he secrets aboard. Nevertheless, Melville spares some of Ahab's "humanities" (79) by displacing the captain's perverse destiny and haunted fatalism onto Fedallah's spectral body. A figure of evil fate who remains "a muffled mystery to the last" (231), Fedallah is connected with Ahab as a shadow to its substance. Melville yokes them together "an unseen tyrant driving them" and they remain in that condition in death, attached by whale-lines to the plunging Moby Dick, who absorbs their bodies within his living orbit and diving depths (538). Throughout his late poetry, Melville continued to distill Asian characters into suspicious sorcerers whose uncanny influence bodied forth a dark and primal antagonism.

Melville uses the language of *Othello* to intimate the malignity of the Leviathan that sheared off Ahab's leg with the "seeming malice" of a "turbaned Turk" (184). Melville compares finding this white whale in the oceans of all the world to recognizing "a white-bearded Mufti in the thronged thoroughfares of Constantinople" (201), and describes Moby Dick's majestic first appearance as occurring "far out on the soft Turkish-rugged waters" (548). The white whale is also islamicized as an inscrutable figure of evil fate when Ahab loses his life. As Ahab throws out his last harpoon, "the flying turn caught him round the neck, and voicelessly as Turkish mutes bowstring their victim, he was shot out of the boat, ere the crew knew he was gone" (572). These islamicist references at the key locations of the whale's irruption into the story suggest the special resonance invested in its mysterious capacity, like Babo's staring white skull, to symbolize the exotic and ungraspable opacity ascribed to Islam. As an alien presence who freely swims the oceans surrounding the Americas, Melville's Moby Dick intimates "That intangible malignity which has been from the beginning; to whose dominion even the modern Christians ascribe one-half of the worlds" (184).

Assuming the identity of Ishmael, Melville affiliated his narrator with a figure most widely known in the nineteenth century as the Abrahamic ances-tor of the Arabs. The islamicist stance of making Ishmael the only survivor empowered Melville to criticize Christian civilization from a position that, although biblical, was also one aligned with Islam, one from which he could speak with the contentious power of an established outsider. Melville's Book of Ishmael integrates the infidel renegade and slave into the center of his narrative, and ultimately into the canon because of *Moby-Dick*'s importance to U.S. literature.[45]

All three of these works from the 1850s locate spaces peripheral to the circumscribed systems from which they can launch their critiques of slavery in the Americas. Setting these narratives in impenetrable swamps in the interior of the U.S. South or, in Melville's case, onboard ships off the coast of Chile ("Benito Cereno") or in the open ocean waters near the Muslim archipelago of Indonesia signifies the ends to which these authors had to go to figure the fate of freedom in the landed Americas with its hierarchical racial economies. The infidel challenge of Islamic difference intimated by these maroons, fugitives, and castaways signified both the militancy of their violent dissent and their authors' ability to engage Islamic latitudes to imagine temporary loopholes of transnational liberty.

Over the Edge: Islam and the Limits of American Interculturalism in the 1940s

By the middle of the twentieth century, African Americans had found more sustainable latitudes of freedom by connecting with the global resource of Islam in ways that signified the stirrings of a revivified civil rights movement in the United States "'Man, if you join the Muslim faith, you ain't colored no more, you'll be white,'" Dizzy Gillespie remembers jazz musicians saying in New York during World War II. "You get a new name and you don't have to be a nigger no more."[46] In his autobiography called *To BE or Not . . . to BOP*, Gillespie explains how a large number of jazz musicians turned to Islam in the 1940s because it provided them with the power of a religious faith which also served as a social act enabling escape from the stigma of color and criticism of a Christianized culture complicit with the system of segregation. Muslims were allowed to mark W (for white) instead of C (for Colored) on their police cards, thereby opening the door to establishments which otherwise refused service to blacks. "When these cats found out that Idrees Sulieman," Gillespie explained, "could go into these white restaurants and bring out sandwiches to the other guys because he wasn't colored, and he looked like the inside of the chimney, they started enrolling in droves" (291). Malcolm X told a similar anecdote about how a dark-skinned friend put a turban on and was served in a segregated restaurant in Atlanta. "He asked the waitress, 'What would happen if a Negro came in here?' And there he's sitting, black as night, but because he has his head wrapped up the waitress looked back at him and says, 'Why, there wouldn't no nigger dare come in here!'"[47]Although Gillespie saw no need to transcend his blackness by becoming a Muslim (he claimed that "WC is a toilet in Europe" and later became a Bahá'í), he was "quite intrigued by the beautiful sound of the word 'Quran,' and found it 'out of this world,' 'way out,' as we used to say" (292). *Life Magazine* conned Dizzy Gillespie into posing for a picture on a prayer rug bowing to Mecca as part of its strategy to write him off as "too strange, weird and exotic to merit serious attention" (293). Although he was resentful of this particular manipulation, this islamicist stance resembles the latitude of dissent that Gillespie created for himself by performing his innovative music. The improvised style of Bebop, whose hip defiance, Eric Lott says, "bucked the regulations of accepted articulateness" (598), vibrated a creolized space of alternative performance signified by Dizzy's riffing on Hamlet's existential soliloquy in the title of his memoirs.[48] At one point, Gillespie embodied this liberty by wearing a turban when traveling abroad. "Sometimes Americans think I'm some kind of Mohammedan nobleman," he commented. "I like to pretend I don't speak English and listen to them talk about me."[49]

Dizzy Gillespie figured his fellow musicians as turning toward Mecca to get beyond the hurt of racism and personally employed Muslim resources to exult in the fluid feel of a foreign freedom. By contrast, Langston Hughes appropriated jazz style even while figuring "Be-Bop Boys" as cashing in on the currency of exoticism in a short four-line poem: "Imploring Mecca/to achieve/six discs/with Decca."[50] However, it was Malcolm X who exemplified most publicly the full irruptive force of Islam as a radical reorientation of conventional racial realities. This substitution is reflected at the most basic level in Malcolm X's effacements of his birth surname (Little) and his street nicknames, their replacement with a letter whose mysterious obscurity symbolized both an absence and a turning of the Cross on its axis, and ultimately the full eclipse of his American identity when he became a Muslim named El-hajj Malik El-Shabazz, in honor of an ancient tribe of black people in the Near East. Some call this disowning process reversion instead of conversion because it replaces the markers and misnomers of second-class Negro citizenship with transnational freedoms signified by a Muslim power that existed in Africa prior to enslavement. The most prominent case was that of the boxer Cassius Clay, who, by erasing his association with the white nineteenth-century abolitionist for whom he was named, became Muhammad Ali and was celebrated in a different arena as the greatest man on earth because of the talking of his fists. Reverting to Islam empowered some African Americans in the mid-twentieth century to protest the exclusions of racism. African Americans were able to perform alternative freedoms that elided national and hemispheric racial categories by restoring transoceanic genealogies of religious faith and subaltern power and imposing these Islamic lineages within American situations.

While the adoption of Islam by African Americans in the 1940s invoked the unfulfilled dream of black emancipation, the literary works of the expatriate U.S. author Paul Bowles at the same time narrated stories that dramatized the paralyzing limits of Americans' intercultural understanding when confronted with their incomprehension of Islamic cultures. In the same years during which Henry Luce called U.S. Americans to assume their role as a global superpower, and the Americas were opened to displaced persons from the hellish fallout of post-World War II Europe, Bowles spelled out—in such works as the novel *The Sheltering Sky* (1949)—the abrupt end of American authority when confronting the radical and alien difference of African Islam in its Saharan hinterlands.

Bowles's story "A Distant Episode," originally published in the *Partisan Review* in 1947 as the Cold War was ensuing, narrates the violent degeneration into madness of a professor of linguistics who travels into the interior of North Africa in leisurely pursuit of varied dialects of Moghrebi, the local language.[51] After being led into an abyss while in search of souvenirs, his tongue is cut out by the Reguibat, a Muslim tribe known for aggressively resisting French colonization and called the "blue people" for their robes of indigo dye. They capture him, dress him in a clownish costume comprised of strings of tin cans, and force him for a full year to perform antic gestures and "fearful growling noises" before paying audiences. Bowles's comment that "he existed in the middle of the movements made by these other men" exemplifies the professor's complete loss of agency (46). Revived into painful consciousness after hearing the Arabic spoken by a man who purchases him, the professor finally refuses to perform, causing the man to seek out and murder the Reguibat who had made the transaction, and be arrested in turn for this act of revenge. Alone and starving, the professor slowly deciphers the French words on a calendar in the house where he is held captive—"he had the feeling he was performing what had been written for him long ago." Roaring and smashing his way to escape from his fate, he "gallops" through the town while "his yelling rose into an indignant lament as he waved his arms more wildly, and hopped high into the air at every few steps, in an access of terror" before leaving the gateway of the town and disappearing in the desert as "the lunar chill was growing in the air" (48–49).

This stunning story, the most anthologized of all of Bowles's work, dramatizes a horrible hybridity through which an arrogant and ignorant Westerner is stripped of all his authority and knowledge except the animalistic bellowing of his own inarticulate outrage and the terrible oblivion of his shapeless identity. Unlike Jim's temporary masquerade as a sick Arab, Bowles's professor performs his tragic loss of cultural agency only to exhibit the primitive helplessness of a slave who can neither speak about nor make sense of the world he inhabits. Bowles's story dramatizes the horror that ensues when Americans reach the ends of their hemisphere and confront the abyss of another half that makes no sense. As Jorge Luis Borges does in his short fiction, Bowles in "A Distant Episode" turns the process of enslavement around on its axis to reveal the destabilizing vertigo that ensues when purported cosmopolites reach the limits of their spheres of intercultural understanding. Bowles wrote in the moment when the Cold War came to constitute a new global bipolarity that divided the globe into first and second worlds representing opposing ideological camps. Like the moon in its cycles, however, Islamic opacity has survived that colossal system of world order. As Wallace Stevens suggested in his poem, the haunting "lunar chill" marks the alien horizons in whose margins we must learn to live even as the new hemispheric studies rescues Americans from other insularities of their own international imaginations.

NOTES

1. Wallace Stevens, "Notes Toward a Supreme Fiction," *The Collected Poems of Wallace Stevens* (New York: Vintage Books, 1954), 382–383; *Letters*, ed. Holly Stevens (New York, A. A. Knopf, 1966), 434. (Asterisks not in original.) Thanks to George Lensing.

2. Roland Greene, "New World Studies and the Limits of National Literatures," *Stanford Humanities Review* 6:1 (1998): 88–110; Claudia Sadowski-Smith and Claire F. Fox, "Theorizing the Hemisphere: Inter-Americas Work at the Intersection of American, Canadian, and Latin American Studies," *Comparative American Studies* 2:1 (2004): 5–38; Anna Brickhouse, *Transamerican Literary Relations and the Nineteenth-Century Public Sphere* (New York: Cambridge University Press, 2004); Paula M. L. Moya and Ramon Saldivar, "Fictions of the Trans-American Imaginary," *MFS: Modern Fiction Studies* 49:1 (2003): 1–18; Sandhya Shukla and Heidi Tinsman. "Editors' Introduction, Special Issue: Our Americas: Political and Cultural Imaginings," *Radical History Review* 89 (Spring 2004): 1–10.

3. Elena Glasberg, "Antarcticas of the Imagination" (Ph.D. Dissertation, Indiana University, 1995).

4. The "Third Space" of Homi Bhabha *("neither the One nor the Other but something else besides")* has an earlier expression in the philosophy of Charles Sanders Peirce, who spoke of the medium of "thirdness" as a mode of being that "is that what it is owing to things between which it mediates and which it brings into relation to each other" (Homi Bhabha, *The Location of Culture* [New York: Routledge, 1994], 28; Charles Sanders Peirce, *Collected Papers of Charles Sanders Peirce*, 8 vols., Vols. 1–6, ed. Charles Hartshorne and Paul Weiss [Cambridge, Mass.: Harvard University Press, 1931–1958], 1:356). On islamicism, see Timothy Marr, *The Cultural Roots of American Islamicism* (New York: Cambridge University Press, 2006).

5. Christopher Columbus, "Journal of the First Voyage of Columbus," *The Northmen, Columbus and Cabot, 985–1503, Original Narratives of Early American History*, ed. Julius E. Olson and Edward Gaylord Bourne (New York: Charles Scribner's Sons, 1906), 89–90.

6. Enrique Dussel, *The Invention of the Americas: Eclipse of "the Other" and the Myth of Modernity*, trans. Michael D. Barber (New York: Continuum, 1995), 34; see also 88–90.

7. Pedro de Castañeda, "The Narrative of the Expedition of Coronado," in *Spanish Explorers in the Southern United States, 1528–1543*, ed. Frederick W. Hodge (New York: C. Scribner's Sons, 1907), 313–337.

8. Christopher Marlowe, *Doctor Faustus: A Two-Text Edition*, ed. David Scott Kastan (New York: W. W. Norton, 2005), 11.

9. Max Harris, *Aztecs, Moors, and Christians: Festivals of Reconquest in Mexico and Spain* (Austin: University of Texas Press, 2000), 23.

10. Sylviane Diouf, *Servants of Allah: African Muslims Enslaved in the Americas* (New York: New York University Press, 1998).

11. Domingo Faustino Sarmiento, *Facundo: Civilization and Barbarism*, trans. Kathleen Ross (1845; Berkeley, University of California Press, 2003).

12. Christina Civantos, *Between Argentines and Arabs: Argentine Orientalism, Arab Immigrants, and the Writing of Identity* (Albany: State University of New York Press, 2005).

13. Jorge Luis Borges, *Collected Fictions* (New York: Penguin, 1998). See also Ian Almond, "Borges the Post-Orientalist: Images of Islam from the Edge of the West," *MFS: Modern Fiction Studies* 50:2 (2004): 535–559.

14. Ana Castillo, "The Ancient Roots of Machismo," in *The Massacre of the Dreamers: Essays on Xicanisma* (Albuquerque: University of New Mexico Press, 1994), 63–84; Milton Hatoum, *Relato de um Certo Oriente* (São Paulo, Brazil: Companhia das Letras, 1989), English version: *The Tree of the Seventh Heaven*, trans. Ellen Watson (New York: Atheneum, 1994); Hatoum, *Dois Irmãos* (São Paulo, Brazil: Companhia das Letras, 2000), English version: *The Brothers*, trans. John Gledson (New York: Farrar, Straus and Giroux, 2002).

15. Louisa May Alcott, *Little Women* (1868; reprint, New York: Bantam Books, 1983), 184.

16. Mark Twain, *The Adventures of Huckleberry Finn* (New York: Harper, 1912), 109.

17. Henry B. Wonham, "'I Want a Real Coon': Mark Twain and Late-Nineteenth-Century Ethnic Caricature," *American Literature* 72:1 (2000): 144.

18. Mark Twain, *Innocents Abroad; or, The New Pilgrim's Progress* (Hartford, Conn.: American Publishing, 1869), 547.

19. Booker Taliaferro Washington, *Up from Slavery: An Autobiography* (Garden City, N.J.: Doubleday, 1900), 103.

20. Kareem Abdul Jabbar (with Alan Steinberg), *Black Profiles in Courage: A Legacy of African American Achievement* (New York: William Morrow and Co., 1996), 1–13.

21. Joseph Roach, *Cities of the Dead: Circum-Atlantic Performance* (New York: Columbia University Press, 1996), 36.

22. Bernth Lindfors, "'Mislike Me Not for My Complexion . . .': Ira Aldridge in Whiteface," *African American Review* 33:2 (1999): 349.

23. Herbert Marshall and Mildred Stock. *Ira Aldridge: The Negro Tragedian* (New York: MacMillan, 1958), 14–16.

24. Lindfors, "'Mislike Me Not,'" 347.

25. Dutton Cook, "Strange Players." *Appleton's Journal* 11 (September 1881): 273.

26. Théophile Gautier, *Voyage en Russie*, 254–256, translated in Marshall and Stock, 230–231.

27. Frances Ellen Watkins Harper, *Iola Leroy; or, Shadows Uplifted* (Philadelphia: Garrigues Brothers, 1893), 84.

28. Joel Chandler Harris, *The Story of Aaron (So Named) The Son of Ben Ali* (Boston: Houghton, Mifflin, 1896); *Aaron in the Wildwoods* (Boston: Houghton, Mifflin, 1897).

29. Joel Chandler Harris, "The Sea Island Hurricanes, The Relief," *Scribner's Magazine* 15, no.3 (19 March 1894): 274.

30. Michael A. Gomez, *Black Crescent: The Experience and Legacy of African Muslims in the Americas* (New York: Cambridge University Press, 2005), 159. See also Keith Cartwright, *Reading Africa into American Literature: Epics, Fables, and Gothic Tales* (Lexington: University Press of Kentucky, 2002), 80–89.

31. E. Merton Coulter, *Thomas Spaulding of Sapelo* (Baton Rouge: Louisiana State University Press, 1940).

32. Cartwright, *Reading Africa*, 170–173; Gomez, *Black Crescent*, 152–159.

33. Ronald A. T. Judy, *(Dis)Forming the American Canon: African-Arabic Slave Narratives and the Vernacular* (Minneapolis: University of Minnesota Press, 1993), 227.

34. William McFeely, *Sapelo's People: A Long Walk into Freedom* (New York: W. W. Norton, 1994), 36.

35. *The Life of Omar ibn Said, Written by Himself*, with introd. and trans. by Ala A. Alryyes, in *The Multilingual Anthology of American Literature*, ed. Marc Shell and Wernor Sollors (New York: New York University Press, 2000), 58–93; Ghada Osman and Camille F. Forbes, "Representing the West in the Arabic Language: The Slave Narrative of Omar ibn Said," *Journal of Islamic Studies* 15:3 (2004): 331–343; and Allan D. Austin, *African Muslims in Antebellum America: A Sourcebook* (New York: Garland, 1984), 445–523.

36. *Boston Massacre, March 5th, 1770: the day which history selects as the dawn of the American Revolution, Commemorative festival, at Faneuil Hall, Friday, March 5, 1858. Protest against the Dred Scott decision . . .* (1858). Broadside at the American Antiquarian Society, Worcester, Massachusetts. Thanks to Thomas Doughton.

37. João José Reis, *Slave Rebellion in Brazil: The Muslim Uprising of 1835 in Bahia*, trans. Arthur Brakel (Baltimore, Md.: Johns Hopkins University Press, 1993); Selwyn D. Ryan, *The Muslimeen Grab for Power: Race, Religion, and Revolution in Trinidad and Tobago* (Port of Spain, Trinidad: Imprint Caribbean, 1991).

38. Harriet Beecher Stowe, *Dred; A Tale of the Great Dismal Swamp*. 2 vols. (Boston: Phillips, Samson and Company, 1856), 1:255.

39. William Tynes Cowan, *The Slave in the Swamp: Disrupting the Plantation Narrative* (New York: Routledge, 2005).

40. David Hunter Strother, "The Dismal Swamp: Illustrated by Porté Crayon," *Harper's New Monthly Magazine* 13:76 (September 1856): 452–453.

41. Herman Melville, *Moby-Dick; or, The Whale* (Evanston and Chicago: Northwestern University Press and the Newberry Library, 1988), 483.

42. Herman Melville, *The Piazza Tales and Other Prose Pieces, 1839–1960* (Evanston and Chicago: Northwestern University Press and the Newberry Library, 1987), 828.

43. Melville, *Piazza Tales*, 87. See also Timothy Marr, "Melville's Ethnic Transcriptions," *Leviathan* 3:1 (2001): 1–25, esp. 21–24.

44. Herman Melville, *Mardi and a Voyage Thither* (Evanston and Chicago: Northwestern University Press and the Newberry Library, 1970), 142.

45. Marr, "American Ishmael: Melville's Literary Islamicism," in *Cultural Roots*, 219–261.

46. Dizzy Gillespie (with Al Fraser), *To BE, or not . . . to BOP: Memoirs* (Garden City, N.Y.: Doubleday, 1979), 291.

47. *Malcolm X Speaks: Selected Speeches and Statements*, ed. George Breitman (New York: Pathfinder, 1989), 36. This space of possibility is alluded to in Ralph Ellison's *Invisible Man* when the narrator experiences a chaotic fluidity without boundaries when he is mistaken as Rinehart: "I recalled a report of a shoeshine boy who had encountered the best treatment in the South simply by wearing a white turban instead of his usual Dobbs or Stetson, and I fell into a fit of laughing" (New York: Vintage, 1995), 499.

48. Eric Lott, "Double V, Double Time: Bepop's Politics of Style," *Callaloo* 36 (Summer 1988): 597–605.

49. Richard O. Boyer, "Bop," *The New Yorker*, 3 July 1948, 31. Further academic inquiry is needed into the extent to which the musical aesthetics of jazz, blues, be-bop, cool, and rap have been derived from diasporic Muslim cultures.

50. Langston Hughes, *The Collected Works of Langston Hughes. Volume 3: The Poems 1951–1967* (Columbia: University of Missouri Press, 2001), 51.

51. Paul Bowles, "A Distant Episode." *Collected Stories* (Santa Rosa, Calif.: Black Sparrow, 1989), 39–49.

14

Of Hemispheres and Other Spheres

Navigating Karen Tei Yamashita's Literary World

KANDICE CHUH

Always a stranger, you move through these places, and you find the things that are recognizable from the places that you've already been.

–Karen Tei Yamashita, *Circle K Cycles* (2001)

Although Asian American literary studies has in recent decades taken the "transnational turn" that Shelley Fisher Fishkin has described of contemporary American studies generally,[1] the particular rubric of "hemispheric studies" has not found as much traction in the field as, for example, "diasporic" or "Pacific Rim studies." Aside from a smattering of works that attend to Canada in a substantial way, most transnationally inclined criticism in Asian American studies has been more involved in mining understudied or otherwise occluded east-west connections than in looking critically north or south. This turn toward the transnational has also been accompanied by a certain amount of anxiety over the consequences of losing focus on the historic and continuing power of the U.S. nation-state in racializing and regulating Asianness within its borders.[2] Moreover, because of the distinctive ways in which Asianness has been racialized as immutably foreign despite nativity, citizenship, or acculturation within the U.S. frame, a critical wariness attaches to any semblance of a presumed commonality of experience or identity across specific sites. In the absence of racial essentialism, in other words, there exists no prima facie case for connecting the expressive cultures of Asian Americans with Asians elsewhere.

I open this essay with this brief rehearsal of some of the conditions and concerns that attend debates about the spatial logics animating Asian American literary studies in order to provide a point of departure for understanding how they might participate in and perhaps advance hemispheric studies. Understood in its broadest sense, hemispheric studies prompts a collaborative and dynamic link among studies of the Americas writ large. While critically mindful of and geared toward negotiating substantial unevenness in political and economic power, hemispheric studies as proposed by such scholars as Claudia Sadowski-Smith and Claire Fox complements "other emergent national, regional, and global perspectives in American, Canadian, and Latin American studies."[3] Such a model attempts to decenter the U.S. nation and critical approaches based on or derived from U.S.-centered studies even as it acknowledges the influential material power of the United States.

My broad aim in this essay is to explore that complementary space between Asian American studies, conceived as a "national perspective" that seeks to understand the link between the national and the global, and hemispheric studies, understood as paradigmatically concerned with the relationship of the Americas to the local or national. Asian American studies offers a national perspective insofar as its primary objectives have been geared toward illuminating U.S. culture and politics from the particular vantage of a domestic racial minority. It is, in other words, the specific site of the U.S. nation and the processes of racialization that have shaped the various practices and structures of the U.S. nation-state that have been the grounds upon which Asian Americanist critics have sought to interrogate the United States' relation to the world. Because the histories of Asian racialization in the United States have been so closely tied to its relations with Asian nations, it makes sense that transnationalism in Asian American studies has focused attention on what Gary Okihiro has described as the "East-West filaments" of Asian American history.[4] Hemispheric studies poses a different kind of challenge, a different set of critical questions for Asian Americanists: in what ways can hemispheric studies enhance the study of racialization in the United States? How might such a perspective advance Asian Americanist efforts to critique the U.S. nation's reliance on and creation of racial difference? This exploration suggests that hemispheric studies articulated through Asian American literary studies underscores the need to look within and among but also *beyond* the Americas and specifically to Asia in critical efforts to challenge the discursive centrality of the United States.

This essay, then, underscores the complexity that Sadowski-Smith and Fox identify as characterizing "attempts to rethink the field [of American studies] outside and beyond national boundaries."[5] For, it points to the ways that hemispheric approaches derived through the minority discourse/ethnic studies-based institutional history of Asian American studies might look quite different from those bearing the legacy of institutionalized American studies. Ascribed with an indelible foreignness, Asian Americans have long argued for recognition as U.S. Americans. Relatedly, Asian American studies has had to disarticulate itself from Asian studies as part of its efforts to show the centrality of Asian Americanness to the formation and sustenance of the U.S. nation.[6] Where American studies arguably has moved from a secure place of unquestioned belongingness to and representativeness of the U.S. nation in reaching out toward extranational perspectives, Asian American studies has been actively working to move "inward," to claim such standing as commensurate with American studies. Asian Americanists continue to argue the importance of seeing Asian Americanness as a distinctly national formation, and even as we negotiate the insights of transnational and other extranational critical approaches, we continue to place primacy on the importance of recognizing the ways that Asian Americanness is both historically and contemporarily dis-identified from the United States. The blunt instrument that is the construct of "American Studies" cannot thoroughly attend to these differences between "American Studies" and "Asian American studies." And in alignment with the work of the other essays constituting this volume, this recognition implicitly suggests that a U.S.-derived hemispheric studies must take as a critical point of departure the radical diversity of the United States. Doing so can also, importantly, remind us of the falsity of the homogeneity implied by any national or other category of identity.

To illustrate the particularity of what an Asian Americanist hemispheric literary criticism might look like, I focus here on the prose writings of Karen Tei Yamashita.[7] A Japanese American writer who lived in Brazil for nearly a decade, during which time she married a Brazilian architect and had two children; who later lived in Japan for six months with that family, a trip that resonated with her earlier longer stay in Japan as a student; and who, before Brazil and after, and before Japan and after, lived (and lives) in her native California; Yamashita bears a biography that reflects the consistent interest in her writings in movement, migration, and transformation. Although she identifies herself specifically as an Asian American writer, and while her work appears in anthologies of Asian American literature and has been repeatedly critically praised for the extraordinary imagination and literary crafting it registers, Asian Americanist literary discourse has only loosely become a home for Yamashita's work, primarily because of the geography of her writings. Apart from her most recent novel, *Tropic of Orange* (1997), which is set partially in Los Angeles, Yamashita has used Brazil as the setting for most of her creative prose. The centrality of Brazil to Yamashita's creative work immediately marks its eccentricity to the usual regimes of U.S. American literature. As a writer for whom nation and, to some extent, hemisphere are categories utterly inadequate to the task of capturing the geographies of her imagination, Yamashita proves an ideal subject through which we might consider the impact of hemispheric approaches on Asian American literary discourse, and the impact of Asian American literatures on hemispheric studies.

Yamashita's work encourages an opening out of U.S. boundaries in different registers (the political, the imaginative, the critical) and multiple directions (south and west, especially). Her writings are coherent wholes without insisting upon or privileging unity, and the energy and narrative pleasures of the work issue from the plotlines and characters that manage to be at once surprising and deliberate. Commitment to a thematic and generic eccentricity and a formal elasticity whereby protagonists transform into minor characters and the latter enlarge into central actors characterize Yamashita's work. Likewise, her settings regenerate repeatedly under pressures of forces both local and global, mounted at the hands of both human agents and non-human (and sometimes inhumane) ideologies. Together, these representational strategies enable her work to resist delimitation by specific geography even as it attends with intimacy to a sense of particular place.

As Asian Americanist discourses have critically acknowledged the inadequacy of the frame of nation to account for the complexities of Asian American histories, subjectivities, and cultures, such pressures on the boundaries of Asian America and of Asian American studies have resulted in efforts, as Rachel Lee notes in her incisive assessment of these critical directions, to embrace the spatial reorganization represented by such terms as "the Pacific Rim" and "the Asia-Pacific," which are effectively representations of "a displacement of the [U.S.] American optic."[8] One of the problems Lee rightly marks with respect to these efforts is that, "[t]hough partly motivated by a desire to enable Asian Americanists a wider area of study" than had been possible by the dominance of such paradigms as cultural nationalism, which insisted on the belongingness of Asians in the United States, "paradoxically, [they] establish new boundaries around their subjects by evoking reformulated regions that might be substituted as the proper domain of Asian American Studies."[9]

Distinctly informed by Latin American literary traditions, which she identifies as her most formative influences as a writer, Yamashita's work falls neither neatly nor completely into the territorial logics that have historically shaped and that currently underlie Asian American studies. In that way, her work helps us avoid the reterritorialization of discourse—the establishment of new boundaries—that Lee highlights. At the same time, though, it clearly engages Asian American literary traditions by, for example, employing and revising such familiar Asian American tropes as railroad labor and immigration and the challenges of acculturation.[10] Yamashita's interest in the epistemological effects of shifting paradigms,[11] especially those like nation and hemisphere that are spatially organized, registers in the space between what is familiar and foreign to Asian American literary studies.

For present purposes, I focus in this essay on two characteristics of Yamashita's prose writings. I begin by showing how Yamashita initiates a hemispheric perspective by her rendering of Brazil, especially through her novel *Brazil-Maru*. That novel anticipates the contemporary concerns of hemispheric studies to find ways of grappling with the irregular emergence of modernities across the Americas. I then move on to emphasizing the ways that, across her writings, Yamashita provides occasion for triangulating the processes of national identity formation unfolding in the United States, Brazil, and Japan in the early and toward the end of the twentieth century. In so doing, she insists upon the integration of an east-west aspect to hemispheric American studies. In addition to prompting U.S. Americanists southward, Yamashita thus implicitly calls for greater critical attention on the part of Brazilianists to the distinctive histories of Japanese immigrants and their Brazilian descendants.[12] Her work compels coordination of efforts among scholars working in specific sites to produce collaborative knowledge.

That discussion is followed by an effort to delineate Yamashita's method of moving beyond a nation-based frame of analysis. Working primarily with *Circle K Cycles* (2001), I show how Yamashita's writings guide us toward a comparative imagination through their explorations of the motivating desires, complex historic negotiations, and variegated costs to self and other, of making home. Her creative visions reject the progression-orientation of a world mapped in two dimensions (the flat world of modernity that bifurcates neatly into North and South, East and West, modern and not). Instead, they demarcate a *circumoceanic* spatial logic characterized by cyclicality and infinite connectivity.[13] Cultural hybridization, intersectionality, and most of all, change—in place, identity, and worldview—dominate in Yamashita's literary world. These characteristics mark the fluid terrain of the circumoceanic space she articulates.

New Civilizations/Emerging Modernities

Yamashita's Brazil emerges as a result of empirical knowledge combined with the fantastic world of the imagination. Yamashita first went to Brazil in 1975 under the aegis of a Thomas J. Watson Fellowship. She had lived for a year and a half in Japan as a student who, inspired by the identity movements unfolding in the United States at that time, sought to research her family's history. During that time, she explains retrospectively in *Circle K Cycles*, she learned to perform Japaneseness well enough that she effectively "passed" as a native, "[b]ut every now and again, I would be questioned in a roundabout way about my ancestry, about my parents and their parents until my story ended in Gifu, Tokyo, and Nagano. The questioner would then exclaim with surprise: *Ah, then you are a pure Japanese!*" (12). The desire to understand "what being a pure Japanese might be" partly inspires Yamashita's journey to Brazil. As a third context (additional to the United States and Japan) for investigating and experiencing Japaneseness, Brazil was to bring into relief the qualities of "pure Japaneseness" that are occluded for her in her native United States, and that are seemingly inaccessible even in Japan. Accordingly, while in Brazil, she conducted extensive interviews at several Nikkei (of Japanese descent) farming communes in addition to other Japanese Brazilian communities. She would later fictively recreate what she learned in *Brazil-Maru*, published in 1992.

The novel is the result of multiple wholesale revisions of "the larger story of an entire immigration" she intends to tell, according to Yamashita.[14] Explicitly a rendering of the historical migration of Japanese to Brazil in the early twentieth century, *Brazil-Maru* may be seen to register Yamashita's understanding that the legacy of her journey to Brazil was, finally, not the revelation of Japaneseness, but rather the insight she was afforded into the nature of home. "It is a work of fiction," writes Yamashita as part of her prefatory opening to the novel, "and the characters are also works of fiction. Certainly it cannot be construed to be representative of that enormous and diverse community of which it is but a part. And yet, perhaps, here is a story that belongs to all of us who travel distances to find something that is, after all, home." Initially drafted before though completed and published only after she and her family had relocated to California and after Yamashita had published *Through the Arc of the Rain Forest*, *Brazil-Maru* narrativizes the history of early twentieth-century Japanese emigration to Brazil from a perspective that is simultaneously internal and external to Brazil.

Such a doubled, hybridized perspective is perhaps especially appropriate with respect to Brazil. A postcolonial and radically diverse nation that has long identified as a "racial democracy"—a functional racial paradise—despite the fact that its social demographics belie such an idealized self-portrait, Brazil bears an extended history of miscegenation that complicates the discrete categorization of races. The historic context immediate to the Japanese immigration with which *Brazil-Maru* is concerned includes the emergence of Brazilian and Japanese modernities in the mid- to late nineteenth century. The entry of Japan into the modern world system in 1868 with the installation of the Meiji government conditioned massive emigration, as, by the end of the nineteenth century, there was a call for the establishment of Japanese settlements overseas in order especially to broaden Japan's market bases. Japanese emigrants settled in Brazil as early as 1908, and by the end of World War II, about 250,000 Japanese emigrants had moved to Latin America, some 189,000 of them to Brazil, mostly as labor on coffee plantations.

The relatively newly established Federal Republic of Brazil (dating to 1889) welcomed Japanese immigrants as a way of bolstering its own needs to create external markets for export. According to Jeffrey Lesser, Japan was valorized by members of the newer republic as an ideal model of the modern nation-state. "Imagining Brazil's future via Japan was a convenient way for intellectuals and policy makers to extract day-to-day pressures from ideological disputes about national identity," explains Lesser.[15] Brazilian travelers to Japan likewise produced representations that "tended toward emulation," even as, at the height of Japanese immigration in the 1920s and continuing to 1945, sociopolitical conflict erupted regarding the place and belongingness of these immigrants.[16]

Partly a consequence of major shifts in the political leadership of the nation during that time, Brazil's alignment with the Allied forces and corollary severing of ties with Japan during World War II intensified anti-Japanese sentiment. Paralleling the fissures within Japanese American communities wrought by the United States' relationship to Japan during the war, Nikkei communities in Brazil fragmented under the pressures of this anti-Japanese sentiment. Japanese-language newspapers were shut down by the government, and because many Nikkei could not read or speak Portuguese, they were largely isolated from the progress of the war, leading some to reject altogether the idea of Japan's defeat. Cut off from connection to their former homeland and unsettled by the anti-Japanese tensions in their present home, Nikkei formed a group in transition in this era, figuratively if not literally dislodged from their moorings.[17] Yamashita's novel animates this history of movement into and residence in Brazil. And it does so in such a way as to link the experiences of Nikkei in the United States with those in Brazil.

Brazil-Maru begins with a prefatory brief rehearsal of the arrival of Japanese to Brazil, one that emphasizes the impact of exclusionary U.S. immigration policies on that migration. Yamashita, in other words, frames the novel for U.S. audiences for whom the story of Japanese migration to Brazil may be seen as foreign. The novel's opening chapter emphasizes this interconnectivity as Ichiro Terada, Part I's narrator, recalls the arrival of his family to Brazil in 1925, having journeyed aboard the ship the *Brazil-maru*. Visited by a Christian evangelist, Momose-sensei, while living in the mountains of central Japan, Ichiro's parents, he explains, saw destiny in the evangelist's vision of Brazil as holding the future for Japanese: "Momose-sensei has lived in America, but he was very clear in his meaning. He said our future is in Brazil. . . . Anyway, we've missed our chance to go to America now. The Americans signed an Exclusion Act that won't allow us in'" (6). Brazil is immediately cast in contrast to the United States as bearing the potential for "a new civilization." Yamashita pursues the imaginative possibilities lying in that construction and reverses the historic-legal exclusion of Japanese from the United States literarily, by bringing that narrative to a U.S. readership. Within the context of the cultural nationalist driven identity-movements in the United States of the 1980s and 1990s, Yamashita found she was unable to publish work that focused on Japanese in Brazil. Thus prompted to make the connections that would facilitate U.S. interest in these non-U.S.-based histories and stories, Yamashita establishes these grounds for comparison early on in the novel.

If in this way Yamashita has opened a border between the United States and Brazil, she extends the scope of this work even further to serve as a broader comment on modernity's emergence and ideals. Each of the four major parts and the epilogue of *Brazil-Maru* open with an epigraphic quotation from Jean-Jacques Rousseau. Even more pointedly, Part I is titled "Emile" in explicit reference to Rousseau's *Emile, or On Education*, published in 1762. Ichiro is figured as the eponymous Emile, so much so that he is referred to as "Emiru" by other characters. Their familiarity with Rousseau is Yamashita's nod to their historic counterparts' expressed enthusiasm for the philosopher's writings, uncovered by Yamashita through her interviews. As we follow these migrants in their efforts to create Esperança, a farming commune, in part because of these invocations of Enlightenment philosophy, we are led to recognize the allegorical function of the immigrant stories Yamashita offers.

Such communes as represented in *Brazil-Maru* were historically a manifestation of one strategy for negotiating the question of assimilability that arose as Brazil attempted to cohere a national identity during the first half of the twentieth century. Communes allowed for a continuing valorization of Japaneseness as emblematic of modern industriousness without requiring social or spatial integration of Nikkei residents. They thus functioned as one way in which what was foreign could be made Brazilian, which describes a strong philosophical thread structuring Brazilian national identity formation in this era. The *brasilidade* movement took hold in earnest in the 1920s and '30s as Brazilian cultural nationalists attempted to distinguish Brazil from Europe in order to move beyond the close identification to European culture that resulted from its colonial past. Even as, following the lead of sociologist Gilberto Freyre, Brazil embraced hybridity as its defining characteristic, Nikkei in residence in Brazil found assimilation to be an extremely uneven process.[18] Yamashita's representation of the communes and the experiences of her characters in variously acculturating and assimilating may, against this backdrop, be seen to comment on precisely that unevenness. In that respect, her representations as the novel progresses seem increasingly oriented more toward illuminating Brazilian identity formation than on Nikkei experiences per se.

This illustration of unevenness is made especially apparent by Yamashita's strict regulation of narrative control in *Brazil-Maru*. The narrators of each of the novel's five parts (including an Epilogue) wax and wane in prominence as they more or less become minor characters in the sections narrated by others. For example, while Ichiro remains part of this novel to its end, he effectively becomes a minor character bearing the function of illuminating the central figures of the remaining parts of the book—those who were secondary to Ichiro in Part I. Ichiro's narrative closure—his enlightenment—is conveyed in a section narrated by a different character (Part III), a displacement of narrative control that is one of the strategies by which Yamashita shifts focus from individual characters to their relation to each other as well as to the overarching story unfolding.

Yamashita's characters, in other words, might better be understood as *character-spaces*. Character-space, as articulated by Alex Woloch in his study of the function of minor characters in nineteenth-century realist novels, refers to the "particular and charged encounter between an individual human personality and a determined space and position within the narrative as a whole."[19] Woloch offers this term as part of his argument that characters may best be seen not as individuals interacting within a fictional world, but rather as "*intersecting* character-spaces, each of which encompasses an *embedded*

interaction between the discretely implied person and the dynamically elaborated narrative form" (emphasis in the original).[20] The conceptualization of
characters as character-spaces Woloch proposes displaces the assessment of
individual importance and motivation in favor of assessing how their dynamic
interrelations together constitute the narrative. Yamashita's comparative
imagination formally manifests in her thematic and structural emphasis on
this narratological negotiation.

By the end of Part II, Brazil clearly functions as the narrative frame that
animates the relations between Yamashita's characters. This is punctuated by
the fact that the Nikkei of her world find in a character called the Bahiano an
enormous generosity that becomes the defining feature of Yamashita's Brazil.
The leader of the town closest to the commune and a man reputed to be both
dangerous and powerful, the Bahiano entered into business dealings with the
commune and refused anti-Japanese sentiment and activity even during the
war. Instead, he embraced the colonists immediately as "people [who] came
here to settle. We've got no argument with them. We're all in this together.
What's it to us if those others want to fight thousands of miles across the sea?"
(94). Because wartime law made it impossible for one of the commune to serve
as its official leader, the Bahiano took up that role for Esperança. During that
time, the Bahiano learned the communal business and life practices of Esperança and was transformed by that knowledge. In that sense, the Bahiano per-
sonifies the "Brazilianization" of foreignness of the era—the process through
which what had been foreign had been adopted and embraced as an element
central to Brazilian identity. The vastly differing relationships that the Nikkei
characters have with the Bahiano serve to mark the irregularity characterizing
this process of Brazilianization.

If in this way Yamashita guides her U.S. readers to and into Brazil, thus
familiarizing us (the United States) with both Nikkei and Brazilian identities,
it is by marking the border between the narrative and the act of narration that
she prompts literary critics to make the analogous move to accept responsibility for making what feels foreign familiar. As Kantaro, the commune's leader
and narrator of Part III, asks, "Who can look back on the passage of their lives
and tell such stories, speak of such struggles, remember that they were the
participants in a great dream, remember that they pursued a life of ideals,
lived their lives as a cup brimming over?" it becomes clear that the only possible answer to this question is Yamashita, who bears ultimate responsibility
for creating the networks of relation and affiliation among characters and their
defining spaces, who in that way creates order through emplotment. Authorship and interpretation are invoked in a way that recalls Yamashita's prefatory
enjoinder to consider this novel as simultaneously historic and universal, ethnographic and distinctly fictional.

Yamashita has explained that she was moved to write fictively upon
reflecting on the research she had conducted in Brazil, for she found the idea

of offering a primarily empirical account of the immigration history with which she was concerned inadequate to the task of capturing the complex emotions and ideas she found emergent from the stories she had gathered. In that decision and the novel that resulted from it, Yamashita exemplifies an Asian Americanist hemispheric practice characterized by a heightened awareness of the contingent nature of knowledge itself. Even as she moves us beyond the United States by means of representations that she creates based on both experience and education, Yamashita cautions against the idealization of representations of any kind. Thus, by the end of *Brazil-Maru*, she has unsettled her own narrativization of this particular history.

The end of the novel reminds us of the violence that has attended the emergence of modernity. This closing contextualizes the ideals and desires that have motivated the immigrant imaginations articulated in the novel within a sense of the irretrievably complicated ironies that describe and inscribe the circumoceanic space underwriting the subjectivities represented. We learn at the novel's end that a character named Genji Befu, Part IV's narrator, has died. Genji is an artist who found Esperança stifling, who thus attempts to kill himself to escape that life, and who becomes lost in Mato Grasso, a region of Brazilian forest, following a plane crash that kills the commune's leader. Outside of Esperança and deep in the Brazilian forest, Genji disappears except to leave iconic markers in the form of sketches for others to find. The epilogue ends with a quotation from a news article which serves as the final words of the novel:

> Three days ago, the so-called Indian of the Lost Tribe was found dead, killed probably while helping himself to someone else's food or store of hidden goods. He was described as a very slight, bowlegged, unkempt man with long black hair, thin strands falling in a tangled beard from his face. He was found shot through the head and clutching a rusty old carbine, empty except for the red earth pushed into the tip of its disintegrating barrel. (248)

That Yamashita further displaces narrative authority with these closing words, having created a disembodied voice that comes out of Mato Grasso, acknowledges the limited explanatory ability of the trope of immigration to account for the histories of displaced indigeneity associated with the emergence of Brazilian and Japanese modernities. The novel's conclusion thwarts expectations that narrative closure will be found in the success or failure of the immigrants. Instead, Yamashita's narrative is hybridized as it unfolds and becomes a history of the red earth—of the claims to land and attendant and often violent movements of people that ensued. Yamashita's awareness of the infinite other stories existing beyond the bounds of this novel and beyond the trope of immigration, which are as yet unrepresented and perhaps unrepresentable within the economy of visibility marked by national, transnational, or global epistemic frames, registers in this figuration.

The communes fictionalized in Yamashita's novel have survived, as is accurately recounted in the epilogue, though they are contemporarily much less isolated from the rest of Brazilian society. And as is also recounted, in the later twentieth century, which has been characterized by enormous joblessness in Brazil, Japanese Brazilians have found themselves migrating to Japan in search of work. The journalistic sense of the novel's epilogue suggests Yamashita's desire to draw a tangible link between the earlier and later migrations to and from Brazil, and allows a sense of history's ironic, disjunctive movements to close the novel.

As the novel follows this course, we see that Yamashita has staged a series of overlapping and interdependent narratives, each of which sends us in search of the next story. Each part of the novel is narrated by a different character, and none of the sections tells a complete story. Rather, it is in their interaction that the textures of communal life emerge. Yamashita's interest, in other words, is not in detailing the individual stories that constitute the history of Japanese immigration to Brazil, but is rather in articulating the variegated sets of relations among persons and places that animate the individual narrative. This emphasis on relationality as leading to a sense of the incompleteness of narrative—there is always another story waiting to be told—refuses and refutes claims to definitive, discrete knowledge. Understanding emerges from precisely the sites of intersection of individual stories, which are those spaces in which individual authority erodes in favor of collaborative storytelling.

By highlighting the limitations of singular authorship, Yamashita conceptualizes what I think of as interdiscursive or interdisciplinary practices as those that respect specialization even as they incisively demarcate its limitations. Analogously, her work then helps us understand that moving analytically beyond the frame of nation does not entail a displacement or disavowal of the continuing importance and effect of national identities and national identity formation. Rather, as Yamashita does by means of articulating a relation between the histories of Nikkei immigration to Brazil and the United States in *Brazil-Maru*, it may productively lead toward the identification of the broad schemas within which such relations are emplotted. Thus, a hemispheric Asian American studies serves at once as a technology for reflecting critically on U.S. culture and politics and as a vehicle for analyzing the irregular emergence and kinds of modernities across the Americas. Against the concerns that transnational paradigms will detract from specific emphasis on the United States, this model apprehends that specific knowledge as but one element in a story that requires both myriad narrators and a commitment to ceaseless interrogation.

Navigating Differences

Yamashita's prose corpus reflects what I am describing as an interdisciplinary sensibility across as well as within texts. In a thoroughly intertextual way,

Yamashita's most recently published long work, *Circle K Cycles*, picks up where *Brazil-Maru* leaves off. *Circle K Cycles* collects the pieces that Yamashita wrote for an Internet travel journal while she and her family lived in Japan in 1997, and puts them alongside short fiction, collages, photographs, and maps "in an effort to paint as varied and textured a portrait as possible of the life I saw and experienced during that time" (11). Rather than being strictly focused on her direct and immediate experiences, however, *Circle K Cycles* uses the occasion of those experiences to contemplate and compare facets of life in Brazil, the United States, and Japan. Echoing her initial travel to Brazil, Yamashita moved to Japan for this period "to meet and understand the Brazilian community living in Japan" (11).

Yamashita's interest in *Circle K Cycles* in the ever-increasing difficulty of correlating identities and homes with singular locations continues not only the story begun in *Brazil-Maru*, but also the formal conventions she uses to explore that issue in *Through the Arc of the Rain Forest* (1990). Written amid the extended drafting and revision required of *Brazil-Maru*, *Through the Arc of the Rain Forest* offers a fantastical tale set in Brazil. Like *Brazil-Maru*, this novel is also partly an immigrant narrative, and despite the radical stylistic differences between them, it uses narrative strategies that resemble those appearing in *Brazil-Maru*. This is not unexpected given the contemporaneousness of their drafting, but is significant in its indication of what Yamashita finds to be important. Namely, their similarity speaks to Yamashita's deep affection for Brazil both as a real place and as an imagined space where such characters as Kazumasa Ishimaru, who has a whirling sphere invisibly attached to his forehead; a three-armed U.S. American transnational capitalist named J. B. Tweep; and, a three-breasted French ornithologist, Michelle Mabelle, would find acceptance and the possibility of realizing home.

I highlight this commonality across novels to suggest that *Brazil-Maru*'s invitation to U.S. readers to enter Brazil as a way of expanding our horizons of knowledge is made more substantial by Yamashita's work in *Through the Arc of the Rain Forest*. This is a novel that deftly illustrates the multilateral and often unpredictable impact of various forms of globalization. As Ursula K. Heise has suggested, of central concern to *Through the Arc of the Rain Forest* is the question of how attachments to place occur and manifest under conditions of globalization.[21] If the flows of culture, people, and capital characteristic of globalization have prompted a reconsideration of the importance of the local in the context of the global as the academic discourses heralding globalization would suggest, what remains is the need to assess the importance of place—of the significance of the here and now.

Heise invites us to recognize the ways that Yamashita derives some of her narrative strategies from Gabriel Garcia Márquez's *Cien años de soledad* (1967) and Mário de Andrade's *Macunaíma* (1928) in investigating these issues. Reading these earlier works as classics of Latin American literature, Heise suggests that Yamashita revises their narratives such that the stories of, respectively, a small town (Márquez's Macondo) and lonesome figure (Andrade's Macunaíma) that are transformed by contact with the worlds beyond their localities, function more generally as an interrogation "of local identity in an age when lasting attachments to a specific environment have become difficult to sustain."[22] Where Márquez's and Andrade's novels were specifically addressed to the formation of national and regional Latin American identities, Yamashita's work concerns itself with the irrelevance of such boundaries to some forms of globalization. What will be expressly articulated later in *Circle K Cycles* as a curiosity about the transformations effected in the contact between Japanese Brazilians and Japan finds implicit expression in this novelistic form.

While the syntax of magical realism and the revising of Latin American literary tropes allow Yamashita in *Through the Arc of the Rain Forest* to emphasize the possibility of otherworldliness, in *Circle K Cycles*, generic hybridity structurally enables her to place variegated worldviews side by side. In this way, Yamashita specifically triangulates the United States, Brazil, and Japan, making each significant, though differently so. That is, the interpretive flexibility required by the nonequivalence of *Circle K Cycles*'s constitutive pieces is a textual iteration of traveling through difference. Comparisons are drawn not toward synthesis of differences or in an easy celebration; rather, they are left open to signification. This space of comparison is the space between the ability to read and the ability to understand a language; it marks the differential knowledge necessary to move into the realm of fluency, of access to worldview.[23]

Yamashita's structuring of *Circle K Cycles*, in other words, both prompts and models the movement into difference that hemispheric studies in one sense represents. "You piece your recognition together like reading abstract art," Yamashita writes of viewing written Japanese: "That looks like a cow. That looks like a violin. Hey, this is the gas bill!" (17). The epiphany of realization of the communicative function of the writing performs a movement through difference into some level of understanding. Importantly, though, that initial critical transformation is insufficient to guarantee future knowledge, Yamashita suggests in an essay titled "Circling Katakana," because languages are themselves living entities. Thus it is that native speakers of Japanese find themselves referring to *katakana* dictionaries—of Japanese, Yamashita explains that there are three character systems used in writing: *kanji*, adopted from China; *hiragana*, native to Japan; and *katakana*, which contemporarily serves to transcribe phonetically foreign words. (Thus, for example, "pasokon" [personal computer] and "borantia" [volunteer] find their way into the Japanese lexicon through katakana.)

Contextualized by this description, Yamashita's explanation that seeing her name written always in katakana in the translated editions of her work becomes legible as a commentary on the erasures of mutability suggested by the written word. The hybridity she sees in her name—"Yamashita" and "Tei" transcribable in kanji and hiragana, respectively, while "Karen" seems appropriately to require katakana—evaporates in these printed translations. While regretting the loss of that hybridity, Yamashita reflects, "Since I cannot read the translation of my work, I don't know how much of it, other than my name, is apportioned to katakana, but it's a curious thought; maybe I am writing in katakana" (54). This thought with which she closes the essay immediately recoordinates the association of a language with a stable identity. Foreignness and nativity are irretrievably enmeshed in the katakana system, a system in which identity is positioned precisely at the site of their incorporation. Katakana in this way serves as a useful metaphor for understanding the work of moving beyond the United States without losing sight of particularity—or to put it differently, of recognizing the contingent nature of foreignness.

Yamashita's work thus suggests that the kind of comparative work integral to hemispheric studies requires a nonassimilative approach to foreignness—to attending to difference. She makes this particularly clear by following "Circling Katakana" immediately with one of two sets of pieces in *Circle K Cycles* that appear in two different languages. First is "Zero Zero Hum . . . aravilha," written in Portuguese, which is paired with "Zero Zero One-derful," written in English. This set uses the conceit of the telephone conversation organized into three conversational tracks to weave together the experience of *dekasegi*—Nikkei migrant workers in Japan—in terms of sexualized economics.[24]

Almost entirely presented as one-sided conversations being conducted simultaneously on separate phone lines by Maria Maravilha, the only external perspective afforded is a narrative that unfolds through a series of short reports offered in italicized print and marked off by lines above and below the entries. These reports initially describe what seems to be a series of different but similar characters—Maria Madelena Oliveira Shinbashi of São Paulo, Maria Madelena Yoshiwara Shinbashi of Curitiba, Madelena Shinbashi of Rio de Janeiro and Tokyo, and Maria Maravilha Shinbashi—to settle finally on Maria Madelena Shinbashi. Respectively described as a dancer, a sex worker, a performer and hostess, and an embezzler, they read as multiple names and identities for one person by the work's ultimate focus on Maria Madelena Shinbashi. This figure continues to be unstable, though, as she is reported to have been seen in various places, everywhere from Bahia to Singapore. Rumor becomes definitional and image replaces person by the story's end in this track of the narrative: images of her have been published in *Playboy* and a video as well as "her holographic image on a keychain" are available for purchase (80).

The staging of this piece allows Yamashita to play with visibility and its association with knowledge. In lieu of a physical person, the personality on the phone maps into a preexisting image, while in the other direction, the pornographic and holographic images are insufficient to articulate complexity. The dekasegi community, too, is simultaneously visible and unseen, according to this work: "Now you see me, now you don't," concludes Maria Maravilha (80). The end of this piece refers back to the recognition that a Portuguese and an English version of it appear side to side. The likely monolingual U.S. readers for whom Yamashita is writing can acknowledge the presence of the Portuguese, but cannot render it intelligible: now you see me, now you don't.

The other twinset is titled, in its English version, "July: Circle K Rules" (the journal entries in the collection are indicated by such titles that identify months prior to a more thematic subtitle). Its companion is written in Japanese. This doubled iteration structurally performs not only the difference that different languages make to representation, but also the possibility of the incorporation of radical difference without its eradication. The interpretation of the polyglot reader fluent in English, Portuguese, and Japanese is not prioritized in this scheme. Rather, it evokes conversation; it requires the forming of relations across differences in order to produce greater collective knowledge. Here, again, the relevance of Yamashita's work to conceptualizing hemispheric studies emerges: The internal structures of the text reproduce this representation of a unified field of differences in a way that approximates the idea of a nonassimilative hemispheric studies.

The importance of allowing for difference within such a practice is underscored by "July: Circle K Rules," which articulates cultural differences in terms of rules and rituals. Shadow boxes set off "Japanese Rules," "Brazilian Rules," "American Rules," and finally, "Circle K Rules." Between these boxes, discussions unfold regarding such matters as the different ways in which residential lifestyles characterize and physical space is inhabited by Japanese, Brazilian, and U.S. American people. In loosely ethnographic style, Yamashita proffers these sets of rules as a way of demarcating differences only to suggest finally that individual experience and interpretation make them meaningful. She concludes with "Circle K Rules":

1. Immigrate into your own country.
2. Learn to cook your favorite meals.
3. Ask the next question. (114)

Denaturalizing the relationship between self and nation, between identity and culture, by means of the first two rules, Yamashita identifies common process rather than origins or arrivals as the cohering principle of migration. The cryptic final rule opens the idea of migration out rather than serving as a definitive conclusion, implying endlessness to the process of immigration: "You" might by this third rule be either the asker or the one asked, effectively unsettling the idea of finite arrival. For Yamashita, immigrants are always ethnographers, not so much of others, but of their own relationship to place.

Yamashita's structuring of *Circle K Cycles* as well as the ways in which she thematizes cultural differences in its constitutive pieces compellingly and simultaneously illuminate the value of multilingual facility and insist that being monolingual need not be a definitive barrier to cross-cultural knowledge. She echoes in this way Gayatri Spivak's reminder that comprehension of difference does not require complete fluency. Rather, what is important is the effort to become fluent—to move into another's (or, an other's) worldview by moving into another language. The crucial element here is a commitment of time and energy, an understanding that even when the cow becomes recognizable as a gas bill, the work of apprehension is never complete. Here, again, collaboration and conversation are prioritized as key words in a critical practice that operates heterotopically.

Circle K Cycles closes by returning to the questions that prompted Yamashita's travels, now with a heightened attention to location:

> The food, the culture, okay, but, geographically speaking, what exactly makes a Nikkei? For example, if you are born in Japan, go to the Americas and live, maybe even forget your Japanese language, then come back, are you Nikkei? . . . Or if you get an eye job and a fake passport? . . . I thought the literal translation of Nikkei is "of the Japanese tribe," but "real" Japanese never refer to themselves as Nikkei. So who's Nikkei? (145).

These questions lead to others—on the determination of beauty, on what counts as home, to end finally with the idea of "Nikkei on the move" (147). Nikkei has transformed from a designation of ethnicity to an unpredictable route through identity and difference. Yamashita invites us to see it as a marker of transformation rather than stable identity, one that can illuminate temporally specific connections between persons and places. Functioning in this way as a term that recognizes the radical instability of identity, the term *Nikkei* and its critical consideration allow for appreciation of even the ironies inhering in those chronotopic links—of, that is, the unpredictable ways that movement and place shape our understanding of identity and difference.

Toward—And Beyond—An Asian Americanist Hemispheric Practice

I have been suggesting throughout these analyses that Yamashita's work possesses a heightened awareness of narrativity, that it promotes the drawing of an analogy between travel and interpretation, between narrative space and discursive field. She explodes paradigmatic confinement by the heterotopic imagination articulated in her writings, and privileges difference as a key facet of comparative practices. By opening Asian Americanist literary critique into the space of the Americas, and by opening the Americas to Asia, Yamashita creatively and effectively cautions against critical parochialism of any kind. She takes delight in finding commonalities, in associating familiarity to new places; but her work—in exemplary literary fashion—also relishes the estrangement of familiar grounds. This interplay between the familiar and the foreign is arguably the defining quality of Yamashita's work, and it precisely for that reason that her works might productively serve as a base upon which we might formulate an Asian Americanist hemispheric studies. By providing us with literary models through which concepts key to the idea of hemispheric studies—the significance of spatial location, the negotiation of linguistic differences, the impact of variegated histories, for example—are explored, Yamashita articulates a relationship between the United States and the other communities and nations constituting the Americas as equally unknown entities. Each site must be studied anew in light of the particular relation being drawn in a given iteration of hemispheric studies, and none can be conceived as an unchanging or homogeneous entity.

Perhaps it is the strong attention that Asian Americanist discourse has paid to arguing the irresolvable heterogeneity of (Asian) Americans that implicitly influences Yamashita's rendering of this version of thinking beyond the nation that emphasizes change and diversity. Or perhaps it is the awareness that Asian American studies brings to understanding the pitfalls of extranational paradigms in relation to U.S. histories of Asian racialization that percolates through Yamashita's insistence on deep recognition of differential histories and cultures across locations. But the value of reading Yamashita in this context is not, I think, in drawing these connections of influence to Asian American studies. Rather, it is in showing us that however far Asian Americanist discourse has taken us, an imagination unbounded by territorial constraints can take us infinitely further.

NOTES

I thank Caroline Levander and Robert Levine for truly helpful editorial guidance. I am also grateful to Zita Nunes for her illuminating feedback on an early draft of this essay, and to the American Studies Department at the University of Minnesota, Minneapolis, for giving me a forum to present and terrific responses to this work as it was developing. Especially, I thank Kale Fajardo, Rod Ferguson, and Josephine Lee in that regard.

1. Shelley Fisher Fishkin, "Crossroads of Cultures: The Transnational Turn in American Studies Presidential Address to the American Studies Association, November 12, 2004," *American Quarterly* 57 (2005):17–57.

2. Erika Lee's recent essay, "Orientalisms in the Americas: A Hemispheric Approach to Asian American History," *Journal of Asian American Studies* 8 (Oct. 2005): 235–256, is a notable exception; in that regard, see also Evelyn Hu-DeHart's "Concluding Commentary: On Migration, Diasporas, and Transnationalism in Asian American History," *Journal of Asian American Studies* 8 (Oct. 2005): 309–312. Sau-ling Cynthia Wong's oft-cited essay "Denationalization Reconsidered: Asian American Cultural Criticism at a Theoretical Crossroads," *Amerasia Journal* 21 (1995): 1–27, which cautions against "denationalization," exemplifies the kinds of concerns provoked by extranational approaches to Asian American studies.

3. Claudia Sadowski-Smith and Claire Fox, "Theorizing the Hemisphere: Inter-Americas

work at the intersection of American, Canadian, and Latin American Studies," *Comparative American Studies* 2 (2004): 5–38, 7.

4. Gary Okihiro, "Turning Japanese Americans," in *Encyclopedia of Japanese Descendants in the Americas: An Illustrated History of the Nikkei*, edited by Akemi Kikumura-Yano (Walnut Creek, Calif.: Alta Mira Press, 2002), 25.

5. Sadowski-Smith and Fox, "Theorizing the Hemisphere," 6.

6. This tack has not been without troublesome consequences. By holding Asia at a critical distance, Asian American studies in one sense effectively reproduced the ideological inclinations of the postwar U.S. nation and the postwar academy, the inclinations that were made manifest in the creation of "areas" for study (area studies) in an effort to master knowledge of those deemed immutably different (i.e., "the other") putatively to ensure the safety of the nation. American studies as a distinctive field is rooted in this same history insofar as its early objectives were shaped by Cold War politics and thus reflected an us-versus-them mentality. As area studies (including American studies) have albeit unevenly engaged the process of renovation to reflect an oftentimes more progressive politics in the past several decades, and as terms like "diaspora" and "transnationalism" have increasingly gained ground in academic discourse, the outdatedness of this particular strategy of claiming the uniqueness of Asian America and Asian American studies has become clear. I develop this argument more fully in chapter 3 of *Imagine Otherwise: On Asian Americanist Critique* (Durham: Duke University Press, 2003), and I do so by drawing especially on Pheng Cheah's "Universal Areas: Asian Studies in a World in Motion" and Naoki Sakai's "The Dislocation of the West," both in *Traces: A Multilingual Journal of Theory and Translation* 5 (2000). See also the introduction to *Orientations: Mapping Studies in the Asian Diaspora* (Durham: Duke University Press, 2001), co-edited by Karen Shimakawa and me.

7. The three novels of Yamashita referenced in this essay were all published by Coffee House Press in Minneapolis, Minnesota. *Through the Arc of the Rain Forest* was published in 1990; *Brazil-Maru* appeared in 1992; and *Circle K Cycles* was published in 2001. Page references to these volumes will be supplied parenthetically in the main body of the essay.

8. Rachel C. Lee, *The Americas of Asian American Literature: Gendered Fictions of Nation and Transnation* (Princeton, N.J.: Princeton University Press, 1999), 107.

9. Lee, *The Americas*, 108.

10. See Lee's *The Americas* (chapter 4) for extended discussion of "what is Asian American" about Yamashita's writings.

11. As Caroline Rody has suggested of *Tropic of Orange*, the work itself allegorizes "imaginative 'paradigm shift'" in its literalization of the idea of globalization. "The Transnational Imagination: Karen Tei Yamashita's *Tropic of Orange*," in *Asian North American Identities*, ed. Eleanor Ty and Donald C. Goellnicht (Bloomington and Indianapolis: Indiana University Press, 2004): 130–148, 132. For excellent discussions of Yamashita's *Through the Arc of the Rain Forest*, see also Lee's *The Americas*, chap. 4; and Molly Wallace's "Tropics of Globalization: Reading the New North America," *Symploke* 9 (2001): 145–160. I thank Shaundra Myers for the phrase "geographic protocol."

12. Jeffrey Lesser's *Negotiating National Identity: Immigrants, Minorities, and the Struggle for Ethnicity in Brazil* (Durham: Duke University Press, 1999) identifies the absence of scholarship on Asians in Brazil and Latin America more broadly, and offers studies that begin to address that lack. See also Hu-Dehart's "Concluding Commentary."

13. I mean the term "circumoceanic" to recall Joseph Roach's conception of a "circum-Atlantic world (as opposed to a transatlantic one) [which] insists on the centrality of the diasporic and genocidal histories of Africa and the Americas, North and South, in the creation of the culture of modernity" (see Roach's *Cities of the Dead: Circum-Atlantic Performance* [New York: Columbia University Press, 1996], 4).

14. Michael S. Murashige, "Karen Tei Yamashita: Interview," in *Words Matter: Conversations with Asian American Writers*, edited by King-kok Cheung (Honolulu: University of Hawaii Press, 2000), 320–342, 332.

15. Lesser, *Negotiating National Identity*, 148.

16. Ibid.

17. See Jeffrey Lesser, "Japanese, Brazilians, Nikkei: A Short History of Identity Building and Homemaking," in *Searching for Home Abroad: Japanese Brazilians and Transnationalism*, ed. Jeffrey Lesser (Durham: Duke University Press, 2003), 1–20.

18. David Cleary provides a helpful overview of the significance of Freyre to the formation of Brazilian national identity in the early twentieth century in "Race, Nationalism, and Social Theory in Brazil: Rethinking Gilberto Freyre," Working Paper 99-09, David Rockefeller Center for Latin American Studies, Harvard University, online at www.transcomm.ox.ac.uk/working%2520papers/cleary.pdf (accessed January 5, 2006).

19. Alex Woloch, *The One vs. the Many: Minor Characters and the Space of the Protagonist in the Novel* (Princeton, N.J.: Princeton University Press, 2003), 14.

20. Ibid., 17–18.

21. Ursula K. Heise, "Local Rock and Global Plastic: World Ecology and the Experience of Place," *Comparative Literature Studies* 41 (2004): 126–152.

22. Ibid., 139.

23. See Rody's "The Transnational Imagination" for a discussion of *Tropic of Orange* as a "border novel" in the tradition of Chicano literatures.

24. An estimated 200,000 dekasegi currently live in Japan, mostly in Japanese Brazilian communities, which are the communities that are of particular interest to Yamashita. Daniel Touro Linger's *No One Home: Brazilian Selves Remade in Japan* (Palo Alto: Stanford University Press, 2001) offers an illuminating study of the dekasegi phenomenon and experience.

15

The Northern Borderlands and Latino Canadian Diaspora

RACHEL ADAMS

The title of Carmen Aguirre's play *¿Que Pasa with La Raza, eh?* (2000) entices us with a provocative fusion of linguistic and cultural referents.[1] *La raza*, a synonym for *la gente* or *el pueblo* (the people), refers to the imagined community of Latin American people of diverse races and backgrounds. The juxtaposition of English and Spanish words implies an audience familiar with both languages. Most intriguingly, the interjection "eh" at the end of a question written largely in Spanish gestures to a Canadian interlocutor. Beginning with the inverted question mark particular to Spanish and ending with Canadian English, Aguirre's title announces a drama that will span the hemisphere. In its representation of Latino community, the play itself addresses such familiar themes as the struggle for cultural expression, the perils of border crossing, the exploitation of migrant workers, and encounters with racism.[2] What makes *¿Que Pasa?* distinctive is that, where we might expect it to be set somewhere in the southwestern United States, it actually takes place in Vancouver. Its Latino characters' search for self-definition unfolds in the context of a critique of Canadian multiculturalism, and it refers to "America" as a synonym for the entire hemisphere rather than for the United States alone. Throughout the play, an enormous, upside-down map of Latin America hangs behind an otherwise bare stage.[3] At the beginning, a slide projects the words "South America," also upside-down, onto the map, introducing a performance that will confuse the familiar geographies of Latino diaspora. But rather than literally turning the map on its head, as this image might suggest, *¿Que Pasa?* moves the border north, giving center stage to Canadian Latino communities that are virtually unknown south of the 49th parallel.

Despite the relatively small size of those communities, it is worth paying attention to the cultural representations they have generated because they can lead to new perspectives on the relationship between hemisphere and nation that is one of the principal subjects of this volume. The hemisphere has become an attractive framework for Americanists eager to shake off the field's association with the nation-state. Acknowledging the plurality of Americas that lie beyond U.S. borders has been a healthy corrective to the tendency within American Studies to conflate America with the United States. Many efforts to remap the field have found particular inspiration in Chicano Studies, which treats the U.S.-Mexico border as a transnational contact zone linking the United States to Latin America. However, Canada is rarely mentioned in such scholarship, and virtually nothing has been written about Canada's Latino population within the context of the hemisphere.[4] In what follows, I will argue that drawing Canada into this emerging interdisciplinary conversation is not simply an additive move, but one that has the potential to alter the way we currently think about the borderlands and the Americas.

Looking at the hemisphere from a perspective that grows out of U.S.-Mexico border studies, we tend to see borders in an entirely negative light. Borders restrict human mobility, perpetuate inequalities, and create artificial divisions among peoples and environments. However, borders can also be a means of protection and a guarantor of rights and services to those who reside within them. In the nineteenth century, crossing the U.S.-Canadian border was so important to escaping slaves that they equated Canada with the Promised Land. In the twentieth century, many Canadians look to the border as the last line of defense against the hegemony of U.S. culture and politics.[5] Their calls for more stringent regulation of the border are motivated by quite different political convictions than those articulated by the U.S. conservatives who advocate the erection of a massive fence along the border with Mexico. Without romanticizing Canada as the antithesis to all that is wrong with the United States, we can still acknowledge that including it in our understanding of the hemisphere encourages us to think about American borders in more nuanced ways. Canada adds an important third term to scholarship on the hemisphere, which is often framed in terms of a dichotomy between the United States (or the more amorphous North America) and Latin America. With Latin American nations, Canada shares concerns about free trade, the regional impact of globalization, and the ubiquity of U.S. culture. But like the United States, it has become a major destination for immigrants because of its political stability and promise of economic opportunity. Globalization and changing patterns of migration are creating new and more direct ties between Canada and Latin America. Recognizing these circumstances offers a way out of the bilateral framing of most conversations about the hemisphere, which, much like foreign relations in the region, tend be mediated through the United States.

As is often the case, cultural critics are guided by insights that are already latent in literature and the arts. My contribution to this conversation will take place via a consideration of the Argentinian Canadian author Guillermo Verdecchia, whose plays and short stories imagine an America that extends from Toronto to Tierra del Fuego. Although he is clearly conversant in U.S.-Mexico border studies, Verdecchia seeks to transform its symbolic geographies by deemphasizing the United States, while explicitly incorporating Canada into a symbolic mapping of the American hemisphere. I focus on his short story collection, *Citizen Suarez* (1997), and his play *Fronteras Americanas: (American Borders)* (1993), which are about the different forms of human mobility—migration, travel, flight—that link Canada to Latin America. Canadian history, settings, and cultural referents crop up frequently in these works, as if to highlight the fact that they are *not* about the United States. Verdecchia thus reminds us that the United States is not the only endpoint for immigration from Central and South America, nor is its border with Mexico the only meeting ground for Anglo- and Latin Americas. Hemisphere and nation are thus salient categories for understanding his work and, because the nation that most concerns him is Canada, his writing, in turn, provides an opportunity to think further about what it would mean to incorporate Canada into prevailing understandings of the American hemisphere.

Ultimately I argue that Verdecchia's expansive view of American borders must be understood, in part, as a form of situated knowledge that emerges from his location in Canada. Unlike the United States, Canada has only one border of any consequence, and the majority of its population lives within 100 miles of it.[6] It has no border region comparable to the U.S. Southwest, with its distinctive culture and distance from centers of national power. Instead, Canada as a whole is often characterized as a "border society." As Roger Gibbens explains of the Canadian border region, "the most important impact comes not from proximity of the international boundary itself, but from the more general proximity of the United States."[7] I suggest that Verdecchia's view of the borderlands as a pervasive cultural phenomenon, rather than a geographically specific one, has much to do with the fact that Canada is his adopted home. Verdecchia's work thematizes the connections between Canada and Latin America, while also offering a model for thinking more broadly about the hemisphere from the perspective of Canada.

Latino Canadian Diasporas

Citizen Suarez and *Fronteras Americanas* are about a Latino population in Canada that has largely gone unnoticed in the United Sates. This oversight is not surprising, given that Latinos constitute a far larger and more significant demographic presence south of the Canadian border. Whereas there are some 35 million Latinos in the United States, comprising 12.5 percent of the total population,[8] there are only 500,000 to 800,000 in all of Canada.[9] And whereas Mexican Americans have occupied the southwestern borderlands region since before it belonged to the United States, the majority of Latinos in Canada arrived during the second half of the twentieth century. Their numbers began to increase as political dissidents fled the Cuban Revolution in 1953, then the military dictatorships that rose to power in the 1970s and 1980s in Brazil, Uruguay, Chile, and Argentina. In the 1980s, civil wars in Nicaragua, Guatemala, and El Salvador drove Central American migrants north in search of refuge and economic opportunity. Canada, which was seeking to augment its labor force, proved a more welcoming destination than the United States, which turned away many Latin American political refugees because of their suspected communist leanings.[10] Today, the largest number of Spanish-speaking migrants live in Quebec, although there are also sizable Latino communities in Vancouver, Toronto, Ottawa, Edmonton, and Winnipeg.[11]

Among the migrants from Latin America are significant numbers of authors, artists, and intellectuals. Until recently, many maintained the stance of political exiles who continued to identify with the home country, seeing their residence in Canada as a necessity rather than a choice.[12] Writing as exiles, they presumed the place of origin as a primary site of identification. Much of their work was concerned with the violence and repression in their home countries, nostalgia for the people and places they had left behind, and the difficulties of adjustment to a new environment. Others turned to forms of modernist experimentation that were devoid of all references to the immediate social or political context. Only more recently has there been an attempt to move away from the experience of exile and toward cultural forms that express a hyphenated Latino Canadian identity. As Alberto Gomez explains of a young generation of Latino artists:

> Often the sons and daughters of political refugees fleeing dictatorships in the southern cone, bitter wars in Central America, or economic impoverishment, they did not choose to settle here. Yet their formation of language and identity is also shaped by experiences of growing up in Canada. Caught between history and place, memories of political conflict clash with the pull of consumer culture. Living between languages and dreams, they sense they are "aliens" in the society in which they exist and from which they come. In Latin America they are identified as "different" for the way they speak Spanish and for their North American acculturation; in Canada, they are immigrants, newcomers, hyphenated citizens.[13]

Unable to identify completely with either Canada or particular Latin American homelands, this second generation seeks modes of belonging that are not tied to the nation-state. Declaring themselves members of *la raza*, they recognize connections to Latinos from many different parts of the American hemisphere. At the same time that they are determined to stay in Canada, they challenge the myth of the nation as a harmonious, multicultural mosaic by speaking out about their encounters with injustice and racial prejudice.

Verdecchia announces himself as a part of this new sensibility when he proclaims at the end of *Fronteras Americanas*: "I am a hyphenated person but I am not falling apart, I am putting together. I am building a house on the border."14 With this statement, he declares his intention to make a home where he is, rejecting both the exile's longing for an unattainable point of origin and the traveler's belief that constant movement can solve his problems. Such sentiments are thematized in *Citizen Suarez* and *Fronteras Americanas*, his most autobiographical works. From a variety of different perspectives, they portray his boyhood experiences as an Argentinian immigrant, and his subsequent efforts to build a career as a well-respected member of Toronto's theatrical and literary communities. In their choice of genre, both works manifest a commitment to the representation of collective experience. *Citizen Suarez* uses the short story form to encompass many different geographic locations and points of view. *Fronteras Americanas* gives voice to two characters from distinct economic and social backgrounds who suggest the diversity of Latino Canadian populations. Verdecchia's work thus provides multiple examples of the contemporary phenomena that tie Latin America and Canada together, painting a revised portrait of the American hemisphere in which Canada plays an integral role.

"Have We Crossed a Border?":
The Hemispheric Americas of *Citizen Suarez*

Verdecchia's short story collection *Citizen Suarez* exports "the borderlands" from its expected location along the U.S.-Mexico border to multiple settings in Canada, the United States, and Latin America. This collection treats borderlands not as a specific region, but as the many places where multiple cultures encounter, fuse, and clash with one another. Some stories deal with the literal crossing of national borders: the difficult adjustments of the eponymous Suarez family after moving to Canada from an unspecified Latin American country; a troubled Canadian traveling through northwest Argentina; a Mexican Canadian who drives to California and then continues south to his father's birthplace in Morelos, Mexico. Others are scattered with evidence of the more diffuse effects of human and cultural migration throughout the hemisphere: a store selling Peruvian goods in downtown Toronto; Spanish-language TV in Anglo-American homes; a Latin American general who tortures a suspected political dissident using techniques learned at the U.S. sponsored School of the Americas. In a paradigmatic scene from the story "Letter from Tucuman," the unnamed protagonist writes:

> The bus stops. In the middle of nothing. We are all asked to get out and proceed to the little shack on the side of the road. Have we crossed a border? Not that I know of [. . .]. But here are a bunch of soldiers looking very bored in rumpled uniforms checking our passports and chain smoking cigarettes. No explanation is offered. Nothing exciting happens; no questions are asked. We all troop back onto the bus. (78)

On the one hand, this passage identifies the protagonist as a traveler who observes, but remains untouched by, the potentially "exciting" disruptions endured by those living under an oppressive military regime. Although the soldiers seem ineffectual, their presence is a reminder of the militarization of many American borders. On the other, this scene might serve as an allegory for a collection that understands American borders as far more dispersed and inchoate than the literal boundary lines between neighboring nations. "Have we crossed a border?" could thus serve as a refrain for virtually every story in the collection.

In *Citizen Suarez*, Latin America is a source of nostalgia and literary inspiration, as well as an appealing travel destination. But it is also torn by political crises and economic instability that make permanent residence there untenable. With the exception of two stories that take place in Argentina, references to Latin America are vague, suggesting that the problems depicted in individual stories could apply to any number of national contexts. For example, the collection opens with a dark satire about the unwitting martyrdom of a university student named Oscar. His problems begin when he wears a necktie that violates the code of mourning imposed by the state after the death of "La Señora," a thinly fictionalized Eva Peron. The breech of sartorial protocol that begins as a joke is soon taken up by various opposition groups, setting off widespread rebellion and prompting harsh retaliatory measures by the ruling military dictatorship. In the end, Oscar is tortured and shot, and "his body, along with several others, [is] heaved into a pit in a garbage dump" (22). So arbitrary and seemingly commonplace is Oscar's death, the story suggests, that he is treated as household garbage, his tie blown away by the wind. The violence and repression of an unnamed Latin American country are similarly depicted in a story called "Winter Comes to the Edge of the World," which is narrated through the flashbacks of a political dissident who has sought refuge in Canada. There, she thinks obsessively of her disappeared comrades, detention camps, "Falcons cruising the street" (122), and her rape by government soldiers. In the title story, "The Several Lives of Citizen Suarez," Octavio Suarez is a math professor who leaves his homeland after struggling against censorship and anti-intellectualism in his university position. The collection ends with a story that is harshly critical of the elite citizens of a fictional Latin American nation named Ixturria. Living in gated compounds, surrounded by imported luxuries, the characters are oblivious to the class warfare and political turmoil taking place around them. After a friend affiliated with the political resistance is murdered, the protagonist completes his retreat from reality by marrying a member of his close-knit social circle. These stories provide a rationale for the Latino Canadian diaspora by showing that, whatever the difficulties of life in the new country, returning to the place of origins is not a viable option.

Despite the fact that it offers a refuge from the crises plaguing many Latin American countries, Canada, in these stories, is hardly a panacea. In "Citizen

Suarez," the prosperous Toronto suburbs are banal and colorless. The protagonist of "Winter Comes" appreciates that Canada provides her refuge from
political repression, but also feels that she is "exiled to the edge of the world"
in an "empty white and grey place" (123). Here, the rather clichéd reference
to Canada's coldness and whiteness takes on added resonance when it is used
to describe racial intolerance, as well as the weather. The story "Money in
the Bank" further develops the portrait of Canadian racial insensitivity in its
depiction of a Latino actor struggling for professional legitimacy. On the set of
a TV movie-of-the-week, the makeup artist paints his face brown, prompting
him to reflect incredulously, "I have nothing against brown but if they wanted
brown they could have hired a brown actor, no? I ask Make-up why she's going
so dark with the face and she says 'You're the Cook aren't you? The Latino
Cook?'" (87). Her questions equate Latinidad with dark skin and manual labor,
underscoring the racial biases that persist despite Canada's official rhetoric
about being a mosaic of different ethnic groups. The protagonist is caught in a
vicious cycle: although he is trained to be a serious actor, his livelihood relies
on broadcast television, where the one-dimensional roles he is forced to play
will be seen by thousands of Canadian viewers, thereby reinforcing the stereotypes that limit his acting opportunities. "Money in the Bank" thus takes us
beyond the new immigrant's feelings of isolation and exclusion to depict the
more abiding prejudices faced by non-Anglo Canadians.

These dilemmas are crystallized in the struggles of Fernando Suarez,
the ambivalent "citizen" of the title story, who seeks to maintain his position on the border, uncomfortably straddling multiple cultures. Although
disillusioned with life in Canada, his parents are determined to assimilate
by becoming Canadian citizens. By contrast, the teenaged Fernando longs to
remain poised between two worlds. He resists claiming membership in any one
national community, attempting to preserve the parts of his identity—and the
special forms of knowledge—that have come through the experience of a trans-
formative move from one place to another. When his parents inform him that
the entire family will become citizens, he fears that he will lose "his position
as a foreigner and his knowledge of the double or perhaps multiple lives he
has lived [which] was for him a recondite and marvelous wound" (46). Unable
to stop them from completing the process, he feels a deep sense of loss at the
possibilities he has given up. Fernando is representative of many characters
in Verdecchia's fiction who affirm the perspective that comes through being
"a hyphenated person" who does not fit easily into any one place. At the same
time, his story underscores the fact that such ambivalence can only be appreci-
ated from the relative safety and comfort of Canada, where one does not have
to worry about being beaten, shot, or imprisoned for failing to fit in.

In its multiple portraits of the encounter between Anglo and Latin America, *Citizen Suarez* compellingly illustrates the portability of the borderlands,
showing why this concept has become an organizing paradigm for recent

comparative work in American, Canadian, and Mexican Studies.[15] But it also raises the kinds of questions that have been asked by Chicano/a critics about whether something gets lost when a specific locale—and the populations, history and culture associated with it—is translated into a more general figure for cultural and geographical crossings of all kinds.[16] The borderlands, as influentially described by Anzaldúa and others, refers to the "third country" along the 2,000 mile border between the United States and Mexico. Border culture emerged out of the rich fusion of the many different ethnic and national groups that passed through and settled in an area where daily life was influenced by conflicts over land, repressive immigration policies, the exploitation of migrant workers, and racial intolerance. For a critic like Anzaldúa, the borderlands is both an actual place and a state of mind that comes from bearing "the emotional residue of an unnatural boundary."[17] Although the stories in *Citizen Suarez* are narrated from many different points of view, the collection tends to focus primarily on well-educated, middle-class migrants and travelers, meaning that the struggles of the most marginalized border crossers are muted. Chicano/a literature often seeks to give voice to populations that have been denied representation, telling the stories of colonization of land, perilous border crossings, and constant fear of *la migra*. Many of the stories in *Citizen Suarez* are also about an underrepresented population of Latin Americans in Canada. But these characters travel across national boundaries with relative ease. The friction they experience comes more from the psychological effects of cultural dislocation than from encounters with the law, dire poverty, or intolerable working conditions. Latin American migrants travel by plane rather than crossing dangerous rivers and deserts by foot. They come to a place with relatively generous immigration policies, particularly toward those who are white and middle class, and who have the resources to arrange their arrival in advance. They must work for a living, but they are professors, actors, and writers rather than manual laborers. Thus, they may feel the same emotional frisson that Anzaldúa describes, while being spared the material suffering associated with U.S.-Mexico border crossings.

When issues of class friction arise in *Citizen Suarez*, they surface as unexpected eruptions, rather than being the center of narrative attention. For example, in "The Several Lives," Fernando remembers an encounter that took place before the move to Canada, when a lunch at a restaurant with his father was interrupted by a boy begging for food. Fernando "believed he was related to the boy in some way [. . .]. The boy was Fernando in some way, the boy Fernando might have become if they hadn't emigrated perhaps" (45). The confrontation might have taught Fernando an enduring lesson about inequality and the potential of empathy to reach others across class lines. But there is no evidence that Fernando's fantasy of identification is reciprocated, or that the meeting has any marked influence on the subsequent course of his life. The story suggests that, with Canadian citizenship, he will be freed from the prospect of such economic want. Poverty and starvation are relegated to the margins of a narrative that is filtered through the perceptions of relatively privileged middle-class characters. So, too, in "Letter from Tucuman," a Canadian traveler turns down an offer by his taxi driver to tour an Argentinian city. Later he realizes that the driver needed the money to buy a birthday present for his daughter. Instead of doing anything to rectify the situation, he sinks into depression, "incapacitated, by all the sadness ever: the lonely dead no one ever mourned; the hundreds of thousands of lost souls, hurled into salty darkness in the bottom of a man-made lake or a cold stinking cell. I am sad for all those whose turn will never come, those who wait and wait and wait" (81). This is not a productive response, but the melodramatic and self-indulgent sadness of a traveler who has enough of life's basic comforts that he can wallow in his own emotional pain without translating it into any meaningful effort to help others. "Letter from Tucuman" is representative of a more general pattern in *Citizen Suarez*, in which the kind of racial and economic tensions that arise in the U.S.-Mexico borderlands surface at the margins of stories concerned with more middle-class problems. Moments of narrative friction remind us that such inequities exist, but they are not the central concern of any of these stories. With *Fronteras Americanas* Verdecchia confronts these issues more directly as they surface beyond the U.S.-Mexico border, while also exploring the potential of theater to serve as its own kind of borderland, where Canada and the Americas meet up with one another.

Fronteras Americanas: A Hemispheric View of the Borderlands

First performed in 1993, Guillermo Verdecchia's one-person play *Fronteras Americanas: (American Borders)* coincided with the signing of the North America Free Trade Agreement (NAFTA). With its focus on trade and investment, NAFTA did not legislate matters of culture, nor did it make provisions for the many North Americans whose lives relied on the regular crossing of national borders. *Fronteras Americanas* is about the human consequences of regional integration. At one point in the play, a slide projected onto the stage quotes Carlos Fuentes: "Every North American, before this century is over, will find that he or she has a personal frontier with Latin America" (54). Fuentes's pronouncement suggests that "American borders" can no longer be understood to refer exclusively to the particular region around the U.S.-Mexico border, since the entire continent has become a contact zone where Anglo- and Latin America meet up, clash, and interpenetrate. As a character named Verdecchia explains to the audience, "when I say AMERICA I don't mean the country, I mean the continent. Somos todos Americanos. We are all Americans" (20). His assertion echoes Latin American thinkers from Simon Bolivar to Jose Martí, who argued for the importance of regional solidarity under the banner of a collective American identity. But what makes it new is that Verdecchia speaks as a Latin American in Canada; his reference to the continent positions Canadian themes and settings within a broader American framework. This agenda is underscored when he delivers a monologue called "An Idiosyncratic History of America" that lists the War of 1812, the establishment of the Dominion of Canada in 1867, and the Montreal Canadiens' winning of the Stanley Cup for hockey in 1969 alongside important moments in United States and Latin American history (29–32). The inclusion of these events carves out a role for Canada in historical narratives that have traditionally focused on other parts of the Americas.

These more explicitly pedagogical revisions of continental history are interspersed with the monologues of two individuals living in Canada, whose experiences form a bridge between Anglo- and Latin America. One is Verdecchia, an anxiety-ridden, middle-class character who laments that he feels lost, although he can locate himself quite specifically "in Toronto, at 30 Bridgman Avenue" (20). As the play continues, he delivers a series of confessional speeches that describe his family's departure from Argentina, childhood encounters with cultural intolerance as a Latino immigrant in Kitchener, Ontario, and his eventual return to the place of his birth. "I Am Going Home—all will be resolved, dissolved, revealed" (36), he tells himself as he plans to visit Argentina for the first time as an adult. But there is reason to believe that his quest will be unsuccessful, since he discloses that his knowledge of "home" has come largely through travel guides, Spanish classes, friends, and three screenings of the film *Missing*.

It is not surprising, then, that Verdecchia's fantasy of homecoming is shattered, since his goal of recovering an authentic point of origin is an impossibility. In Buenos Aires, his foreignness is manifest in a bout of food poisoning. His vomiting is a literal symptom of his inability to digest Argentinian culture, regardless of how fervently he believes that it should be familiar and palatable. The experience of childhood dislocation followed by many years of identification with a lost homeland have left him in a state of uncomfortable liminality. When he announces, "All sides of the border have claimed and rejected me" (51), he suggests that the border is less a specific location than a powerful metaphor for those who understand themselves as belonging to more than one culture, and thus unable to feel at home in any one geographical place. He finds this realization painful, but by the end of the play he claims to have translated his angst into something more productive: "I am learning to live the border. I have called off the Border Patrol. I am a hyphenated person but I am not falling apart, I am putting together. I am building a house on the border." He then turns to the audience with a direct challenge: "And you? Did you change your name somewhere along the way? Does a part of you live hundreds or thousands of kilometres away? Do you have two countries, two memories? Do you have a border zone?" (78). Verdecchia's confessional narrative ends when he ruptures the divide between performer and spectator, his questions implicating the viewer by suggesting that living on a "border zone" of some kind has become a virtually universal American condition.

To understand what is happening when Verdecchia breaks through the fourth wall, it is useful to follow Diana Taylor's distinction between the archive and the repertoire. She describes the archive as a storehouse where documents and other types of material evidence are preserved for posterity. The alternative is the repertoire, a repository of living, "embodied memory," such as "performances, gestures, orality, movement, dance, singing," forms of expression that are considered to be "ephemeral, nonreproducible knowledge."[18] Describing such inter-American repertoires as Spanish *pastorelas* (shepherds' plays) and mock battles between *moros y cristianos* (Moors and Christians), Taylor argues that "the repertoire allows for an alternative perspective on historical processes of transnational contact and invites a remapping of the Americas, this time following the traditions of embodied practice."[19] In contrast to the static artifacts of the archive, the contents of the repertoire can evolve in response to different historical contexts and geographic locations. *Fronteras Americanas* foregrounds these forms of embodied knowledge when it becomes a collaboration between actor and spectators, who must continually reenact the discovery of borders named by its title. As Verdecchia explains in the preface, "*Fronteras Americanas* is part of a process, part of a much larger attempt to understand and invent. As such, it is provisional, atado con alambre [strung together with wire]. In performance, changes were made nightly depending on my mood, the public, our location, the arrangement of the planets" (13). Relinquishing control over the production of his work, Verdecchia writes, "I hope that anyone choosing to perform this text will consider the possibilities of making (respectful) changes and leaving room for personal and more current responses" (13). Framing the play in such terms ensures that it will function as a repertoire of collective experience, evolving over time and in reaction to current events.

Fronteras Americanas is less a narrative than a collage of voices and "found objects" such as quotations, video and film clips, and sounds and images lifted from other sources. What holds these disparate materials together are monologues delivered by Verdecchia and his alter ego, a Chicano character named Wideload. Both parts are played by the same actor, a device that gestures to a *latinidad* that transcends national borders. This decision is significant for Verdecchia, an actor whose elite training has allowed him to escape the kind of ethnic typecasting that he encountered during his early career.[20] But instead of passing as part of the cultural mainstream, Verdecchia outs himself through his identification with an unmistakably Latino character. His deployment of stereotypes about Chicanos is strategic. As Michelle Habell-Pallán explains, Chicano popular culture has been appropriated by a new generation of Latino Canadians, who have seized on its association with militant oppositionality to articulate an ethnic identity that resists the cozy version of cultural pluralism promulgated by the state.[21] If Verdecchia represents the internal conflicts of

the assimilated, middle-class Latino Canadian, Wideload is his unruly, irre-
pressible double and the two cannot be disentangled. Through the presence
of this abrasive, working class character, *Fronteras Americanas* offers a more
heterogeneous representation of Canadian borderlands than *Citizen Suarez*.

Although his dialect is clichéd, Wideload's speeches challenge Anglo
stereotypes about Mexicans by claiming aggressively that south of the border
"dere's no pinche Taco Bell for thousands of miles" (22), critiquing representations of Latinos in American popular culture, and debunking propaganda
surrounding the War on Drugs. While many aspects of this character are
unsurprising, what makes the Chicano Wideload remarkable is that he lives in
Canada and that Canadian culture is central to his subjectivity as an occupant
of the borderlands. When he says that he lives "in the border," he explains
"for you people from outa town" that he means "Queen and Lansdowne," an
ethnically and economically mixed Toronto neighborhood. Here, he speaks
to audiences beyond his own local community, challenging them to confront
entrenched racial assumptions, but also serving as a guide who can introduce
them to unfamiliar geographies. His character is thus a testament to the
Chicanos' growing geographic dispersal, as well as the diversity of Latinos in
Canada. Chicanos can no longer be described by reference to a single region,
since they have come to inhabit many different parts of the American continent. In doing so, they have expanded the perimeters of the borderlands and
its varied cultures.

Together, the monologues of Wideload and Verdecchia attest to the diversity of Latin American experiences in Canada and to the growing significance
of Canada to a broader understanding of American history and culture. The
dense network of inter-American relations traced out by *Fronteras Americanas*
makes a convincing case for the inclusion of Canada within any comprehensive portrait of America's border cultures. While it shares the conclusions
drawn by *Citizen Suarez*, the disparities between its two central characters,
as well as its use of live performance, make the play the more compelling
of the two works. Because Wideload and Verdecchia are so different in class
and cultural capital, the play ultimately offers a more varied portrait of the
Latino/a presence than the short story collection, with its nearly exclusive
focus on well-educated, middle-class characters. And because it is meant to be
performed, *Fronteras Americanas* can change to incorporate the experiences of
audiences from different geographic and cultural backgrounds, enacting—as
well as explaining—the transformation of the hemispheric map by redrawing
the line dividing North and South America so that points of encounter could
occur virtually anywhere.

* * *

For certain audiences, Verdecchia's endeavor to translate "the borderlands"
from a single geographic region into a flexible metaphor for the increasing

interpenetration of north and south might be controversial. Some critics have protested that the ubiquity of border studies at once overlooks and enacts a kind of "violence" against those who struggle with harsh conditions along the U.S.-Mexico border. Yet (in its own version of U.S. exceptionalism) this argument ignores the prolific scholarship on international borders in many other parts of the world, as well as the fact that North America is divided by two borders that are best understood in relation to one another. In my reading of *Citizen Suarez* I have noted Verdecchia's tendency to marginalize the problems of poverty and exploitation that are so central to representations of the U.S.-Mexico border. Read alone, this collection might seem to have little to say to readers of Chicano/a literature. However, it becomes more meaningful when read alongside *Fronteras Americanas* so that the two works together offer a varied portrait of Latino diaspora. Verdecchia's more recent play about the Gulf War, *A Line in the Sand* (with Marcus Youssef, 1997), examines borders in a more global context through the story of a Canadian soldier and a Palestinian teenager who meet on a line in the Qatari desert.[22] Together, these works depict Canada's increasing involvement in international affairs, suggesting that its status as a border nation is not only relevant to its relations with the United States, but with the rest of the world.

As I have suggested, Verdecchia's deterritorialization of the borderlands may be explained, at least in part, as the product of his experience as a Latino living in Canada, rather than the United States, where the border with Mexico has become virtually synonymous with the very notion of borderlands. His comparative approach to the borderlands allows him to imagine the need for solidarities among Canadian Latinos, U.S. Chicanos, and other Latin Americans that might be less apparent in a place dominated by a larger and more singular Latino presence. His work is also an example of how Latino Canadian culture complicates the U.S.-centric view that "the border" refers exclusively to the place where the United States and Mexico meet. Drawing on the oppositional connotations of U.S.-Mexican border culture, it unmoors the borderlands from their particular location to show how the hemisphere itself has become a crucible for the complex intermixture of Anglo- and Latin Americas. It does so without losing sight of the nation, which has the power to enable liberating forms of movement, to force the desperate flight of its citizens, and to constrict routes of freedom and economic opportunity. By introducing Canadian characters and settings, Verdecchia's work makes a strong case for the inclusion of Canada within our study of the American hemisphere, giving new meaning to "the North" while at the same time disrupting the binary between north and south with a necessary third term.

NOTES

1. Carmen Aguirre, *¿Que Pasa with La Raza, eh?*, in *Along Human Lines: Dramas from Refugee Lives* (Winnipeg: Blizzard, 2000).

2. Michelle Habell-Pallán, "'Don't Call Us Hispanic': Popular Latino Theater in Vancouver," in *Latino/a Popular Culture*, ed. Michelle Habell-Pallán and Mary Romero (New York: New York University Press, 2002), 174–175.

3. This set is an allusion to the original upside-down map of the Americas, drawn by the Uruguyan modernist Joaquín Torres-García in 1943.

4. See for example, Kirsten Silva Gruez, *Ambassadors of Culture: The Transamerican Origins of Latino Writing* (Princeton: Princeton University Press, 2002); Gretchen Murphy, *Hemispheric Imaginings: The Monroe Doctrine and Narratives of U.S. Empire* (Durham, N.C.: Duke University Press, 2005); George B. Handley, *Postslavery Literatures in the Americas: Family Portraits in Black and White* (Charlottesville: University of Virginia Press, 2000); Anna Brickhouse, *Transamerican Literary Relations and the Nineteenth Century Public Sphere* (Cambridge and New York: Cambridge University Press, 2004); Gustavo Pérez-Firmat, ed., *Do the Americas Have a Common Literature?* (Durham, N.C.: Duke University Press, 1990); José David Saldívar, *Border Matters: Remapping American Cultural Studies* (Berkeley: University of California Press, 1997).

Some notable exceptions that incorporate the more inclusive model of the hemisphere I am imagining are Earl Fitz, *Rediscovering the New World: Inter-American Literature in a Comparative Context* (Iowa City: University of Iowa Press, 1991); Claudia Sadowski-Smith, "Border Fictions: Transnational Writing from U.S. Borders, Globalization, and Inter-American Studies" (unpublished ms.); Claudia Sadowski-Smith, *Border Fictions: Globalization, Empire, and Writing at the Boundaries of the United States* (Charlottesville: University of Virginia Press, 2008); Sarah Casteel, *Second Arrivals: Landscape and Belonging in Contemporary Writing of the Americas* (Charlottesville: University of Virginia Press, 2007); and the special issue of *Comparative American Studies* on "Canada and the Americas," edited by Rachel Adams and Sarah Casteel (3:1 [March 2005]).

5. Bryce Traister, "Risking Nationalism: NAFTA and the Limits of the New American Studies," *Canadian Review of American Studies/Revue canadienne d'ètudes amèrucaines* 27.3 (1997): 191–204.

6. Roger Gibbins, "Meaning and Significance of the Canadian-American Border," *Borders and Border Politics in a Globalizing World*, ed. Paul Ganster and David E. Lorey (Oxford: SR Books, 2005), 153.

7. Gibbins, "Meaning and Significance," 157.

8. Online at http://pewhispanic.org/files/factsheets/2.pdf (accessed 14 June 2006).

9. Online at http://migration.ucdavis.edu/MN/more.php?id=3071_0_2_0 (accessed 14 June 2006).

10. Thomas C. Wright and Rody Oñate, *Flight from Chile: Voices of Exile* (Albuquerque: University of New Mexico Press, 1998).

11. Hugh Hazleton, "Quebec Hispanico: Themes of Exile and Integration in the Writing of Latin Americans Living in Quebec," *Canadian Literature* no. 142–143 (Autumn–Winter 1994); and Andrew Machalski, *Hispanic Writers in Canada: A Preliminary Survey of the Activities of Spanish and Latin-American Writers in Canada*, ed. Michael S. Batts (Ottawa: Department of the Secretary of State of Canada, 1988).

12. Habell-Pallan, "'Don't Call Us Hispanic,'" 175; Alberto Gomez, "Where the South and the North Meet: Latino Identity and Cultural Heterogeneity," *a-r-c* 2 (November 2000) http://a-r-c.gold.ac.uk/a-r-c_Three, 33 (accessed 22 June 2006).

13. Gomez, "Where the South and the North Meet," 3.

14. Guillermo Verdecchia, *Fronteras Americanas: (American Borders)* (Toronto: Coach House Press, 1993), 77. All subsequent references are cited parenthetically in text.

15. See, for example, Frank Bonilla, ed., *Borderless Borders: U.S. Latinos, Latin Americans, and the Paradox of Interdependence* (Philadelphia: Temple University Press, 1998); W. H. New, *Land/Sliding: Imagining Space, Presence, and Power in Canadian Writing* (Toronto: University of Toronto Press, 1997); Deborah Castillo and Maria Socorro Tabuenca Cordoba, *Border Women: Writing from La Frontera* (Minneapolis: University of Minnesota Press, 2002); Marc S. Rodriguez, ed., *Repositioning North American Migration History: New Directions in Modern Continental Migration, Citizenship, and Community* (Rochester, N.Y.: University of Rochester Press, 2004).

16. See, for example, Mary Pat Brady, "The Fungibility of Borders," *Nepantla: Views from the South* 1 (2000): 171–190; Claire Fox, *The Fence and the River: Culture and Politics at the U.S.-Mexico Border* (Minneapolis: University of Minnesota Press), 199; and Castillo and Tabuenca Cordoba, *Border Women*.

17. Gloria Anzaldúa, *Borderlands/La Frontera: The New Mestiza* (San Francisco: Aunt Lute books, 1999), 25.

18. Diana Taylor, *The Archive and the Repertoire: Performing Cultural Memory in the Americas* (Durham, N.C.: Duke University Press, 2005), 20.

19. Ibid.

20. *Canadian Theatre Encyclopedia* http://www.canadiantheatre.com/dict.pl?term= Verdecchia%2C%20Guillermo (accessed 21 May 2007).

21. Habell-Pallan, "'Don't Call Us Hispanic.'"

22. Marcus Youssef and Guillermo Verdecchia, *A Line in the Sand* (Burnaby, Canada: Talonbooks, 1997).

Afterword

The Times of Hemispheric Studies

SUSAN GILLMAN

In 1998, on the occasion of the centennial of the Spanish-American/Cuban War, there was a flurry of attention in U.S. studies to things hemispheric. This turned out to be just one of many moments of identity crisis for the field. The self-questioning extended from the objects of study to the very name of "American Studies." From 1998, looking both backward and forward, first (roughly speaking), during the canon busting of the 1970s and 1980s, it was our texts that came under scrutiny and, almost simultaneously, under the pressures of New Historicism, our contexts; then, with the concept of imagined communities and increasing attention to the phenomenon of nationalism, the category of nation came under fire, and a search ensued for alternative units of study, including, as it transpired, borders, diasporas, hemispheres, and oceans. Once the nation was questioned, other categories came into view, namely empire or the absence thereof, in the study of U.S. literature (it's a chicken-and-egg problem: which came first, the visibility of nation or of empire?). The turn to the "cultures of U.S. imperialism" was also coextensive with the "transnational turn," thence to "globalization"—and here we are!

In the context of this mini-history of a field in constant crisis, the moment when "hemispheric studies" emerged has proven to be notably long-lasting. With important origins in the middle decades of the twentieth century, it was revitalized in 1995 with the centennial of the death of the poet, patriot, and father of Cuban independence, José Martí. Relatively little known at that time in U.S. literary studies, Martí, as Cuban nationalist, architect of the hemispheric pan-nationalism of "Our America," and longtime exile in New York City, offered multiple avenues to the "comparative," "post-" or "trans-" national approach to U.S. studies that was sought by humanists and social scientists alike. Above all, perhaps, from today's perspective, Martí's role as translator (of fiction and other writing in English and German) points to the as yet untapped potential for making central to the ongoing transnational turn the study of language in the Americas. This means a decisive departure from the homogenizing of global English and toward what critic Jonathan Arac calls the multicultural babel of the many languages of world literature—including, within the rubric of "American" literature, languages other than English. The goal here would be a Martíean "critical, cosmopolitan polyglot way of working with the literature of the United States."[1]

Thinking hemispherically through Martí, however, reminds us of the strange career of such seeming cosmopolitanism in the Americas. "Hemisphere" has the imperious Monroe Doctrine-aire ring that gave area studies such a bad name in the context of Cold-War Latin America. This was the model of area studies in which coverage masquerades as comparison, language acquisition substitutes for method, and the nation-state becomes a stand-in for other conceptions of region and perhaps even for theory itself.[2] Likewise, with comparative studies, whether in history or literature, the potential as a model for a transnational hemispheric Americas studies is fraught. The comparative framework itself has a history as a mode of analysis that favors the nation as both the object and the frame of study itself—an exclusive focus apparent in the longstanding tradition of "two-country" pairings. Questioning the category of nation is one thing—and there's been a big salutary boom in ocean studies (Black Atlantic, circumcaribbean, rejuvenated Atlantic World)—but there are limits, we know, to an approach that relies simply on counter units-of-study. Nor can aspiring comparative Americanists rely on what has been traditionally called "Comparative Literature," since the bases of comparison, which were ascendant in Cold War culture, are no longer in place as they once were in the 1960s and 1970s. As modes of analysis, all of these fields—area studies, comparative history, and comparative literature—are currently undergoing their own internal and interdisciplinary critique, parallel to that of American Studies. In fact, all four might even be undergoing what Gayatri Spivak heralded in 2003, in her book calling for a rebirth of comparative literature, as the "death of a discipline."[3] The field is dead; long live the field! Yet to paraphrase Mark Twain, perhaps the rumors of these deaths have been greatly exaggerated.

Aside from the fact of concurrent crises, what do these various comparative programs really have in common? Although no one would consider today's hemispheric studies to be the equivalent of yesterday's area studies, still, as Arac and Spivak demonstrate and Levander and Levine confirm, the comparison is itself instrumental.[4] We have a lot to learn both from the pitfalls and the possibilities of these comparative fields, theories, and methods. Together, they bring into focus the structure of "comparability" itself and the problem of interpreting space and time that is critical to it. Considerations of space (meaning geography and place) and time (meaning temporality and history) help to develop a different comparative perspective, based on uneven development and incommensurability, than that which emerges from the usual linearity and symmetry. Comparability in these terms would address the ways

that local, regional, and national histories are invariably crosscut by their location in sometimes surprising and conflicting global geographies. The various
invocations of the "Global" or "Hemispheric" South in this essay collection,
for example, contain the residue of such earlier, perhaps more provincial and
unexamined space-time locations as the Old, New, and Great South. In turn,
these markers point to the related, even broader and more foundational, pair-
ing of Old and New World. As such, the possibilities for "Comparative Southern
Studies" entail a theory of space and time that would recognize the "palimpsestuous" quality of the present, where multiple times exist simultaneously
within and across the same places or coexist as uneven temporalities.[5]

"Hemispheric Studies," as it is experimentally deployed, questioned, and,
at times, jettisoned in this volume of essays, is poised to make a difference
to thinking about comparative U.S. studies. It is not just that the term, when
used to bring into focus so many different phenomena (not only geographic
locations but also cultural routes, genealogies, imaginaries, cities, and, finally,
the conception of spheres themselves), produces a salutary set of anomalous,
non-parallel elements that aggressively resist conventional comparative models. More than that, different kinds of space-time frameworks emerge from the
materials themselves, so that both geographic space and temporality can be put
into play, though this doesn't necessarily mean mobilizing these coordinates
as parallel or symmetrical. Such approaches suggest the possibilities of hemispheric studies in multiple dimensions: rather than assuming a geographical
unit of study that privileges space at the expense of time, "hemisphere" should
perhaps be defined—as it is, even provisionally, in many of these essays—as
a spatiotemporal unit. Hemispheric studies would always operate not just in
two or even three dimensions but in multiple, asymmetrical, and non-parallel
dimensions, multiply related and arrayed.

Thus, each spatial dimension could and does have a specific temporal twin
or analogue. If the unit is the *old* circumcaribbean realm or the related Black
Atlantic, as it is for Brickhouse, Greeson, and Guterl, then it's the history of
goods, persons, ideas, and culture that circulates through the time zones, and
former routes, of the triangular trade; if, on the other hand, it's the *new* "African American Hemispherism," then it's the same products tracked through
the history of transnational black activism (Nwankwo, Stephens); if the unit
is the Gulf of Mexico, then it's the differing, historical moments of abjection,
marked by a strange sense of temporality, of Latinos both in the United States
and points farther south (Gruesz, Lazo, Alemán); if it's Asia-Pacific, then
the temporal analogue points to the elusive, apparently anachronistic links
between the waning empire of Spain and the emerging colossus of the United
States (Marr).

"Hemisphere" as limned by this collection can thus embrace Asia-
Pacific as well as the circumcaribbean/Atlantic world. This is in part a consequence of the comparative perspective based on uneven development and

incommensurability, both of which characterize the global reach of these different regional, national, imperial, and neocolonial histories. As such, the collection avoids one common pitfall of comparative studies, the misleading symmetry and static synchronicity of spatial and temporal units, such as slavery, or "race relations," thought of as social institutions, cutting indifferently across geographical or national regions, when their coherence or consistency across time and space cannot be taken for granted. In contrast, an approach taking incommensurability as a central, constitutive element registers instead the uneven developments and anomalies characteristic of the field of Americas studies. For example, we're used to hearing "Latin America and the Caribbean" said in one breath, but this yoking often implies parallel terms confusing the different linguistic traditions associated with each: Spanish and Portuguese with Latin America, the Caribbean with Spanish, French, and English. The linguistic differences similarly cascade into uneven historical legacies of colonialism, and the different neocolonialisms of three overlapping but distinct imperial histories. All of these coalesce suggestively in the "Latin American Year," as Deborah Cohn shows in her essay on the cultural politics of the 1966 PEN Congress, when Latin American "Boom" literature, translated and marketed in the United States, had its celebratory moment during the "American century."

To take only one, extended example of such disjunctive comparisons: many would assume a ready-made comparison between the two great artist-activists and founding fathers of the modern Cuban and Philippine nations, José Martí and José Rizal, who are linked by their premature deaths, barely a year apart, at a transitional moment in their respective national struggles for independence from Spain and the looming neocolonial threat, foreseen by both writers, from the United States. Yet as Benedict Anderson has suggestively pointed out, despite the fact that "the Cuban example was crucial" to the Filipinos in mobilizing a national revolution, the differences in the personal and political histories of the two founding fathers are as striking as the "possible parallels"; similarly, the divergences between the Cuban and Filipino colonial situations (in relation to the mother country, specifically their relations to the metropole in terms of language, legal system, and insurrectionary tradition) suggest that between the two otherwise seemingly analogous histories, "there is nothing remotely comparable," as Anderson puts it.[6] We need a reading practice attuned to such a multidimensional, multidirectional comparability that can effect a union of temporality with its spatial complement, but not necessarily as equal partners. Some of the essays already lend themselves to this bi- or multidimensionality, particularly when their method follows from and is indebted to the object of study. They suggest how the space-time relations of particular texts and contexts can help to define and shape our comparative methodologies.

Jennifer Greeson's argument on the paradoxes of local color's global reach includes a series of suggestive possibilities for defining a temporal version of that predominantly spatial paradox. She argues provocatively that far from an "insular, backward-looking" genre, local color of the 1870s spoke perfectly to the "expansionist, forward-marching" temper of the times, a linking of space with time that was achieved through what she calls transatlantic "transposition" or "comparison." Tracing the nineteenth-century formulation of the "Great South"—the title of a popular U.S. travelogue, imitating Henry Morton Stanley's account of his Africa expedition—as a sort of domestic Africa, Greeson stresses the mechanism of comparison, or better yet, transposition, that, in moving from the Mediterranean to the Gulf of Mexico, "transposed a surrogate experience of European empire into a more immediate projection of United States empire to come." The complex of spatiotemporal relations outlined here, in which the South is imagined both as a place and a time, a surrogate experience of European empire transferred into a projection of U.S. empire to come, suggests the possibilities of a hemispheric studies based on disjunctive comparability. In tracing the circuit from the Great South (then) to the Global South (now), we can imagine inserting yet another well-known formation, the Old/New South as an unrecognized stop in-between. There is a hemispheric history, Greeson implies, of the putatively domestic periodization of Old and New Souths that would show how its spatialization/temporalization is both alternating and simultaneous.

Just so, Matthew Guterl's "American Mediterranean" lays out the ways that such oceanic transferences produce comparisons that equate the geological residues of the past (the French, Spanish, and English empires of the Caribbean) with reflections or projections of the future (the expansion of the United States into the slaveholding South). In this canny spatiotemporal analysis of the "hemispherics of the mid-century South," New Orleans is the capital of a "great nation of futurity" and Cuba and Haiti are twin imagined futures, feared and/or desired, of the slaveholding world of the American Mediterranean. Like Greeson's Reconstruction South, the site of a transatlantic transposition of European imperial space to future American time, Guterl's American Mediterranean is a transoceanic projection of a future time onto a palimpsestic space, Havana a "sister city of sorts" to Mobile, and Cuba "the *boulevard* of the New World." The essence of these formulations that link spaces of surrogacy to projected times is their fundamental reliance on and reversal of the machinery of the comparative, for both liken the United States to a European space-time while rejecting the usual hierarchy or priority of Old and New Worlds.

What's thus striking about both of these Southern transpositions is how comprehensively they manage the "specter" or "demon" of comparison that haunted Rizal. His term, *el demonio de las comparaciones*, was coined in his famous nationalist novel *Noli Me Tangere* (1887) to convey the disorientation of the young mestizo hero as he realizes that his vision of the botanical gardens in Manila is permanently shadowed by their Spanish counterpart, the first to which they come second, the original to their copy, much as both the time and space of the New World are haunted by the "Old."[7] Marking one limit of the comparative imperative in a transnational context, Rizal's specter offers a provocative contrast to the hemispheric comparativism of this collection. Guterl's American Mediterranean is a global temporal and spatial transposition in which the antebellum South was Rome, the Mississippi the "*mare nostrum*," and the comparison that creates the fatal doubled vision for Rizal instead becomes a means of historicizing—expanding, simultaneously, backward and forward—the space-time of the world history of slavery and freedom, revolution and rebellion. Likewise, the Great or Global South that emerges in several of the essays, including Kirsten Silva Gruesz's "mercurial space of 'Central' America," a place of underdevelopment which is both belated and a harbinger of a potential future, is formed through, not despite, the specter of comparison. This South, like the New World itself, may be read, the essays show, as a set of spatial and temporal manipulations that are right on the surface, part of the very contemporary machinery of comparison, an essential element rather than a haunting residue. Extending this logic to the other space-time frameworks in the volume suggests the scope of future work to be done in a thoroughly disjunctive, comparative hemispheric studies.

Accounts of space and time also demand an attention to language. What if we thought of language itself as a space-time archive? Verb tenses, for example, are a simple clue to how the expression of time is keyed to expression in language. They provide a kind of shorthand for the grammatical sense of continuing action between present and past/future.[8] Far from merely a formal, syntactical marker, verb tenses are critical to our sense of both pastness and futurity. Put differently, from a linguistics standpoint, "tense is the grammaticalization of time."[9] Time distinctions are not identical with language but, through the category of tense, a few of the major distinctions can be embedded in the grammar of a language. Verb tense is thus constitutive of rather than simply incidental to the sense of historical consciousness that flows from language.

Extending that logic and taking it further (into the hemisphere of comparative multilingual and transnational studies), we would focus on the linguistic aspect of temporal conception and expression. Going deeper with that insight into the territory of "hemisphere and nation," we'd get access to a different, even broader, linguistic-temporal relation through the travel and translation of verb tenses: how is time structured differently in different languages, and how does translation reflect that difference? Languages are not all equal in so many ways, not least of which is the relative weight and richness of their own temporal structures. Some languages have a wealth of tenses in contrast with others, while some languages lack tense entirely. It may be a surprise to learn that English has only two tenses, what are traditionally termed "past" and "present," and it has even been argued that "non-past" would be a better name for the latter, mostly used for talking about present and future time.[10] The question of how different "American" languages handle tense and time leads, perhaps unsurprisingly, to a view of the uneven capacity for thinking pastness through tense structures.

The "perfect inequality" of language thus makes translation a key both to the limits and possibilities of thinking through time as a linguistic phenomenon.[11] Another way to put this reciprocal relationship: language produces temporality through tense, and time is inscribed in, limited, and bound by the horizons of language. Apprehensions of time, keyed to language, especially verbs, are inflected by tense structures and their capacity to express pastness and futurity. Different languages apprehend and convey time differently—discerning these differences is one of the challenges of translation. What would it mean for those working within and across disciplines to develop similar such interpretive skills and practices?

Anna Brickhouse's essay, "Hemispheric Jamestown," is suggestively attentive to the linguistic and cultural play of language—the translational mediations of Spanish Jesuit accounts of native informants translated into English—as it covers and inhabits the colonial space-time of Jamestown. In so doing, she develops new coordinates for a fetishized place (Jamestown) and new modes of access to the ambivalent history of "Spanish colonial priority and Native-Creole biculturalism at the site of the future nation's ostensible English founding." In this reading, "Jamestown" is not only a space and a time but also, critically, a linguistic complex.

So, too, does Gruesz mobilize the uses of translation to mark the strange temporality of our hemispheric spaces, in her case the newly "Latinized" Gulf Coast, suddenly a place of massive migration of Spanish-speaking workers from Central America. Invoking performance artist Guillermo Gómez Peña's equation in "The Last Migration: A Spanglish Opera" of New Orleans with Honduras (the last line in a litany of such Americas comparisons), Gruesz pairs it suggestively with an earlier poem, in Spanish, by Honduran Guillermo Bustillo Reina, "Viaje a Nueva New Orleans" (Voyage to New Orleans). Providing her own translation, she comments that one of Bustillo Reina's words, *prolongación* (extension), has the same temporal and spatial resonance in both languages, so that the phrase grammatically reverses the temporal priority that has characterized Anglo-American apprehensions of Central America since the nineteenth century. Gruesz's temporal-linguistic reading through translation is echoed in Rodrigo Lazo's invocation of the place and time of nineteenth-century "Hispanophone Philadelphia." For Lazo, Spanish-language translations of key U.S. political texts from the 1770s through the 1820s were among the many marketable commodities that helped to make Philadelphia into a thriving city in the early republican United States. All three of these locations—Brickhouse's Jamestown, Silva Gruesz's New Orleans, and Lazo's Philadelphia—dramatize the ways that this collection links language and translation to space and time, suggesting how translation might become a central and not simply an incidental aspect of hemispheric critical practice. All three notably touch on the challenges of linguistic and cultural translation: the gaps, infelicities, and instabilities that define the grounds of translation.

Let me conclude here with a return to the uses of a disjunctive comparability, or better yet, "incomparability," as it is reflected in the mistranslatability of language that Brickhouse, Gruesz and others in this collection bring into view. Mistranslation would provide a linguistic analogue to seeking the incomparable in comparative studies: those events, figures, times and places that are characterized by a reluctance, resistance, or refusal to compare. The Martí-Rizal relation is just one example of such elusive comparisons. Rizal's *el demonio de las camparaciones* became the mistranslated "specter of comparison," which says worlds about our own demons in today's comparative study. By approaching mistranslation in this way, as a critical phenomenon with intellectual integrity in its own right, rather than assuming that it is unavoidable and lamentable, we gain insight into the disjunctive comparability that's so striking in the collection. Simply putting mistranslation to critical use would avoid not only the tyranny of fidelity to the original but also the homogenizing, or faux egalitarianism, of language study—treating languages as though they're equals—that so often accompanies the implicit hierarchizing of the world's prestige languages. Honoring mistranslation in this way would gain access to the linguistic differences and inequalities that characterize the grammar and structure of language. Most of all, this would banish the specter of comparisons that haunts language study and comparative study alike.

In seeking out unevenness and situations that at their outer limit appear to be beyond compare, *Hemispheric American Studies* goes a long way toward a kind of self-critical, skeptical comparative study that would rather not be a member of the club. It seems closer to the spirit of this kind of critical comparativism to call it "incomparability"—not in the sense of a unit of analysis, like the nation, which claims an irreducible uniqueness, leaving only trivial differences as the basis of comparison. Nor in the sense simply of the unlocated pre/post of the new American Studies. Moving beyond the nation in this collection means being confronted with seemingly incomparable situations and events, texts and contexts: the American Mediterranean, Hemispheric Jamestown, and the many, unknown "other spheres" that will emerge from the future space-time of hemispheric American studies.

NOTES

1. Jonathan Arac, "Global and Babel: Two Perspectives," *ESQ: A Journal of the American Renaissance* 50 (2004): 95–120.
2. See Harry Harootunian, "Some Thoughts on Comparability and the Space-Time Problem," in "Problems of Comparability/Possibilities for Comparative Studies," ed. Harry Harootunian and Hyun Ok Park, *boundary* 2:32 (2005): 23–52.

3. Gayatri Chakravorty Spivak, *Death of a Discipline* (New York: Columbia University Press, 2003).

4. As Paul Bové puts it even more bluntly: "can American Studies be Area Studies?" The expected answer is "no"—American Studies, a player in the cultural sphere, lacks the explicit political clout essential to the State Department–driven *realpolitik* of area studies. See "Can American Studies Be Area Studies?" in Masao Miyoshi and Harry D. Harrootunian, eds., *Learning Places: The Afterlives of Area Studies* (Durham: Duke University Press, 2002), 206–230.

5. See Harootunian, "Some Thoughts on Comparability," 47. The term "palimpsestuous" was coined as the French *palimpsestueuse* by Philippe Lejeune in *Moi Aussi* (Paris: Editions de Seuil, 1986), 115.

6. Benedict Anderson, *Under Three Flags: Anarchism and the Anti-Colonial Imagination* (London and New York: Verso, 2005), 131, 141.

7. See Benedict Anderson, *The Spectre of Comparisons: Nationalism, Southeast Asis, and the World* (London and New York: Verso, 1998), 2; on the mistranslation of the phrase, "specter of comparisons," see also Anderson, *Under Three Flags*, 32.

8. For two literary and cultural histories that, suggestively, make a play on verbs, a shorthand for relations between past and present, see Mark C. Carnes, *Past Imperfect: History According to the Movies* (New York: Henry Holt, 1995); H. Bruce Franklin, *Future Perfect: American Science Fiction of the Nineteenth Century* (1966; expanded and rev. ed., New Brunswick: Rutgers University Press, 1995).

9. R. L. Trask, *Language: The Basics* (2nd ed., London and New York: Routledge, 1999), 58–59; Trask, *Key Concepts in Language and Linguistics* (London and New York: Routledge, 1999; rpt. 2004), 311.

10. See Trask, *Language*, 60.

11. Edward W. Said, "Living in Arabic," *Raritan* 21 (Spring 2002): 235; qtd. in Arac, "Global and Babel," 111.

NOTES ON CONTRIBUTORS

Rachel Adams is Associate Professor of English and Comparative Literature and Associate Director of American Studies at Columbia University. She is the author of *Sideshow U.S.A.: Freaks and the American Cultural Imagination* (2001), and she is working on a new book that seeks to reframe American Studies through the lens of the continent rather than the nation-state.

Jesse Alemán is Associate Professor of English at the University of New Mexico, where he teaches nineteenth-century American and Chicano/a literatures. He is the editor of Loreta Janeta Velazquez's *The Woman in Battle* (2003) and the co-editor, with Shelly Streeby, of *Empire and the Literature of Sensation* (2007). He is currently working on a book on the literature of the U.S.-Mexico War.

Ralph Bauer is Associate Professor of English at the University of Maryland. He is the author of *The Cultural Geography of Colonial American Literatures: Empire, Travel, Modernity* (2003) and the editor of *An Inca Account of the Conquest of Peru. By Titu Cusi Yupanqui* (2005) and (with Jose Antonia Mazzotti) *Creole Subjects in the Colonial Americas* (forthcoming).

Anna Brickhouse is Associate Professor of English at the University of Virginia. She is the author of *Transamerican Literary Relations and the Nineteenth-Century Public Sphere* (2004).

Kandice Chuh is Associate Professor of English and an affiliate faculty member of the American Studies Department and the Asian American Studies Program at the University of Maryland. She is the author of *Imagine Otherwise: On Asian Americanist Critique* (2003) and an editor of *Orientations: Mapping Studies in the Asian Diaspora* (2001).

Deborah Cohn is Associate Professor of Spanish at Indiana University, Bloomington. She is the author of *History and Memory in the Two Souths: Recent Southern and Spanish American Fiction* (1999) and the co-editor, with Jon Smith, of *Look Away!: The U.S. South in New World Studies* (2004). She recently received a National Endowment for the Humanities fellowship for work on a book entitled *Creating the Boom's Reputation: The Promotion of the Boom in and by the U.S.*

Claire F. Fox is Associate Professor of English and International Studies at the University of Iowa. She is the author of *The Fence and the River: Culture and Politics at the U.S.-Mexico Border* (1999), and she is currently working on a book about hemispheric cultural policy during the Cold War period.

Susan Gillman is Professor of Literature at the University of California, Santa Cruz. She is the author of *Dark Twins: Imposture and Identity in Mark Twain's America* (1989) and *Blood Talk: American Race Melodrama and the Culture of the Occult* (2003), and co-editor, with Alys Weinbaum, of *"Next to the Color Line": Gender and Sexuality in the Work of W. E. B. Du Bois* (2007). She is working on a book tentatively titled *Unfaithfully Yours: Adaptation Theory and Americas Studies.*

Jennifer Rae Greeson teaches American literature in the English department at Princeton University, where she holds the Class of 1936 Bicentennial Pre-ceptorship. She is completing her first book, *Our South: Domestic Geography and Global Imagination in United States Literature, from Independence to The Birth of a Nation.*

Kirsten Silva Gruesz teaches nineteenth- and twentieth-century literatures of the Americas at the University of California, Santa Cruz. The author of *Ambassadors of Culture: The Transamerican Origins of Latino Writing* (2002), she is currently working on a book on ideologies of Spanish-language acquisition over the past three centuries, as well as a study of the Gulf of Mexico as an Anglo-Latino border space.

Matthew Pratt Guterl is Director of American Studies and Associate Professor of African American and African Diaspora Studies at Indiana University, Bloomington. He is the author of *The Color of Race in America, 1900–1940* (2001) and *A World without Slaves* (forthcoming) and the co-editor, with James T. Campbell and Robert G. Lee, of *Race, Nation, and Empire in American History* (2007).

Robert McKee Irwin is Associate Professor in the Department of Spanish and Portuguese at the University of California, Davis. He is the author of *Mexican Masculinities* (2003) and *Bandits, Captives, Heroines and Saints: Cultural Icons of Mexico's Northwest Frontier* (2007), and the coeditor of *Hispanisms and Homosexualities (1998), The Famous 41: Sexuality and Social Control in Mexico, 1901* (2003), and *Diccionario de estudios culturales latinoamericanos* (forthcoming).

Rodrigo Lazo is Associate Professor of English at the University of California, Irvine. He is the author of *Writing to Cuba: Filibustering and Cuban Exiles in the United States* (2005), and he is currently working on a book-length study of the hemispheric dimensions of Spanish-language print culture in the early nineteenth-century United States.

Caroline F. Levander is Professor of English and Director of the Humanities Research Center at Rice University. She is the author of *Voices of the Nation: Women and Public Speech in Nineteenth-Century American Literature* (1998) and *Cradle of Liberty: Race, the Child, and National Belonging from Thomas Jefferson to W. E. B. Du Bois* (2006), and the editor (with Carol J. Singley) of *The American Child: A Cultural Studies Reader* (2003).

Robert S. Levine is Professor of English and a Faculty Affiliate in American Studies at the University of Maryland, College Park. He is the author of *Conspiracy and Romance* (1989), *Martin Delany, Frederick Douglass, and the Politics of Representative Identity* (1997), and *Dislocating Race and Nation* (2008), and the editor of a number of volumes, including *Martin R. Delany: A Documentary Reader* (2003), *The Norton Anthology of American Literature, 1820–1865* (2007), and (with Samuel Otter) *Frederick Douglass and Herman Melville: Essays in Relation* (2008).

Timothy Marr is an Associate Professor in the Curriculum in American Studies at the University of North Carolina at Chapel Hill. He is the author of *The Cultural Roots of American Islamicism* (2006).

Ifeoma C. K. Nwankwo is Associate Professor of English at Vanderbilt University. She is the author of *Black Cosmopolitanism: Racial Consciousness and Transnational Identity in the Nineteenth-Century Americas* (2005) and is currently working on a comparative book-length study of African American and Caribbean vernacular poetry and music lyrics and an edited collection (with Mamdou Diouf) on music and dance of the Afro-Atlantic world.

Michelle A. Stephens is Associate Professor of English at Colgate University. She is the author of *Black Empire: The Masculine Global Imaginary of Caribbean Intellectuals in the United States, 1914–1962* (2005), and she is working on a book-length project entitled *Black Acts: Performances of Race and Masculinity across the African Diaspora*.

INDEX

Page numbers in *italics* refer to illustrations.